LONGFELLOW REDUX

CHRISTOPH IRMSCHER

Longfellow
Redux

UNIVERSITY OF ILLINOIS PRESS

Urbana and Chicago

© 2006 by the Board of Trustees
of the University of Illinois
All rights reserved
Manufactured in the United States of America
∞ This book is printed on acid-free paper.

C 5 4 3 2 1

Library of Congress Cataloging-in-Publication Data
Irmscher, Christoph. Longfellow redux / Christoph Irmscher.
p. cm.
Includes bibliographical references and index.
ISBN-13: 978-0-252-03063-5 (cloth : acid-free paper)
ISBN-10: 0-252-03063-X (cloth : acid-free paper)
1. Longfellow, Henry Wadsworth, 1807–1882.
2. Poets, American—19th century—Biography.
I. Title.
PS2281.I76   2006
2005028931

For my father,
Hans Dietrich Irmscher

In these challenging times, we must rededicate ourselves
to Longfellow's ideals [and] think beyond
our own experience.

—Senator Edward M. Kennedy

SEPTEMBER 14, 2002, ON THE THIRTIETH ANNIVERSARY
OF THE LONGFELLOW NATIONAL HISTORIC SITE
IN CAMBRIDGE, MASSACHUSETTS

CONTENTS

ILLUSTRATIONS

ACKNOWLEDGMENTS

This is a book about a poet who, on a cold, bright New England afternoon in March 1854, would write in his journal, as if he had nothing more important to report: "Drive to town; my principal business being to buy Alice a doll, which I accomplish, to her vast delight." I cannot explain why this passage touches me whenever I read it—but my reaction probably has something to do with the fact that I began writing *Longfellow Redux* when my son Nicholas had just been born, and that I finished it, four years later, after the birth of my daughter Julia.

Somewhere else in his journals, Longfellow says that one should even enjoy the noise that one's children make—a sentiment I admire but have found a bit harder to emulate. Still, I can say with complete honesty that I have learned more from my children than from all the books I have read in my life. And as I stumble on in this incredible, lifelong journey called fatherhood, I'm also understanding more and more about just how much of himself my own father, the gentlest man and the finest scholar I know, has given me over the years. This book is for him.

My friends, family, and colleagues have given freely of their time to help with this book. Frank Kearful volunteered to read the manuscript not once but twice. My wife, Lauren Bernofsky, also made numerous suggestions for improvement. As always, my mother, Elisabeth Irmscher, has supported me in more ways I can mention. Lawrence Buell and George Hutchinson wrote many letters on my behalf, though all I could promise them in return was a free copy of the finished book, and Werner Sollors encouraged me to carry on. When I mistakenly thought I was almost done, the participants of a seminar at the Folger Shakespeare Library, directed by Steven Shapin, forced me to clarify my thinking about issues of intellectual biography and history.

I thank my colleagues in the English Department at the University of Maryland, Baltimore County (UMBC), particularly Jessica Berman, Chris Corbett, and Raphael Falco, for their interest and their friendship. My former chair, Kenneth Baldwin, has supported me for several years now, both directly and indirectly. He made sure that I found the time to complete the manuscript and then very generously provided the funds that made it possible to include the illustrations. A summer fellowship from the National Endowment for the Humanities and a summer stipend from my own university got me started on the book; a UMBC Research Fellowship, awarded under the auspices of the university's provost, Arthur Johnson, allowed me to complete it.

My exemplary editor at the University of Illinois Press, Willis Regier, helped me—to modify a phrase from a Wallace Stevens poem—"uncrumple" a "much-crumpled" manuscript and saw to it that it became a book. Two anonymous readers for the Press encouraged me to refine my argument, and Robert Dale Parker gave his support when it most counted. I'm grateful to Richard Poirier and Stephanie Volmer, who accepted and edited an embryonic version of this manuscript for publication in *Raritan,* and to Massimo Bacigalupo, who invited me to Genoa and has now allowed me to reuse portions of a lecture I gave there (which first appeared in his *America and the Mediterranean*) in this book. Richard d'Abate of the Maine Historical Society invited me twice to talk about Longfellow to remarkably tolerant audiences in Portland, Maine. I also would like to thank Rosella Mamoli Zorzi and Marino Zorzi for their help with the translations from the Venetian in chapter 3. Adriana Proser of the Asia Society in New York talked me through a passage in Longfellow's "Kéramos" that otherwise wouldn't have made sense to me. Longfellow's biographer, Charles Calhoun, took a chance when he first invited me to speak at one of the Maine Humanities Council's Great Books weekends; he hasn't been able to get rid of me since. My conversations with him have added substance and detail to my argument.

I thank the office staff of my department (Patty Bach, Susan Harrell, and Mary Welsh) for many and often life-saving favors. My student and research assistant Ilse Schweitzer, herself a remarkable scholar of medieval literature, helped prepare the index and saved me from several errors. As the years go by, I become ever more conscious of how long it takes for a murky outline to grow into the shape of a printed book—which is why I am most appreciative of the excellent work done by Angela Burton and the staff at the University of Illinois Press, who have helped me stay on track. Photographer Tim Ford, with the consummate professionalism and good humor I have come to expect from him, prepared all the illustrations for publication. Tim, Angela, and book designer Copenhaver Cumpston have made me and my book look better than both of us deserve.

My greatest debt is to the long-suffering librarians and archivists who answered my questions and obtained books, manuscripts, microfilms, and negatives for me. Harvard's Houghton Library is second to none, and so are the people working there, and I take great pleasure in thanking them once again, especially Tom Ford and Susan Halpert. I am also grateful to Anita Israel at the Longfellow National Historic Site in Cambridge, who provided me with photocopies from Fanny Longfellow's "Chronicles of the Children of Craigie Castle," and Rachel Shapiro in the Interlibrary Loan Department of UMBC's Albin O. Kuhn Library, who has perfected the art of extending supposedly firm due dates. Leslie Morris, the curator of manuscripts at Houghton Library and literary executor of the Longfellow estate, helped me in ways too numerous to mention here and, last but not least, generously allowed me to quote from the Longfellow Papers. I can't help but think that the dedication of the wonderful people who take care of Longfellow's legacy in Maine and Massachusetts is somehow a tribute to a poet who was known for his capacity for friendship and his hospitality. I have profound admiration for Jim Shea, Nancy Jones, and Paul Blandford of the Longfellow National Historic Site in Cambridge and Richard d'Abate, Steven Bromage, and Sara Archbald of the Maine Historical Society in Portland.

Let me add a quick disclaimer here. Throughout the book I will be referring to the reader of Longfellow's works as "she." Now why would I—obviously a male critic and reader myself—presume to do that? I would ask that *my* readers take my preference for the female pronoun as nothing but a convenient fiction: one that will allow me to make fun of the old patriarchal pretence that serious literature is written for guys only while it will also keep my sentences from becoming submerged in a flood of "his or hers."

Good, clear prose matters. I wouldn't have written a line of this book without the man who taught me that, although I have never been able to match him: Daniel Aaron, my mentor and friend. Dan, whose essays on

Longfellow remain unsurpassed, always seemed to know better than I did what it exactly it was that I wanted to accomplish. He also told me when it was time to finish. As Longfellow once quipped, "Let us be grateful to writers for what is left in the inkstand."

A NOTE ON QUOTATIONS

All quotations from Longfellow's journals come from the unpublished manuscripts in the Longfellow Papers (MS Am 1340) at Houghton Library, Harvard University. Unless otherwise indicated, the excerpts have not been edited. To save space, entries are only referenced by dates, not by the call number of the volume in which they appear. Quotations from Longfellow's published works follow the "Craigie" edition, *The Complete Writings of Henry Wadsworth Longfellow,* 11 vols. (Boston: Houghton, Mifflin, 1904), and are identified by parenthetical references, citing only the number of the volume and the page. Longfellow's letters (cited as *Letters*) are taken from Andrew Hilen's edition, *The Letters of Henry Wadsworth Longfellow,* 6 vols. (Cambridge, Mass.: Belknap, 1966–82). Longfellow's anthology *Poems of Places,* 31 vols. (Boston: Osgood; later Houghton, Osgood, 1876–79), is abbreviated as *Places.* References to Samuel Longfellow's biography (*Life of Henry Wadsworth Longfellow, with Extracts from his Journals and Correspondence,* 3 vols., Boston: Houghton, Mifflin, 1891) are preceded by *Life.*

LONGFELLOW REDUX

INTRODUCTION

In a recent column published in *Newsweek*, writer Bruce Wexler asked, somewhat disingenuously, "Is poetry dead?" Predictably, his answer was yes. Perhaps less predictably, Wexler went on to acknowledge the part that he personally had played in killing it. Though he had once been hooked on Robert Lowell and John Berryman, his life since college had taken a turn in which there simply was no time for the twenty readings a good poem needs before it begins to make sense: "I got married, had children, pursued my career, bought a house. With apologies to Frost, I began to find more relevance in articles about interest rates than essays on the sprung rhythm of Hopkins." Today he couldn't, he admitted, name even a single living poet. "April was National Poetry Month, a fact I know only because it was noted in my younger daughter's school newsletter. I celebrated by finding out the name of our poet laureate (Billy Collins) and reading one of his poems. This may not seem like much, but I have television shows to watch, bestsellers to read and Web sites to visit before I sleep." Didn't poets and poetry critics realize, too, that their cherished art was done, finished, over?[1]

Apparently not. Though others had announced the end of poetry before, Wexler's piece, for some reason, got the adrenaline of even the mildest-mannered poet pumping.[2] Soon the World Wide Web was abuzz with angry refutations of Wexler's heresies. On web sites with evocative names such as "turkshead.com," "bookslut.com," and (my favorite) "mysterium.aqualyrica.com," poor Mr. Wexler was attacked as a "schlemiel" who didn't know "poetry from petunias," mocked as a lazybones, light on research and heavy on bigotry, who prefers falling asleep while watching *The Late Show* to putting his nose into a book that could change his life, and lambasted as a mindless "yahoo from Chicago" with no sense for the finer things in life. Irony was lost on the infuriated poets who posted messages solemnly protesting Wexler's verdict. Many of them had taken issue precisely with his observation that the number of poetry's practitioners today far exceeds that of its appreciators. But, funnily enough, the extent of the rage they were now directing at nonpoet Wexler somehow confirmed his tongue-in-cheek dismissal of a literary genre that he thought had remained alive mostly for those who kept producing it.

It seems to me that both Wexler and his attackers are right. And then again, perhaps they are both wrong. Poetry today is neither dead nor fully alive. Certainly, the kind of poetry that bears (or, rather, *demands*) rereading isn't widely appreciated anymore. Take a look at a Waldenbooks near you. To some extent, this is the result of the idea promoted by English departments for over a hundred years now—that literature is difficult and that understanding it properly requires proper training, an attentiveness to nuances that must go beyond the bristling of the skin A. E. Housman felt when remembering a particularly good line of poetry.[3] As Wexler puts it, succinctly, "Poetry takes work." In this view, the college-educated reader who dreamily recites Yeats's "The Wild Swans at Coole" and the muse-kissed hipster who, copies of her latest self-published chapbook under her arm, lines up for her turn on open mic night don't have much in common with the old lady who, while shopping at her local Safeway store, picks up a Hallmark card because its rhymed message so perfectly expresses her own joy over her new grandchild's birth. The disdain with which the literary establishment has greeted Maya Angelou's decision to launch her own line of Hallmark greeting cards proves my point (Billy Collins angrily claimed Angelou was "lowering the understanding of what poetry can actually do").[4]

But this is, of course, only one side of the story. Remember Bob Dylan, who once said that Smokey Robinson was "America's greatest living poet"? In a recent essay, Dana Gioia, speaking from the pulpit of new chairman of the National Endowment for the Arts, offers an even more provocative assessment. He claims that poetry has been experiencing a revival lately as a public and largely auditory art form, at poetry slams, cowboy poetry festivals, and rap concerts. For many people, the poet as the sleep-deprived creator of carefully crafted lines has been, argues Gioia, replaced by the "amplified bard" on a well-lit stage. Ironically, the emphasis on poetry as oral performance has also meant a return to more traditional formal patternings—take the four-stress accentual line used by rappers or the ballad stanzas favored by the cowboy poets. A former marketing executive for General Foods (where he was responsible for advertising Jell-O) as well as a formalist poet, Gioia has an ulterior motive here. Elevating the new "public poetry" allows him to criticize all those ivory tower–dwelling poets who think that snide disdain for the untweedy masses already constitutes artistic rebellion. It also gives him another chance to tackle the English professors, who persist in writing about poetry in the unintelligible "mandarin code" of literary criticism.[5]

Longfellow Redux is intended to remind us of a poet who pretty much invented poetry as a public idiom in the United States and abroad and who was later shunned by the literary and academic establishment precisely because of it. Longfellow's reputation did not depend on a mystification of the writer's office. His accessibility and lack of arrogance were proverbial. "I am glad to speak to a poet," an Irish mason informed the author of *Evangeline* and *Hiawatha* when he ran into him in the streets of Cambridge, Massachusetts, because "I have meself a brother in the Port, who is a drunkard and a Poet" (June 4, 1867). In his own day, Longfellow's works appealed to bespectacled university professors and servant girls alike. At the height of his fame, the man whom the New York diarist George Templeton Strong regarded as the American Coleridge commanded an audience that was, if not the largest, then certainly the most inclusive one that poetry has ever enjoyed in the United States and elsewhere.[6] (When Longfellow visited England in 1868, at the height of this fame, Charles Dickens noticed that wherever he went, "the workingmen" were "at least as well acquainted with his books as the classes socially above them.")[7]

The first chapter of this book, "Strangers as Friends," reconstructs Longfellow's relationship with his audience, as manifested, for example, in the voluminous correspondence he maintained with his fans both at home and abroad, a community that included the king of Brazil as well as a nine-year-old girl from Ohio. I ask what features of Longfellow's poetry might have encouraged so many of his readers to think of themselves as writers of poetry, too (and then to share generous samples of it with the man they called the "Poet of the Heart"). The second chapter, "How Marbles Are Made," suggests links between the domestic arrangements in Longfellow's household, notably his democratic view of fatherhood, and his conception of himself as an author who is less the godlike creator of unique meaning than the competent redistributor of cultural goods. Being

American, for Longfellow, meant not being limited to just one viewpoint. "Mad for Travel," the third chapter, looks at the roots and effects of Longfellow's obsession with travel and his insistence that the American experiment never be regarded as an exclusively Anglo-Saxon one. Longfellow's many translations, the subject of the book's final chapter, "It Whirls Me Away," further rendered fluid the boundaries between national cultures, just as they blurred the line dividing so-called original literary work from an activity mocked as merely reproductive.

Today, Longfellow's erstwhile fame is a distant memory. The title of my book, *Longfellow Redux,* is not meant to imply that I hope to restore Longfellow to a literary greatness some think he may have never possessed. What it does suggest is that, on the eve of the two-hundredth anniversary of the Cambridge poet's birth, the time has come to take another look at him. When I first began to circulate parts of my manuscript among friends and colleagues, some of my more academic readers challenged me to deliver better proof of why Longfellow was a "major" writer after all, someone who should be restored to his place in the canon from which twentieth-century American poets and critics, his distant relative Ezra Pound among them, had successfully gotten him expelled. But my contention in this book is that terms such as "major" or "minor" do not, in fact, apply to Longfellow. They do little to characterize the challenges his non-egocentric concept of authorship, his rejection of the notion that an author be the sole originator and proprietor of his or her work, pose to the ways in which we continue to think about literature and literary history.

Virginia Jackson, in a compelling essay published a few years ago, claims that Longfellow himself might have been responsible for his own disappearance from the canon. Jackson has little patience for the likes of Dana Gioia who are hankering, "with jealous awe," after the unparalleled mass appreciation Longfellow once enjoyed. As she sees it, Longfellow, by suggesting that his poems wrote and told themselves, ironically made them so accessible that soon enough no one indeed needed access to him or his poetry—and, for that matter, to any poetry—anymore.[8] Was it *Longfellow,* then, who killed poetry first, long before Mr. Wexler and his friends did? Perhaps unintentionally, Jackson's argument further bolsters the notion that poetry, to remain poetry at all, must be difficult—that it is, as Wallace Stevens once said, "the scholar's art."[9]

I began writing this book at a time when I found myself becoming increasingly uncomfortable with that assumption. I was thinking then not just about my own, personal identity (as an immigrant to the United States and as the father of a young son) but also about my role, or rather my role*s*, in the profession I have chosen, who I was and who I wanted to be as a reader, writer, researcher, and teacher. In a sense, this book marks a watershed for me. I have learned a great deal from previous scholarly treatments of Longfellow, a debt my endnotes might not always reflect. But my primary purpose in writing *Longfellow Redux*—which I like to think is more of an essay in four parts than a traditional monograph—was to take the discussion of Longfellow's importance beyond the conversation of specialists and to see what he has to say about the business of literature in general.

We have read much about Longfellow's failings, artistic as well as ideological. His contemporaries faulted him for being too imitative and too popular, and, although we have added a few more items to the list of grievances, it seems we still haven't quite forgiven him for his success. *The Reader's Companion to American History,* published in 1991 by Houghton Mifflin, the same firm that once counted Longfellow among its stars, complains that he was so popular mostly because his "mellifluous poems challenged no one's prejudices"—well, other poems written at the time didn't challenge them either, yet their producers were never able to match Longfellow in terms of audience appeal.[10] From a modern perspective it would have been nice indeed if Longfellow had written about, say, the Middle East, translated extensively from the Chinese, and actively campaigned for the survival of Native Americans instead of inappropriately romanticizing their demise. We know that he didn't—what we don't know so well is that being "Eurocentric" could be considered a rather provocative stance at a time when even the president of Harvard was hoping to never receive another letter from Europe. Rather than on what he failed to achieve, I will focus on what I think Longfellow *did* achieve and what I think might still be relevant today. My hope is that a somewhat different Longfellow will emerge from the following pages: not the poet "of little depth" the *Reader's Companion to American History* describes but a highly self-conscious writer with a clear and coherent understanding of what he was doing, a writer who, apart from being more cosmopolitan, was in some ways perhaps even more American than Whitman.

In an incisive essay that has crucially influenced my own approach to the subject of this book, Steven Shapin points out that cultural historians, when describing the contributions of individuals, invariably prefer the "isolated knowers fabricating their culture out of thin air and personal circumstance" to the "cultural dopes," the docile practitioners of culture "doing nothing more than reflecting existing knowledge."[11] In *Longfellow Redux,* my plea on behalf of one of American literature's most effective and self-effacing practitioners, I raise my voice in protest against this persistent pattern of cultural evaluation. To return to the infamous *Newsweek* column, both the poetry-shy Mr. Wexler and his emphatic attackers would benefit, I think, from including Longfellow in the perennial debate about the death (or the survival) of poetry. His example will not only help us clarify what is really at stake here, it will also give us a better understanding of the hierarchies that still affect us and our thinking about literature and the arts today.

To be sure, Longfellow would have cringed at the explicitness of contemporary rap songs. And while it is hard to imagine him tapping his feet even to a languid Mary Chapin Carpenter ballad, I am nevertheless certain that America's first "pop" poet would have found utterly congenial the modern singer's desire to find "a soft, familiar rhythm in these swirling, unsure times."[12] After all, as Longfellow once said himself, in a poem about a sculptor who wanted to carve an image of divine sublimity and finally realized that the best material was right in front of him, a glowing piece of wood in his own fireplace: "That is best which lieth nearest."[13]

ONE

Strangers as Friends

LONGFELLOW AND HIS READERS

Liking to Be Liked

On August 22, 1879, Henry Wadsworth Longfellow was standing at the front door of Craigie House, his residence on Brattle Street in Cambridge, enjoying the morning. A thin lady clad in black approached him and demanded: "Is this the house where Longfellow was born?" "No," responded Longfellow, recovering from his surprise, "he was not born here." Pondering the next option that would endow with due significance the landmark she had come to inspect, the visitor suggested, unfazed: "Did he die here?" "Not yet," responded the seventy-two-year-old poet. Since Longfellow had apparently neither originated nor passed away in the building before her, the lady now concluded that he must still be living there. In fact: "Are you Longfellow?" Now, finally, she got an answer that satisfied her, but she felt the need to add, reproachfully, "I thought you died two years ago."

This story appears in the last volume of Longfellow's journals. The brazen tourist, equipped with the stern confidence that comes from ignorance, could have been created by Mark Twain—an "innocent at home," as it were. She is representative of the hordes of fans that made the pilgrimage to the Georgian mansion, once George Washington's headquarters and now the residence of the "Poet of the Heart."[1] As the diary passage shows, Longfellow knew how to make fun of his admirers. But more than a smidgen of this irony here seems directed against himself. The impudent lady's somber attire transforms her into something a little sinister, a kind of demotic Cassandra figure, sent to confirm the picture of the prematurely petrified poet, paralyzed by his own conventionality, as it had been evoked by some of his less well-meaning contemporaries. As another visitor to Craigie House mentioned in Longfellow's journal during the previous year put it bluntly, when apprised of the poet's actual age: "I have seen a good many men of your age, who looked much younger than you do" (October 10, 1877).

Longfellow lived in Craigie House for more than four decades, from August 1837, when the newly minted Harvard Professor of Modern Languages from Portland, Maine, rented two rooms from the eccentric Mrs. Craigie, to the day he died. The house was a wedding present from his father-in-law to Longfellow and his wife, Fanny Appleton. Here he raised his five children and produced eleven collections of poetry, two novels, three epic poems, and several plays and dramatic poems. Here he completed his translation of Dante's *Divine Comedy* and answered thousands of letters from readers all over the world. Here he compiled four major anthologies and prepared his Harvard lectures, until he was able to resign his position in February 1854, when he was making enough money as a poet to support himself and his family. Here his wife died on July 10, 1861, after a horrific accident, and here Longfellow himself passed away more than twenty years later, in the afternoon of March 24, 1882. Just a few days earlier, he had written his last two lines of poetry: "The world rolls into light / It is daybreak everywhere" ("The Bells of San Blas," 3:331).

Longfellow was a man of quiet contradictions. Although he liked travel, he barely left his house after 1842, when he returned from taking the "water-cure" in Germany; although he was politically one of the most tolerant of nineteenth-century American writers (an abolitionist, pacifist Unitarian liberal and avowed multiculturalist), he shunned all occasions on which he would have had to declare his opinions publicly and declined all invitations to give speeches. And although he was a deeply private man, he opened the doors of his residence, where he always kept a box of his autographs on his mantelpiece, to hundreds of adoring fans.

Longfellow liked to have his books liked, as he told Richard Henry Stoddard in 1878 (*Letters* 6:359). While Poe, a kind of "Byron in a tea-pot," as Longfellow called him, threw down his gauntlet to the public, "scorning alike its praise and censure" (November 29, 1845), Longfellow went out of his way to court his readers' sympathies, encouraging the kind of absorptive reading, accompanied by warm, pleasant feelings, that modern academics have loved to scorn. He knew how permeable the walls of his "ideal home-world of Poetry," his "Palace of Song," were (November 14, 1845), rattled not just by the wild gusts of wind and rain so characteristic of the fearsome New England weather that so often gave him splitting headaches but also by the very precariousness of the writer's position in America at a time when, as the narrator of Henry James's *Aspern Papers* (1887) said, "literature was lonely there and art and form almost impossible."[2]

His own father, Stephen Longfellow, a Harvard-educated, well-respected lawyer and congressman for the state of Maine, had warned him early on about his career choice, pointing out, in a letter written from Washington, that while "a literary life . . . must be very pleasant," there really "wasn't wealth enough in this country to afford encouragement and patronage to merely literary men." And to drive home his point that literature wasn't really a profession but a pastime that could be practiced by anyone with a little education, his father singled out some anonymous work he had seen printed in a newspaper, which he suspected to have come from his son's pen, for closer scrutiny: "It is a very pretty production, and I read it with pleasure. But you will observe that the second line of the sixth verse has too many feet. 'Beneath the dark and motionless beech.' I think it would be improved by substituting *lonely* for *motionless*."[3] In a subsequent letter, Stephen Longfellow, in lawyerly fashion, cautioned his son that he was rushing his "poetical productions" into print: "If you re-examine them you will find some defects which would have been corrected if you had adopted the course I recommend" (*Life* 1:57).

Longfellow later made it clear, in turn, what he thought of the legal profession. Among the stories and doodles he did for his children, now preserved in Harvard's Houghton Library, is a business card, originally given to his friend Charles Sumner by Frederick Adolphus Sawyer. Longfellow added, "Is a Lawyer" and adorned the card with a gallery of somewhat forbidding faces (fig. 1). But although he recognized that "there never was a better opportunity offered for the exertion of literary talent in our own country" (*Letters* 1:95), Longfellow for the first three decades of his long career didn't appear to be too sanguine about living the poet's life either. In fact, he held on to his teaching job until he was too exasperated to continue. Given his father's and his own doubts, it is perhaps not surprising that his first major book, the travelogue *Outre-Mer: A Pilgrimage by the Sea* (1835), ended with the twenty-eight-year-old author castigating himself for hop-

FIGURE I

Doodlings by Henry Wadsworth Longfellow, from his "Drawings
for the Children," Longfellow Papers, Houghton Library, Harvard
University, MS Am 1340 (164). By permission of the Houghton Library,
Harvard University.

ing that his book might last. "Dost thou covet fame? Vain dreamer! A few
brief days, and what will the busy world know of thee?" As if entranced
with the idea of imminent oblivion, the young author continued: "Alas!
This little book is but a bubble on the stream; and although it may catch
the sunshine for a moment, yet it will soon float down the swift-rushing
current, and be seen no more!" (7:326).

Longfellow's self-pitying prophecy was not to come true. Over the
next few decades he became better known than any American writer before or after him. His expanding readership spanned social classes, generations, and continents. In 1846, Ticknor in Boston published the second
edition of Longfellow's *Outre-Mer,* prepared from stereotype plates that
the author retained and paid for himself. The handsome edition in duodecimo format, bound in chocolate-colored cloth, sold for $1.00.[4] Thirty
years later, the book was still in print, advertised at a price of $1.50 in the
catalogue of Ticknor's successor. The little "bubble on the stream" had
lasted. Not bad for a first book.

Although some of his contemporaries might have managed to sell more books,[5] Longfellow for quite some time was America's, if not the world's, most widely recognized poet, so well-respected locally that he could not clap his hands in the theatre without everybody else noticing and the newspapers writing about it the next day,[6] so famous nationally that he was asked for his opinion when a name for a new state in the Union had to be found,[7] so revered internationally that a letter from Italy addressed merely "to Mr. Greatest Poet Longfellow" reached him without any problem.[8] Though he would come to care little about it, Longfellow, to his father's satisfaction, had been equally successful in his academic career. At the age of eighteen, he was offered the position of professor of modern languages at Bowdoin College in Maine, which he took up only after several years of preparatory travel in Europe. In 1835, he moved on to Harvard, where he had been appointed the Smith Professor of Modern Languages and Belles Lettres. Longfellow was the first college teacher in the United States to teach a class on Goethe's *Faust,* the first American translator of Dante's entire *Divine Comedy,* a "poeta doctus" fluent in multiple foreign languages, who, in spite of his stupendous learning, always remained in touch with the general reader, never forgetting that the real criterion for success was "the recognition of the public" (to Horace Harper, February 15, 1854; *Letters* 3:411). And after his resignation, he dared to become a professional poet at a time when, as Lawrence Buell points out in one of the best modern essays on Longfellow, "no one in America had ever made a living by poetry before."[9]

By any measure, Longfellow's life *was* a success story. It seems richly symbolic that one of the period's most famous racehorses, the legendary thoroughbred "Longfellow," winner of thirteen races, including the Saratoga Cup, was named after him. Longfellow's popularity soared with *The Song of Hiawatha,* published the same year as Whitman's *Leaves of Grass.* But while Whitman was forced to review his own book in hopes of increasing its meager sales, Longfellow's Indian epic was an immediate hit. Actresses in Chippewa costumes toured the country and, posing against painted backgrounds that featured leafy forests and quaint wigwams, belted out Longfellow's thumping trochees to sold-out theaters. Steamships were named after the protagonist and his demure mate, Minnehaha, and a drink called "Hiawatha" was offered in a New York bar with the unambiguous promise to "make the imbiber fancy himself in the happy hunting grounds." A popular item, the "Hiawatha" sleigh, had a scene from the poem painted on the back.[10] Longfellow's Indian protagonists became transethnic popular culture icons. In 1921, the Jewish comedienne Fanny Brice, while performing at the Ziegfeld Follies, brought down the house with a song called "I'm an Indian," in which a certain Rosie Rosenstein pretended that she was "a Yiddishe squaw": "I'm Minnehaha / Minnie-who? / Minnehaha / Ah ha."[11]

Longfellow's works easily transcended ethnic as well as national boundaries. At the height of his fame, his poems had been translated into French, Italian, German, Spanish, Portuguese, Dutch, Swedish, Danish, Chinese, and even Icelandic.[12] In the preface to his 1857 translation of *Hiawatha,* the German poet Ferdinand Freiligrath declared that Longfellow's poetry had, as if for the first time, helped Americans "discover" America.[13] Given the extraordinary success of *Hiawatha* in Freiligrath's own country, it is fair to say that many Germans also first discovered America through Longfellow's lines. And not only the Germans. On July 4, 1868, Longfellow was Queen Victoria's guest at Windsor Castle. "I noticed an unusual interest among the attendants and servants," the Queen later told Theodore Martin, Prince Albert's biographer, finding it a bit hard to believe that

> they so generally understood who he was. When he took leave, they concealed themselves in places from which they could get a good look at him as he passed. I have since inquired among them, and am surprised and pleased to find that many of his poems are familiar to them. No other distinguished person has come here that has excited so peculiar an interest. Such poets wear a crown that is imperishable.[14]

Julis Margaret Cameron's well-known photograph of Longfellow, taken during the same trip to England, when Longfellow was visiting Alfred Lord Tennyson, her neighbor on the Isle of Wight, reflects the public appreciation that was now extended to Longfellow wherever he went, as a poet and even more so as a person. The image shows the poet at his most poet-like (fig. 2), contradicting all those who thought he looked too much like a "tailor" or, as a compositor who once typeset *The Golden Legend* for him quipped, "a comfortable hotelkeeper."[15] Cameron's portrait was intended to make him look like Longfellow, or at least like many of his fans thought Longfellow should look. Tennyson is said to have warned his American visitor: "Longfellow, you will have to do whatever she tells you. I'll come back soon and see what is left of you."[16] The result of the session was a photograph that is indeed highly individualized. At the same time, Cameron

FIGURE 2

Julia Margaret Cameron, *Henry Wadsworth Longfellow*, 1868. Albu-
men photoprint. Special Collections, Albin O. Kuhn Library,
University of Maryland, Baltimore County, Acc. 75-15-001.
Courtesy of Special Collections, University of Maryland,
Baltimore County.

gave it the kind of general appeal that Longfellow's devoted readers trea-
sured. The composition, one of only a few in which Cameron included a
sitter's hand,[17] is striking because it sends the viewer looking in two different
directions at once: the face, shown entirely in profile, is turned to the left,
while the hand points us to the right. The loose, almost unkempt-looking
white beard and long, straggly strands of hair covering the neck serve as a
light frame for the darker-seeming skin and, by way of contrast, emphasize

the tautness of the lines and wrinkles around Longfellow's mouth and nose, giving his appearance a sternness of purpose and focus.

Upon closer inspection, though, the hand seems more relaxed than the face. The thumb partially disappears into the folds of the poet's dark cape, and the fingers lie lightly on the fabric, indicating the region of the heart. While Longfellow's leonine head is upright, rigid, even fierce—an image of control—his loose hand signals the place where we can always approach, even understand, him. Should we remember here also that this is the hand that holds the pen?

This, to be sure, was the "Poet of the Heart," revered by readers everywhere. Viewers more familiar with Longfellow's personal circumstances would have remembered, too, the touching story behind the impressive beard. The fire that killed his wife in 1861 also singed his hands and face when he tried to rescue her, making it difficult for him to shave. Cameron herself thought the "Profile likeness very fine indeed & therefore worthy of you."[18] Her photograph was a memorable representation of the man William Dean Howells called the "white Mr. Longfellow," "charitable in the immediate sort which Christ seems to have meant." Part resplendent Old Testament prophet, part modest Messiah, aged in body perhaps but youthful in spirit—a gifted poet, yes, but one who feels our pain, too, one whose heart is, as Howells put it, "open to all the homelessness of the world."[19]

And the world responded. "We need him as a tired child needs a soothing nurse," crooned the Reverend T. T. Munger in the *New York Independent,* in an essay titled "The Influence of Longfellow on American Life."[20] Charlotte Fiske Bates's compilation *The Longfellow Birthday-Book,* a medley of Longfellow quotations adorning a calendar with blank spaces for names and dates of birth, sold nineteen thousand copies in its first year of publication.[21] After his death, when the poet's portrait, draped in black, could be seen in many shop windows in Cambridge, the *Independent* ran a story about a group of people traveling aboard a French steamer bound for Marseille, who became engaged in an animated conversation about who was the world's most "universal poet." One passenger suggested Victor Hugo. "How can you, an American, give to him the place that is occupied by your own Longfellow?" demanded a Russian lady, who immediately began to quote from Longfellow's poem "The Bridge," adding that she would "long to visit Boston so that I may stand on the bridge." Then, the other passengers, among them an English captain, a gray-haired Scotsman, a Greek living in England, and finally the French captain of the ship, took turns reciting, in their respective accents, passages from Longfellow, until the Russian lady triumphantly concluded, with the (richly symbolic) lights of Napoleon's birthplace, Ajaccio, glimmering in the background, "Do you suppose there is any other poet of any country, living or dead, from whom so many of us could have quoted? Not one. Not even Shakespeare or Victor Hugo or Homer."[22]

The passengers expressed what had become a kind of global consensus about Longfellow—a poet both greater and, in his greatness, humbler than the others. In 1883, George Lowell Austin would end his four-hundred-page biography of Longfellow with a fulsome tribute to a man whose "sunny nature" and "serene," "blameless" life had rendered him immune to "the turbulence that made the lives of Byron and of Poe miserable."[23]

No wonder that, even during Longfellow's lifetime, some of his literary peers began to be a bit impatient with all the praise heaped on a writer whose real gifts and accomplishments they considered limited when compared to their own. For Edgar Allan Poe, Longfellow's global renown had been bought at the price of shameless plagiarism, the real secret behind Longfellow's uncanny productivity. Though no slouch himself when it came to pilfering other people's words and ideas, Poe used the willing pages of the *Broadway Journal* and the *Aristidean* to mount a full-scale attack on Longfellow, calling him, in a memorable review published in April 1845, the "GREAT MOGUL of the Imitators," the perpetrator of works that were "exceedingly feeble," "very singularly silly," "insipid," "schoolboyish," "sickening," and "scarcely worth" the pages they occupied. Longfellow's poems were "nothing," suitable only as bedside reading for the "negrophilic old ladies of the north."[24] Poe's review disintegrated into meanness and calumny: "the author of 'Outre-Mer,' is not only a servile imitator, but a most insolent literary thief." If by any chance Longfellow came across an original idea, exclaimed Poe, now attacking not only the poet himself but his entire côterie ("abolitionists, transcendentalists, and fanatics in general"), he would strut about the barnyard cackling "like a little bantam hen, who, by a strange freak of nature, had laid a second egg on the same day."[25]

Some of the sharpest barbs came from Margaret Fuller, who reviewed Longfellow's poems in the *New York Tribune* on December 10, 1845. Packing terms of abuse into the form of a more general reflection on the purposes of poetry (the greatest poets are "the prophets of the manhood of man") and employing the first person plural throughout, Fuller insinuated that her dim view of Longfellow's talents was shared by all readers with good taste: "Such works as Mr. Longfellow's we consider injurious only if allowed to usurp the place of better things." Mercilessly Fuller made fun of the typical Longfellow poem with "its Preciosos and Preciosas, its Vikings and knights, and cavaliers, its flowers of all climes, and wild flowers of none." In her opinion, Longfellow was a poet solidly "of the middle class," and although this sobriquet was supposed to define and denigrate his rank among his fellow writers, one feels that Fuller was also taking aim at his readers.[26]

In the eyes of his literary opponents, then, Longfellow had spent a lifetime repeating "his name" to an "admiring bog" (to use a phrase from an Emily Dickinson poem).[27] He fit to perfection the description of the poet as "lyrist" offered in Emerson's essay "The Poet" (1844): "a man of subtle mind, whose head appeared to be a music-box of delicate tunes and rhythms" but who does not "stand out of our low limitations, like a Chimborazo under the line, running up from the torrid base through all the climates of the globe, with belts of the herbage of every latitude on its high and mottled sides." According to Emerson, the mind of a poet of such modest gifts is not a mountain[28] but the size of a dainty formal garden, complete "with fountains and statues, with well-bred men and women standing and sitting in the walks and terraces."[29] What one encounters in such poetry is "the tone of conventional life" (Emerson believed that one couldn't have a real conversation with Longfellow, because he lived in a palace surrounded by servants and exquisite, differently colored wine bottles).[30]

And the sounds of conventional life are what Emerson's disciple, Walt Whitman, heard, too, when he was reading Longfellow's poetry. Although he would occasionally profess respect for him, especially after he was dead, he more typically thought of Longfellow as an "adapter and adopter," a writer who "never travelled new paths" and "shrank from unusual things."[31] And as Whitman's star began to rise, at least in Europe, Longfellow's fame was slowly fading, both at home and abroad. On March 25, 1882, a day before Longfellow's funeral, the *London Times*—recognizing that, in spite of Mr. Whitman's "questionable morality," *Leaves of Grass* might be the "nucleus of the literature of the future"—declared that Longfellow, the author of many "dulcet verses," had never in fact belonged "to the same strong, swift-souled race as Byron or Shelley." More serene than Byron, perhaps, but greater, no, not by a long shot.

An even less ambivalent rejection of Longfellow's work, as if admiring it stamped the reader as a different, more "rudimentary" form of life, came from Alice James. Propped up by her cushions, in all her "black-goggled, greenery-yallery loveliness," James had seen several applicants for the position of nurse and companion for her pass through the rooms of her London apartment, becoming increasingly convinced that "*haves*" like herself could never "hope to enter remotely into the inspiring motives of the *have-nots*." The worst of the lot, she said, had been the "intelligent" nurse she had once tried out. Thinking that a "literary" remark would "meet the requirements of the situation," this woman made the mistake of mentioning that "Longfellow was such a *deep* poet." Alice recoiled in horror and sent her packing: "Altho' she showed such tact in choosing my native geniuses," she observed with withering irony, "we parted shortly most amiably and expensively, to continue on so high a key was too great a strain."[32] Liking Longfellow's work, over the years, had become synonymous with a shocking disregard for the necessity of social as well as cultural boundaries, a form of improper reaching for the laurels of intellectual refinement by those who, in the eyes of Alice James and her peers, clearly weren't entitled to it.

Today, the complaint muttered by the lady in black at the gate of Craigie House ("I thought you died two years ago") seems weirdly prophetic, except that for many academic critics Longfellow has been dead for so long that he is now mummified. At the latest, Longfellow's decline began with the onset of the twentieth century, when his works were considered representative of what philosopher George Santayana had mocked as America's "genteel tradition." Limp examples of poetic conventionality, they entered the "trajectory of extinction" from which Barbara Herrnstein Smith has told us canonical texts are normally protected.[33] Eminently recitable, Longfellow's lines held on for a bit in the high school and college curricula, but not for long. In 1998, the *New York Times*—ironically in an article about the alleged "historical amnesia" of the Canadians—misidentified the author of *Evangeline* as "William Wordsworth."[34]

The modern attempts to denigrate him, along with the readers who enjoyed his works, are surprisingly consistent in the desire to eliminate all the Longfellow-admiring nurses from the halls of literary criticism. Liking Longfellow has become improper because he is too insufferably proper, too likely to be admired by people who have no business commenting on literary works. When in the 1920s I. A. Richards had his Cambridge students write about several anonymous poems, ranging from John Donne to D. H. Lawrence and to "Woodbine Willie," the one that fared the worst was poem no. 13, Longfellow's "In the Churchyard of Cambridge" (3:25–26). The poem is an ambivalent elegy for a member of the Vassal family that built the house in which Longfellow lived. It begins *in medias res,* with a brief description of what the speaker is contemplating, the grave of a lady in the old Cambridge cemetery, who had herself buried with a slave at her feet and a slave at her head, apparently so she wouldn't have to get by without their services in the afterlife. Longfellow's speaker asks a series of questions about this shocking arrangement (was the lady so in love with "foolish pomp" to have demanded such a manner of burial? Or did it show her Christian humility?), all of which are rejected in the penultimate stanza:

> Who shall tell us? No one speaks;
> No color shoots into those cheeks,
>   Either of anger or of pride,
> At the rude question we have asked;
> Nor will the mystery be unmasked
>   By those who are sleeping at her side.

The final stanza of the poem recommends that the reader remember her "own secret sins and terrors" rather than focus on the dead lady's flaws.

"Indignation rose high in the case of this poem," remembered Richards in his *Practical Criticism: A Study of Literary Judgment* (1925). Students called the work "commonplace," "dead," "sentimental," "weak-kneed," "maudlin," "beneath contempt," "artistically insincere," "ludicrous," "written in a state of semi-somnolence by a man with St. Vitus's dance," "not worth much effort on the part of the reader because the underlying emotion is not of sufficient value." Since the lady was now covered in dust, asked one student, how could the poet have known that her eyes were beautiful? The poem was so serious and naïve, another student observed, that it had to have been written by an American. At least one member of the class wondered if indeed Longfellow was responsible for "this gush of sentiment and evangelical piety." All the students felt that the emotions described in the poem were commonplace, of a kind that could have been experienced by anybody. None of them, lamented Richards, showed any appreciation for the poet's "easy kind of humour," his light play on social conventions, his urbane rejection of ready-made judgments. Readers of Wordsworth, Shelley, or Keats rather than Dryden, Pope, or Cowper, these young men wanted poetry to be "a mystery," something that ultimately defies (and should defy!) explanation.[35]

As seemed clear even then, Longfellow's works hadn't stood the test of time. "Who, except wretched schoolchildren, now reads Longfellow?" demanded Ludwig Lewisohn in 1932. Longfellow didn't even deserve to be called a "minor" poet: "The thing to establish in America is not that Longfellow was a very small poet but that he did not partake of the poetic character at all."[36] Herbert Gorman's extraordinarily hostile biography of Longfellow, first published in 1926, had paved the way for such merciless verdicts. Here, Longfellow appears as a tattered and ridiculous relic from the past, an unpleasant reminder of a time when America hadn't yet come into her own. True enough, Longfellow was the grandson of a state senator (on his father's side) and of a Revolutionary War general (on his mother's side). For Gorman, however, in spite of this impeccably American pedigree, Longfellow never developed an authentically American perspective. He became the emblem of a displaced, sadly anachronistic Eurocentrism, "kindly benign," "moral," and "safe," "the sheltered enthusiast of a culture that is not congenitally American." "Henry," as Gorman insists on calling him, had faults galore, but he wasn't aware of them; he rarely felt the "pangs of his own feebleness" as a writer. Unembarrassed by his lack of poetic originality, sliding gracefully "over the surface of life," he composed his trifling poems at a "polished library table," surrounded by other people's books, childishly attached to the warm comforts of domestic life.[37]

When F. O. Matthiessen, in his 1950 introduction to the second edition of the *New Oxford Book of American Poetry*, called on his readers to "smash the plaster bust" of Longfellow's "dead reputation," he was really, as Lewisohn would have put it, "slaying the thrice slain."[38] Few readers since have bothered to pick up the pieces. As Malcolm Bradbury and Richard Ruland concluded about Longfellow: "Unless our conception of poetry changes significantly, he will never again be thought great."[39] No significant body of academic Longfellow criticism has ever developed. Today he leads, when he is included at all, "a shadowy existence in anthologies."[40] His poetry occupies barely a page and a half in the latest edition of the *Norton Anthology of Poetry*. And the first volume of the much-anticipated *New Anthology of American Poetry*—praised as "the most comprehensive and innovative anthology of American poetry ever published" and as the first such collection to demonstrate "how a succession of canons of American poetry have evolved"—contains exactly two poems by Longfellow (and predictable choices they are: "The Psalm of Life" and "The Cross of Snow").[41] Other recent efforts to revive him—among them a new edition of Longfellow's poetry published by the Library of America and edited by the poet J. D. McClatchy—have elicited only a whisper from the American literary establishment. Longfellow, the first American writer to be included in Westminster Abbey's Poet's Corner, had, in effect, become the first white male author to be kicked out of the canon. In a recent essay, Barbara Everett reasserts what has now become a commonplace: "It could be said that before Whitman, no American poet of real gifts wrote American literature."[42]

Longfellow has always had his defenders, of course. "Whatever the miserable envy of trashy criticism may write against Longfellow," fumed Cornelia Walter, the editor of the *Boston Evening Transcript*, on January 19, 1846, "one thing is most certain, no American poet is more read." Two years after Longfellow's death, Julia Ward Howe took Margaret Fuller to task for her harsh criticism of Longfellow, suggesting that we also remember the many good things he did for his readers. Even though Longfellow might have lived in the "beautiful house of culture" (a "hothouse," as Fuller would have said), he had always remained "sensitive to the touch" of ordinary humanity that one would invariably find "encamped around it."[43]

But such arguments permanently lost their power when the New Critics went ahead and banned all "personal registrations," such as "spiritual ecstasy," "the flowing of tears" and "visceral or laryngeal sensations," from the discussion of literary works, putting more astringent aesthetic standards in their place.[44] The last important critical monograph on the man once celebrated as the "American Minnesinger" was Newton Arvin's *Longfellow: His Life and Work,* published in 1963. Arvin, formerly professor of English at Smith College, was a quiet, unassuming man leading a quiet, unassuming life until he was arrested and publicly exposed as a homosexual and the owner of a substantial collection of gay erotica, some of which he would regularly share with more or less closeted younger colleagues. He was, one would think, an unlikely interpreter of Longfellow's poems. But it is hard not to discover the disgraced Arvin's own covert longing for the kind of life he had never enjoyed in his description of his subject as a "poet of acceptance, rather than of rebellion and rejection."[45] Arvin did emphasize the "emotional and physical distress" of Longfellow's early years, perhaps the result of "sexual tension" after the death of his first wife Mary. Still, there were always "great and profoundly real satisfactions" available to compensate and console a man of Longfellow's "warm" and "kind" disposition—his friendship with Hawthorne, for example, or his marriage to Fanny Appleton, which gave him two decades of "almost pure felicity" (54). In other words, Longfellow *wasn't* like Arvin. He couldn't have followed Hawthorne into the "dark reaches" of his mind (53); nor did his melancholy partake of the "wildness of terror or fierceness of anger" that Arvin had uncovered in Melville, who was, "of course," superior to him in power. Sensitive to pain but averse to tragedy, Longfellow clung to neat little moralizing "lessons," without ever abandoning himself to the "evidence of his sensibilities" (67).

In itself, this argument was nothing new. Although Arvin, in many subtle readings of the poems, considerably complicates the image of the poet as an inoffensive purveyor of poetic padding for the common man's comfort zone, he ultimately reestablishes the tone of critical condescension practiced by more "exacting" readers from Poe onward. As Emerson once phrased it, a poet must aspire to being more than "a warming pan at sick beds" and balsam for "rheumatic souls."[46] In his epilogue, Arvin finds that Longfellow "spoke too directly to the general taste of his own age ever to have a great claim" on later ages. Though not a "poetaster," he was, after all, a "minor poet." So there, Dr. Lewisohn.

In more recent years, scholars have been more interested in historicizing than in evaluating Longfellow's artistic achievements, and a more balanced view of Longfellow's cultural importance has emerged. The name of the Longfellow Institute at Harvard, founded in 1994 and dedicated to literature written in the United States in languages other than English, is a tribute to Longfellow's multilingual interests, an aspect also foregrounded in a brand-new biography of the poet (the first in forty years!) by the Maine-based historian Charles Calhoun.[47] Perhaps the most persuasive attempt to reinvigorate critical interest in Longfellow is Mary Louise Kete's *Sentimental Collaborations,* where Longfellow appears alongside Lydia Sigourney and Mark Twain as well as Harriet Gould, a nineteenth-century amateur poet from Vermont related to Kete's husband. Longfellow's and Sigourney's poetry, according to Kete, deployed the language of sentimentality to initiate an exchange of sympathies between authors and readers, which in turn helped alleviate contemporary anxieties about what it meant to be American. Kete distances herself from all those readers who equate "sentimental" with saccharine and emphasizes the political, utopian dimensions of the term. As a "dialect of common sense," in Whitman's phrase, sentimentality succeeded where the enlightened insistence on reason had failed miserably, namely in bringing about a sense of national togetherness. Moved by Sigourney's and Longfellow's poems of mourning, readers turned loss into gain and learned to experience themselves as Americans.

This is good and interesting, but one wonders if some of the old prejudices against sentimentality don't creep in through the critical back door here, especially in view of Kete's initial retelling of Al Gore's story about his son's nearly fatal accident in a mall parking lot—proof that the sentimental mode has not lost its relevance today. Presenting his experience as a "story of grief and solace," Gore the privileged upper-class American was able to reinvent himself as an ordinary, mall-shopping citizen worried sick about his family. In the context of Gore's public speech, the "deployment" of sentimentality unmasks itself as what Kete's noun already suggests it really is—a ploy. And this is exactly what, according to Kete, sentimentality also meant for Longfellow, the privileged scion of a well-connected New England family, who legitimized himself in the still somewhat dubious profession of poet by using the power of language to "model what the middle-class American would feel like, wear, and think." Under the guise of "sentimental collaboration," Longfellow and Sigourney "coerced" their readers into joining them "in the articulation of a shared vision of America."[48]

But Kete's brilliant model, apart from glossing over the differences between Sigourney and Longfellow (more about this later in this chapter), does not account for Longfellow's vast popularity outside America or, for that matter, in more localized areas of the world, such as French Canada. Most important, it doesn't explain the unique relationship between Longfellow and his fans, who, as we shall see, showed few signs of feeling "coerced" in their responses to his poetry. "Sentimentalism," for Longfellow, was less a sinister trick than a name for a series of interactions between a writer and his readers, the nature of which I will attempt to sketch out in the rest of this chapter.

In 1941, T. S. Eliot wrote an introduction to a selection of the works of Rudyard Kipling, a perhaps equally popular writer who admired (and parodied) Longfellow.[49] Eliot proposed that, in this particular case, "the critical tools which we are accustomed to use in analysing and criticising poetry" (and weren't these the tools that Eliot himself had helped to establish?) "do not seem to work."[50] I suggest that Eliot's caveat also applies to Longfellow. But what critical tools *would* work, then? The clue to understanding Longfellow's position in American literature lies with his readers—not so much with his Cambridge peers as with the men, women, and children who read and memorized his poems in New England, Ohio, Iowa, Nebraska, and Wisconsin as well as abroad, a public that Whitman could evoke only on paper, while Longfellow commanded it in real life. If we return, for a moment, to the lady in black introduced at the beginning of this chapter and look at her not as a prophet of doom but as a not easily intimidated member of Longfellow's audience who feels that she is entitled to the right answer, we will also notice the somewhat startling fact that—although he might have been amused, perhaps even irritated, by his visitor's behavior—Longfellow never challenges her right to question him so sharply in front of his own house.

Not Pleased with Milton

America's first "pop" poet enjoyed the kind of celebrity status that nowadays would win him the devoted attention of the *National Enquirer* or *Star* magazine. He was a public poet,[51] admired and, in a sense, "owned" even by those who did not read him. George Lowell Austin tells the story of Thomas Buchanan Read's painting of Longfellow's three daughters, which depicted Annie Allegra, the youngest of his children, in such a misleading position that she seemed to have no arms. Disseminated throughout the country in thousands of photographic reproductions, the image (fig. 3) gave rise to ludicrous anecdotes about the poor Longfellow daughter, who was showing so much fortitude in the face of adversity. One day, James Russell Lowell, riding a Cambridge horse-car, overheard "one woman repeating to another the story of the armless child." "My dear woman," Lowell reprimanded her gently, "you are greatly mistaken. I am an intimate friend of the family, and I know that the facts are not as you represent." Unfazed and "with the air of someone not willing to be set right," the lady shot back: "I have it, sir, from a lady who got it from a member of the family."[52]

Before the full weight of modern academic criticism came crashing down on him, Longfellow was read in Copenhagen, where Hans Christian Andersen counted himself among the poet's devotees,[53] in China, where an admirer laboriously inscribed the text of "The Psalm of Life" on a delicate fan,[54] and in Calcutta, where an enthusiastic reader named Syud Hossein discovered that he could rely on Longfellow's poetry to cure one of his friends of his "predilection for airy castle-building." (Apparently Longfellow's poem had impressed this young man so much that he "immedi-

FIGURE 3

Longfellow's daughters, portrait carte-de-visite of a
painting (1859) by Thomas Buchanan Read, date unknown.
Author's collection.

ately took a copy from me: and I hope has by this time got it by heart and
begun to act in its spirit.")[55] Some particularly committed readers wrote in
to thank Longfellow even for poems he didn't write.[56]

What do we in fact know about these self-described "argent admirers" (Longfellow's correspondents were not always flawless spellers.)[57] Between 1821 and 1882, the year of his death, Longfellow received more
than twenty thousand letters, and this number does not include the more
than thirteen hundred requests for autographs and hundreds of birthday
greetings.[58] The letters to Longfellow (from 6,223 identified correspondents) preserved in Harvard's Houghton Library fill seventy-three boxes
or thirty-six linear feet of shelf-space.

Still, even this collection doesn't begin to give us an idea of the actual extent of Longfellow's correspondence, enormous even for a time in which access to a writer was not controlled by agents and publicists. Longfellow himself admits that he misplaced at least some of the letters he received.[59] And certainly not all of his fans had the courage to write to him. For example, Mrs. Harrison Otis once told Longfellow that her German servant girl was completely hooked on his *Voices of the Night* and refused to read anything else (*Life* 1:394).

If, for lack of an alternative, we consider the Houghton collection to be representative, the average Longfellow reader was white and almost as likely to be a woman as a man. Out of Longfellow's 6,223 correspondents, 1,579 (by my rough count) can immediately be identified as female, though the actual number of letters by women is probably much higher, especially if we include the hundreds of birthday greetings and requests for autographs Longfellow received. This is an impressive record, given that Longfellow's close friends and academic colleagues (who, from George Washington Greene to Charles Sumner, make up a large part of his more regular correspondents) tended to be male. The youngest of Longfellow's identified correspondents was six,[60] the oldest seventy-eight. Quite a few of the correspondents were foreigners; the writers of the letters I have read include a nine-year-old girl from Hamilton, Ohio, as well as Dom Pedro II, the emperor of Brazil.

Many of Longfellow's followers read his lines with glistening eyes, and some of them even told him so. Tears were shed by Mrs. Otis's maid as well as Abraham Lincoln, whose cheeks were said to have moistened when Noah Brooks recited Longfellow's poem "The Building of the Ship."[61] Longfellow himself witnessed Fanny Kemble "trembling, palpitating, and weeping" as she was performing his poetry in public (February 12, 1850). In a letter of June 16, 1851, Kemble, who had been struggling with depression after she had lost custody of her two children to her "intolerable" ex-husband Pierce Butler,[62] confessed to him the intensely personal significance his poetry had for her:

> Some little while ago I took up a volume of your poems and a load
> of most miserable suffering that had literally hardened my heart appeared to me to relax its pressure while I read it—for the first time for
> many months the iron grasp of sorrow seemed to relax and I experienced a moral relief which is indescribable but for which I blessed

you most earnestly and prayed that the benefit that you had done me might be restored to you in your need a thousandfold.[63]

Kemble had opened a door to establish intimacy between them, and Longfellow, in turn, walked right through it. In the response he sent her, he mentioned the tears that *he* had shed while reading her letter. Superficially, this exchange—tears produce a poem that makes a reader cry whose response then again makes the author weep—fits perfectly Kete's model of "sentimental collaboration." But Kemble also recognizes that the author, far from being the untouchable guarantor of meaning, is not exempt from what he describes: that he, too, under changed circumstances, might be the one in need.

Clearly, something in the dealings between Longfellow and his audience made him different from his contemporaries: a kind of leveling of the usual relationship between the author (as the one holding the "authority" over his work) and his readers (as the passive recipients of the author's words of consolation), which puts the reader in a position from which she can freely address, argue with, extend advice to, and even request favors from the person who produced the "sentimental" work that had moved her in the first place.

One of the most startling facts about the letters from America, England, France, Germany, Greece, Hungary, India, Italy, and Russia that poured in at Craigie House was the familiar, even intimate, conversational tone the correspondents felt free to adopt, as if, like the lady in black and the passenger in the Cambridge horse-carriage, they knew facts about him that Longfellow himself didn't. In 1862, Syud Hossein at first said he wanted ed to "appologize [*sic*] for writing to you from the other end of the world without ever having had the honor of your acquaintance." But then he immediately went on to justify his intrusion: "I can only say that any one who has read, & reading appreciated your charming and instructive poems and tales cannot but feel as if he needed no introduction in addressing you."

Writing in 1878, Mrs. Caroline P. Holden from Frankfort Station in Wile County, Illinois, skipped the apologetic stage. She sounded a confident note right from the beginning of her erratically punctuated message from the "Holden Homestead." "You will probably not be surprised to receive a letter from an entire stranger," she wrote on June 24. "I have been impelled many days, to write you, as would a loving daughter." Longfellow knew nothing about her, Holden conceded, but she, whose sons were now old enough to vote, had known Longfellow from the earliest days of her childhood. "Not your face, your form, but your heart, your soul, the secret springs of your God-given nature, as they have flowed out in verse, all over ours, & other lands." The recent death of William Cullen Bryant had inspired Holden to put pen to paper and write directly to her idol, to assure him that, after he too will have passed over to "the other shore" (Longfellow had turned seventy-one earlier that year), the encomiums now lavished on Bryant would seem "as drops beside a shower, compared to those that will be given to you." Mrs. Holden said she wasn't offering such promise of posthumous praise lightly, and she concluded her letter by inviting Longfellow to come out and pay her a visit before it was too late (remember, Bryant was already dead!). Allow not, she urged him, even "one inspired thought to go unwritten, for there will never be another mind & heart cast in the same mould of the Poet, Longfellow." Her husband also sent his regards.[64]

A year later, Elizabeth S. Crannell of 9 Hall Place in Albany, New York, also fretted about what she perceived as the poet's fast-approaching end—but not enough, apparently, to keep her from asking for Longfellow's "honest opinion" regarding her own literary talents. Appropriately, Miss Crannell's gentle *memento mori* came in the form of a poem. In case Longfellow wanted to see more, she could provide him with "any number" of poems of approximately "the same merit." Three stanzas from Crannell's piece lauding "the sweetest bard, our land hath known" will suffice here:

> "It is not always May," ye sung;
> But oh, if Winter ever brings,
> A faith so pure, a heart so young,
> As through thy forms, throbs and sings,
> Then grieve not for the May-day flight;
> Nor for the waning of the Year:
> Nor for the coming of the night
> When He shall say, "Lo I am here."
>
> Not like dumb cattle hast thou trod
> Nor yet with tears, sown earth's green face.
> But flowers of joy spring from the sod,
> Where e'er thy song hath left a trace.[65]

Note the allusions in Miss Crannell's verse to famous lines by Longfellow himself ("It Is Not Always May"; "The Psalm of Life"). Interestingly, she was using the poet's own images to console *him.*

Other correspondents were less interested in *giving* than in receiving life advice. A perhaps extreme case in point is Ida M. F. Livingstone, originally from Washington, D.C., and now of Randolph, Massachusetts, who was manifestly less concerned about the poet's well-being than about her own. She wasted not much time on the preliminaries: "Your worldwide renown, and your name that is a beautiful household word, must be my appology [*sic*]," she informed Longfellow right at the beginning of a letter dated June 18, 1880. It turned out that Mrs. Livingstone was *in extremis* and needed help. In her sprawling, bold handwriting (fig. 4), vigorously underlining several of her words, she demonstrated her entitlement to Longfellow's advice also by quoting from his works (in this instance, appropriately, from the second part of his trilogy *Christus: A Mystery):*

> I have come now, in this dark hour of my adversity to you, Sir, who have written such sublime poems,—who have had such marvellous thoughts;—who have uttered words of such eternal pathos, that they will live on forever in a thousand hearts; To you who have said "Faith alone can interpret life, and the heart that aches and bleeds with the stigma Of pain, *alone bears the likeness of Christ,* and can comprehend its dark enigma"—I reach out imploring arms.[66]

Having established a suitable precedent for her own suffering, Mrs. Livingstone went on to tell Longfellow, in some detail, of her first husband's decease shortly after she wed him, of the property that she lost, her father's death, her unfeeling sister's removal to Missouri, and, finally, her ill-advised choice of a new husband-to-be, "a gentleman of high social position" who had deserted her as soon as his previous entanglement with another lady had come to light. In horror, Mrs. Livingstone had fled to the "lovely quiet" of the "suberban [*sic*] Towns about Boston." But here she couldn't find any peace either. "Oh, Mr. Longfellow," she moaned, underlining her words once more, "*I can not rest!* I am so tempest tossed. My dreams, my ambitions, my hopes,—all are gone." And, inspired by her choice of imagery, she went on: "I am left on a desolate shore—anchorless, rudderless, alone!"[67] With her life a shambles, she knew that, in the words of her favorite poet, she had to rally herself and, again, be "up and doing."

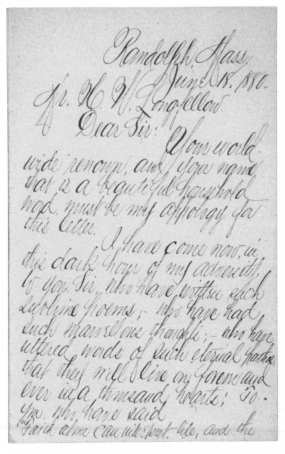

FIGURE 4

Ida Livingstone, page from a letter to Henry Wadsworth
Longfellow, June 18, 1880. Longfellow Papers, Houghton
Library, Harvard University, bMS Am 1340.2 (3472). By
permission of the Houghton Library, Harvard University.

But this was more easily said than done. She had been, said Mrs. Livingstone, a correspondent for several newspapers but "there seems to be
so very little money I can make in this manner." Wasn't Mr. Longfellow
("all the great world knows *you*") aware of something profitable that she
could do—work as a governess, for example, or as a traveling companion? "I have—I think—quite a pleasant disposition." There really were few

places in the vast world for abandoned ladies of good character like her, even if they were equipped with the ambition of a Napoleon. And Mrs. Livingstone picked up her nautical imagery again. Appealing once more to Longfellow's "beautiful heart," she asked him if he couldn't spy the "white gleam of a little sail" on the vast sea of uncertainty that surrounded her. Comparing herself, for the second time, to the savior on the cross ("I am no more to blame for having been thus unfortunate than Christ for being crucified") and, for good measure, also to Alexander the Great ("Alexander in parcelling out his spoils, left himself '*hope*.' I also have that alone, left me"), Mrs. Livingstone distinctly envisioned the possibility of a visit to Longfellow's house in the near future: "I shall board for a few days on Chester Square."

Longfellow must have panicked. His reply, dated June 21, 1880, was far shorter than usual and ended by pointing out that since he was about to depart for the seaside, he was afraid he wouldn't have the pleasure of seeing Mrs. Livingstone before his return in September (when he could be reasonably sure that her temporary stay in her Boston "suberb" had ended). Obviously, his correspondent's penchant for dramatic images as well as for casual allusions to literature and world history had not escaped his notice, and he advised her to "cling rather to the letter-writing for the papers" (*Letters* 6:615).[68]

But Mrs. Livingstone's confidence in her abilities was unshaken. Several months later, on December 29, 1880, she responded, revealing, not to Longfellow's surprise, that she fancied herself a bit of a writer, too. She was now living in Missouri and doing much better. Her once rusty knife had been *sharpened* (some energetic underlining here), and now she was eagerly anticipating the publication of a small volume of poems and "many beautiful thoughts in prose," to which she was hoping Longfellow would contribute a prefatory poem. "Just think, dear Mr. Longfellow, you have only to sit alone for a half hour, one of these snowy Winter days, and you will *think* a poem! It seems to me that *half* your thoughts must be poems." The anticipated favor would, she assured him, "happify" her "*so much*" (more underlining).[69] It is not clear if, intimidated perhaps by the reference to the sharpened knife, Longfellow ever replied.

One of Longfellow's most undaunted correspondents was the Vermont poet Julia Caroline Ripley Dorr, who had the considerable advantage of actually having met her idol in person. Dorr's encounter with Longfellow overwhelmed her, and she dramatically re-created her feelings in a letter dated January 1, 1879. "I find there is nothing I recalled with more delight than the few moments I spent under your roof one bright day last November," she gushed. "You have forgotten it, maybe; but what do you suppose it was to me to stand face to face with one whom I had reverenced from my very childhood, and whose songs had been to me all my life long an inspiration and a delight?" Longfellow wouldn't be able to know the feeling, she said, almost reproachfully, "unless you remember what it would have been to you, forty years ago, to have looked upon the face of Milton, to have clasped hands with Shakespeare, to have heard the voice of Dante." Dripping with emotion, Mrs. Dorr's reminiscence peters out in an excited staccato of sentences separated by dashes before she comes to a surprising conclusion: "—My heart was so full that I could not talk—I could only feel—But now to business."

It turned out that Mrs. Dorr had produced a poem, called "The Three Ships," an "almost literal description of a sunset scene, with three dark schooners slowly sailing into its fiery depths," a spectacle she had witnessed "from the deck of a steamer on Lake Superior." She would, said Mrs. Dorr, really like to see the poem included in one of the forthcoming volumes of Longfellow's anthology-in-progress, *Poems of Places* (1876–79). We do not know if Longfellow wondered about what a "literal" description of a fiery sunset should have been like ("The sun lay low in the glowing west / With bars of purple across his breast," Mrs. Dorr had written, apparently more reluctant to be "literal" at the time than she was now willing to admit. "And all the air was a luminous mist, / Crimson and amber and amethyst"). We do know, however, that her request had not fallen on deaf ears. On January 18, Longfellow wrote back saying that he would be "only too happy" to include the poem, which would find its place in the volume on the *Western States* under "Superior, the Lake" (*Letters* 6:437; *Places* 29:231–33).

It is easy—too easy, perhaps, as some of my own attempts at paraphrase have shown—to smile at Longfellow's fans, smirk at their skewed images, laugh out loud about the confidences they shared with him and ridicule their attempts (fumbling at best, by the standards of modern criticism) to convey their feelings in verse, too. True poetry, Randall Jarrell once said, in an attack on the general public accustomed to find fault with the "obscurity" of modern literature, must be read with "an attitude that is a mixture of sharp intelligence and of willing emotional empathy." It seems that Longfellow's readers had plenty of the latter and almost nothing of the former. And yet, Longfellow's correspondents, from Mr. Hossein in

Calcutta to Mrs. Livingstone in Charlotte, Missouri, did something Jarrell complained the modern foes of literary complexity don't do anymore.[70] They *read poetry,* and since poetry mattered so much to them, they felt compelled to try their hands at writing it, too, thus obliterating the boundary that separates good work from that produced by good intentions.

Longfellow's literary colleagues were dismayed by the rampant "cacoethes scribendi" that, for some reason, seemed to seize especially those who weren't at all qualified to write.[71] Why, howled George William Curtis from the "Editor's Easy Chair," his column in *Harper's,* were there so many people in this country, women especially, possessed by the yearning, "for it seems to be more than a desire," not only to write but to see their works in print as well?[72]

It must have occurred to some of the harbingers of "high" art in America that Longfellow, with his almost proverbial accessibility, might have been to blame for all those deeply felt, passionately expressed poems that were now mushrooming in the humblest households. Poet Richard Henry Stoddard saw the link and, in *Scribner's,* decided to come to Longfellow's defense, sort of. Employing the familiar Coleridgean distinction between "imagination" (good) and "fancy" (bad) to explain what had in fact induced so many readers to imitate him, Stoddard singled out what he admitted was a bad habit of Longfellow, namely his penchant for inappropriate conceits. Consider "A Gleam of Sunshine," where the sun pouring in through the blinds is compared to the "celestial ladder" in Jacob's dream (1:215). But Longfellow's minor lapses of judgment became major disasters in the hands of his less capable fans: "It was the fancy of Mr. Longfellow, and not his imagination, which commended his poetry to our poetasters of both sexes, and what was excellent in him—and is excellent in itself, when restrained within due bounds—became absurd in them."[73]

The "fanciful imagery" of Longfellow's poetry might explain why writing verse suddenly didn't seem all that hard anymore to his readers. Find a great-sounding simile—or, better still, a couple of them—and you have yourself a poem. But this theory doesn't begin to explain the fan mail. Why did so many of Longfellow's fans feel comfortable addressing him as their *friend,* discussing with him subjects as delicate as his declining health? Why did they not shy away from asking the very man they would readily compare to Shakespeare for help with their own personal disasters and their own paltry literary efforts? Usually, the very existence of the work was evoked as enough of a reason: You, Mr. Longfellow, showed us your "friendship" by writing the poems that speak to us, and now we take you at your word. "I find the courage to address you as I would a friend," explained James Whitcomb Riley, the future perpetrator of "Little Orphant [*sic*] Annie," in a letter accompanied by several recent samples of his poetic output, "since by your works you have proven yourself a friend to the world."[74] The final entry in Longfellow's journals, written on January 31, 1882, less than two months before his death, was about another such self-declared "friend," whose request was only slightly more outlandish than most: "Received this morning a postal card from a gentleman in Falls City, Nebraska," wrote Longfellow. "He 'is not pleased with Milton's Paradise Regained,' and wishing me 'to take up the poem where he left off, and continue it to the Millenium; never mind his style; give your own, and oblige a friend. W. F. Cunningham.'"[75]

In his journals, Longfellow sometimes hinted that such communications worried him, especially the privileged knowledge of his character they presumed. Nevertheless, he seems to have regarded his bulging files of letters as a kind of occupational hazard, to be borne willingly by a poet of his wide public appeal. It wasn't easy. His correspondents not only wanted him to take an interest in their problems but also expected him to use his own stamps. The "letters from all sorts of people" that arrived at Longfellow's house seemed to have one thing in common: "No hesitation—no reserve—no consideration or delicacy! What people! And they often leave me to pay the return post" (May 15, 1855). On particularly bad days, Longfellow imagined himself surrounded by his "unknown correspondents," their "loud halloo" ringing in his ears (*Letters* 6:116), and he felt he could see them taking aim at him from a distance ("My life is made unsafe—completely riddled by their merciless sharp-shooting," May 9, 1856). From everywhere, the ghostly voices of yet unanswered letters were beckoning: "I no sooner sit down to rest and meditate upon something I have in mind," Longfellow wrote on March 13, 1877, "than I am haunted by the spectre of some unanswered letter, and start up, exclaiming like Hamlet, 'Ha ha boy! say'st thou so? art thou there, true-penny?'"[76] His correspondence became something of a nightmare, in which he beheld letters pouring in from all sides, a many-headed, many-limbed monster intent on suffocating him. "Up to my armpits in unanswered letters," he wailed in September 1877 (in a letter, no less), "a con[s]tantly increasing mass of unprofitable reading" (*Letters* 6:303).

And these letters were from men and women completely unknown to him! The "Perfect Stranger" had become a familiar presence in the Long-fellow household:

> Letters, letters, letters! How they come, and how they consume one's time! Not from friends,—I do not mean that, for it is always a plea-sure to hear from them;—but the "perfect stranger," as he is fond of calling himself, and who always has "an axe to grind," and wants you to turn the grindstone. A charming Essay might be written on the "Perfect Stranger." (April 14, 1862)

Given such impositions, it seems nothing short of remarkable that Long-fellow spent hours at his desk every day writing letters, sometimes as many as twenty a day, to the "semi-literate" or "subliterary" American public mocked by Herbert Gorman and Ludwig Lewisohn.[77] Toward the end of his life, when the steady stream of "letters on all subjects, which annoy and perplex me" showed no signs of letting up, he did contemplate, briefly, "the uncivil resolution of answering none of them."[78] Which implies that he had always considered it a sign of "civility" to respond. (In Camden, New Jersey, Walt Whitman, unhampered by conventional ideas of deco-rum, found it easier to deal with the celebrity seekers who hounded him late in life: "I practically never answer them," he told Horace Traubel. "I make what use I can of the return stamps and let the rest of the matter go.")[79] In November 1881, finally, four months before his death, Longfel-low had a circular printed in which he informed his correspondents, par-ticularly those who would begin their letters identifying themselves as "an entire stranger," that Mr. Longfellow, on account of his illness, found it "impossible to answer any letters at present." An immense relief, he told his friend George Washington Greene (*Letters* 6:750).

At least he knew why he had kept trying for so long. While some people regarded the pen as mightier than the sword, Longfellow was well aware that it wasn't a particularly "safe staff to lean upon," not safe enough at any rate not to worry about what his readers might think of him.[80] Didn't Buffon array himself "in full dress for writing his Natural History"? Thus we should do also when writing letters, Longfellow informed his publisher James T. Fields on March 17, 1871, so that we may always be "courtly and polite" and say "handsome things to each other." In fact, he told Fields, he was writing these lines "arrayed in my dress-coat, with a rose in my button-hole, a circumstance I think worth mentioning" (*Letters* 5:409).

Many of the letters Longfellow received were simple customer service requests. For example, a lady in Ohio announced that she was planning to host a party at her house celebrating Longfellow's birthday and included a hundred blank cards for him to sign, "as she wishes to distribute them among her guests" (February 23, 1881). More challenging were those letters that contained specific queries from committed readers, frequently asked at the behest of a book club or some other community organization. Was *Evangeline,* a schoolteacher from Marlboro, Massachusetts, wanted to know, founded on fact or the poet's imagination?[81] Had he been thinking of Goethe's *Faust* when he wrote "The Psalm of Life"? inquired Mr. Sawyer, a member of a literary club in Brooklyn.[82] And what did the title of *Hyperion* really mean, wondered Mrs. Redman Abbott, from Chestnut Hill, near Philadelphia, who confessed to having read the novel, "well—innumerable times." Would he be "so very kind as to be the Oedipus to solve our riddle"?[83] Several correspondents, like Nebraska's Mr. Cunningham who didn't like the ending of *Paradise Regained,* proposed tasks and topics for future work, which seems less strange when we remember that Longfellow kept a "Book of Suggestions" for just that purpose on his desk.[84]

Particularly inane letters at least entertained him. In January 1850, a gentleman wrote asking Longfellow to pen a valentine for him, because he wanted to return a valentine from a young lady received last year. Commented Longfellow, "He does not like to show the white feather in the poetic way; and wants to show what he can do, with the help of my white feather" (January 31, 1850). Or take the note from J. H. Fenstermacher in Pottsville, Pennsylvania, which Longfellow mentioned in a letter to his daughter Annie on March 25, 1877. Apparently Mr. Fenstermacher had "of late read a good deal about you being the best of American poets" and was now hoping or, rather, demanding that Longfellow consider composing an "oration" for him. "State your price," said Mr. Fenstermacher, "and if satisfactory I will let you write one for me" (*Letters* 6:260).[85] Then there was the correspondent who, amusingly, begged him for an "autograph written with your own hand" (February 22, 1881), or, for that matter, Mr. Lewis Cruger of Washington, "an unreconstructed rebel," who encouraged Longfellow to defray the expenses of publishing his "Analytical Essays on the Great Poets," judged by his friends to be on a level with "the most eloquent and beautiful compositions in the English language" (August 11, 1877).[86]

Many of his readers, inspired by Longfellow's prodigious output, sent along samples of their own work, from the farmer in Michigan who asked that Longfellow endorse his own epic on the Iroquois so that no one would think "it must be in some sort a copy or imitation of the Song of Hiawatha" (September 6, 1859) to the gentleman in Maine who enclosed, for the poet's inspection, a work on the Creation, "done up in about six hundred lines" (March 18, 1870), to Mr. Tracy of Buffalo, who included his poem titled "The Rhyme of the Tempest Fiend" ("Hardly fair, that," mumbled Longfellow, "as I do not know him," December 2, 1845).[87] Occasionally, readers would get an apologetic note saying that Mr. Longfellow on principle couldn't review such works.[88] But a majority of Longfellow's muse-kissed fans were given noncommittal, patient, and polite advice, even when he didn't really like what they had sent. Cautiously and favorably, Longfellow commented either on the general mood he said he had perceived in a poem or zoomed in on tiny details, counseling William Martin in western Ontario not to rhyme "dawn" with "morn" and assuring Moody Currier in New Hampshire that he did appreciate the "spirit" in which his poetry was written ("and that, as Göthe says, is the main thing in every performance").[89] He would encourage fellow poets like Julia Dorr in Vermont to try her hand at rhymed couplets ("the metre most agreeable to the English ear") and would inform James Whitcomb Riley in Indiana that in line 13 of his poem "Destiny" he'd really meant to say "*supine*" and not "*prone*," which, Longfellow reminded him, means "face-downward."[90]

John Greenleaf Whittier, often compared with Longfellow because he, too, was a "fireside poet," believed that it was the mail from his fans that eventually killed Longfellow: "My friend Longfellow was driven to death by these incessant demands." Whittier knew what he was talking about. Since the publication of *Snow-Bound* (1866), which catapulted him to instant stardom, literary "pilgrims" had been showing up unannounced on his doorstep, too, and Whittier was finding it difficult to handle his "unhappily increasing correspondence." For every letter he answered, "two more come by the next mail."[91] During the last five years of his long life, when he was battling numerous health problems, Whittier wrote over nine hundred letters. That this should have happened to someone who would "rather chop wood than talk poetry, with strangers" is richly ironical.[92]

When asked to comment in detail on a correspondent's poetic efforts, Whittier tended to be less careful than Longfellow. He would note, for example, a writer's lack of skill "in the mere mechanism of verse" and give cold comfort to a sailor who thought he has been kissed by the muse: "Few men can be poets in the true sense of the term." But then Whittier himself didn't really believe in "making literature the great aim of life," as he wrote, perhaps somewhat pointedly, the New Hampshire poet Celia Thaxter, after praising a poem she had published in the *Atlantic Monthly*.[93]

Looking at the sheer extent of Longfellow's correspondence with his fans, the modern reader is reminded of his predecessor in the American public's favor, the Connecticut poet Lydia Sigourney (1791–1865). In letter 14 of her autobiography, *Letters of Life* (1866), Sigourney lamented that her correspondence sometimes amounted to "a yearly exchange of two thousand letters." The letters she had received ranged from some "elegiac verses" required by the owner of a canary "which had been accidentally starved to death" to a particularly thrifty correspondent's request that she write some very general commemorative lines for him, since his wife's health was failing and they also had a young baby and he wanted something he could use in the event that both should be "taken by death." A distraught father needed an elegy for his baby, volunteering as the only bit of information intended to inspire his "tuneful Muse" that his child had been "drowned in a barrel of swine's food." A more inventive correspondent, who claimed he had a strong "dislike to the business of punctuation, finding that it brings on a 'pain in the back of the neck,'" asked her to insert the missing commas in a manuscript volume of no less than three hundred pages.

Most of these requests, with the exception perhaps of the invitation that she act as an umpire of a baby show in the city of New York, concerned Sigourney's services as a writer, sometimes in the most basic sense of the word: "Desired to assist a servant-man not very well able to read, in getting his Sunday-school lessons, and to 'write out all the answers for him, clear through the book, to save his time.'" All in all, the demands on Sigourney as a writing master had done little, she admitted, to get her out of the drab "kitchen in Parnassus." Still a servant, she was forced to officiate as an "aproned waiter" in the house of poetry, obliging her customers where the members of other professions would have said no:

> Do we go to a milliner, and say, "You have earned a good name in your line. Make me a bonnet and a dress. I should prize them as proofs of your skill?" Do we tell the carpet manufacturer, "You assort your colors better than others. Weave me a carpet for my study?" Do we address the professed cook with "You have a high reputation. I am to have a party. Come and make my jellies and confections?"

Would those functionaries, think ye, devote time, toil, and material to such proposals, without compensation? I trow not.[94]

The moral to be inferred here is not that the writer should do as the carpet manufacturer would and charge the appropriate fee for services rendered. For Sigourney, a writer was supposed to have loftier goals in mind. Consider the context in which the quotations from her fan mail appeared. Sigourney's *Letters of Life* is an epistolary autobiography, cast in the form of fourteen letters to a "dear friend," which ostensibly have no other purpose than to reaffirm, to all those who care to know, the intimacy of their connection, marked by the kind of sentimental affection that in reality doesn't even need all "these poor instrumentalities of pen and ink." The proper mode of writing letters, and of producing literature, is thus contrasted with the improper one, as practiced by the favor-seeking correspondents, so deficient "in the sense of propriety." Lest the message be lost on her readers (who are of course supposed to distance themselves from the canary owner or the father who let his own child drown in swine food), Sigourney adds that the true rewards for her dedicated service in the field of letters have come to her from abroad rather than from home: "scarcely any profit has accrued to my literary labors in this vicinity, or indeed in the whole of my own New England."[95]

In terms of sheer volume of mail, at least another one of Longfellow's female colleagues could have competed with Sigourney: "Fanny Fern," born Sara Payson Willis in 1811, four years after Longfellow and in the same city of Portland, Maine. Determined to make a living for herself and her children through her writing, Fanny Fern became the first weekly newspaper columnist in the United States. Her book, *Fern Leaves from Fanny's Portfolio* (1853), a collection of articles she had written for several periodicals, sold seventy thousand copies in the United States and twenty-nine thousand copies in England in less than a year.[96] In 1855, Robert Bonner contracted Fern's exclusive services for the *New York Ledger,* whose circulation, within a few years, shot up to four hundred thousand.

According to Fern's granddaughter, the writer's mailbox at 303 East Eighteenth Street in Manhattan was constantly overflowing with fan mail. However, these letters came as responses to her newspaper columns in which Fern talked directly about the specific problems besetting herself and her readers: from comparatively trivial matters, such as the risks of feeding too much candy to children and the experience of having a furnace installed in one's house, to personal tragedies, such as her daughter Grace's death in December 1862, to serious social issues, such as the treatment of the insane on Blackwell's Island or the discrimination against women in everyday life.

Although the letters she received were often pressingly personal, Fanny Fern preferred to answer them in her weekly column. The following article, published on February 18, 1860, tells us something about the extent of Fern's fame, reaching as it did from the streets of Manhattan to the prairies. It also clearly shows her determination to keep the interaction between herself and her readers as public as possible, thus avoiding the kind of one-on-one encounters, either by mail or through social contact, that both irked and intrigued Longfellow:

> Don't you suppose I feel grateful to the man who sent me a box of nice, warm soles to slip in my boots this cold weather? Don't you suppose that the mother who sent me a daguerreotype of her dead boy, made my heart glow with that sweet and touching proof of confidence toward a stranger? Don't you suppose that the little girls off in the prairies who sent me some flower-seeds in a nice, little letter, made me very happy? Don't you suppose I would have written a love letter for that entranced young man, to the girl he adored yet was afraid of, had I time? ... Do you suppose I wouldn't read several MSS. a month, give my opinion, and find a publisher, were the days longer, and my head stronger? (Warren 258)

It was only in the safe space of her column that Fanny Fern extended her "woman's hand," clasping "yours in sympathy."[97] The whole spectrum of America's problems seemed to be represented here, as the examples included in Fanny Fern's autobiographical novel, *Ruth Hall* (1855), also prove—they cover everything from grief over a beloved dog's death to the request to write up a story that will help expose and embarrass a deceitful ex-lover ("I will furnish all the facts").

Like Longfellow's readers, the letter-writers felt that their idol "Fanny Fern" was "a stranger, and yet *not* a stranger" to them. After all, they had read, as one of them phrased it, "your heart in your many writings."[98] Unlike Longfellow, however, Fanny Fern vigorously resisted any contact that went beyond the intimacy she so successfully staged in her public writings. Requests for autographs annoyed her as much as they did Sigourney. On a single sheet of paper sent back to one of her fans, she signed her name explicitly "without pleasure," and in one of her columns she lambasted the strangers who pursued her in public, attempting to "pry open" her "humble Fern leaves."[99]

Neither Sigourney nor Fern was willing to dispense with the boundaries that protected them from the groundlings. Aware of the female writer's precarious situation in American society, they claimed to have no pretensions to high art. But they also used the excesses displayed by their fans to distance themselves from purely instrumentalized views of the purposes of literature.[100]

It is not surprising that Sigourney, author of widely popular advice books such as *Letters to Young Ladies* and *Letters to Mothers,* would have been the recipient of requests for poems made to order. Small wonder too that, inspired by the pseudointimacy achieved in the virtual space of her *New York Ledger* column, Fanny Fern's fans would bare their souls in letters to a woman they had never met. But why a volume like Longfellow's *Voices of the Night,* prefaced by a quotation from Euripides (in Greek!), should have elicited confessions of similar intensity from eager readers everywhere is more puzzling and not easily explained by references to the "sentimental" nature of the poetry.

Even more remarkable is, perhaps, the sheer number of people who weren't content with letter-writing but showed up on the poet's doorstep. In 1881, Hawthorne's son-in-law, George P. Lathrop, in an article for *Harper's,* scoffed at the hordes of visitors, well known to the residents of Cambridge, who were tramping up the garden path to Craigie House: "The days follow in something like a continuous levee at this old colonial mansion, whose heavy brass knocker is plied (or more often gazed at by a deteriorating generation, in ignorance as to the mode of handling it) by a long stream of pilgrims of high and low degree, drawn by reverence, or curiosity, or the wish for literary advice."[101]

Collectively, these intruders—some of whom were, even by our modern standards, quite strange—took the Victorian ritual of "calling" beyond acceptable limits. On occasion, people would address Longfellow on one of his walks through Cambridge and were then invited to come home with him: "I met in the street some young ladies who ask if they may shake hands with me. Bring them in, with a silent gentleman and his wife, who seem to have charge of the party, to see the house. They are from Philadelphia, but I do not learn their names" (April 2, 1866). More frequently, the visitors came unbidden, like the traveler who dropped in on October

18, 1866, wondering "if Shakespeare did not live somewhere about here" (Longfellow told him that "I know no such person in the neighborhood"). Some of Longfellow's callers had decidedly ulterior motives. On March 28, 1876, a "clamorous woman," whose one distinction was to have married into the family of the Van Rensselaers, showed up "with a book to sell" and didn't leave before Longfellow had indeed purchased the item, "which I do not want." Other visitors, like Mrs. Randolph from Louisiana, who visited on February 24, 1881, apparently just wanted to let off steam. The Bostonians were, observed Mrs. Randolph, "cold and stiff." Why on earth were the ladies at the Brunswick Hotel not speaking to her?

Then there were the foreigners, a sheer endless stream of them: Italian beggars, Cuban abolitionists, a longhaired German poet, a Norwegian writer, and a Polish count "with a fifty Ogre power of devouring time" (December 15, 1850). A lady with a strong German accent stopped by to recite "The Building of the Ship," which she referred to as the "Lunch of the Sheep," and threatened to perform the poem in public as well (April 27, 1877). More amusing than annoying was a tipsy, scruffy Frenchman who stumbled in one afternoon, quoting Virgil, Horace, and Homer in their original languages as he made himself comfortable. Though he spoke no English at all, he was hopeful that the poet would employ him as a secretary (March 30, 1866). What had he done, Longfellow asked himself in a letter to Sumner, to deserve his role as the good "*Oncle d'Amérique*" and "general superintendent of all the dilapidated and tumble-down foreigners, that pass this way" (*Letters* 4:130)?

Longfellow's substantial income, "far exceeding that which is generally supposed to fall to the lot of poets,"[102] was public knowledge, and Craigie House rapidly became a magnet for all sorts of confidence men, as a British visitor had occasion to observe. He was particularly intrigued by a man with his arm in a sling, who claimed to have been injured "in the service of his country" but then indignantly refused to let the somewhat skeptical Longfellow inspect his wound: "if that is the light in which you look at the matter I would rather not be beholden to you for assistance, and so I wish you good morning."[103] Some of these more or less amiable villains Longfellow rather liked, even if they turned out to be repeat offenders. There was, for example, an English gentleman named Hamilton, a "cool plausible man," who appeared, along with his wife, on Longfellow's doorstep on a lovely, bright day in 1868. Longfellow remembered him well: "When he was here in 1863 or 64, he called himself Burr." After his last visit, a clerk from one of Boston's mercantile houses had called to inquire about him and said they had "paid a draft for him, which had come back protested." Apparently, Mr. Burr-Hamilton, the placid bouncer of checks, had paved the way for his fraud by speaking of Longfellow as a "friend" (February 8, 1868).

Others were simply lunatics. My personal favorite is a somewhat deranged lady who paid a visit in February 1881, identifying herself as a descendant of John Locke, blessed with a remarkable "memory of facts and dates." She hinted that she was in the process of establishing a "Society for the suppression of Cruelty to Letter Carriers" and explained that, on the basis of her reading of Ezekiel 36, she had reached the conclusion that the plant known as "hollyhock" should be called "holly-flock." Longfellow was disconcerted enough to look up the verse when she was gone: "As the holy flock, as the flock of Jerusalem in her solemn feasts; so shall the waste cities be filled with flocks of men" (February 23, 1881). The prize for maniacal persistence, however, goes to the lady who showed up at Craigie House with several suitcases and announced that she was married to the great poet and had now come to live with him, an episode clearly remembered decades later by Longfellow's son Ernest. She had to be forcibly removed by the Cambridge police.[104]

What are we to make of these visits? If Longfellow really abhorred them as much as he often said he did, why then did his house remain always open to everyone who wanted to enter?[105] "Never send word 'not at home,'" warned the formidable Mrs. Abell in a widely used etiquette book, "it is an immorality when you are only engaged, and has a bad influence on the servants."[106] But the reasons for Longfellow's relentless availability went beyond social convention. He must have secretly enjoyed at least some of these visits, so detailed are his accounts of them in the journals. (And he *did* try out the "magic belt" one of his callers brought—a surefire cure for neuralgia, he said, if kept on overnight. "To-day my head is better," the mystified poet reported the next day, on February 27, 1875, after "seven hours of painless sleep." Go figure.)

Of course, the practice of making calls or, to use a less class-specific term, visiting, was not limited to the Victorian bourgeoisie. Nor was it originally a leisure activity. In antebellum New England, visits were a way of strengthening and deepening community ties. Women as well as men met not only to socialize or to entertain each other but also to exchange important services. Industrial capitalism would place crucial limits on such opportunities to visit. It transformed the social lives of countless families by measuring the time of most men in hourly wages and confining women to the domestic space. But Longfellow, whose "business" *was* the home, obviously did not, and could not, easily separate domesticity and work, the humdrum life of a father and citizen from the higher goals of literature. His willingness to receive visitors at the house that was also his place of work indicates that to him writing was less a privilege than a civic obligation or, even less glamorously, a business—in a sense, *everybody's* business. This is the tenor of a remark made by his daughter Annie that Longfellow recorded in his journal. Comparing her father's work to that of the fishermen of Nahant, Annie said, "in a mysterious whisper": "The trade of Poet is better, because you can do it all Winter" (January 18, 1861). The "mystery" was that there was none. Longfellow's little daughter intuitively classified the profession of the poet as something that is not different from other types of work. If anything, it has the added advantage that it can be practiced even in inclement weather and, even more important, at home. Here, the public and the private spheres intermingle, opening up not just the poet's house but even his heart to the inquiring looks of his readers.

Longfellow's study, featured in numerous contemporary illustrations (fig. 5), became famous as "the room sacred to the Muses almost above all others on American soil."[107] The tools of the writer's trade, among them the inkstands (Longfellow used quill pens), eventually became as well known as the crayon portraits of Emerson, Sumner, and Hawthorne that were also displayed there. Longfellow owned not just one but three of these writing implements: his own, one that had belonged to Coleridge, and one formerly used by the Irish poet Thomas Moore, whose small wastepaper basket was nearby, on the seat in the window. Along with the glass-encased fragments of Dante's coffin, Liszt's portrait, and a first edition of Gray's poems, these inkstands were among the carefully selected symbols of culture with which the poet surrounded himself.

The very fact that these items, as material objects, were publicly written and talked about already erased some of their uniqueness and dispelled their aura. They were not part of a shrine[108] but rather lent authenticity to the work that was going on in this study. "High culture" doesn't serve as a mark of distinction here, as a barrier separating a godlike producer of literature from his awestruck readers, pausing before the golden knocker on the poet's front door. And the small statue of Goethe on the poet's writing stand indicated to everyone that literature was not creation *ex nihilo*

FIGURE 5

"Henry Wadsworth Longfellow in His Study," Cambridge, Massachusetts.
Warren's Portraits (415 Washington Street, Boston), 1872–74. Courtesy
of Historic New England/Society for the Preservation of New
England Antiquities (neg. number 15745-B).

but something achieved in patient dialogue with those who had come before. Several visitors commented on how untidy Longfellow's workplace
seemed, strewn as it was with papers, proofs, and books.[109] Interestingly,
though Longfellow also owned a standing desk, contemporary engrav-
ings and photographs typically show him sitting at his round central table,
which was covered with a patterned cloth—a visible reminder of the link
he wanted to preserve in his work between domesticity and literary professionalism. Craigie House was prominently featured, in an adoring article by
George William Curtis, when George Putnam published his *Homes of American Authors* in 1853. The residences described in the book (from Audubon's
Minnie's Land to Daniel Webster's Marshfield) were supposed to show
the American public as well as interested readers abroad that American
"literary laborers" were "comfortably housed" and that "authorship in
America, notwithstanding the want of an international copy-right, which

has been so sorely felt by literary laborers, has at last become a profession which men may live by."[110]

That Longfellow might have thought of the "trade of poet" as a profession like others is confirmed by at least one other anecdote reported in his journal of November 1847, shortly after the publication of *Evangeline.* Longfellow had made one of his frequent trips to Boston, this time to buy some hats for his children. As he was paying for his purchase, the clerk beamed at him: "You will get part of your money back tomorrow for one of your books" (November 9, 1847). A trade indeed.

Silence: Longfellow's Journals

To the modern reader, the sheer volume of visitors filing in and out of the homes of Victorians seems daunting. Frequently, diarists of the time recorded who showed up and when rather than who said what and why. Longfellow's journals seem to fit that category. They were "almost insipid," opined Horace Traubel, the faithful transcriber of Whitman's rants and raves and bellyaches.[111] More recently, William Charvat found them "almost completely unrewarding," matched in dullness only by the poet's correspondence, which Charvat called, with some exaggeration, the "most barren of all literary letters in the nineteenth century."[112] To prove his point, Charvat quoted a passage from the 1853 journal, in which Longfellow, looking back on another year of listless journalizing, acknowledged: "How brief this chronicle is, even of my outward life. And of my inner life, not a word. If one were only sure that my Journal would never be seen by anyone and never get into print, how different the case would be. But death picks the locks of all portfolios and throws the contents into the street" (December 14, 1853).

There is reason, though, to assume that Longfellow's guardedness was temperamental and not the result of his fear of posthumous publication. According to Annie Fields, an overzealous dinner guest once exclaimed: "Longfellow, tell us about yourself; you never talk about yourself." "No," Longfellow responded, "I believe I never do." The guest persisted, "And yet, you confessed to me once—" Longfellow interrupted him, "No . . . I think, I never did." And a French visitor who quizzed him extensively about his public life and then said, "Maintenant, monsieur, quelques anecdotes, s'il vous plaît, de la vie intime?" ("And now, sir, some anecdotes, please, about your innermost life?") was told in no uncertain terms that the subject was off limits: "That," said Mr. Longfellow, "is just what I cannot tell you."[113]

"Rather a silent man" (June 3, 1861), Longfellow kept his problems to himself. Disasters in his personal life, such as the death of his daughter Fanny, barely two years old, in 1848 or the accident that ended the life of his wife in 1861, left few traces in his journals and even fewer in his poetry. Even when he *does* write about his dead daughter, the contained plainness of his language gestures at what he does not and indeed *cannot* say: "I miss very much my dear little Fanny. An inappeasable longing to see her comes over me, which I can *hardly* control" (November, 12 1848). The poem inspired by little Fanny's death, "Resignation" (1848), avoids the first person singular entirely and hides the poet's private grief behind generalized observations on mortality and immortality (1:303–5). After his wife's death, when he was "inwardly bleeding to death" (to George William Curtis, September 28, 1861; *Letters* 4:245), several pages of Longfellow's journal are covered not with words but with small crosses. When he does attempt to write an entry, he does so only to express how inarticulate he has become: "I can make no record of these days. Better leave them wrapped in silence" (February 10, 1862). The moving sonnet devoted to his wife's memory, "The Cross of Snow," with its comparison of the speaker's private grief to the vast snow-cross that he had seen in a photograph of a ravine in the Rockies, remained in Longfellow's portfolio until his brother published it in his 1886 biography. Writing, for Longfellow, was not primarily a form of self-expression. His reluctance to use what he called "that objectionable pronoun" ("I") made his work as well as his life the mirror of the aspirations of every one of his readers.[114]

As Peter Gay has shown, among Victorians "the secret life of the self" had grown into "a wholly serious indoor sport." For them, diaries were notebooks of the heart, to modify a phrase coined by the German playwright Friedrich Hebbel.[115] Often extending over the course of a lifetime, they became a kind of serial autobiography. But if we approach the twenty-plus volumes of Longfellow's journals with such expectations in mind, they are bound to disappoint us. Even when he is talking merely to himself, Longfellow frequently gives us more information about the weather than about his emotional needs or intellectual interests. Transcripts of a busy social life, Longfellow's journals consist of notes, often tedious to the modern reader, on the people he encountered and the meals he consumed, lists of things done and left undone, books read and left unread, with vague comments such as "interesting" (on Hawthorne's tales) or—the negative verdict—"heavy" (on Byron's *Lara*) attached to individual items. Readers looking for profound remarks on literature will be disappointed. Longfellow had nothing much at all to say about Thoreau's *Walden* ("Evening, read 'Walden,'" August 30, 1854), which apparently captivated him less than the German writer Nikolaus Becker, author of the "Song of the Rhine," perhaps "not a great poet" but at least someone who "had the felicity to touch the hearts of his countrymen" (October 1, 1845). When recounting the meetings of the illustrious Saturday Club, Longfellow notes the presence of other distinguished members but, irritatingly, does not mention what topics were discussed.

This is not to say that the journals are merely *aides de mémoire*. Side by side with plodding passages of unrelieved boredom—in which we learn, for example, that Longfellow had to sit through an entire church service with wet feet or that he was annoyed when the voice of the prompter was "altogether too predominant" during a performance of Bellini's *Norma* (June 2, 1847)—we find sections of extraordinary beauty, especially when he is writing about life in his summer retreat, Nahant.[116] More often than not, however, Longfellow's entries deteriorate to the level of the daybook: "Like all other Sundays. Morning at Chapel; afternoon at home" (May 2, 1847). He professed to be amused by Samuel Pepys's obsession with "trivialities, from Lady Castlemain's [*sic*] petticoats hanging out to dry, down to his own periwig, and velvet cloak" (March 25, 1860). But Longfellow's own jottings in the journals betray a similar fascination with dress—minus, of course, Pepys's salacious details. Longfellow noted, for example, the "french-gray or lavender trousers and gaiter-boots" of the geologist Edouard de Verneuil, who had come to visit him (May 22, 1846), or the "hugest stripes" on the trousers of the pianist Leopold de Meyer (October 18, 1846), without in either case imparting much about the conversations he had with the wearers of these garments.

Occasionally, a reader will come across passages that reveal a different side of Longfellow. There, instead of the napping professor, we find the avid opera fan and wine connoisseur, who liked long, solitary walks and in the winter would skate "till the ice began to crack in the snow" (December 13, 1845). Unkind remarks about his students (teaching college was, Longfellow thought, like "the pulling of hair from the camel's back," April 3, 1848) alternate with sentences that show the deep concern of a rather nontraditional father for his wild and wayward son Charlie, whom he nevertheless, to the dismay of the people of Cambridge, refused to rein in. Other sections remind us that Longfellow was a thoroughly modern man in many ways, the first in Cambridge to have a shower bath in his house, which his friend, Senator Charles Sumner, enjoyed greatly when stopping by on June 14, 1846 (as the water was cascading down his body, Sumner seemed like a new Adam to the fascinated Longfellow).

Such entertaining asides are more than outweighed, however, by passages in which Longfellow almost willfully foregrounds the mundaneness of his existence, moments when, though he was in the middle of writing a poem, he was called to dinner, for example,[117] or when the stomping of his children through the house interfered with his attempts to channel what little inspiration he felt at that time into an acceptable poem. "Saturday is a bad day to buy playthings for children," Longfellow noted on October 12, 1853, when his two boys were noisily riding up and down the hallway on two velocipedes he had acquired that day. Among these notes of writerly frustration, entries in which Longfellow comments on the spurious nature of the whole "tedious" enterprise of journal-keeping itself are particularly prominent (March 1, 1855). In a satirical poem scribbled in his journal on June 10, 1847, Longfellow made fun of the conventions of diary-writing:

> It has become a bore infernal,
> To be always writing in this Journal,
> Page after page, and day after day,
> When I have nothing at all to say.

Taken as a whole, Longfellow's journals seem to indicate that he lived his life the way William Dean Howells said his handwriting looked, "quite vertical, and rounded, with a slope neither to the right nor left, leaving but a soft impression on the page" (Howells 166). Less charitably inclined readers will find plenty of material here to corroborate their notion of Longfellow the tame and timid traditionalist, leery of the excitement of the artist's life, given instead to an existence marked by "quiet self-control,"[118] a petty pilferer of other people's ideas and words rather than a creator and independent thinker. It will come as no surprise to them that one of his favorite gifts was a cushion made by an admirer from England, Mrs. Frances Farrer, who had stitched a lotus on it, "full of rest, and suggestions of peace and quiet" (June 23, 1855).

But what should we in fact expect from a writer? Protracted, intense suffering, superior insight, stupendous psychological depth, constant activity, continuing evidence of a richly significant inner life? That he be discriminating, always relevant, and relentlessly honest in the letters he sends, the diary notes he keeps, and scrupulous in the selection of his friends and visitors? Longfellow himself once summarized these romantic stereotypes, with both residual envy and the kind of detachment that came from the growing realization that his own makeup was fundamentally different. "I read with wonder and admiration of those, who amid sorrow and sickness and privation, have toiled up to immortality," he wrote on November 13, 1835, a day when he felt quite out of sorts because of a bad cold. He knew the type: "Enduring much—laboring much—accomplishing much," such writers will finally, "with shattered nerves and the sinews of the mind unstrung," lie down in their graves, "and the world talks of them during their slumber." But Longfellow in reality had little patience for people whose tempestuous inner lives spilled over, unfiltered, into their works: "Some people write," he complained in an entry made a few weeks earlier, "as if they had thrust their goose-quill into their brains, and let all the strange fancies, that dwell there, gush out through it in a steady stream upon paper" (September 27, 1835).[119]

This assessment never changed during Longfellow's long career. "Who wants to be a Crabbe [*sic*] Robinson"? he asked on October 17, 1869. He was alluding to the friend of Blake and Coleridge, Henry Crabb Robinson (1775–1867), the busybody among the diary-scribblers, who had died two years earlier, leaving behind thirty-five volumes of dignified chatter about the literary exploits of his contemporaries.[120] Like Longfellow's journals, Robinson's day-by-day account of his leisurely existence betrays little about the writer's "inner" feelings. For the compulsive talker Robinson, his journal was less a reflection of life than a substitute for it, the only place where he could hold forth uninterruptedly for as long as he pleased. In Longfellow's case, however, the journals are merely one part of the larger matrix of personal, familial, and cultural activity, part and parcel of a busy writer's everyday life.

In his journal entries, Longfellow seems like the rest of us, voluble and needlessly precise when it comes to trivial matters, reticent or vague about affairs of the heart. But in the economy of his dealings with readers and visitors, his baffling silence, or "speechlessness," as Annie Fields called it,[121] became a necessary part of the de-emphasis of authorship that is characteristic of his work in general. Read for what they are rather than for what they obviously aren't, Longfellow's journals offer a sustained critique of the Emersonian notion of the poet as the "liberating god" of his world.[122]

Middlebrowsing

The nineteenth century, so the story goes, saw an increasing separation of work from family life, a division between the public sphere, where men, as the detached but dedicated providers, worked to make a living, and the private home, which was the empire of the woman and the mother, "hermetically sealed off from the poisonous air of the world outside."[123] Paid production and patriarchal power here, unpaid reproduction and feminine submissiveness there. Obviously, such a rough-and-ready model doesn't do justice to the actual complexity of gender relations in Victorian America, especially at a time when the home, in publications like Catherine E. Beecher's *Treatise on Domestic Economy for the Use of Young Ladies at Home and at School* (1841), was also beginning to be identified as a workplace, not simply as the gentleman's "retreat from the cares of the world" and "a place to be at ease."[124]

If we want to understand Longfellow as a writer, we need to see him embedded in a network of relationships (maintained through his letters and the visits, however reluctantly tolerated) that connect him to a community of *readers,* native as well as foreign. On another level, he was also part of a community of other *writers,* native as well as foreign, living as well as dead. "Insist on you," Emerson had told his fellow Americans, "never imitate."[125] But Longfellow's works, published and unpublished, were pervaded by borrowings, sometimes explicit, more often unacknowledged, from other authors—so much so that on occasion it even seemed to him they hadn't been written by anyone in particular. This was, his opponents claimed, plagiarism raised to the level of fine (or perhaps not so fine?) art. Edgar Allan Poe, Longfellow's critical nemesis, unkindly pointed out that in *Voices of the Night,* his first volume of poetry, Longfellow had plagiarized even Sir Philip Sidney's line that one should never plagiarize: "Look, then, into thine heart, and write!" ("Prelude," 1:17).[126]

With Longfellow, such literary pilfering was, as Daniel Aaron, one of the poet's most astute critics, has said, temperamental rather than accidental, the way a sponge soaks up rather than repels liquids.[127] Even in his journals, where he so frequently confronts us, his unbidden audience, with an interiority that never really seems fully interior, Longfellow reminds us that all utterances—even the laments over a life not worth recording in a journal—have their literary antecedents. On April 11, 1857, for example, Longfellow reflected that, "I might almost fill up my diary as Louis XVI did his: Monday: Nothing. Tuesday: Nothing. Wednesday: Nothing. and so on to the end of the week." In *The Innocents Abroad* (1869), Mark Twain would later wittily comment on the diary that he said he kept as a boy, in which the entries, becoming scarcer and scarcer as time went by, all read: "Got up, washed, went to bed," until he reached the sensible conclusion that startling events were really too rare in his life "to render a diary necessary."[128]

Longfellow's reluctance to "insist" on himself corresponds to his conviction that everything in this world exists "in duplicate"—including the notion, shared by Louis XIV, Longfellow, and Mark Twain, that one's life simply doesn't yield events startling enough to be written about. This insight, as sobering as it can be exhilarating, came to him when he discovered that Schelling's essay on Dante, which he had thought had never been translated by anyone except himself, had already been translated by someone else into Italian: "whatever one is doing he may be pretty sure that some one else is doing the same, in some other part of the world" (March 20, 1847).[129] Indeed, he'd had plenty of evidence. For example, in 1835 Longfellow discovered that the title he had chosen for his travelogue, *Outre-Mer,* had been used, at just about the same time his book was published in America, by somebody else in Paris, for a book about the West Indies.[130] And, as he was idly leafing through an issue of the *Revue des deux Mondes* one day, Longfellow stumbled across "La Chanson du Cloutier," a poem about a blacksmith by Auguste Brizeux (1803–1858), the last lines of which sounded suspiciously like the fifth stanza of his own "The Village Blacksmith" (1839). For all he knew, Monsieur Brizeux had never seen his poem (September 16, 1846).

If writers like Melville claimed that it was better "to fail in originality, than to succeed in imitation,"[131] Longfellow must have felt that it was often difficult *not* to imitate, both for him and other writers. In the poem introducing his mega-anthology *Poems of Places,* he cast this observation in more positive terms, arguing that it can be more advantageous to see with someone else's eyes, even to use, on occasion, someone else's words, "than mine own."[132] Compare that with a terse entry in Emerson's diary for October 1832: "I will not see with others' eyes." All his mistakes, Emerson clarified in a later entry, had come from "forsaking my station & trying to see the object from another person's point of view."[133]

Taken seriously, Longfellow's vastly different position does not indicate pathological loss of self-assertiveness. Instead, it has important implications for his understanding of the work of poetry itself. "Originality," for romantics and modernists alike, was the defining feature of poetry. As Wallace Stevens put it, any objection to "originality in poetry is an objection to poetry itself because originality is of the essence of the thing."[134] Postmodernism might have taught us to "handle convention lightly" and not to place too much emphasis on the distinction between an original and its copy.[135] But deep down most of us, as Janice Radway has shown in her work on the Book-of-the-Month Club, probably still believe in the Romantic notion of the author as a lonely, heroic battler against the norm, the creator of original, irreproducible, inspired works, beholden to no one but himself.[136] Listen to how William Wordsworth, well aware of his superior talent and training, once defined his relationship with his audience— namely by distinguishing himself from them. A poet is, he wrote in 1802, "a man . . . endowed with more lively sensibility, more enthusiasm and tenderness, who has a greater knowledge of human nature, and a more comprehensive soul, than are supposed to be common among mankind."[137] And now hold against this Annie Longfellow's definition of her father's work as a trade like others, better only in that it can be carried out regardless of the weather.

When Robert Graves first met Ezra Pound from Idaho, "plump, hunched, soft-spoken and ill at ease," he asked T. E. Lawrence: "What's wrong with that man?" Lawrence's answer was: "Pound has spent his life trying to live down a family scandal: he's Longfellow's grand-nephew."[138] From a modernist point of view, Longfellow epitomized nineteenth-century parlor propriety; any association with him had to be embarrassing. Fortunately, a renewed interest in Victorianism, as manifested in Peter Gay's five-volume exploration of the nineteenth-century "bourgeois experience," has shattered some of the old monolithic views of that period. It has dispelled some of the stuffiness that, like a bad odor, has seemed to hang over it, emanating from the letters people wrote, the books they wrote and read, the houses they furnished, and the paintings they collected. Lawrence Levine and others have questioned the cultural hierarchies and the modes of writing associated with them that emerged in the course of the nineteenth century, most specifically the distinction between "highbrow" (writers published, or desperately eager to get published, by the *Atlantic Monthly)* and "lowbrow" literature (written by hacks who produced sensational novels conveyor-belt style). And they have also shown how some writers were trying to bridge the gap that seemed to open up between the interests of an increasingly detached cultural elite and the needs of the ordinary reader.[139]

Longfellow was intrigued by, if somewhat nervous about, the fast-developing market for mass-produced works of literature. In his journal, he describes running into the novelist Joseph Holt Ingraham, "a young, dark man with soft voice," then the author of eighty novels and counting. He was impressed when Ingraham boasted that he could write two chapters a day, "one before dinner, one after," and that such work brought "him something more than three thousand dollars a year" (April 6, 1846). But Longfellow was no slouch either when it came to marketing his wares. In 1845, he took the unusual step of purchasing the plates of his books from his publisher. From then on until about 1865, Longfellow owned the plates of all his books (a notable exception was *Poets and Poetry of Europe),* and publishers had to buy the right to print any Longfellow titles from the author himself, an arrangement that brought his royalties (which had been an unusually high 13 percent anyway) up to an average rate of 18 1/4 percent.[140] Between 1845 and 1850 alone, Longfellow's yearly earnings were almost $2,000, close to what Ingraham made per year from writing trash. And while Longfellow's royalties might have declined a bit after 1855, his market value clearly did not. A tally he jotted down in his journal on March 31, 1857, indicates how pleased he was: in the United States alone, *The Song of Hiawatha,* released just two years earlier, had sold 50,000 copies, followed by *Voices of the Night,* his first volume of poetry (43,550), and *Ballads and Other Poems* (40,470). *Evangeline* had scored 35,880 copies, not bad at all for a book that had been on the market for a decade. In 1874, he received a whopping $3,000 from Robert Bonner, the editor of the *New York Ledger,* for a single poem, "The Hanging of the Crane." And he hadn't even had to ask for it. A year later, Longfellow signed a contract with his publisher Osgood that guaranteed him $4,000 annually from sales of his old books.

But although he wasn't above celebrating the Blue and Gold edition of his poems as "a handsome little heifer" that would yield "a good deal of milk" (*Letters* 4:108), Longfellow always distinguished his own work from such "mechanical" productions as Ingraham's hastily assembled novels. He refused to write down to a "low level," as he told an aspiring novelist in 1877. "I do not believe in such writing. . . . The sensational is for the moment only." And he added a hilarious example of his own, to show how a trashy title could do a writer in: "A novel with the title of 'The Yellow-haired Clerk of the Howling Wilderness,' would certainly stamp the author with infamy, however it might captivate the crowd" (*Letters* 6:297). A writer should neither prostitute nor seek to immortalize himself, he had decided early on in his career. Rather, he should attempt "to make a salutary and lasting impression on the minds of others" (January 22, 1836). As William Charvat has pointed out, Longfellow until 1854, the year of his long-desired resignation from his professorship at Harvard, did not depend on royalties for his survival and therefore had no reason to think of himself as a "Messalina debauched by the public street."[141]

And yet his savvy dealings with publishers show how he gradually re-fashioned himself as a poet who would appeal also to readers with smaller purses. *Voices of the Night,* for example, when it came out in 1839, sold for 75 cents (about $12 today), was reprinted in 1844 in a "shilling edition" by G. H. Clarke in London. It was published again in 1845, with double columns printed on cheap paper, by Robert Redding in Boston, at the price of only 12½ cents (about $2.28 today). The irony is that this inexpensive edition proved rather dear to Longfellow. He paid $72 for the plates and received only $60 from the publisher,[142] an indication that he had wanted to publish the paperback for other than pecuniary reasons. In fact, Longfellow loved his cheap editions. Like "light and well trimmed vessels," he told Joseph Bosworth, his paperbacks would "run far inland up the scarcely navigable streams, where heavier ships of the line cannot follow them" (February 28, 1844; *Letters* 3:27). He would have known that a girl working in the Lowell textile mills earned less than $2 per week and a tailor in Boston barely $5.[143]

I own a highly unusual edition of Redding's 1845 paperback edition of *Voices of the Night,* which once belonged to the Maclure Library Association in Pittsford, Vermont (fig. 6). Free to all inhabitants of Pittsford who were willing to pay (as a small sticker pasted inside the front cover of the book tells us) "twenty-five cents half-yearly in advance" and who agreed to return the books as well as pay for "all damages they may sustain in their hands," this remarkable little library was founded in 1839 in the middle of rural Vermont by Thomas H. Palmer, a citizen of Pittsford. According to the town's official historian, Palmer hoped that "a large and well-selected" collection of books would "give a decided impulse to the intellectual and moral improvement of the people" of Pittsford.[144] He managed to wangle $400 out of a wealthy merchant, William Maclure, formerly of Philadel-

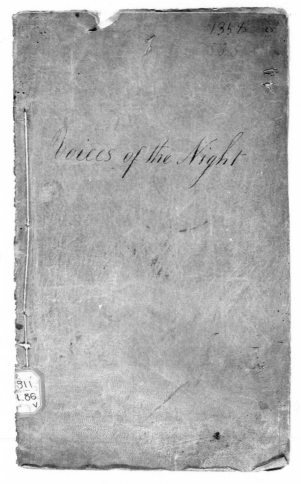

FIGURE 6

Henry Wadsworth Longfellow, *Voices of the Night* (Boston:
Redding, 1845). Handmade cover. Author's collection.

phia, extracted another $600 from local residents, and the "Maclure Library Association" was on its way. Subscribers were able to keep books for four weeks, and, as an added benefit, could attend free lectures at the library. The Pittsforders must have bought *Voices of the Night* shortly after it came out, since the loan periods, fines, and fees listed on the paste-in are still pretty much the ones mentioned in the Association's original by-laws, although instead of only 5 cents, patrons apparently were now being charged 10 cents for each week a book was late, "until the fine amounts to twice the cost of the book."

Maybe it was the fines, maybe the citizens of Pittsford cared enough about Longfellow's poetry—either way, this copy of *Voices of the Night* is in excellent shape today, given the cheap format in which it was originally published. Although the pages, their edges curling with age, show signs of frequent use, including occasional small food stains and little splotches of ink, the book is remarkably free of the telltale tears, scratches, and more or less enlightened marginalia left by previous users that normally give away the ex-library book. Indeed, someone at the Pittsford library must have cared enough about the volume to glue the original and not very durable paper wrappers to an outer layer of flexible, light-brown calfskin. Probably the same person then stitched Longfellow's pages to the new cover. On the front, after drawing a more or less straight horizontal line (later erased), he or she wrote across the cover, in beautiful handwriting, "*Voices of the Night.*" Longfellow, the inveterate advocate of authorial anonymity, would have been pleased to see that the librarian forgot to include the poet's name.

The same year that Redding's edition of *Voices of the Night* was published, Longfellow contracted with Carey & Hart in Philadelphia for a fancy illustrated edition of his poems. Poe was mentally rubbing his hands together. Here, finally, was the secret of Longfellow's success, the annoying "indiscriminate approbation" extended to the pilfering Harvard professor. The posh packaging of the product—the "fine paper and large type," the "morocco binding and gilt edges," and the poet's "flattering portrait of himself"—substituted for literary quality.[145] But Longfellow had in fact asked Carey & Hart if they would consider what his friend Charles Sumner had called a "dog-cheap edition" of his works, one that would "penetrate the common mind, and common heart of the country."[146] When Abraham Hart refused, Longfellow authorized Harper & Brothers to bring out his poems in the form of a 50-cent paperback (for which he reused the Redding plates of *Voices of the Night*): certainly out of reach for a laborer but still one of the most inexpensive books by a contemporary American author on the market. The cheapest such item in the 1846 catalogue of Ticknor, the Boston firm that would publish all of Longfellow's future books, was James Colman's collection *The Island Bride, and Other Poems,* which sold for 75 cents.

Poe wouldn't have been too terribly impressed by a "cheap" version of Longfellow anyway. When he heard about Redding's 12½ cent *Voices of the Night,* he readily condemned it in the *Aristidean,* calling it "a bad move." Relishing the role of the moral arbiter, he added disingenuously that "the dignity of poetica[l] letters should be maintained."[147]

Longfellow's disconcertingly wide-ranging presence on the market continued. In April 1850, Ticknor first brought out a two-volume, board-covered edition of Longfellow's *Poetical Works* in sextodecimo format, priced at $2 and comprising everything from *Voices of the Night* to *The Seaside and the Fireside.* The famous Blue and Gold editions of Longfellow's poetry and prose works, in two handsomely bound volumes in the rare trigesimo-secundo format with an engraved portrait of Longfellow by W. H. Smith and priced at $1.75 each, were added in 1857; the edition of the poems eventually outsold every other item in the series except Tennyson's poems.[148] In subsequent years, the firm of Ticknor, in its various permutations (as Ticknor, Reed, and Fields, then Ticknor and Fields, then Fields, Osgood and Co., then James R. Osgood and Co., then Houghton, Osgood and Co., and, finally, Houghton, Mifflin and Co.), would let general readers choose between as many as eight different trade editions of his poetry, starting with the duodecimo Diamond edition (which was printed in double columns and cost $1 in 1878) and ending with the Illustrated Holiday edition, published in royal octavo format, over five hundred pages long, with three hundred engravings, the author's portrait, and an ornate design on a stylish cover ($10 in 1878). Houghton Mifflin's "cheap editions" of *Hyperion* and *Outre-Mer* sold for 15 cents each.[149]

Leo Marx has argued that it was Longfellow's uncanny sense for "the attractiveness of upward social mobility in an expanding capitalist society" that made him vastly more popular than Whitman, despite the latter's desire to be the "mate and companion of people."[150] However, as the publication history of Longfellow's books shows, the story of his success is more complicated. Poe thought that Longfellow's poetry was too inferior to deserve the morocco binding reserved for "high art," but he apparently also thought that his work was too dignified to be put out in a shilling edition: too low for "highbrow" art, Longfellow was too high for the "lowbrows." But Longfellow purposely addressed himself to readers ranging over the entire economic spectrum, acknowledging the degree of flux that made it possible for a former sign-painter like James Whitcomb Riley to become a successful poet and for Miss Crannell from Albany to dispense poetic advice to a writer who had been a Harvard professor. Longfellow's readers were, to assign them a term invented in the twentieth century, "middlebrows," keenly interested in what often wasn't available to them, the "standards and ideals of High Culture," and fiercely determined to appropriate those in diluted form—"watered down," as Dwight Macdonald sneered.[151] Macdonald was not alone in his disdain for such cultural imposters. Virginia Woolf declared that she would take her pen and stab dead anyone who dared to call her a "middlebrow." She knew she had nothing in common with those men and women "of middlebred intelligence" who spent their lives "betwixt and between," sauntering "now on this side of the hedge, now on that, in pursuit of no single object."[152] One need only remember here the indefatigable Mrs. Livingstone, her mind a veritable squirrel's nest of quotations from the Great Men of the Past, including Alexander the Great, Jesus Christ, and, of course, Longfellow.

Still, even writers with the highest ambitions could occasionally be seen hawking their wares on the less acceptable side of Woolf's literary hedge. But they never stayed there for long. The first issue of Whitman's *Leaves of Grass,* for example, with a gilded ornamental leaf and vine design stamped on a tasteful olive-green cloth jacket, seemed as if it had been designed with readers like Miss Crannell from Albany in mind. But there the similarities ended. The book's interior, which featured a provocative picture of the bare-necked bum in street clothes, a rambling preface printed in newspaper columns, and then a multitude of free-flowing, idiosyncratically punctuated lines of uncouth, prose-like verse touting rough individualism and democracy, was intended to wreak havoc on all conventional expectations of bourgeois comfort.[153] Longfellow, who in Whitman's eyes was merely the effeminate "expresser of common themes," a singer of "little songs of the masses,"[154] appeared to seduce his readers into thinking that with a bit of effort they, too, could write like him. But Whitman, the proud purveyor of "songs of vital endeavor and manly evolution" intended to foster future "races of outdoor athletes,"[155] was shouting at his audience that it wasn't enough to cross boundaries on paper or to become upwardly mobile in one's stunted imagination. He was convinced that all social and cultural distinctions had to be dissolved.

Ironically, Whitman, whom Andrew Carnegie celebrated as America's greatest poet,[156] became a vocal proponent of capitalist expansion, praising America's "captains of industry" and their "undaunted armies" and finding his muse "install'd amid the kitchen ware" ("Song of the Exposition," 1871). While Whitman's Big Book continued to expand, Longfellow's volumes remained short—so short, in fact, that people could read them at one sitting, as he told John James Piatt.[157] In Longfellow's own day, the "Dedication" at the beginning of *The Seaside and the Fireside* (1850) did perhaps more to reduce the barriers between a poet and his audience than the mocking taunt issued at the end of Whitman's "Song of Myself," where the "untamable" speaker warns his readers that trying to understand him will take a lifetime of effort. "You will hardly know who I am or what I mean," Whitman said, but, never mind, the reader should keep on trying: "Failing to fetch me at first keep encouraged, / Missing me one place search another, / I stop somewhere waiting for you." And while the self-obsessed Whitmanian speaker, in love with the "sound of the belch'd words" of his own voice and, shockingly, even the odor of his armpits, promised his readers that he would "do nothing but listen," he in fact continued to hold forth, "hoping to cease not till death" (*Leaves* 78, 27, 46, 48, 26). And so, as the Good Gray Poet himself was gaining in years, his book kept growing in size: "*Think not we give out yet, / Forth from these snowy hairs we keep up yet the lilt.*"[158]

Whitman was proud of his role as the filterer and refiner of the "long dumb voices" of his disadvantaged contemporaries, who he felt depended on his vocalizing to be heard at all (*Leaves* 46). Ironically, for all the looseness of Whitman's style, the reader of *Leaves of Grass* invariably remains the grateful recipient of the favors of a poet who is always one if not several steps ahead of her. As Longfellow projected the relationship between himself and his readers, it was, by contrast, the *poet* who found himself at the receiving end:

> As one who, walking in the twilight gloom,
>   Hears round about him voices as it darkens,
> And seeing not the forms from which they come,
>   Pauses from time to time, and turns and hearkens;
>
> So walking here in twilight, O my friends!
>   I hear your voices, softened by the distance,
> And pause, and turn to listen, as each sends
>   His words of friendship, comfort, and assistance.
>
> ("Dedication" 1:275)

At the end of "Song of Myself," Whitman's poetic persona invites the reader to follow him up a knoll, where he will embrace her ("My left hand hooking you round the waist") and point out to her the "landscapes of continents, and the public road" (*Leaves* 72). In Longfellow's "Dedication," on the other hand, the poet takes self-humiliation almost beyond bearable limits and imagines himself not as a guide but as a hushed traveling companion, a humble beach-walker, lingering and listening wherever he is invited to stay. Whitman wanted to enter his readers' bodies, inhabit their souls, and if his ultimate goal was to embrace them as his "lovers," his identity as a prophet or "shaman," a giver of insight as well as a sharer of pleasures, depended on his separateness from his audience. He, unlike them, had already been "initiated into the mysteries upon which his power is based."[159] Longfellow once said that in his life, too, there had been "things of which I may not speak,"[160] but in his poetry he preferred to cast himself in the role of a contemplative friend, close to his readers yet far enough away to respect their privacy, *their* separateness:

> Therefore I hope to join your seaside walk,
>   Saddened, and mostly silent, with emotion;
> Not interrupting with intrusive talk
>   The grand, majestic symphonies of ocean.
>
> Therefore I hope, as no unwelcome guest,
>   At your warm fireside, when the lamps are lighted,
> To have my place reserved among the rest,
>   Nor stand as one unsought and uninvited!

Banking on the "hopes, and fears, and aspirations" shared by all, Longfellow's poetry dealt mostly in generalized emotions. Longfellow said himself that his antislavery poems were "so mild that even a Slaveholder might read them without losing his appetite for breakfast."[161] His readers could easily presume to be on familiar terms with him because the sentiments that he offered were ciphers, empty vessels to be filled with the readers' own feelings. Longfellow was, wrote William Charvat, "the first poet to arrive at a clear understanding of his relation to society," casting himself in the role of the average citizen. Here was someone who, like everybody else, needed friends, family, and things around him, someone who would publicly share the private "weight of care" that depresses the ordinary man or woman.[162] If the poet was a welcome visitor in their emotional lives, Longfellow's readers also had a standing invitation to inhabit his poems, as welcome guests, not the infinitely malleable disciples Whitman envisioned.

Even though he was perfectly able to see through the many conventions that governed his life as well as his art, Longfellow remained reluctant to relinquish them. Not for him, really, was the "Life of Genius" (*Letters* 2:334), a fact he memorably conveyed in one of his most popular works, "Excelsior" (1841). The poem features a somewhat anemic traveler hell-bent on perfection, "resisting all temptations," to quote Longfellow's own interpretation of the poem in a letter to J. G. Jarvis, "laying aside all fears, heedless of all warnings and pressing right on to accomplish his purpose" (*Letters* 2:500–501). Hurrying through an Alpine village, the impulsive young man pays no attention to the free advice given by more ordinary-minded citizens:

> In happy homes he saw the light
> Of household fires gleam warm and bright;
> Above, the spectral glaciers shone,
> And from his lips escaped a groan,
>   Excelsior!

> "Try not the Pass!" the old man said;
> "Dark lowers the tempest overhead,
> The roaring torrent is deep and wide!"
> And loud that clarion voice replied,
>   Excelsior!

> "O stay," the maiden said, "and rest
> Thy weary head upon this breast!"
> A tear stood in his bright blue eye,
> But still he answered, with a sigh,
>   Excelsior!

> "Beware the pine-tree's withered branch!
> Beware the awful avalanche!"
> This was the peasant's last Good-night,
> A voice replied, far up the height,
>   Excelsior! (1:90)

Predictably, Longfellow's antisocial hero, his goal unreachable, freezes to death. By contrast, his creator, who had stayed up too late to complete the poem, came down merely with a "dreadful cold." Longfellow, for one, wasn't suited to "disregard the happiness of domestic peace" (to Jarvis, *Letters* 2:501), and the secret of his success was, perhaps, that he communicated something like that to his readers as well.[163]

Longfellow, like most of his fans, was more comfortable on the shores of the Charles in Cambridge than on the rocks of Niagara Falls, the mere sight of which was "too much" for him when he visited it in 1862. "My nerves shake like a bridge of wire. A vague sense of terror and unrest haunts me all the time. My head swims and reels with the ceaseless motion of the water. It would drive one mad to stay here a week" (June, 9 1862). The vantage point from which he and his readers would view the world and the often deviant behaviors of its less predictable inhabitants was always that of the "norm," a word that, in its modern sense, entered the language around the middle of the nineteenth century.[164] While the more scholarly-minded debated whether the electrifying refrain "Excelsior" was correct Latin or not (shouldn't he have used "Excelsius," the comparative of the adverb *excelse?*),[165] the majority of Longfellow's readers soon knew the work by heart. Along with his fascinated fans, the poet-speaker himself would contemplate from a safe distance the "banner with the strange device, / Excelsior!" that the young man brandishes, his eyes "flashing" like those of Coleridge's Kubla Khan, as he heads for the "spectral" glaciers of death. Flirting with the grand idea of heroism, Longfellow, by gesturing toward the "happy home" the young man has shunned, toward the "household fires gleam warm and bright" he has left behind, also helps to relativize it.

Parodies soon abounded, among them a version known as "Paddy's Excelsior," in which the somewhat intoxicated speaker prefers the maiden's soft embrace to certain hypothermia in the glaciers of Switzerland:

> "Faith, I meant to kape on till I got to the top,
> But as yer shwate self has axed me, I may as well shtop.
> Be jabbers!"[166]

In the musical setting used by the Hutchinson Family singers, Longfellow's "Excelsior" quickly became part of American popular culture, and the title of the poem itself, correct Latin or not, also made it into *Webster's Dictionary* (as "more lofty" and "ever upward").[167] Nothing in Longfellow's poem (or, for that matter, the Hutchinsons' musical version, which reminded listeners of a chorale or chant) seemed to encourage the average citizen to forsake home and hearth and, like the crazed speaker, scramble to the nearest mountaintop, where he or she would then die a lonely death. The Excelsior Life Insurance Company in New York, for one, could not have been too concerned that their customers would misread the poem's message (and risk their well-insured lives in foolish endeavors), because they reprinted Longfellow's text in an advertising brochure illustrated by Frederick T. Vance.[168]

Perhaps the poem's most peculiar use occurred in the form of a booklet bound in glazed green wrappers that was published in 1873 by D. H. Brigham and Company, clothing merchants in Springfield, Massachusetts.[169] Presumably working from the same plates as Excelsior Life Insurance, Brigham and Company printed Longfellow's stanzas side by side with glowing praise for their superior store ("we congratulate ourselves that we are ready in every particular") and the complete line of fine furnishings for gentlemen of all sizes and descriptions they had to offer (including "Fat Men's suits, up to 500 lbs."; "Tall Men, up to 7 Feet"; "Black Cloth, adapted to Clergymen").

The publication helpfully informed interested parties, next to a picture of the damage done by the "awful avalanche" (fig. 7), that in their establishment "*no one can be cheated or dissatisfied,* as we sell strictly at *One Price* (except to clergymen), exchange goods promptly, and refund money if not satisfactory." This system had "done wonders," the brochure said smugly. On the page facing a picture of the poor monks of Saint Bernard struggling up a slippery mountain slope, customers were assured that the Brigham products for children were "all sponged before having them cut, thereby securing a perfect fit until the garment is worn out" (fig. 8). In fact, the stock they had in this department was so comprehensive that Brigham and Company were able to cater to the needs of both "*Stout and Slender Boys.*" At the end of the pamphlet, the view of the dead body of Longfellow's protagonist, "half-buried in the snow," is considerably lightened by the announcement, on the opposite page, that Brigham and Company could be trusted for the "Best Fitting White Dress Shirt" (fig. 9). The youth's heroic banner became a business recommendation of sorts when juxtaposed with the announcement, printed on the same page as the illustration, that "OUR STORE is known and acknowledged to be the best arranged, best lighted, and with our five floors, decidedly the largest Retail Clothing House in this country" (fig. 10). Brigham and Company knew what they were doing: they had taken the famous poem's description of an

From D. H. Brigham and Company, *Excelsior, Illustrated* (1873). Author's collection.

MEN'S DEPARTMENT.

After years of experience in the Custom Clothing trade, we are fully convinced that our present stock of Ready-Made will compare favorably with ordered work, and at a much lower price.

Extreme Sizes, both Fat and Long,

added this season, for business and dress purposes, adapted to all classes.

SUIT AND OVERCOAT DEPARTMENT

SPECIALLY ATTRACTIVE.

No one can be cheated or dissatisfied,

as we sell strictly at *One Price* (except to clergymen), exchange goods promptly, and refund money if not satisfactory.

OUR C. O. D. SYSTEM,

a great success, satisfies both buyer and seller. This, with polite attention, has done wonders.

D. H. BRIGHAM & CO.

Beware the awful avalanche!"
This was the peasant's last Good-night,
A voice replied far up the height,
Excelsior!

D. H. BRIGHAM & CO'S

Youths', Boys' and Children's

DEPARTMENT

Is one that demands a wider range of styles and prices than men's, and yet we feel confident that we are fully equal to the demands.

Largest Retail Stock in New England.

OUR GOODS ARE ALL SPONGED

before having them cut, to prevent shrinking, thereby securing a perfect fit until the garment is worn out.

In this, as well as in the men's suits, we have made provision for the *Stout and Slender Boys*.

We are confident, in point of style and quality of fabric, we are fully up to Custom-Made garments.

D. H. BRIGHAM & CO.

At break of day, as heavenward
The pious monks of Saint Bernard
Utter'd the oft-repeated prayer,
A voice cried through the startled air,
Excelsior!

A traveler by the faithful hound
Half-buried in the snow was found,
Still grasping in his hand of ice,
That banner with the strange device,
Excelsior !

There in the twilight cold and gray,
Lifeless, but beautiful, he lay ;
And from the sky, serene and far,
A voice fell, like a falling star,
Excelsior !

extreme experience and applied it to what the writer of the catalogue characterized as the availability of *"Extreme Sizes, both Fat and Long."*

The Brigham catalogue seems admirably suited to appall the purists
among the modern students of American poetry. But we can safely assume that it was no shock to Longfellow; at least in the case of the Excelsior Insurance Company, we know that he actually gave them permission
to use his text.[170] Why this venture into advertising? Early in his career,
Longfellow once disputed that he was writing for the "kitchenmaids" of
America (March 29, 1836). But he had an equally strong dislike of all writing that he called, in a deliberately chosen slang phrase, "too high-faluting"
(July, 29 1854). A purveyor of fine poems that were intended to fit readers
of all sizes, he could not regard literature as something high and dry. Far
from being, in Carlyle's phrase about Emerson, a "Soliloquizer on the eternal mountain-tops only," he maintained an infinite relish for the middle of
muddled humanity.[171]

That's why he simply couldn't be unkind to the befuddled young man,
"an entire stranger to me, who showed up one evening in July 1848, quite
hilarious with wine and wassel [*sic*]." Introducing himself as Homer, the
young man avowed himself the author of "a poem called 'Upward,' which
he called a translation—(meaning imitation) of 'Excelsior,' and which he
said Mr Whipple pronounced superior to the original." When Homer tried
to recite his production, however, "he broke down and said he was too
modest" (July 1, 1848).[172] Longfellow was sympathetic. All in all, his work
was intended to create and map out an acceptable middle ground between
the sensational and the "high-faluting," between Joseph Holt Ingraham
and S. T. Coleridge, something all the aspiring Homers of America would
like and, however wretched the results, feel inspired to emulate.

"O happy Poet! by no critic vext!" Longfellow once said, probably not
expecting that academic critics would indeed, for the most part, stay away
from him (though I don't think he would have too much minded their absence).[173] But I contend that Longfellow has much to say to critics, as well
as general readers, today. As Françoise Meltzer has shown, literary history,
even in its more revisionist guises, still insists on the importance of the
new, the true, the boldly innovative.[174] Longfellow invites us to question
the assumptions that still underlie most accounts of how literature devel-
ops and changes.

In 1846, he happened to be reading somewhere that the age was "still
looking for its Poet," apparently someone who "should be hailed by accla-

mation as the Seer of this nineteenth century" (February 11, 1846). What did people want? he wondered. That the advent of such a genius be "heralded by signs and wonder"? For Longfellow, literature was nothing "major" or "minor," nothing "old" or "new." In the course of his long career, he began to see himself less and less as an "original" creator than as the competent redistributor of common cultural goods, whose relationship with his audience was based on a system of exchange, both monetary and emotional, governed by civility and mutual respect. In 1831, Alexis de Tocqueville, powerfully attracted to and made just a little nervous by American democracy, pondered the literature he saw evolving there, and found that he disliked authors who saw literature as "nothing more than an industry." For every "great" American writer (and weren't such geniuses few and far between?), there were "thousands of retailers of ideas."[175] And isn't this exactly how we have been trained to look at Longfellow, too? Take a look at the anthologies. Our children in school and college still learn to celebrate the history of American literature as the inexorable march toward linguistic unity, cultural independence, and national self-sufficiency—notions that Longfellow's work gently undermines. It seems richly ironic, by the way, that one of the earliest proponents of what has become the current canon of "major" American writers should have been a traveling Frenchman.

Longfellow's relentlessly accessible texts—written, in Pierre Bourdieu's terms, for a general, "non-producing" audience—dispute the notion that aesthetic experience is limited to "high cultural" works.[176] In their own time, they empowered his readers to think of themselves as poets too, from Miss Crannell in Albany, New York, whose verses instructed Longfellow not to be afraid of death, to the young Emily and Austin Dickinson in Amherst, Massachusetts, who, inspired by the faint eroticism of Longfellow's novel *Kavanagh*, kept a copy of the book stashed away in the family piano.[177] "Every province" has its own poet, declared Longfellow in "Vox Populi" (3:77), but the community that his poetry built was neither local nor global. Each of its members was allowed a separate identity and privacy, just as the poet was allowed to hold on to his innermost thoughts.

Richard Brodhead has argued that in antebellum America, reading gradually became a private activity, with individual readers turning into isolated, uncomplaining consumers of mass-produced literary goods, a "huge paying public."[178] The example of Longfellow suggests that there might be some problems with this theory. Consider the notion of reading proposed in his programmatic poem "The Day Is Done," which he used as a poetic preface to the anthology *The Waif* (1844). The text begins on a nostalgic note, not unexpected of a poet who loves the backward glance. The "lights of the village" are still visible, but they already seem far away, shrouded in mist and rain: "And a feeling of sadness comes o'er me / That my soul cannot resist." In Longfellow's hands, poetry does not, as it did for the Romantics, make laws for the world. Instead, it becomes a more subdued form of discourse, something that somehow will help us live our lives, as the old familiar verities (represented here by the village, where one could still feel at ease as part of an ordered community) recede into oblivion. In this situation, the great masters, more interested in realizing themselves and their genius than in connecting with their readers, might ultimately be of less value than writers with more modest ambitions, who feel the same sadness we all do but give us the music that helps us bear it. "Read from some humbler poet," the speaker encourages the reader,

> Whose songs gushed from his heart,
> As showers from the clouds of summer,
>   Or tears from the eyelids start;
>
> Who, through long days of labor,
>   And nights devoid of ease,
> Still heard in his soul the music
>   Of wonderful melodies. (1:247)

As his poem switches from monologue to dialogue, from the "I" to the "you," Longfellow is making a case for the merits of the average talent in poetry—championing not the Mozarts but the Salieris of poetry, in the terms of Peter Shaffer's play *Amadeus*. Though read by individual readers, these lesser writers reestablish the community that was lost when the lights in the village went out:

> Such songs have the power to quiet
>   The restless pulse of care,
> And come like the benediction
>   That follows after prayer.
>
> Then read from the treasured volume
>   The poem of thy choice,
> And lend to the rhyme of the poet
>   The beauty of thy voice.

> And the night shall be filled with music,
> And the cares, that infest the day,
> Shall fold their tents, like the Arabs,
> And as silently steal away. (1:247)

The poem ends with an orientalist cliché, linking as it does wandering tribes of Arabs to troubles that temporarily "infest" our lives. The image seems ethnocentric today, and has been made further so by the intervention of the Zionist Israel Zangwill, who suggested in an article published in 1917 that the Arabs of Palestine should be encouraged to "fold their tents," as is their "proverbial habit," and "silently" leave their lands, traveling expenses to be footed by the Jews.[179] But if we ignore the afterlife of the simile and focus, for a moment, on its original purpose, it is easy to see why Longfellow would have attracted such a vast readership in his time. He is his own and his trade's best advocate: what his speaker does here is contrast the "nomadic" worries that haunt his readers with the stability and collective comfort brought on by the reading of poetry. The "rhyme of the poet" requires the reader's voice to be heard, and when the hand that held the book now seizes the pen (as was the case with Miss Crannell or Mrs. Dorr), leisurely literary consumption may turn into public poetic production. See the critics cringe.

It has become customary to describe what was happening in the course of the nineteenth century as an experience of dislocation, a time when local self-definitions (the world of the "village") were challenged not just by the experience of slavery and war but also by the increasing influx of information. In "every nook and corner," protested Longfellow, those infernal "newspaper correspondents" were lying in ambush, waiting for something to report, "destroying all privacy and retirement, and proclaiming to the world the color of your gloves and the style of your shoe-tie" (August 31, 1849). The fast-developing print media were the means through which many Americans were learning to think about themselves and events elsewhere in the world. "Every mail brings these exciting pictures of carnage," Fanny Longfellow wrote despairingly in 1855, at the height of the Crimean War. "What power an evil thing has."[180] In the face of such an overwhelming potential for disorientation, Longfellow's "The Day Is Done" suggested a simple but effective incentive for individual yet also communal resolve. In the 1890s, the poem was included in an enormously popular anthology, optimistically titled *The Thousand Best Poems in the World,* as an example of what "hundreds of millions" of ordinary people might not only "read to themselves" but also "say to some dear friends."[181]

In *Evangeline* and *Hiawatha*, too, works that both dealt with the destruction of communities and the displacement of a people, Longfellow expertly used the medium of print to circulate stories of courage and resolution in the face of adversity and disorientation that seemed instantly familiar and therefore comforting to his readers, offering them *shared, public* images to contain their *private* grief. No wonder that a picture of Longfellow's Evangeline graced many a college dormitory room, as the *Hamilton Literary Monthly* reported; no wonder, too, that among the debris left on the battlefield at Gettysburg was found a locket with Read's portrait of the three Longfellow daughters. No Longfellow relative is known to have fought at Gettysburg, so we must assume that some "perfect stranger" or "argent admirer" carried the image with him, inside his shirt, a substitute for the family he no longer or perhaps never had.[182]

But Longfellow did more than offer his audience a prescription for meek, "womanly" persistence in the face of brutal adversity.[183] By encouraging his readers to share in the "mystique" of literary production, to take his images and fill them with their own meaning, he broke down the barriers between poet and reader in a way that would irk subsequent generations of poets markedly less concerned about their audiences: "I beg you my friendly critics," declared Ezra Pound, Longfellow's reluctant relative, in *Tenzone* (1913), "Do not set about to procure me an audience."[184] And by systematically exposing them to the experiences of different cultures, Longfellow gave his readers—whether American or not—a chance to imagine themselves, vicariously, as more than just citizens of one country, namely as inhabitants of the world and participants in traditions other than their own.

Longfellow very much liked Abraham Cowley's observation that the main end of poetry was "to communicate delight to others" (May 29, 1847).[185] Seen rightly, books were, he noted, a rather cheap way of buying pleasure (September 25, 1849). More than anything else, it has been this emphasis on pleasing his readers—"entire strangers" he would invariably treat as if they were his friends—that has turned Longfellow into the pariah of the modern pantheon of American literature. In *A Feeling for Books,* her study of the readership of the Book-of-the-Month Club, Janice Radway pointed out that "academic high culture" still largely defines itself "by dismissing the suspect pleasures of the middlebrow."[186] As was to be expected, some members of "academic high culture" quickly took issue with this claim. In a review of Radway's book, James English blithely argued that "the whole supposed conflict between reading for pleasure and reading for work" has in fact been fading from the discipline of English.[187] But it seems obvious that the descendants of Miss Crannell and Mrs. Livingstone still aren't crowding the lecture rooms at MLA conferences today. If academics, in the long wake of Roland Barthes's *plaisir du texte,* have sometimes appropriated "pleasure" as a critical category, this doesn't at all prove that old cultural hierarchies have indeed been eliminated. Rather, such a move might reflect the presumption of literary critics that they have the authority to speak not just for themselves but even for readers who approach texts with very different expectations in mind. Studying pleasure is one of the most effective ways of controlling it.[188]

Longfellow's erstwhile popular appeal, still more embarrassing than interesting to most modern literary historians, teaches us to be wary of the cultural value systems that are still with us today. We should protect him against the conservative admirers he has retained, those who praise his poetry as the embodiment of values (form, skill, decorum) that they think contemporary poetry has, for the most part, shamefully abandoned.[189] But we should also resist the arguments of those who find it hard not to scoff at ordinary readers like Syud Hossein from Calcutta, a man who simply needed a good poem to talk a friend out of his predilection for "airy castle-building" and who, we may assume, was more than happy to pay for it.

TWO

How Marbles Are Made

FATHERHOOD AND AUTHORSHIP

Fathers and Children

Longfellow's many fans were especially fond of a poem that seemed to give them a glimpse of the poet's private life, "The Children's Hour," dated November 2, 1859, in the poet's manuscript. A lasting addition to the Hallmark Hall of Fame, the poem drips with the kind of sentimentality that more sophisticated readers have come to despise about Longfellow. Even worse, the poem unabashedly invites us to identify speaker and author, a move that would make the most laid-back English major nervous.

Before "The Children's Hour" was published in the September 1860 issue of the *Atlantic Monthly,* Longfellow's editor, James Fields, predicted that "the parental public" would "like it hugely."[1] No wonder—the poem so clearly re-creates an autobiographical experience, even mentioning the poet's own three daughters (familiar to readers from the Read painting, fig. 4) by name as they are preparing to "raid" their father's study before night falls. However, in describing his experience of fatherhood, the poem also tells a more complicated story about Longfellow's views on authority and authorship:

> Between the dark and the daylight,
> When the night is beginning to lower,
> Comes a pause in the day's occupations,
> That is known as the Children's Hour.

I hear in the chamber above me
    The patter of little feet,
The sound of a door that is opened,
    And voices soft and sweet.

From my study I see in the lamplight,
    Descending the broad hall stair,
Grave Alice, and laughing Allegra,
    And Edith with golden hair.

A whisper, and then a silence:
    Yet I know by their merry eyes
They are plotting and planning together
    To take me by surprise. (3:63)

For Newton Arvin, "The Children's Hour" was a prime example of Longfellow's "masscult poetry," cheap verse produced to please the general public with a vicarious peep into the poet's domestic life.[2] Yet, with all due respect for Arvin, the little text is less easy than it looks. For starters, the reader at least needs to know who the "Bishop of Bingen" in l. 28 was, on whose identity an understanding of the poem's final stanzas hinges. In 970, Hatto, the archbishop of Mainz, during a great famine, was said to have assembled the poor in a barn and torched them so that there would be enough left to eat for the rich. But an army of mice came after the bishop, who sought refuge in a tower on the Rhine. Unfazed, the mice scaled the walls and devoured the bishop. After refusing to share his food with the rabble, the ungodly bishop had become food himself.

Longfellow's rewriting of the gory legend, transposed into the domestic tranquility of Craigie House, adds an interesting twist to the poem, because here the "bishop," a.k.a. Henry Wadsworth Longfellow, is apparently able to hold his own against the invading "rodents," a.k.a. Alice, Anne Allegra ("Annie"), and Edith Longfellow. The Mouse Tower of Bingen turns into a Bluebeard-like fortress, inhabited by a gentle if firm father-ogre promising not to release his assailants until death do them part:

They climb up into my turret
    O'er the arms and back of my chair;
If I try to escape, they surround me;
    They seem to be everywhere.

They almost devour me with kisses,
    Their arms around me entwine,
Till I think of the Bishop of Bingen
    In his Mouse-Tower on the Rhine!

Do you think, O blue-eyed banditti,
    Because you have scaled the wall,
Such an old mustache as I am
    Is not a match for you all!

I have you fast in my fortress,
    And will not let you depart,
But put you down into the dungeon
    In the round-tower of my heart.

And there will I keep you forever,
    Yes, forever and a day,
Till the walls shall crumble to ruin,
    And moulder in dust away! (3:64)

Longfellow had seen the "Mäuseturm" (mouse tower) of Bingen in May 1829,[3] but in this poem he was also remembering Robert Southey's 1799 ballad "God's Judgment on a Wicked Bishop," in which the mice, for more lurid effect, appear as rats, nibbling their way through the bricks of the bishop's hideout, where they then enjoy their ghastly meal: "They have whetted their teeth against the stones, / And now they pick the Bishop's bones; / They gnaw'd the flesh from every limb, / For they were sent to do judgment on him."[4]

Norman Holmes Pearson once said about "The Children's Hour" that "few parents cannot honestly share it."[5] Really? The introduction of the greedy bishop and his vengeful mice into a poem that starts out in the saccharinely sentimental mode complicates Longfellow's narrative just a bit. The poem ends dramatically, with references to crumbling walls and moldering dust. A stanza eliminated from the final version, following right after the current line 18, shows the father in an even less attractive light, as a figure with dubious intentions, spying on his unsuspecting children under the cover of darkness: "They do not know I am watching, / That every motion I mark, / For they in the light are standing, / While I am hid in the dark."[6] The same stanza also unambiguously identifies the "round-tower of the heart" as a "prison."

The mixture of silliness and solemnity that distinguishes the poem is reinforced by its form. Longfellow's four-line stanzas follow a regular *abcb* rhyme scheme, but he otherwise departs from the traditional format of the ballad, in which the first and third lines are supposed to have four accented syllables and the second and fourth lines three. Throughout the poem, Longfellow also keeps his meter flexible to reflect the liveliness of the scene he describes, allowing for dactyls and anapests to wreak havoc on any too-regular beat pattern: "Íf I | trỳ to es | cápe; they sur | róund me, | / | They séem | to be é | verywhére." While he has fun with the meter, Longfellow also messes with the old myth of the father munching on his children. In this poem, the *children* attempt to "devour" their father, who responds by promising to devour *them*—by incorporating them in his heart. My sweet edible you. These children and their father would love each other "to death," as it were.

The father's possessiveness "matches" the neediness of his little daughters, who, it should be mentioned, are rendered without the usual stereotypes accompanying portrayals of children in nineteenth-century popular literature. (Victorian readers would have noted that the romping "banditti" in the poem were not boys, whom everyone expected to be full of mischief and "general deucedness,"[7] but soft-voiced, blue-eyed little girls.) The point here is not that the father wants to eat up his offspring because he is afraid of being "made redundant" by them, as Marina Warner has described the tradition behind Goya's gruesome painting *Saturn Devouring His Child*.[8] Longfellow's clingy father is concerned less with his potential displacement than with the loss of togetherness. What began as an invasion is actually an invited and more-than-welcome visit, which the father wants to prolong for as long as possible. The space that the poem finally imagines is a "dungeon," but it is not a nasty place: an enclosed area where the needy father and his devouring children with their entwining arms can be forever together, where the "children's hour" lasts a lifetime. (When, many years later, his daughter Edith got married, Longfellow confessed to his sister that, after the wedding guests were all gone, "I could not help saying to myself; 'I have lost my little Edith. How I shall miss her!'" *Letters* 6:328). It is remarkable that in "The Children's Hour" the mother is completely absent from the poet-father's vision of the scene. Longfellow's poem imagines a family in which the father, keeping his children for himself, can be their mother, too. (The poem was written almost two years before Fanny's death.)

What began as a father's report *about* his children ends as a story addressed *to* them. It could be argued that the last three stanzas only re-create the father's *thoughts,* but the poem's pliable meter and the nursery-rhyme-like sound of Longfellow's language ("forever, / Yes, forever and a day") invite us to imagine these lines as being *spoken.* This simple trick serves to drag the reader into the poem. While she is invited to sympathize with the father/speaker (whose allusion to Southey, left unexplained in the poem itself, she might recognize and appreciate), she will also—because the "you" automatically implies her, too—identify with the children. Just as he works to bridge the widening gap between "high" and "low" art elsewhere in his work, Longfellow in "The Children's Hour" also resists the bifurcation of serious writing into texts intended for adults and texts for children, which had been one of the legacies of Romanticism with its treatment of the child as a nostalgic object, separate from the world of the adults and of almost anthropological interest to them, a strange and attractive being equipped with gifts no longer fully comprehensible to hardened grown-ups.

As a writer, Longfellow worked at home—most of the time until August 1854, when he officially resigned from his position at Harvard, and *all* the time after that date. But his study was apparently not the kind of safe retreat from the domestic cares and chores that other self-employed author-fathers such as Emerson were able to claim for themselves.[9] While the poem's title, "The Children's Hour," seems to indicate that there is a special time reserved for children, the text as a whole actually *negates* such an arrangement. The walls of the poet's study—like the walls of Bishop Hatto's tower—are as permeable as the borders of the text. The sphere of work and the sphere of play merge in Longfellow's poem, and the writer who speaks in the poem cannot be separated from the father, and vice versa.

For Longfellow, being an author meant being a father, and that was, as he knew only too well, a particularly "difficult *rôle* to play" (*Letters* 4:130). But a rewarding one, too: in Longfellow's "Children," a poem written on February 1, 1849, the father-speaker listens to his sons romping in their room as he is moping downstairs in his study, "in rather melancholy mood."[10] Longfellow concludes—in a poem, no less!—that children are better than everything that was ever "sung or said," because they are "*living* poems" (3:60; my emphasis). In a letter to Freiligrath, dated January 29, 1857, Longfellow arranged the names of his children as if they were the titles of poems, followed by page numbers (their ages) and a less than serious apology:

Pardon me as an author, I have written them out like the Table of contents to [a] volume of lyric poems. (*Letters* 4:11)

Whoever works as an artist, declared Freud in his study of the wellsprings of Leonardo da Vinci's creativity, "certainly feels as a father" to the products of his efforts.[11] For Longfellow, however, fatherhood had little of the masculinist bias that informs Freud's remark, and, as "The Children's Hour" proves, it certainly was not synonymous with undisputed parental authority. As I will be arguing throughout this chapter, this is no less true of the ways in which he understood what is conventionally regarded as literary paternity or authorship.

For Longfellow, being a father (to one's children, to one's poems) meant being a son first—the humbling recognition that, no matter how great one's longing for superiority and independence, everything has already been done and thought before. Longfellow, who followed his father Stephen's advice not to place his hopes on a "literary life" and to pursue "a profession which will afford you subsistence as well as reputation" (*Life* 1:56), did not conceive of the relationship between a son and his father as an agonistic battle, at the end of which the son replaces his exhausted progenitor and, Oedipus-like, faces the consequences.[12] If T. S. Eliot later came to regard the history of literature as the inevitable foreclosing of opportunities for literary originality (in the sense that all poets, regardless of rank and talent, by fulfilling "some possibility of the language," simultaneously leave "one possibility less" for their successors), Longfellow saw it as progressive, steadily rising enrichment, as the inexorable diversification of subjects and artistic options available to every new writer with enough time to read and the ability to write.[13]

The demand for "originality" in writing really tells us more about an author's audiences than about the author. It draws our attention to the ever-widening gap between on the one hand readers of "sophisticated" taste (a.k.a. literary critics)—who, with the intention of identifying and castigating instances of "plagiarism," prove their refined knowledge by constantly comparing what is being done with what has been done—and on the other hand readers of a more "popular" bent, for whom, as Sir Francis Jeffrey once observed, even the twentieth repetition will have "all the charm of an original."[14] If in the following pages I continue to look at how Longfellow exerted and cheerfully undermined paternal authority in his home, this should also be taken as a reminder that for him literature was not an autonomous discourse but a deeply human transaction. Intertextual relations, to him, were as little separable from interpersonal ones as the author's study was safe from the sudden incursions of his daughters.

American family life had changed fundamentally in the first decades of the nineteenth century. In his essay "Domestic Life," Emerson wrote that if a historian wished "to acquaint himself with the real . . . spirit of the age," he should spend time not in the capitols or courtrooms of the country but in someone's private home.[15] The new ideal of the middle-class family, emerging around 1830, assigned the child a privileged place in the home, where the mother, in the absence of the bread-winning father, assumed the primary function of the child raiser.[16] As some historians have argued, not just physical but also moral nurture became the province of the mothers, while fathers, once the undisputed heads of the households, the sources of intellectual power and stern administrators of corporal punishment, were relegated to an advisory function.[17] "With industrialization and the growth of cities, the economic production that had been central to the household moved out, leaving behind a largely domestic space."[18] Most of the handbooks of the period—such as Lydia Maria Child's *The American Frugal Housewife,* Lydia Sigourney's *Letters to Mothers,* and Catherine Beecher's *Treatise on Domestic Economy*—focus on the woman's role in the house. In Susan Warner's vastly popular novel *The Wide, Wide World* (1850), which sports several prominently placed quotations from Longfellow's work,[19] the father of young Ellen Montgomery is a threatening and forbidding but ultimately irrelevant figure. "Captain" Montgomery's professional obligations are unclear even to his terminally ill wife. "He has agreed to go soon on some government or military business to Europe," she explains vaguely to her daughter, who couldn't care less ("he has been away a great deal before"), except that she now realizes she will be left behind.[20] Not a tear is shed for old Montgomery when his ship is lost on his return from Europe.

The circumstances of Ellen's upbringing (sick mother and absent, uncaring father) have devastating consequences for her, forcing her to adopt the role of an adult before she has even had the opportunity to be a child. In the novel, Ellen reads but never plays. Even by mid-nineteenth-century standards this was strange. As toys manufactured to afford children, in the words of Maria Edgeworth, "trials of dexterity and activity" became widely available (such as tops, kites, hoops, balls, shuttlecocks, and ninepins),[21] Victorian parents recognized their offspring as individuals with specific tastes and demands and a right to their own separate spheres. Numerous handbooks strove to reinterpret authority as affection, and parents were encouraged to apply "a kind of silent, natural-looking power," according to Horace Bushnell's *Christian Nurture* (1847), and to show, as the etiquette guru Mrs. Abell recommended, "the gentleness of Christ" in their dealings with unruly children.[22]

Obedience remained the goal, but among the acceptable disciplinary sanctions, Ichabod Crane's weapon of choice, the rod, was waning in popularity: "Much more common were shaming, playing upon the child's guilt, and depriving the child of company, food, or self-respect."[23] Spare the rod and save the child. Parents were now asked to nourish the "souls" of their children. Emerson reflected in January 1839 that in his dealings with his son Waldo all "my Latin & Greek, my accomplishments and my money" were of no importance: "If I am merely wilful, he . . . sets his will against mine; tit for tat. But if I renounce my will & act for the soul, setting that up as umpire between us two, his young eyes look with soul also; he reveres & loves with me."[24]

At least at first sight, Longfellow's "The Children's Hour" encapsulates neatly the mixture of affection and desire for control with which mid-nineteenth-century American parents approached their children, the freedom within carefully prescribed limits that they extended to them. No wonder that the poem was so successful, spawning countless other publications with similar titles. For Henry James, who thought that "The Children's Hour" should be retitled "The Children's *Century*," Longfellow's poem represented the sickening American adoration of immaturity, which he satirized in his story "The Point of View" (1882). "There is nothing in America but the young people," complains the aptly named Miss Sturdy in James's story to her correspondent in Florence, Mrs. Draper: "People talk of them, consider them, defer to them, bow down to them," even though the little boys will kick your shins and the little girls will slap your face. And these brats had the books to back them up: "There is an immense literature entirely addressed to them, in which the kicking of shins and the slapping

of faces is much recommended." For the childless bachelor James, the pat-
ter of little feet in Longfellow's poem had turned into the steady marching
of millions of spoiled brats, drowning out any and all intelligent exchanges between adults: "several millions of little feet are actively engaged in
stamping out conversation, and I don't see how they can long fail to keep
it under."[25]

The constantly expanding market for children's magazines and books
must have added to James's chagrin. In 1867, a Philadelphia firm started a
popular periodical for children named after Longfellow's poem. The cover
for one of the issues published in 1870 would have raised James's hackles:
several nerdy children eagerly turning, or looking at, the pages in books are
assembled around their mother, who is comfortably placed in an armchair
in her parlor, her skirt billowing out, an image of female nurturing (fig. 11).
Instead of Longfellow's storytelling father we see a mother caring for her
children, in full accordance with the conventional image of nineteenth-
century middle-class family life.

Recent research into the history of fatherhood, however, has suggested that there are significant problems with the common view of the
Victorian American family as a stratified power structure and that it might
be more useful to think of it as an intricate "web of rights, obligations,
prerogatives, and duties" in which fathers were also enmeshed.[26] Unlike
Captain Montgomery in Warner's novel, many fathers understood that
their children needed them to be present in their lives. They offered them
piggyback rides, took them fishing or ice-skating, and played Santa Claus at
Christmas.[27] After the birth of his daughter Blanche in 1845, Longfellow's
friend, James Russell Lowell, became, in his own words, "the personifica-
tion of the maternal principle," tending to her needs day and night. Lowell
vigorously objected to fathers who viewed their children only as after-dinner enjoyment, as "an additional digestif to the nuts and raisins."[28]

Longfellow's diaries are an eloquent testimony to the keen maternal
interest he took in the development of his children. For example, as the
diary for 1846 shows, Longfellow early on celebrated his first-born son
Charley's extraordinary desire for independence, appreciating that the
"splendid boy," though barely two years old, would always aim "for the
street and the largest freedom." And he commended him for his interest in
hearing stories, "tho' he will not allow them to be read from a book. Improvised must they be and instantly, or he begins to kick" (April 19, 1846).
He devoted large amounts of time to playing with Charley, running around

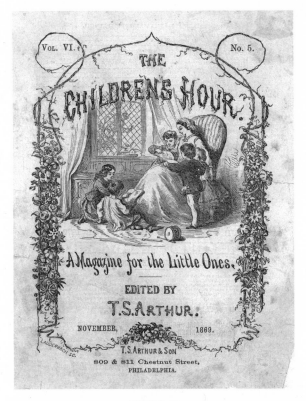

FIGURE 11

Cover of *The Children's Hour* 6, 5 (November 1869).
Courtesy of Patricia Pflieger, English Department,
West Chester University.

with him outside, where he would "nail" dandelions into the grass with a hammer and push around a little wheelbarrow full of lilacs and buttercups (May 13 and 24, 1846). Longfellow would take him to see the crowds, carriages, and omnibuses on Washington Street, which Charley stared at "with dilated eyes" (May 22, 1846), or help him fly his kite (June 2, 1846). Charley, in turn, ran around the house exclaiming "'where is the papa?' all day long," as Fanny Longfellow, who was apparently not at all jealous, reported in a letter to her best friend.[29]

In his journal, the proud father noted carefully any additions to Charley's vocabulary: "Aw! yide!" stood for "ride in the Omnibus, for which he has a passion" (June 6, 1846); "gugle-gugle muck" for "turkey's egg" (July 11, 1846); and "Papa's fat booze" referred to Longfellow's big, wadded dressing gown (September 20, 1846). Longfellow took his son on trips to his Cambridge printing press, where Charley was "struck dumb with astonishment at seeing the steam-presses in motion, their wheels flying about" (December 5, 1846), and to the Harvard College Library, where, to the boy's "infinite delight," he showed him "Audubon's huge book of birds" (December 29, 1846). On evenings when Longfellow came home later than usual, Charley would reluctantly go to bed "with a broken heart because he could not kiss Papa" (November 20, 1846).

Remarks in Longfellow's letters and journals make his study seem more like a family room than a *sanctum sanctorum* where the children may not go. On January 30, 1859, for example, he reminded his friend Charles Sumner in Europe what a typical Sunday afternoon in his study at Castle Craigie was like. While he was writing these lines, "two little girls are playing about the room—A. [Annie] counting with great noise the brass handles on my secretary, 'nine, eight, five, one,' and E. [Edith] insisting upon having some paper box, long promised but never found, and informing me that I am not a man of my word!" (*Letters* 4:118). It was here that the boys used their blocks to build wells with imaginary fountains; here the girls held birthday parties for their dolls.[30] Even when Longfellow wasn't around, his workplace apparently wasn't off limits: returning from his walks, he would be greeted by Charley bursting "out of the study, jubilant, and crying 'There's Papa'" (November 20, 1846). In his own journal, Charley mentions with enthusiasm that on Washington's birthday he had popped corn "on a shovel in the Study."[31]

When his sons became old enough to attend school, Longfellow mourned their daily departure from home, fearing that he had been deposed from his central role in their lives: "I look after them as they go down the gravel walk . . . eager, happy, full of life, and something of sadness mingles with my feelings of joy. I remember how weary school used to be to me. As yet, it has not lost its novelty for them. I do not move them half like schools" (June 10, 1850).

Many journal entries indicate that Longfellow took an especially active part in the care of his children when they were sick. For example, he would readily stay up at night, when "Erny," his pulse "flying and throbbing like quicksilver," was running a fever, wrapping him in wet towels which he "changed every half hour" (December 14, 1846). It was always to the father, that "most kind and indulgent of parents," that the Longfellow children went "in our childish troubles," Erny Longfellow later recalled. "He was very skillful in putting on a bandage for a sore throat or doing up a cut finger, keeping at hand little bandages already rolled up for immediate use. He also doctored us with homopathic remedies for our small ailments, but of course calling in a regular doctor for anything serious."[32]

It seems that some of the Longfellow children rewarded such parental preparedness with even greater recklessness. The trouble they would give their parents is well illustrated by the events of the summer of 1856. Charley had purchased a gun with his pocket money and, unbeknownst to his father, filled it not with percussion caps but with real gunpowder. The weapon exploded, either because Charley overloaded it or because it was cheap, and it permanently maimed his left hand. Longfellow had to stay up and watch over him for a week. "We eat our bread with tears," he wrote in his journal (April 12, 1856). A few months later, on a single day, Alice fell into the water and almost drowned while a sailing vessel, with the barely recovered Charley on it, seemed about to capsize when it was hurled against the rocks off the coast of Nahant. These events prompted Fanny to write to her childless brother, Thomas Appleton: "Ah, they are terrible cares—you are fortunate perhaps not to know the inexpressible anxiety they cause hour by hour. One has no longer any youth after they come."[33]

As wild as his children were, Longfellow claimed that he enjoyed "even their noise" (April 16, 1854). Certainly, he was not the sternest of disciplinarians. An amusing episode recorded on November 4, 1849 reveals that he was likely to side with his children when the humor of a particular situation made it impossible for him to think about its potential pedagogical pitfalls. On that day, Charles Sumner had shown up for dinner, during which Longfellow, with uncharacteristic eagerness, implored him not to seek coalitions that would endanger the "Free Soilers'" antislavery doctrine. Their meal finished, they went for a walk in the garden, where they came across a tethered calf. All talk of politics was forgotten now. "In a bucolic moment of enthusiasm for the fascinations of rural life," Sumner approached the animal, intending to pat it on the head ("he who knows not grass from grain," as Longfellow added mockingly). Grabbing the rope around the calf's neck, he tried to pull it closer to him ("Come here! come here!"). Predictably, the animal took a leap, the rope swept through the grass, and Longfellow, Fanny, and Charley saw a "brief glimmer of gray gaiters high in air, and prone lies the philanthropist in the sod." They laughed, which was not appreciated by the confused politician: "When a friend meets with an accident you ought not to laugh at him; you ought to pity, and sympathize with him!" Sumner's advice sounds as if it had been taken out of a contemporary Victorian parenting handbook. Longfellow's response to Sumner's graceless fall, on the other hand, a mixture of genuine amusement and mild *schadenfreude,* hardly meets the minimal requirements for proper paternal supervision.

For Emerson, "Toil and Want, and Truth and Mutual Faith" were the grim but useful guardian angels of childhood,[34] and he passed on that sobering knowledge to his own children, with whom, as his son later remembered, he rarely romped: "any silliness or giggling brought a stern look." Every new day was, he taught them, a "dewdrop" from the hand of God. If they became unruly, he sent them outdoors so that "the great calm face of Nature would soothe their little grief."[35] Next to the fairly serious, precocious children of Emerson, Longfellow's sons and daughters as they appear in their father's diaries seem almost comically normal.

From the moment of their birth, Waldo, Ellen, and Eddy Emerson were enveloped in cloaks of warm admiration and eager anticipation that made them seem larger than life. Although he mentions moments of paternal solicitude in his diary—for example, lying down at night next to his daughter when she couldn't sleep (June 16, 1842)—the emphasis in Emerson's diaries and in his essay on "Domestic Life" is on portraying children as budding poets, small Adams and Eves in gardens full of flowers, in whose every word sparkles the natural affinity for metaphor that most adults have repressed. "See the cobwebs go up out of the gentleman's mouth," Waldo exclaims when he sees a man smoking a pipe (*Journals* 216). In his lively imagination, "the flowers talk when the wind blows over them" (*Journals* 240), while to his sister Ellen the rain outside seems like "tears on the window" (*Journals* 242). Every once in a while the Emerson children would spontaneously break out into rhyme, as when Eddy, on July 22, 1851, announced that "With my sharp-pointed sword / I will conquer Concord" (*Journals* 426).

For Longfellow, the "law of entail" was not valid on Parnassus, as evidenced, for example, by the unexceptional poetry of Hartley Coleridge ("alas! where is the father's inspiration," July 14, 1846). And yet, in his own way he encouraged his children to think of themselves as writers, too. Among the most moving documents in the Longfellow papers at Harvard are two diaries by Charley Longfellow, one apparently recorded by his father when Charley was only five years old, and a second one, this time mostly in the boy's own hand, that he began when he was nine.[36] In both texts, the father is a much more prominent figure than the mother. He can be seen making molds for Charley and Erny's lead-casting and constructing a wooden roller with an endless ream of paper so that they could draw on it, in the style of painter John Banvard, a huge panorama.[37] Out of stiff brown paper, Longfellow would manufacture soldiers' caps, which Charley then adorned with designs of his own invention: "I painted mine with stars on one side, and three moons on the other; and Erny's with a picture of me shooting at a mark" (June 10, 1850). Longfellow's parental inventiveness becomes evident in Charley's entry for May 5, 1850: "After dinner Papa cut an orange in two, and made me a beautiful pair of golden scales . . . out of the peel of the orange." These scales Charley then put to good use in his toy grocery store, where one of the most loyal customers was, of course, Longfellow *père*.

It is remarkable that Longfellow the author, acting as his son's scribe, would so willingly have subordinated his own voice to that of his son, leaving the child's thoughts, words, and his idiosyncratic spellings intact. A case in point is the entry for May 21, 1850, the record of a meeting with President Taylor in Washington, where Longfellow had taken his family for a visit. The momentous occasion left Charley, then a couple of weeks shy of his sixth birthday, unimpressed: "Went to the White House and saw President Taylor. He shook hands with me; and I shook hands with him." On two occasions, Charley made up songs of his own; one of them was full of visions of military destruction ("The cannons came / Smashing to pieces! / Banners were broken in two! / And the drums made a great noise," April 13, 1850), while the other, based on a picture he had seen "where some people were going away in a vessel," conveyed a more melancholy mood ("It is very sorrowful / To sail away in a ship! / It is very sorrowful / When you get there," April 29, 1850). The latter was set to music by Longfellow, who performed it for Charley, accompanying himself on the piano.

Apart from those moments of accidental artistry, Charley's diaries show a normal child fond of wild games and almost magically drawn to feats of engineering and tools such as hammers and saws. Rather than a writer, five-year-old Charley wanted to be a *printer* of children's books" (my emphasis). But when he was nine, his literary taste had not developed further than stories about terrible "ship-wrecks," as his later diary reveals. In 1852, when the deposed leader of the Hungarian revolution, Lajos Kossuth, visited Longfellow and asked Charley and Ernest what they thought of their father's poetry, it turned out that they could not repeat a word of it (Longfellow to Sumner, April 23, 1852, *Letters* 3:341).

Unlike Hawthorne, Longfellow never published anything that could directly qualify as "children's literature."[38] But the mere fact that his "Book of Suggestions" contains references to stories intended for children proves that he did not necessarily see work of this kind as completely separate from his other plans. In 1847, for example, he was contemplating several projects, among them a story to be titled "Little Merrythought." A year later, he elaborated on the idea: "Title 'Little Merrythought; an Autobiography.' with a portrait of Merrythought in his red cloak, with a cock's feather in his hat like Mephistophiles [*sic*]."[39] Fragments of "Little Merrythought" are now among Longfellow's papers at Harvard. It appears that he continued to work on it for quite a while after 1847, as the original cast of characters expanded beyond Charley to include Alice (born in 1850), Edith (born in 1853), and "Annie" Allegra (born in 1855).[40]

The loose narrative of Longfellow's story revolves around the trials and tribulations of a tiny bone probably taken from a turkey. The beginning sounds like a parody of the orphaning of the hero in such popular novels as Dickens's *Oliver Twist,* except that "Merrythought" quite literally emerges from his mother's corpse—he is, as his name indicates, a wishbone, from his mother's chest untimely ripped: "I was born on Christmas day; on which occasion my mother was invited to dinner, not as a guest but as meat. She was roasted; and brought to table with her gizzard under her wing. When I was taken from her breast she was quite dead." After his bony body has been decked out with new clothes, Merrythought takes evident pleasure in his dapper appearance: "I had a red waistcoat and cloak given me, and a pair of red shoes, like little Erny's, though mine were made of sealing-wax. I had also a red cap, and white cock's feathers; and a black mask; likewise made of sealing-wax. Someone said I looked quite the gentleman."

Longfellow's fanciful illustration (fig. 12) exploits the amusing contrast Merrythought's spindly legs and pointy red shoes form with his huge cloak and the large, flowing feather attached to his hat. As he is standing on "the green meadow of the table-cloth," with four sharp, unrelenting children's eyes trained on him, Merrythought seems like a skeletal reincarnation of Gulliver in Brobdignag. Thanks to his diminutive proportions, he is soon able to assume an interesting role in the household. As a benevolent spy he comments freely on the relations between "Papa" ("a rather portly

FIGURE 12

Title page of Longfellow, "Little Merrythought,"
Longfellow Papers, Houghton Library, Harvard University,
MS Am 1340 (165). By permission of the Houghton
Library, Harvard University.

man, with a bright red waistcoat"), "mama" ("very Beautiful"), and their
children, brown-eyed Erny ("a dreamy little boy; who sucked his thumb")
and the older, boisterous Charley, also known as "Infant Terrible," with
"grey eyes snapping like steel traps." Some promising-sounding chapters,
of which we have only the titles ("How Little Erny lost his two front teeth
and looked like a walrus"), were apparently never written or are now lost,
but the deft vignettes that remain are enough to allow us to piece together
the contours of a charming narrative.

Longfellow took "Little Merrythought" very seriously and, as the entry in his "Book of Suggestions" shows, might even have thought about revising it for publication. As it stands, "Little Merrythought" gives us an unusual glimpse behind the scenes in a household in which an all-too-human and sometimes overwhelmed father is in charge of less-than-obedient, boisterous, and hyperactive children. Interestingly, the mother has a merely supplementary function:

> Presently they began to play, and run about the room. I observed that the effect of dinner was very different upon the children, from what it was on their parents. The latter settled down into large arm chairs, and showed a decided inclination to sleep. But the children were full of sport; and ran about the room with a great uproar. Infant Terrible lay down on the floor, and his brother rolled him over and over, like a barrel. Then he desired his father to toss him up in the air. "Up, up!" said he. "Toss me up so high, that I shall never, never come down again!"

In spite of the pleasing title, there is an astonishing amount of violence in "Merrythought," starting with the hero's induced birth in the first chapter and ending in the gruesome deaths of several household pets in later parts (the causes include poisoning and accidental beheading). Of course, the traditional custom associated with a "merrythought" or wishbone already implies a certain degree of force: people test their luck by pulling, with all their might, at either end of the forked bone until it breaks. Whoever gets the larger piece has his or her wish come true.

Still, in Longfellow's tale, the use of force seems more gratuitous. "Merrythought" is broken apart, too, but this happens when, in a paroxysm of unexplained rage, Charley, a.k.a. Infant Terrible, throws him on the table, "with such violence, that I thought every bone in my body was broken," while exclaiming: "You ugly little fellow! I wish you were dead!" Merrythought, with one of his legs shattered, is instantly shut away in a little box. Despondently, Infant Terrible apologizes and pleads with his father to repair him. Finally, "Papa" takes a match out of a box, which, as he explains, will make a "capital" leg for the little fellow: "It is round and smooth and just long enough. And then he has only to scrape it on the ground, and it will light up, and he can touch off a cannon with it." The fitting of the new prosthetic device is not painful, since "chloroform" is applied to ease the pain: "there was a little smell of sealing-wax, and then it was all over" (we might recall here that, at the insistence of her husband, Fanny Longfellow had been the first woman in Boston to give birth to one of her children with the aid of ether).[41]

If the damage in this chapter is easily repaired, a later vignette suggests that Erny, too, is subject to unpredictable fits of passion. Irascible and boastful, the boy is a formidable tyrant, a vicious insect constantly abuzz, a volcano of misguided energy noisily threatening to erupt:

> Suddenly at times he goes down on his back upon the carpet and buzzes round and round like a fly with his wings burnt off! He also threatened to kill people, and cut off their heads. This morning I heard him saying to his Nurse: "I am stronger than a giant! a great deal stronger than a giant. And if you don't let me go down stairs I will cut your head right off!" And now I understood why the Nurse sometimes called him little Blue Beard!

While Longfellow's educational motto isn't *laissez-faire laissez-allez*, he remains convinced that a father's understanding and support are more productive than drastic interference. The following vignette shows Erny in the throes of another temper tantrum: "Bump! and down went little Erny. He has hurled himself, headlong upon the floor . . . and there he lay on his back, buzzing, bumping, whirling round, and round, like a great bee, that has been stunned, and cannot get upon his legs." The cause of his anger is trivial, "a nothing, something the Infant [Charley] had got and would not give him." The father's policy is to wait until Erny has come to his senses again: "At last he said, amid sobs: 'I will be good. Help me to be good, papa!' Ah yes! help him to be good. That is what children most need. Not so much chiding and lecturing; but a little more sympathy, a little help to be good."

At first sight, this seems very much in line with the new form of parental power, or authority-as-affection, that Richard Brodhead has argued became a disciplinary regimen in midcentury America, when it was virtually impossible for the child to recognize a parent's hidden agenda from the displays of sympathy lavished upon her. The parent's goal was not the "humanization of authority" but, in fact, "a superior introjection of authority with humanization's aid."[42] Like a thief in the night, the autocratic power-hungry parent sneaks in through the back door of warmth and tenderness, seizing the unsuspecting child where it is weakest, in its need for love.

But does he in this case? Several segments of "Merrythought" indeed foreground the child's desire for the parent's love and reassurance. In one of the most moving episodes, "The Town-Clock," "Papa" Longfellow (he had first written "father," which didn't sound affectionate enough) tries to calm down his excitable daughter Annie ("Panzie") by embracing her: "Panzie had her troubles like other little girls and whenever she was troubled her Papa used to take her in his arms and press his heart against hers and say: 'Your little watch is going too fast; come and set it by the great town clock. Tick-tick-tick-tick!'" But Papa's advice is relativized by the admission that even this particular town clock, "if the truth must be told, and of course it must!" was "sometimes too fast, and did not exactly keep time with some other steady old town clocks, but struck too soon and made too much noise." All in all, the role played by Longfellow *père* in "Little Merrythought" is marked by tender sympathy, not smug superiority.

Merrythought, for one, is far from impressed with the head of the household, whose stories he finds boring. The advantage of having a disinterested narrator tell the story of his family is that Longfellow can turn the lens unsparingly upon himself. And what we see there is not always that impressive. One morning, for example, the boys surprise the father as he is shaving in his dressing room, making funny faces under the impact of the freshly sharpened blade. To his children, soapsuds-covered Longfellow looks like a buffalo, "with his horns sawed off." Catching his strange reflection in the mirror, the father "could not help laughing to see what a grotesque figure he really made, with his hair in disorder, and his upper lip projected, as if he were going to whistle. Perhaps he reflected, also, that every morning of his life he made just the same exhibition of himself, without being conscious of it."

But Longfellow's children are not just irascible despots and unpredictable pranksters. They are also eager listeners. During breakfast one day Erny wants to know why marbles are round. And, while the blue eyes of Alice "looked straight and level over the edge of her blue mug, from which she was drinking milk," the "wise Papa" proceeds with the following bogus explanation, a parody of schoolbook prose:

> In Holland there are a great many Windmills. Opposite the city of Amsterdam the whole sea-shore is lined with them. There they stand, and grind all day long, their great white sails going round and round and round, in the sunshine and the mist. Now the millers' boys pick up pebbles on the shore and put them into boxes; and these boxes the

millers fasten to the sails of the mills, and while the corn is ground into flower [*sic*] inside, these pebbles, by rubbing each other in the boxes, are ground into marbles outside, and smoothed and polished and rounded. And that is the way the Toozers and the Alleys and the Agates are made, without much trouble to anybody.

Charley's response is characteristic; rather than appreciate Longfellow's "wisdom," he instantly wishes, his eyes brightening, that his father were a miller and not a poet so that he could manufacture his own marbles in the manner just explained to him. "I would make lots of marbles, I bet I would." Erny remains silent; before his inner eye, plenty of Dutch windmills begin to appear, "whirling round in the mist by the sea-side." One of the favorite books in the Longfellow household was *Don Quixote;* it is hard not to think here of the episode in which Cervantes' "Knight of the Woeful Figure," who has plenty of "wind-mills in his head," comes across the thirty or forty mills that he takes for long-armed giants.[43] Ultimately, though, Longfellow's rendering of the anecdote is determined less by literary considerations or by the adult knowledge that windmills don't make marbles than by vicarious participation in the joy of his sons.

Marbles appear again in a later fragment from "Merrythought," when Edith Longfellow is shown struggling to acquire some knowledge of French. While Emerson and his son Edward plough through *Viri Romae,* Longfellow was interested in plainer, if more contemporary, fare, as evidenced in this hilarious passage from "Merrythought," which comments comically on Longfellow's own pedagogical prowess, or more precisely disinclination to exert fatherly authority, while simultaneously making fun of the many impaired American tourists populating the pages of books about foreign travel, such as George W. Curtis's *Potiphar Papers* (1853) or Mark Twain's *Innocents Abroad.* The best student in a class of one, Edith Longfellow listens to her polyglot father reading to her, bit by bit, the sentence, "Ma mère est aimable." Attempting to translate this rare nugget of wisdom into good English, Edie comes up with an unusual solution, as reported by Longfellow's spy, Merrythought:

> "*Ma Mère,*" said her Papa.
> "My Mother," said little Edie.
> "*Est aimable,*" said her Papa.
> "Ate a marble" said little Edie. "Why! how could she eat a
>   marble? I should think it would hurt her!"

Edith's penalty is far from severe: "her Papa laughed till the tears came into his eyes; and little Edie had to go down to the foot of the class, which was not very far, because, as I said before, she was the only one in it!"

In "Little Merrythought," Longfellow's deflation of parental (and writerly) authority manifests itself also in the playful inclusion of nontextual material, drawings as well as *objets trouvés,* especially in the later sections, which were written for the benefit of the girls and obviously intended as a comment on more serious matters, such as the experience of war: here, their dolls are obliged to go without tea, cannot afford new dresses and have to use paper money. As examples of the currency to be used, Longfellow glues in the label from a matchbox, made by Ezekiel Byam in Boston, and the wrapper from a bar of W. Baker's "Half Vanilla Chocolate" (figs. 13 and 14).

Longfellow took the concerns of his children seriously, refusing to create a fantasy world uncontaminated by the pressures of the outside world. He did not regard his children merely as "proto-people," to be cherished and nurtured for what they might become, but as real human beings with lives of their own.[44] The "banknotes" produced from labels reflect the material world his children would have encountered in their everyday lives. Clearly intended for the girls because of the references to the hardships experienced by the dolls, the story about the "banknotes" also rejects the idea that money is a matter to be handled only by men.

Longfellow might not have had children in mind when he wrote his poetry, but, as Van Wyck Brooks maintained, children were always "his best readers."[45] In Longfellow's "adult" poetry, many images are drawn from the world of a child's imagination, and many of his works became perennial schoolbook favorites. Several poems have children as protagonists or observers—think of the skipper's daughter in "The Wreck of the Hesperus"; the children coming home from school admiring "the flaming forge" in the village smithy ("The Village Blacksmith"); the "gentle boy with soft and silken locks" in "The Castle-Builder," a "fearless rider on his father's knee" who is also "an eager listener unto stories told / At the Round Table of the nursery" (3:77–78); the schoolboy collecting hazelnuts and birds' nests in "Songo River"; the weary little pilgrims in "The Children's Crusade" (1879); and, perhaps most beautifully, the sleepy boy turning 'round to look at his "broken playthings on the floor" in the late sonnet "Nature" (3:227–28).

More than a handful of Longfellow's poems deal exclusively with the experiences of children or, more specifically, his own children. "To a Child" (1:230–37), which Longfellow began writing on October 2, 1845, a month before Ernest's birth, recreates a child's view of the world as it appears in the pictures he sees on the painted tiles of the "ancient" chimney in his room. They show "many a grotesque form and face," a lady with a parrot on her hand, for example, a Turkish pasha, and a Chinese mandarin. But Ernest, a tyrannous Tamerlane rather than a meek disciple of the past, "restlessly, impatiently" striving to be free, cares as little about these exotic images as he does about the fact that in the same house where his nursery is now, the "Father of His Country," George Washington, once walked up and down the creaking stairs, "weary both in heart and head." And the father-speaker soon learns that his speculations about the "undiscovered land" of his child's future ("By what astrology of fear or hope / Dare I to cast thy horoscope") are as futile as his attempts to place his child in a context rife with the patriarchal associations of the past.

Even before his wife's death in 1861, which left him in charge of raising three young girls, Longfellow saw fatherhood not as a tool for domination but as a process, an exchange of sympathies and identities that involved self-understanding as well as understanding the needs of others. Despite the servants with whom he surrounded himself and the differently colored wines that made his house seem so unattractive to Emerson, Longfellow imagined the family not as the playground of patriarchal power or the site of strife and competition but as a potentially egalitarian and dehierarchized space, inhabited by people with different but equally interesting personalities: a space in which the father and his children are, as Longfellow said in "The Children's Hour," "matches" for each other.

I am suggesting in this chapter that this vision—rather unusual even by our standards today—can also be applied to Longfellow's understanding of authorship. Granted, the dream of togetherness expressed in "The Children's Hour," with its references to the dungeon and moldering dust, is not without its problems. But a poet's fantasies have to be taken with a grain of salt. When a nine-year-old admirer of "The Wreck of the Hesperus," in a letter to Longfellow, voiced concerns about the "cabel's [sic] length" the skipper's ship was supposed to have leapt in a storm, the author asked her not to expect "very exact measurements" in poetry. His own mindset, he told her, wasn't all that different from that of a child:

Longfellow, "Little Merrythought," Houghton MS Am 1340 (165).
By permission of the Houghton Library, Harvard University.

new dress. But Ezekiel Byam was a good man, and gave them to everybody who bought matches of him.

Some time after this they got some new bank-notes much more splendid than Mr. Byam's. There came from the Bank of W. Baker, who was also a good man, and gave them to everybody who bought his chocolate. Here is one of them.

"Poets, *like children,* occasionally exaggerate a little, and make things seem larger than they really are; as for instance when they say the waves ran 'mountain high.'"[46]

The Originals Are Not Original

According to Little Merrythought, one of the stories the portly father likes to tell is "the everlasting story of himself when he was a little boy." The perfect expression of this nostalgic impulse in Longfellow's poetry is, perhaps, "My Lost Youth," an unusually autobiographical text, at least by Longfellow's own standards (3:39–42). Although "My Lost Youth" was written in March 1855, the idea for a poem about his native city occurred to Longfellow as early as 1846, when he lay down in the grass near the old fort in Portland and "listened to the lashing, lulling sound of the sea" at his feet and admired the many white sails in the harbor, "coming and departing" (July 26, 1846). In the poem, Longfellow's memories of specific places or landscapes—"the pleasant streets of that dear old town," "the sheen of the far-surrounding seas," the islands off the coast "that were the Hesperides / Of all my boyish dreams," the "black wharves and the ships," "the bulwarks by the shore," the "breezy dome of groves" called "Deering's Woods"—combine with visual and auditory details only a child would have observed with such clarity: the strange-looking Spanish sailors "with bearded lips" arriving from abroad, the drumbeats and bugle sounds wafting over from the fort, the thundering sounds of a confrontation of ships during the War of 1812. These impressions are accompanied by the refrain of an old "Lapland" song, which the speaker claims haunted him:

> I remember the gleams and glooms that dart
>   Across the school-boy's brain;
> The song and the silence in the heart,
> That in part are prophecies, and in part
>   Are longings wild and vain.
>   And the voice of that fitful song
>   Sings on, and is never still:
> "A boy's will is the wind's will,
> And the thoughts of youth are long, long thoughts."

Though it is clearly intended to be a nostalgic poem, "My Lost Youth" ends on a cheerful note. One's youth, decides the speaker, isn't really lost as long as "the dreams of the days that were" can still be wakened, at least for the length of a short poem, and as long as the song, called "wayward," "old," "mournful," "sweet," and "strange and beautiful" in the course of the text, still hums in the speaker's mind.

In his journal, Longfellow mentions that he wrote "My Lost Youth" after a day filled with pain, which he had spent cowering over the fire: "At night, as I lie in bed, and cannot sleep, a poem comes into my mind—a memory of Portland, my native town—the city by the Sea, 'Siede la terra dove nato [*sic*] fui / Sulla marina'" (March 29, 1855). Apparently, Longfellow was haunted by memories not only of *le temps perdu* but of a recent reading experience, in this case the beginning of Francesca da Rimini's lament from Dante's *Inferno* 5. (He only had to change the feminine adjective "nata" to the masculine form "nato" to render Francesca's words applicable to himself.) In Longfellow's own, later translation: "Sitteth the city, wherein I was born / Upon the sea-shore where the Po descends / To rest in peace with all his retinue" (9:46). Francesca's Ravenna indeed hovers uncertainly behind the poem's initial lines, which conjure up both the speaker's longing for the past as well as his uneasy state of mind in the present: "Often I think of the beautiful town / That is seated by the sea."

Some readers might think it a bit strange that Longfellow's quaint northern American birthplace is made to evoke a city as rich in history and cultural associations as Ravenna. We need to remember here, though, that in 1855 Longfellow's reference to Francesca (which, unlike the Lapland song, is not marked as a quotation) would have been recognizable only to a small and fairly elite group of Dante lovers. What both the Dante allusion and the Lapland song do have in common is that they were never, as the poem insinuates, part of the poet's "lost youth." Longfellow encountered them while browsing in Johann Gottfried Herder's *Stimmen der Völker in ihren Liedern* (1778/79). "Die Fahrt zur Geliebten" ("Journey to the Beloved") is the title of the poem he found there, which describes the speaker's insistent longing—stronger than chains of iron and stronger, too, than all other thoughts that could distract him—to be united with his love.[47] Herder himself had encountered the poem not in its original form but, as he says, "aus der dritten Hand," at the second remove from the original source, namely in the pages of Johannes Scheffer's *Lapponia,* a history of Lapland written in Latin and first published in 1673. The song, allegedly sung decades ago, by a Portland boy with poetic aspirations now emerges as the English version of a fragmentary German translation of a

Latin translation of an anonymous source, which itself (as Herder pointed out) was the product of a largely unreliable oral tradition. Along the way, nothing much has remained, to use Herder's phrase, of the "raw Lapland" original.[48]

But Longfellow has substituted something else for it. Herder's German version was a pretty straightforward two-liner, rich in nouns: "Knabenwille ist Windeswille, / Jünglings Gedanken lange Gedanken." Longfellow subtly complicates what Herder casts in the form of a simple sequence of statements. By repeating the adjective "long" and adding a finite verb ("are"), he extends the second line of Herder's version. He translates word for word but still manages to alter the original text, replacing the German "Jünglings Gedanken" (a young man's thoughts) with the longer English phrase "the thoughts of youth," a revision that brings an interesting ambiguity to the line. The English word "youth," unlike the German word "Jüngling," signifies a state as well as a person; grammatically speaking, it can serve as the object as well as the subject of "thoughts." The predominantly dark vowels of the second line enhance the contrast it now forms with the first line's brighter /a/- and /i/- sounds: "A boy's will is the wind's will / And the thoughts of youth are long, long thoughts."

The ultimate effect of Longfellow's editing is that the two lines of the Lapland song now describe a kind of opposition between the boy's fickleness and the grownup poet's enduring, indeed "long," memory of that time in his own life. Youth lost is youth regained. Although Longfellow has in fact added two words to Herder's second line, his translation retains the same number of syllables, a sign of his skill as a translator (more about this in chapter 4). While altering the original he has also, in a sense, preserved it. Longfellow's retouching of Herder's German might seem microscopic, but then he also believed that "real estate on Mount Parnassus should be sold by the inch not by the acre."[49]

"My Lost Youth," a poem supposedly written as a release from acutely felt personal pain, shows Longfellow casually yet competently harvesting the vast repositories of literary tradition, cheerfully blurring the lines between original and copy, source and quotation. To some extent, this desire for self-objectivation-through-quotation reflects the reservations he had about autobiography in general. In his college lectures Longfellow lashed out against writing that he felt was too subjective. For him, Goethe was the prime example of a poet whose works were often *too* personal, who allowed his supersized ego to strut across every page of his works.[50]

The flurry of tautological definitions of literary "subjectivity" we find in Longfellow's 1837 lectures on Goethe betrays just how deeply he cared about the issue: "In the books of a subjective writer we never lose sight of the author. It is the same voice, only somewhat counterfitted; the same face partially concealed, under various masks. They give us constantly portraits of themselves. . . . They exhibit themselves." Like Snug in Shakespeare's *Midsummer Night's Dream,* subjective writers always show enough of their own face beneath the mask to be able to exclaim contentedly: "I one Snug the joiner am!" And like Moonshine in the same play, they feel the need to declare their own involvement in, and ownership of, their texts: "All I have to say, is to tell you, that the lanthorn is the moon; I, the man in the moon; this thorn bush my thorn bush, and this dog my dog."[51]

The objective poet, by contrast, knows that the world gets along just fine without his or her presence. In terms that recall Keats's "negative capability" and anticipate Eliot's impersonality doctrine in "Tradition and the Individual Talent" (1919), Longfellow talks about the loss of personality in the work of the objective writer, who never presumes to speak *in propria persona:*

> Objectivity is the power of losing one's self entirely in any object— or character, and becoming completely identified with it for the moment. The objective writer is an artist, who forgetful of himself, sees only the object he has to describe. All scenes and persons are described without exhibiting the peculiarities of the describer. The author is not seen in his book. He never speaks in his own person; nor are you reminded of him. He is completely swallowed up, and lost sight of.[52]

In his next lecture, Longfellow then turned to a particular problem he thought he had identified in Goethe's writings, namely the German writer's tendency to appropriate the thoughts of others and pass them off as his own. In Sarah Austin's *Characteristics of Goethe,* Longfellow found a revealing comment Goethe made to Friedrich Jakob Soret in 1832:

> What should I be—what would remain of me—if this art of appropriation were considered as derogatory to Genius? What have I done? I have collected and turned to account all that I have seen, heard, observed. . . . Every one of my writings has been furnished by a thousand different persons, a thousand different things.[53]

At first sight at least, Goethe's admission that all his writings have depended on the thoughts and experiences of others sounds suspiciously like Long-fellow's own poetic practice. The important difference is that, from Long-fellow's perspective at least, his liberal use of the past does not serve the purpose of self-aggrandizement (whereas Goethe seems to have regarded his sources as tributes due his genius). Longfellow's constant allusions and quotations draw attention to the fact that a literary work is never anyone's personal property but part of a continuum of shared words and ideas.

While some of Longfellow's borrowings come explicitly labeled as such, many of them are left unidentified. Is it merely a coincidence, then, that the first lines of "My Lost Youth" ("Often I think of the beautiful town / That is seated by the sea") sound a bit like the beginning of Poe's equally nostalgic, if more immediately provocative 1849 poem "Annabel Lee," familiar to most modern readers from Vladimir Nabokov's novel *Lolita* ("It was many and many a year ago, / In a kingdom by the sea, / That a maiden there lived whom you may know / By the name of Anna-bel Lee")?[54] If this was a deliberate echo, "My Lost Youth," containing a subtle plagiarism inflicted on the critic who had most loudly accused him of plagiarism, might have been one of Longfellow's craftiest rejoinders to Poe. Ironically, Longfellow's borrowed refrain from "My Lost Youth" was later borrowed, without further acknowledgment, by yet another poet: Robert Frost, probably unaware of the complicated literary genealogy of the phrase, appropriated Longfellow's "Lapland song" for the title for his first volume of poetry: *A Boy's Will* (1913).

"Make no quotations or references to other writers," Walt Whitman once advised his fellow writers.[55] But for Longfellow, writing poetry in-evitably meant quoting other poets. His was a poetry of detachment from immediate autobiographical concerns, even in works that seem clearly based on his own life, like "The Children's Hour" and "My Lost Youth." If he was indeed one of the "versifiers" slighted by Emerson, a poet who, "contented with a civil and conformed manner of living," would write about himself only "at a safe distance" from his own experience, the many quotations and allusions in his work, from the Lapland song to a Robert Southey ballad, served him as the convenient tools by which he achieved such self-distancing.[56]

Given this penchant for quotation, Longfellow's lifelong flirtation with anonymous publication makes sense, too. Whereas Goethe, in the statement Longfellow excerpted for his lecture, derived visible satisfaction from the power and dignity his own name would bestow on a text, no matter how many people had contributed to it, Longfellow felt, he told an aspiring author, a "keener joy" in publishing his poems anonymously "than I have ever felt in printing a whole volume with my name" (*Letters* 3:411). In *Outre-Mer,* he directs his reader to the forgotten songs of the medieval poet-musicians of central and northern France, the "Trouvères," noting that there are indeed "few characteristic marks by which any individual author can be singled out and ranked above the rest" (7:113). He quotes an anonymous Old English poem on the passage of time, "copied from a book whose title I have forgotten, and of which I have but a single leaf, containing the poem" (7:506). And he praises the "ancient ballads of Spain," composed by bards no one remembers, and adds another turn of the screw by soliciting the opinion of an anonymous critic: "These poets . . . have left behind them no trace to which the imagination can attach itself" (7:200). Even more than such literary examples, Longfellow found he liked the inscriptions on tombstones, authorless poems in miniature, as it were. He singles out, for its brevity, lucidity, and immediate appeal, one he found in a cemetery in Bologna: "'*Lucrezia Picini / Implora eterna pace.'* Lucretia Picini implores eternal peace!" (7:277).

Not surprisingly, the form of the anthology, with its multiple opportunities for the diffusion of authorship and vicarious traveling it offered, became one of Longfellow's favorite genres, from *The Waif* (1844) and *The Poets and Poetry of Europe* (1845), to *Tales of a Wayside Inn* (1863–73), Longfellow's answer to Boccaccio and Chaucer, and, finally, the thirty-one-volume *Poems of Places,* the most comprehensive collection of poems ever published in the United States. For Longfellow, the anthology was not an instrument for separating the wheat from the chaff, as the note introducing *Poets and Poetry of Europe* makes clear: "in order to render the literary history of the various countries as complete as these materials and the limits of a single volume would allow, an author of no great note has sometimes been admitted, or a poem which a severer taste would have excluded. The work is to be regarded as a collection rather than as a selection."[57] In *The Waif,* all entries appeared anonymously, even the ones whose authors *were* known—one had to turn to the table of contents to ascertain the source. In addition, neither here nor in the volume's sequel, *The Estray* (1845), do we find references to the work Longfellow had performed as an editor. Only the introductory poems, later published separately as "The Day Is Done" and "Pegasus in Pound," carry his signature. Reviewing *The Waif* in the *New-York Weekly Mirror* on January 15, 1845, Edgar Allan Poe accused Longfellow of having written the allegedly anonymous poems in the volume himself. And he complained that he had purposely excluded such American writers as Edgar Allan Poe—presumably so that he could more safely imitate (*"is* that the word?"), or rather plagiarize, their styles and themes.[58] In his journal, Longfellow retaliated in verse: "In Hexameters sings serenely a Harvard professor / In Pentameter him damns censorious Poe" (February 24, 1847). Since these two lines imitate, as he very well knew, an epigram by Friedrich Schiller, he thus both confirmed and mocked Poe's angry allegations.[59]

Margaret Fuller clearly recognized that the anthologizing impulse extended to Longfellow's own, ostensibly "original," work ("a tastefully arranged Museum"). But she phrased her insight cynically, implying that one couldn't even call Longfellow a "plagiarist," since this would presuppose that somewhere somehow in his work there might be hidden an original idea: "We have been surprised," she wrote, "that anyone should have been anxious to fasten special charges of this kind upon him, when we had supposed it so obvious that the greater part of his mental stores were derived from the work of others. He has no style of his own, growing out of his own experience and observation of nature. Nature, with him, whether human or external, is always seen through the windows of literature."[60]

I contend that Longfellow was fully aware of the mediated, irrepressibly allusive nature of his literary work, recognizing the presence of a universe of texts and traditions to which his "individual talent" (I'm deliberately using T. S. Eliot's much later terminology here) had to subordinate itself. For Emerson, the poet was a "teller of news"; Longfellow defined him as the competent administrator of all that had been said before.[61] At a time when Walt Whitman felt that "there was never any more inception than there is now,"[62] Longfellow knew that every line he produced would inevitably become part of a past that had, in effect, already anticipated and predicted him and his work. Take the protagonist of Longfellow's first novel, *Hyperion,* a young American traveler named Paul Flemming, who, after some unspecified heartbreak, has retreated into the "great tomb of the Past" with a passion that amazes and amuses his German friend, the Baron von Hohenfels:

> it often astonishes me that, coming from that fresh green world of
> yours beyond the sea, you should feel so much interest in these old

things; nay, at times, seem so to have drunk in their spirit as really to live in the times of old. For my part, I do not see what charm there is in the pale and wrinkled countenance of the Past, so to entice the soul of a young man. It seems to me like falling in love with one's grandmother. Give me the Present,—warm, glowing, palpitating with life. (8:159)

But in a patched-together novel,[63] which, among other things, contains a whole chapter lifted and translated from another book ("Johannes Kreislers des Kapellmeisters Musikalische Leiden" from E.T.A. Hoffmann's *Phantasiestücke in Callots Manier*),[64] Flemming doesn't really stand a chance of being "original." As it turns out, he is a sort of quotation from the past himself, since he bears the name—though in a variant spelling—of a German baroque poet, Paul Fleming (1609–40). "So you are from America," the German sculptor Dannecker exclaims when he meets Flemming. "But you have a German name. Paul Flemming was one of our old poets" (8:323).

His journals show that Longfellow himself was puzzled by the extent to which phrases and images he thought he had invented had a tendency to turn up, with almost comical regularity, in the works of writers he was sure he hadn't even read. On December 8, 1846, a "soft, vapory, rainy day," he had picked up a volume of poems by the Connecticut poet John Gardiner Calkins Brainard (1796–1828). His glance fell on a poem called "The Mockingbird," and more specifically, the following passage, which he immediately copied into his journal:

> Now his note
> Mounts to the play-ground of the lark—high up
> Quite to the sky. And then again it falls,
> *As a lost star falls,* down into the marsh.

Didn't that last image (Longfellow underlined it) sound suspiciously like the one he had used in "Excelsior": "A voice fell like a falling star"? Longfellow knew that Brainard's poem had not been on his mind when he wrote this passage. "In all probability," he hadn't even read it yet. And this wasn't the first time he had seen the phrase, right? His friend, the classicist Cornelius Felton, had "said at the time, that the same image was in Euripides or Pindar, I forget which. Of a truth one cannot strike a spade into the soil of Parnassus, without disturbing the bones of some dead poet" (December 8, 1846). And so Longfellow went ahead and recruited Brainard's bird (appropriately a species that imitates the calls of others) to do even more work: he used it as a model for the "delirious music" of the mockingbird in the second part of *Evangeline*.[65] All his thoughts were, he said, "after-thoughts," echoes of things thought by people long before him (November 2, 1846).

There were numerous other such coincidences. On September 15, 1850, for example, Longfellow discovered a line from his "Ode to a Child," in slightly different form, in Wordsworth's poem "On the Power of Sound." On December 12, 1851, during one of his early morning walks, he thought of a beautiful metaphor ("The houses hearsed with plumes of smoke"). When, after his return home, he looked up "hearsed" in his dictionary, he found, to his surprise, a reference to a poem by Richard Crashaw: "This line I never saw before. The idea rose up in my mind unsought, at the scene before me," he protested. But he knew that "if I ever print that line it will be called a plagiarism."[66] The unpleasant discovery, however, apparently did not prevent Longfellow from using the image later, namely in his moving threnody for Nathaniel Hawthorne, where he remembers Hawthorne's funeral in Concord as a surreal dream-scene: "I only see—a dream within a dream—/ The hilltop hearsed with pines" (3:138).

The issue of literary originality was of considerable importance to Longfellow's literary contemporaries. Oliver Wendell Holmes's alter ego, the amiable lecturer in *The Autocrat of the Breakfast Table*, seemed obsessed with this topic, conceding that whenever he had written a good line, he immediately worried that he had seen it somewhere else: "the moment after it was written it seemed a hundred years old."[67] Even Ralph Waldo Emerson, the prophet of a home-grown American identity, belatedly realized that there were problems with the notion of originality. In 1868, he admitted that the sepulchers of the fathers he had mocked at the beginning of *Nature* might, after all, contain something valuable: "Our debt to tradition through reading and conversation is so massive, our protest or private addition so rare and insignificant,—and that commonly on the ground of other reading or hearing,—that, in a large sense, one would say there is no pure originality." All great minds quote, decided Emerson, and "the originals are not original." However, faced with the dangerous notion that all literature is "eavesdropping," Emerson, after much example-giving, pointed out that it all depends on how we quote—whether we do it timidly and furtively or honestly and bravely. Used by an independent spirit, even a trite quotation can assume "a new and fervent sense." Originality, then, is not a textual feature; it is a state of mind. Seen in this light, a true author can still lay claim to a phrase he has found in another writer's work, while "admirable mimics have nothing of their own."[68]

Longfellow drew a different conclusion from the "coincidences" of phrasings and meanings he stumbled across in his own work. Rather than deploring the absence from his work of the original force of authorship, he became attuned to a vision of literary history as a colorful pageant of texts that, in one form or another, replicate or imitate each other. On the one hand, being a writer meant placing oneself into the sad situation of Don Quixote, tottering under the weight of other people's ideas and images. On the other hand, it meant holding interesting conversations with writers long gone and places far away. Instead of feeling crushed by the burden of the past and the realization of his own pathetic belatedness, Longfellow time and again toyed with the idea of an "authorless" literature. In one of his journals Longfellow transcribed an amusing but revealing fantasy involving a text that in a way had written itself. At the end of 1854, as he was getting worried that he had written nothing for a month, he fell asleep and dreamed that he was in New York, "delivering a lecture, and in the middle of the first sentence, fell asleep." The lecture, however, apparently continued without interruption, "for on awaking I found myself in my room at the hotel, and some friends congratulating me on my success" (December 8, 1854). Far from disabling and emasculating him as a writer, the realization that all writing is, to some extent, re-writing and thus to a large extent beyond the author's conscious control seems to have had a liberating effect on Longfellow's imagination.

Superficially, the attitude toward literary production outlined here contradicts Longfellow's shrewd management of his rights as an author and his royalties (see chapter 1). But it appears that Longfellow first had to empty authorship of most of its spiritual connotations to establish it firmly as what he thought it primarily was—hard work. Longfellow's insistence on literature as a profession that requires craftsmanship also helps dispel accusations usually leveled against those found wanting in originality: that copying "does not entail much labor."[69] As Longfellow put it in a letter to Thomas Gold Appleton on July 14, 1872, alluding to Milton's sonnet on his blindness: "They also work, who only sit and read" (*Letters* 5:565).[70]

Authorship Deferred

Consider, in the context of the definition of authorship I have been sketching out here, Longfellow's much-maligned Indian epic *The Song of Hiawatha,* or the "Song That's By-No-Author," as it was mocked by one of the many parodists.[71] Composed during the same year as "My Lost Youth," Longfellow's epic virtually insists on its own derivativeness: "This Indian Edda—if I may so call it—is founded on a tradition prevalent among the North American Indians," he began his the notes he attached to the poem, as if he wanted to draw attention to the fact that what he had concocted was nothing new but a mixture of various preexisting sources, Indian folklore stirred in with Norse poetry and a generous helping of Greek myth (2:379).

The use of such explanatory footnotes in connection with Native American themes in itself was not new. Lydia Sigourney's *Pocahontas* (1842), for example, had come equipped with tidbits of anthropological wisdom, early American history, and suggestions for further reading.[72] But the cornucopia of sources assembled in Longfellow's critical apparatus—from Henry Rowe Schoolcraft's *Algic Researches* to George Catlin's *Letters and Notes on the Manners, Customs, and Conditions of the North American Indians* to *The Narrative of the Captivity and Adventures of John Tanner* and John Wells Foster and Josiah Dwight Whitney's *Report on the Geology of the Lake Superior Land District*—went beyond normally acceptable limits, suggesting that the author had indeed sacrificed all pretensions to literary originality in favor of pseudoscholarly fact-collecting.

His intention had been, Longfellow claimed, to "weave together" the different "beautiful traditions" of his Indians into a new whole.[73] But the finished product would make some readers think less of an intricately woven tapestry than a lukewarm soup made from random leftovers. Unconcerned about ethnographic fact, Longfellow had gone ahead and combined one mythical story shared by several tribes—that of "a personage of miraculous birth, who was sent among them to clear their rivers, forests, and fishing-grounds, and to teach them the arts of peace"—with "other curious legends," apparently for no other reason than that he had found all these in one convenient package in the writings of the Bureau of Indian Affairs officer and amateur ethnographer Henry Rowe Schoolcraft, "to whom the literary world is greatly indebted for his indefatigable zeal in rescuing from oblivion so much of the legendary lore of the Indians" (2:379).

To make matters worse, Longfellow's cheerfully eclectic *Hiawatha* does not just borrow from native sources; it replicates and reflects, directly or indirectly, themes from many different western traditions. The poem's status as a mélange of quotations is made obvious in its very title, which recalls the *Chanson de Roland* and perhaps also the beginning of the *Odyssey*. Hiawatha's magic mittens and enchanted moccasins (not mentioned in Schoolcraft) remind the reader of the invulnerability cloaks and seven-league boots of Grimm's fairy tales. His adventures resemble the trials of Prometheus and the labors of Hercules, the harrowing experience of Jonah, Christ's temptation in the desert, and King Arthur's departure from Camelot. Finally, Hiawatha's wooing of Minnehaha, the daughter of an arrow-maker from the hostile tribe of the Dakotahs, invites comparisons with the story of Romeo and Juliet.

Longfellow felt that such eclecticism was justified by the uncertain status of the original Native American myth itself. Even in tribal cultures, "Hiawatha" was, as Longfellow explained, an elusive, multifaceted figure, who was familiar, in different guises, under many different names: "Michabou, Chiabo, Manabozo, Tarenya-wagon, and Hiawatha" (2:379). In fact, not even the name "Hiawatha" offers a guarantee of authenticity. "Manabozho" (a variant spelling) was the title Longfellow had originally chosen for his work-in-progress (June 25, 1854), an appropriate designation, it seems, given that the poem is set among the "Ojibways on the southern shore of Lake Superior." But he soon settled for the Iroquois name "Hiawatha" (to be pronounced "He-ah-wah'thah," as he advised a reader),[74] thus dragging in a new set of stories derived from a completely different tribal tradition about the semimythical founder of the Iroquois Federation. Manabozho and Hiawatha had already been conflated by Schoolcraft, but even if Longfellow had been aware of the error, he probably wouldn't have cared. He readily admitted that he preferred the new name because it sounded better: "Hiawatha is Iroquois," he informed his German translator Freiligrath, "I chose it . . . for sake of euphony" (*Letters* 3:517).

As if such eclecticism weren't enough, Longfellow served up this stew of legends in a form borrowed, at least in part, from the pseudoarchaic Finnish epic, the *Kalevala,* compiled by the physician Elias Lönnrot (1802–84) after decades of collecting the songs of the unlettered peasants in Northern Finland. Lönnrot had hoped that his poem would be understood as the belated Finnish answer to the *Iliad* or the *Edda,* a thought that must have intrigued Longfellow as he was looking for a subject that would address the crisis of a nation he feared was self-destructing.[75]

It appears, too, that Longfellow had not even consulted the *Kalevala* in its original form. What little Finnish he had picked up during a brief stay in Sweden in 1835 had evaporated by the 1850s, and he had come to know Lönnrot's thumping rhythms only through a German verse translation by Anton Schiefner (1852). Still, the similarities between the *Kalevala* and *Hiawatha,* in terms of content as well as form, were so striking that America's resident expert on the Finnish epic, Thomas Conrad Porter, a professor of natural science at Franklin and Marshall College, felt it necessary to intervene. "Plagiarism," he exclaimed, hiding his identity behind the initials "T.C.P.," in *The Washington National Intelligencer* of November 27, 1855.[76] Longfellow confessed, at least in private, that the "charge of imitation" mounted by "T.C.P." irked him. In one of his most explicit comments on the matter, a letter written to Charles Sumner on December 3, 1855, Longfellow doesn't deny that he lifted the meter as well as some of the stories from Lönnrot. But he rejects any personal culpability, suggesting once again that the coincidences of literary and cultural history, unsurprising to someone who had studied them closely, should not be misunderstood as literary theft: "As to having 'taken many of the most striking incidents of the Finnish Epic and transferred them to the American Indians'—it is absurd." He knew the *Kalevala* very well: "that some of its legends resemble the Indian stories preserved by Schoolcraft, is very true; but the idea of making me responsible for that is absolutely ludicrous!" (*Letters* 3:507).

Longfellow claimed that he could give "chapter and verse" for all of the Indian legends. But his reworking of the Schoolcraft material is in fact highly idiosyncratic. In *Oneóta,* Schoolcraft had argued that the distinguishing feature of Native American myth was its originality, a point he reasserted in one of his letters to Longfellow.[77] Yet Longfellow's revisions of the stories he had found in *Algic Researches* seem geared to destroy all the original power of his sources in favor of a carefully sanitized, westernized version of tribal mythology. Schoolcraft's retelling is itself hardly an accurate representation of native lore, as Margaret Fuller recognized early on.[78] However, it gives the reader at least a hint of Manabozho's unpredictability, his trickery, and his talent for deception.[79] He is an "evil genius," always "fond of novelty" and with a penchant for elaborate schemes of deception, a "dirty fellow" as well as a god. In one particularly memorable scene, he has several animals dance in a circle around him, with their eyes closed, and proceeds to eat one at a time as they pass by—a plan that works well until the little duck blinks and sees what he is up to.

Longfellow's Hiawatha, on the other hand, grows up in complete harmony with nature around him, marveling at the stars above him and making friends with the creatures around him, who later help him build his magical canoe. When still a boy, he shoots a deer that appears to him in the woods, "flecked with leafy light and shadow" (2:148). But this one act of masculine swagger is followed later by a protracted period of fasting, in which Hiawatha asks for the salvation of his people and "not for greater skill in hunting, / Not for greater craft in fishing, / Not for triumphs in the battle" (2:159). Driven by the "consciousness of his power to new trials of bravery, skill, and necromantic prowess" (Schoolcraft 1:154), Schoolcraft's boundary-crossing Manabozho has no mission other than his own advantage, while Longfellow's Hiawatha does what he does "for advantage of the nations" (2:159). And if Schoolcraft's recreation of the Manabozho story concludes with the promise that the trickster-God will reappear some day, "to exercise an important power in the final disposition of the human race" (Schoolcraft 1:139), Longfellow's story ends in departure and death.

Along with Schoolcraft's optimistic finale, Longfellow has eliminated most of Manabozho's moral ambiguity from his version. Hiawatha himself has as little chance to be mean as his grandmother has to be horny (in Schoolcraft's narrative, Nokomis tells him to go away so that she can enjoy her tryst with the long-haired bear).[80] He is a messianic figure, clothed in the radiant light of western hero worship, a bringer of peace during a time of political unrest. The one trickster figure left in Longfellow's poem is Hiawatha's antagonist, the "mischief-maker" Pau-Puk-Keewis, who assumes some of Manabozho's attributes and abilities, transforming himself, for example, into the largest of beavers, just as Manabozho once asked to be turned into the largest of wolves. He is killed off in a rather spectacular way: his skull is beaten to a pulp with war-clubs, and when he survives that, as well as a subsequent Icarus-like fall from the sky, a huge sandstone mountain finally collapses on top of him.

Characteristically, though he is "swift of foot" and "strong of arm," Hiawatha wants to rule by love and patience (2:149, 150, 204). His most intense adult relationships in the book are with men, especially those who flaunt their feminine qualities. His "beloved" friend, the singer Chibiabos, is brave as a man and soft as a woman; his opponent Pau-Puk-Keewis wears his hair "smooth, and parted like a woman's" and "hung with braids of scented grasses" (2:169, 208). And his ritual struggle with the beautiful corn-god, the young Mondamin, is exhausting and dangerous but, strangely, also physically satisfying and rejuvenating. At the golden-haired Mondamin's touch, "new life and hope and vigor" are throbbing through every pore of Hiawatha's body, and on his brow the sweat stands "like drops of dew" (2:162–63). After his victory, which is less the result of Hiawatha's superior strength than of the smiling Mondamin's decision that he has fought enough, he strips the corn-god's body and makes a soft bed for him in the ground, waiting for the maize to sprout from it. Minnehaha's father, the Old Arrowmaker, complains that the heroes of the olden times are gone. "Now the men were all like women, / Only used their tongues for weapons!" (2:199)—a charge that would also apply to the relentlessly speechifying Hiawatha. Many readers have noted that the death of Chibiabos, which causes Hiawatha to moan and wail for "seven long weeks," seems to affect him far more than the passing of his wife Minnehaha, whom he mourns only for "seven long days and nights" (2:240, 281).

It would seem likely that Longfellow's softened version of Indian myth was intended to pander to stereotypes then prevalent in white mainstream America. Thomas Jefferson, in his *Notes on the State of Virginia* (1781/85), had promoted the romantic notion of the American Indian as gifted with the powers of "sublime oratory," namely "such as prove their reason and sentiment strong, their imagination glowing and elevated."[81] Since Native Americans, unlike the blacks so feared by Jefferson, were supposed to be "formed in mind as well as in body, on the same module with the 'Homo sapiens Europaeus'" (Jefferson 187), they appeared to offer white Americans the chance of constructing a genealogy for themselves that would help naturalize their relation with an environment that continued to puzzle them. Ironically, once the Indians had been dignified as "noble," the way had been paved for their removal from the American scene. The "noble savage" turned into the "vanishing Indian" or, often, the vanish*ed* Indian. Native Americans became a popular culture artifact, "a poetical people whose activities took place in a sublime landscape and whose fate aroused sentiment."[82]

Longfellow's *Hiawatha,* which ended with the protagonist meekly drifting off into the "fiery sunset," appeared to confirm this cliché. According to Newton Arvin, there was no "painful complexity, no rich contradictoriness," in Longfellow's portrayal of Native American culture. The best one could say about *Hiawatha,* added Arvin, was that there are "a good many things" worse than it.[83] Not exactly a ringing endorsement.

Is Arvin right? Given Longfellow's vexed approach to the problem of literary originality, I would argue that Longfellow wasn't driven primarily by the quaint desire to "reinforce the antiquity of Hiawatha's time,"[84] by the wish to prettify the past while whitewashing the political sins of the present. Longfellow's modification of Schoolcraft makes sense when we begin to read *Hiawatha* as a carefully contrived performance, an elaborate play on the notions of authorship and authenticity, and therefore of great relevance for Longfellow's rather modern concerns as an American writer. Longfellow's reliance on data collected by others is not the unfortunate result of lack of literary imagination. It is indicative of his desire, evident throughout his work, to downplay the part he had in the composition of a work that he felt was his own only insofar as he had worked on giving it its final shape and form.

The beginning of *Hiawatha* is a clever staging of his dependence on his sources, in the sense that Longfellow both admits and disputes his debt. In an imaginary dialogue with an inquisitive reader, the speaker/author thrice refuses clearly to answer a reader's legitimate request for clarification about his sources ("Should you ask . . . I should answer"). The first hypothetical question concerns most generally the authenticity of his narrative: "Should you ask me whence these stories / Whence these legends and traditions?" Longfellow answers the question the moment it has been asked, immediately suggesting that the very idea of an origin is ludicrous when applied to a narrative that essentially tells itself because it comes not from people but directly from nature. "Nawadaha" (Schoolcraft's Ojibway name) merely transcribed it, which, strictly speaking, would make Longfellow's poem a transcription of a transcription: "I repeat them as I heard them / From the lips of Nawadaha / The musician, the sweet singer" (2:123). Given Longfellow's editing of the Schoolcraft material, the speaker's claim that his poem is nothing but a "repetition" of what he has heard elsewhere is, of course, more than a tad disingenuous.

But Longfellow's hypothetical listener persists in his quest for origins. Now that Nawadaha has been identified as the poem's central source, the next question concerns *his* legitimacy as a storyteller: "Should you ask where Nawadaha / Found these songs so wild and wayward . . ." Longfellow's speaker reiterates his earlier response: turn to the forests and fens, to the moorlands and "melancholy marshes" of the American wilderness. Nawadaha's stories emanate from the North American continent itself, a direct translation into words of the sights and sounds of American nature, "the bird's-nests of the forest," "the hoof-prints of the bison," and "the eyry of the eagle." But Longfellow's imaginary listener still isn't satisfied:

> If still further you should ask me,
> Saying, "Who was Nawadaha?
> Tell us of this Nawadaha,"
> I should answer your inquiries
> Straightway in such words as follow. (2:124)

But again, the speaker's answer is far from "straightway." Not Nawadaha's identity counts, he tells us, but the place he came from, "Tawasentha," a "green and silent valley, / By the pleasant water-courses" (an allusion to the valley in Albany County where Schoolcraft was born). What now?

The carefully staged displacement of original authorship at the beginning of the poem makes *Hiawatha* another Longfellow work critical of the notion of literary paternity. A few cantos into the poem, Hiawatha confronts his own "author" and father, the West Wind "Mudjekeewis." Like Schoolcraft's hero, who complains that "I have neither father nor mother" (Schoolcraft 1:139), Hiawatha is driven by the desire to find out more about his origins. He knows that his life started with his mother's rape and then death. His heart feels like a "living coal" when he finally discovers his "ancient" progenitor at the end of the world, resting on the "gusty summits" of the Rocky Mountains. Mudjekeewis presents an impressive image of patriarchal authority. His streaming hair white like drifting snow, he boasts of his superior strength and, recognizing the features of the beautiful Wenonah in her son's face, basks in belated fatherly pride:

> And he looked at Hiawatha
> With a wise look and benignant,
> With a countenance paternal,
> Looked with pride upon the beauty
> Of his tall and graceful figure. (2:153)

Silently, Mudjekeewis confesses his responsibility for Wenonah's death, bowing "his hoary head in anguish" (2:154). The fight between father and son that now follows assumes mythic proportions:

> . . . the earth shook with the tumult
> And confusion of the battle,
> And the air was full of shoutings,
> And the thunder of the mountains,
> Starting, answered: "Baim-wawa!" (2:155)

The altercation ends when the father, driven into a corner, declares that he had just wanted to test his son's courage and promises him a share of his kingdom after his death. All the bitterness has departed from Hiawatha; assured of his self-sufficiency and absolved of the need to prove himself, he can bring peace and healing to his tribe—not as a patriarchal tyrant but as a friend and brother to his people. This Indian Oedipus will be a better leader: "Go back to your home and people," Mudjekeewis encourages him. "Live among them, toil among them, / Cleanse the earth from all that harms it, / Clear the fishing-grounds and rivers, / Slay all monsters and magicians" (2:156).

Longfellow knew what he was doing when he portrayed Hiawatha as both a tribal shaman and the reincarnation of the Greek god Hercules, as a warrior of superhuman strength as well as a young man with a face of womanly beauty. Like its protagonist, Longfellow's text also resists categorization. Suffused with words taken from Schoolcraft's Ojibway lexicon, *Hiawatha* often reads like a draft of a translation abandoned halfway through, something that is neither "Indian" nor English:

> By the river's brink he wandered,
> Through the Muskoday, the meadow,
> Saw the wild rice, Mahnomonee,
> Saw the blueberry, Meenahga,
> And the strawberry, Odahmin,
> And the gooseberry, Shabomin,
> And the grapevine, the Bemahgut . . . (2:160)

Longfellow is asking the mid-nineteenth-century white American reader to perform more than just an act of retrospective historical empathy. He is requiring her to make several adjustments at once: temporal, cultural, and, most of all, linguistic.

While the landscape of the poem (the southern shore of Lake Superior, between Grand Sable Dunes and the Pictured Rocks) might be familiar to some, its inhabitants aren't, and Longfellow works hard to remind his readers of that. The odd, frequently parodied meter of the poem, which Newton Arvin found monotonous and maddening, is an essential part of this effort. Whether it sounds like a primitive drumbeat or not, it imposes a kind of barrier between the reader and the text, defamiliarizing the events the poem narrates. Drifting through verse awash with strange sounds, the reader remains suspended between the then and the now, between the present in which wonders don't happen, ghosts don't walk, "Indians" have well-nigh vanished, and no one talks in trochaic tetrameters, and a past world where at night "corpses clad in garments," their faces painted crimson by the flames, cower around the fire, where even the stars, glaring like the eyes of wolves, are hungry, and wild geese make noises like "bowstrings snapped asunder."

In this world, a squirrel is called "Adjidau'mo," the whippoorwill "Wawonais'sa," the pigeon "Ome'me," and the dragonfly "Dushkwo-ne'-she," while the strawberry is known as "Odah'min" and rice as "Mahnomo'nee"—terms that envelop them in an aura of mystery and emphasize their difference from the creatures or plants that Longfellow's readers saw in their own backyards and fields. Like Whitman, Longfellow loved the sound of Indian words, but whereas Whitman restricted himself to the use of occasional place names, such as "Mannahatta" or "Paumanok," Longfellow delved deeper into the repertoire of native phrases that he had gathered from Schoolcraft's writings. Among his papers is still a small dictionary of the Ojibway language, neatly written out in Longfellow's own hand, an early form of the glossary that appears at the end of *Hiawatha*.[85] One had to be a "blockhead" to prefer a word like "pigeon" to the more evocative and musical "Oméme," Longfellow excitedly told Charles Sumner after a missionary with his Ojibway wife had visited him at Castle Craigie. He elaborated: "No one—excepting always the blockheads—can hear the word *Opechee*, without hearing at the same time all the forest ring with the song of the birds! and it is not so with its English equivalent *robin*, which suggests the English landscape, groves and cottages, and gardens" (January 14, 1856; *Letters* 3:523).

Most critics, put off by the thumping trochees and the plodding insertion of native words, have not recognized how sensuous Longfellow's poem is, taking us to places where the touch of things is acutely felt, heard, or seen—as if everyone in this poem were in a state of heightened awareness. Here, the squirrel chatters, bullfrogs sob, and ravens caw and crow. Through the clear waters of the lake, bodies of large fish gleam. In the morning, a light breeze plays in the squirrel's fine fur "as in the prairie grasses." In this world, the sun sets by shooting sharp spears of light into the dark corners of the forest. At night the moon rises, "rippling, rounding," from the water. Wails of anguish travel far in this landscape: when Hiawatha learns about the death of Chibiabos, his screams are answered by the howling of wolves. In the winter, snowflakes hiss among withered oak-leaves and the branches of trees creak and groan, "tossed and troubled" by a wintry tempest. We sense the sunlight burning on Hiawatha's shoulders, just as, later in the poem, we also feel a cold breath of air when, their garments rustling, the messengers of death leave Minnehaha's tent. We hear the air coming through Hiawatha's nostrils and imagine the sweat freezing on his brow as, elsewhere, the icy hand of death grasps his wife. When everything is almost over for him, the arrival of the "paleface" invaders is announced by the grating of their canoe on the pebbles of the shore.

Throughout *Hiawatha*, Longfellow tells us what objects are made of and what they are used for, from Hiawatha's bow and his bed made of hemlocks to the flint-tipped arrows he favors, "smoothed and sharpened at the edges," and the bowls of polished bass-wood used at his wedding. We can almost touch the whitened leather used for wigwams, the soft doe-skin of Pau-puk-Keewis's shirt.

This pervasive interest in things and the making of things reminds us of the work that went into the making of Longfellow's poem. *Hiawatha*, despite Longfellow's assertions that all he is doing here is to pass on tales from native oral tradition, is an extremely self-referential text.[86] References to (and examples of) storytelling and literary composition pervade Longfellow's narrative, from the "legends and traditions" mentioned in the prologue to the sweet and tender songs of Hiawatha's poetic friend Chibiabos to Iagoo's stories about "The Son of the Evening Star" and about the ways of the white people.

Hiawatha is first and foremost a story about the poet Longfellow. Not coincidentally, apart from establishing himself as the messenger of peace and unity to warring native tribes, Hiawatha is also the bringer of language or more precisely, of writing, of a system of signs that makes the graves of the fathers speak. The images Hiawatha creates are collectively accessible ones; making the absent present, they preserve a memory of a common past. As Hiawatha points out to his people, "On the grave-posts of our fathers / Are no signs, no figures painted; / Who are in those graves we know not, / Only know they are our fathers" (2:233). It could easily be argued that Longfellow is guilty here of the kind of ethnocentrism identified by Claude Lévi-Strauss in *Tristes Tropiques*. He apparently assumes that the possession of writing "as an artificial memory" necessarily marks an advance over a form of human existence in which people remain "incapable of remembering the past beyond the narrow margin of individual memory . . . imprisoned in a fluctuating history which will always lack both a beginning and any lasting awareness of an aim." Nothing in the history of civilization supports such a view, argues Lévi-Strauss, who also points out that the emergence of writing often goes hand in hand with the creation of empires: "the primary function of written communication is to facilitate slavery."[87]

From a modern perspective, the elegiac ending of *Hiawatha* proves Lévi-Strauss right. Hiawatha's people, from the moment they acquire a way of commemorating the past, seem condemned to become part of the past. That said, Hiawatha's "picture-writing" is *not* represented by Longfellow as a pathetic anticipation of the delights of full literacy but as a completely functional system of signification that seems more concise and elegant than the often cumbersome translations into the "white man's language":

> . . . the last of all the figures
> Was a heart within a circle,
> Drawn within a magic circle;
> And the image had this meaning:
> "Naked lies your heart before me,
> To your naked heart I whisper!" (2:238)

Longfellow later said that what mattered most about a poem was the "general impression" it conveyed,[88] and there is every indication that what he wanted the reader of *Hiawatha* to remember was, above all, a few simple images. In a sense, then, Longfellow too engages in a form of picture-writing, inviting the reader to visualize rather than literally remember his poem:[89] Hiawatha flanked by his two friends, the poet and the strong man; the nude Minnehaha, "unashamed and unaffrighted," dancing around the cornfield; the sleeping giant Kwasind lazily drifting down the river in a boat. And while this strategy does not, of course, make *Hiawatha* a "native" poem, it also considerably complicates the reader's attitude toward the arrival of the white colonizers at the end of a poem that has often been misconstrued as a more or less racist endorsement of Indian removal.

Hiawatha's vision of white settlement is at first quite positive, as if the colonists had come to continue his mission of peace and brotherly love, "restless, struggling, toiling, striving, / Speaking many tongues, yet feeling / But one heart-beat in their bosoms" (2:289). Wherever the white men stepped, Hiawatha said a flower would spring up, a symbol of their achievement, "the White-man's Foot in blossom" (2:289). Longfellow was probably remembering here a passage from Lydia Sigourney's *Pocahontas,* where the speaker imagines "flowers and herbage" flourishing in the "long-trampled dust" left behind by those "erring, red-brow'd men," whose demise is as regrettable as it is historically inevitable.[90]

But most of Longfellow's readers would have known that Hiawatha's vision referred to what was not really a flower but in fact a troublesome weed, the broadleaf plantain, also known as the cart-track plant. Longfellow had learned about it from Louis Agassiz, who, on September 13, 1849, after dinner at Craigie House, had taken him for a little show-and-tell along the roads of Cambridge: "He says that wherever a road or a railway is opened in this country, there European weeds spring up; and as we walked down to the village he pointed out by the roadside a weed called by the Indians 'The White Man's Foot', because it advances into the wilderness with the white man." Weeds accompany the settler's intrusion into the native world. Unsurprisingly, then, Hiawatha's view of white colonization soon darkens as he sees his own people—"scattered, / All forgetful of my counsels, / Weakened, warring with each other"—condemned to a slow and painful death (2:290). His mission has failed. The central image of the poem is indeed the gravestone, whose "half-effaced," "rude" inscription Longfellow insists is like his own poem (2:126). But, in a way, this is also the poet striking a pose. Significantly, the only ones who have trouble expressing themselves in *Hiawatha* are the white Jesuits, whose stammering words of greeting to the natives ("Peace of Christ, and joy of Mary!") are in sharp contrast with Hiawatha's smooth oratory, a fact not lost on contemporary readers.

Hiawatha, successful beyond even its author's imaginings, inevitably spawned an impressive number of parodies. An anecdote popular at the time had a lover respond to a marriage proposal Hiawatha-style: "I will answer, I will tell you; I will have you, I will wed you."[91] As political speeches, sermons, advertisements, and newspaper articles began to be modeled on the meter of Longfellow's Indian poem, pranksters everywhere felt called upon to mock the new fad. Several parodies came out as books; thousands more, briefly appreciated and then rapidly forgotten, were published as newspaper columns, skits, and poems in little magazines. Parodying *Hiawatha* became a sport, so much so that Lewis Carroll prefaced his own attempt with an apology: "In an age of imitation, I can claim no special merit for this slight attempt at doing what is known to be so easy."[92]

Longfellow wasn't always sure what to think of such responses to his work. "A parody or travesty of a poem is apt to throw an air of ridicule about the original," even if it had not been made with this intention, he told a correspondent in October 1870. The problem with parodies was that the better they were, the more damage they did, "for one cannot get rid of them, but ever after sees them making faces behind the original" (*Letters* 5:375–76). On the other hand, we also know that Longfellow was able to quote, from memory, lines from a parody of "Excelsior" that had been sent to him.[93] And he certainly kept track of the many *Hiawatha* spoofs. When Charles Sumner sent him a parody titled "Misch-ko-da-sa," Longfellow recommended that he also take a look at the much better one published in *Punch,* by Shirley Brooks (February 7, 1856; *Letters* 3:526). Longfellow knew that, for better or worse, his poems were public property.

Two of the parodies show clearly that the aspects of *Hiawatha* I have highlighted here were understood by most of Longfellow's readers. The funnier of the two came from the Reverend George Augustus Strong, who took his cue from the fake "Feejee" mermaid on display at Barnum's American Museum and in 1856 presented the public with *The Song of Milgenwater* (called *Milkanwatha* in the second edition), allegedly translated from "the original Feejee" by Marc Antony Henderson, D.C.L., "Professor of the Feejee Language and Literature in the Brandywine Female Academy." (The publisher of the work was identified as "Tickell & Grinne.") Strong alludes to Longfellow's problems with literary originality and ownership right at the beginning of his book, in a "Translator's Preface." At first he simulates generosity and rejects the notion that there might be any direct relationship between this translation from the Feejee "original" and Longfellow's "original" work. But then, introducing a fake distinction between "piracy" and "imitation" and cleverly inverting the relationship between the parodied text and the parody itself, he suggests that the reader, well, should take another look:

> That, in many of its parts, there is a strong correspondence between
> it and Mr. Longfellow's last great work, "The Song of Hiawatha,"
> is too apparent to be overlooked. But so far from basing upon this

similarity of incident and treatment, a charge of *literary piracy* against Mr. Longfellow, as has been done by some who have discovered a much fainter likeness to a poem of Scandinavian origin—the translator recognizes in it only another evidence of that unity of thought which characterizes the human species, and which is a natural consequence of the unity of the races, of which the great family of man is composed. How far the "Song of Hiawatha," may be justly deemed an *imitation,* however, in outline, incident or versification, of the Scandinavian—or of the poem from the Feejee, here presented to our readers—it is for them, and not for the translator, to decide; but it is believed that a careful comparison, one with another, will disclose many curious resemblances in form and feature, which may be thought worthy the attention of men of letters.[94]

The notes that are supplied, like Longfellow's, at the end of Strong's "translation" continue the cheerfully fraudulent game. For example, the "translator" identifies an apparent allusion to *Hamlet*—fevers and chills are the "worst of ills that flesh is heir to"—as in fact derived from a cannibalistic (and unintelligible) work by the Feejee poet "Tremen-jus," in which the speaker complains about tough and juiceless meat: "Of ills flesh be th' heir to, worst much, may be!" And a reference to the hero's "blushing" earlobes is compared to a passage from Keats's *Endymion.*

Strong's parody is set on the island of "Chaw-a-man-up," on the shores of a lake called, none too subtly, "Watta-puddel." The storyline is the same as in Longfellow's poem, with the protagonist's courtship and marriage, Longfellow's creative addition to the native material, given top billing. But the protagonist is now called "Milkanwatha" and his bride-to-be, a descendant of the distinguished tribe of the Noodles, "Pogee-Wogee." As in *Hiawatha,* the protagonist's mate and his friends have to die, ferried away to eternity by "Watta-puddel," whereupon Milkanwatha realizes, not incorrectly, that his days are numbered, too. Strong spices up his narrative with some great fake Indian (or, as the author would claim, "Feejee") words: the flea is called "Sticka-ta-wa-in" and the bluebird "Lingo-sneedel." The cornfield is referred to as "Plow-e-tup," the bullfrog appears as "Opee-pod," the grey goose as "Dab-si-di-do," and the rooster, the most onomatopoetic of all, is called "Doodel-doo." Hiawatha's Chibiabos has been transformed into the wimpy "Sillininkum," and Kwasind is now known as "Beedel," Milkanwatha's "fat man" (rather than his strong man). The androgynous Pau-puk-Keewis is more fittingly named "Papamama." A small glossary in the back, for the reader's convenience, lists and translates all these "Feejee" terms. While Strong's puns often sound a little juvenile, some of the details of his parody show that he had studied Longfellow's poem quite closely, imitating especially the poet's penchant for drawn-out, fully explained similes: "Just as, to a big umbrella, / Is the handle, when it's raining, / So a wife is, to her husband" (40; a note informs the incredulous reader that umbrellas were actually quite common on the Feejee Islands).

At the end of Strong's parody, Hiawatha/Milkanwatha, as he did in Longfellow's "original," drifts off into the sunset, bobbing up and down, like a demented duck, on the reddening waters of "Watta-puddel." Why he has to leave, no one knows. But when he gets to the Land of the Hereafter, here termed "Ponee-rag-bag," he finds all his dead friends, who have in fact been revived by their immersion in "Watta-puddel." *Milkanwatha* ends as a tongue-in-cheek advertisement for the benefits of the plunge-bath, a particularly apt conclusion (though Strong probably did not know this) for a parody of a poem by an author who once had traveled all the way to Europe to seek relief from his neuralgia through the water-cure.

To the second edition of his parody Strong added versions of several other well-known poems, ranging from Tennyson's "The Lotus-Eaters" (here called "The Cigar-Smokers") to Longfellow's very own "Excelsior," retitled "High-er," in which the ambitious youth at the end is just plain dead ("lifeless, defunct, without any doubt, / The Lamp of his Being, decidedly out"). Although he always reprints the first stanza of the parodied text as a kind of epigraph to his takeoffs, in the short preface to this odd collection Strong again vigorously denies that the resemblances between his humble "Feejee" poems and sundry "familiar productions by distinguished authors" are anything other than coincidences, or, to use his own beautiful coinage, "parallelographs." The real danger, pretends Strong, isn't that his poems might be considered imitations. Rather, his readers might suspect that Keats and his colleagues had helped themselves to crumbs from the richly stocked tables of Feejee culture, that is, if the pristine reputation of these luminaries didn't in fact "forbid us to harbor, for one moment, the suspicion that they could descend from their high position as men and poets—to attack a struggling literature like the Feejee, with a weapon so unworthy of their powers as the Parody—so universally condemned by the rules of the literary service" (89).

The Song of Milkanwatha is a rather innocent, good-natured literary spoof, devoid of overt political intent. This is not true of *Pluri-bus-tah* (1865), a bitter satire produced by a writer with a markedly less generous disposition, "Philander Doesticks" (a pseudonym for the *New York Tribune* journalist Mortimer Neal Thomson, 1831–75), who, in his unapologetic "Author's Apology," declares that his main intent was to "break things" and, more specifically, to "slaughter the American Eagle, cut the throat of the Goddess of Liberty, annihilate the Yankee nation."[95] Thomson lashes out against all the participants in the drama of American history, and he has little patience for Longfellow's more optimistic reading of Indian removal, in which the white settlers appear as the at least potentially worthy successors of natives who cheerfully accept that they have reached their sell-by date.

Pluri-bus-tah begins with the mighty Jupiter emitting thick clouds of smoke through his Meerschaum pipe ("a denser, bluer vapor / Ever rising, rising, rising"), a clear reference to the peace pipe smoked at the beginning of *Hiawatha*. The Indians are too busy to notice since they are attending a "Red republican mass-meeting," sponsored by Hiawatha, who has given out free tickets "over all the lakes and rivers." Their ruler, the goddess Miss America, is on her way to complain to Jupiter that the amiable playthings he had given her, the cute Indians who had so nicely and so entertainingly "shot, and killed, and scalped each other / Roasted, broiled and stewed each other," have all been captured by "the poet Henry Wadsworth":

> He took all my Indian subjects,
> All my pretty, playful warriors,
> With their toys, the knife and war-club,
> With their pretty games of scalping . . .
>   *(Pluri-bus-tah, 35)*

John McLenan's illustration for the book shows a long-nosed Longfellow carrying away several diminutive Indians with nose-rings while holding a copy of *Hiawatha* under his left arm (fig. 15). In the background a screaming "Miss America" is visible. In the poem, she blames Jupiter for having allowed "Henry Wadsworth" to scoop up all her pretty Indians to turn them into a book.

The settlement and subsequent government of America by Pluri-bus-tah, the brutal leader of the Pilgrim-fath-us, goes from bad to worse. In the

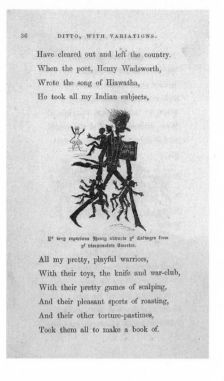

FIGURE 15

John McLenan, "Ye very rapacious
Henry abducts ye Salvages from ye
disconsolate America," from Q. K.
Philander Doesticks, B.P., *Pluri-bus-tah:
A Song That's-By-No-Author* (New York:
Livermore and Rudd, 1856).
Author's collection.

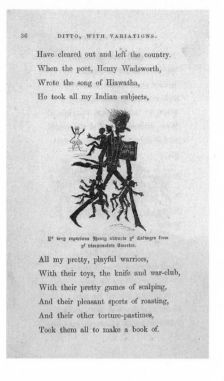

"Yenga" (Yankee) nation, the corn-god Mondamin's influence is felt mainly in the form of "Whisky made of Indian corn-juice," of which Pluri-bus-
tah has to drink half a gallon before he feels manly enough to pummel his
slave, the "sable Cuffee," into submission: "And he whaled away at Cuffee,
/ Injured and astonished Cuffee" (126). Pluri-bus-tah's offspring from his
marriage to the goddess Liberty is the ruthless Yunga-Merraka ("Young
America"), whose immoral shenanigans and "Bowery notions" come to an
end only when slave Cuffee finally retaliates and enslaves *him*. At the end
of the poem, nothing is left of the once powerful "Yenga nation" but its
symbol, the "Almighty Dollar."

    Pluri-bus-tah mocks Longfellow's vision of an America united in broth-
erly love, but it also makes fun of the poem's literary claims. Like "Marc
Antony Henderson," the creator of Milkanwatha, "Philander Doesticks"
seizes on Longfellow's authorial role-playing at the beginning of *Hiawatha*
to ridicule his own claim to authorship, dubious for different reasons.

"Doesticks" pretends that the manuscript was given to him by a pawnshop owner, identified only as "the Uncle," the seedy patron of many a starving American artist. Apparently, the hard-up author had been in desperate need of cash:

> Should you ask *me* where *I* found it?
> Found this song, perhaps so stupid,
> Found this most abusive epic?
> I should answer, I should tell you
> That "I found it at my Uncle's,"
> "Number one, around the corner,"
> In a paper, in a pocket,
> In a coat, within a bundle,
> Tied up, ticketed and labelled,
> Labeled by my careful "Uncle;"
> Placed within a cozy recess,
> On a shelf behind a curtain. . . .
>
> Months had flown, and still the author
> Hadn't yet redeemed his pledges,
> Hadn't paid the two and sixpence.
>
> (*Plu-ri-bus-tah,* xvi–xvii)

"Doesticks" cleverly imitates Longfellow's diction, from the paralyzing tetrameters to the tautologies ("I should tell you, I should answer") to the numbing repetitions ("labeled / labeled by my careful 'Uncle'"). As his "Indian" trochees invaded the American reading public, Longfellow could be certain that at least one of his messages had been understood. *Hiawatha,* the "song that's by no author," had acquired multiple authors; it had become truly everybody's poem. To some extent, this is still true today. One of the more recent spoofs is *The Song of Hakawatha,* written by the pseudonymous F. X. Reid. *Hakawatha,* a computer hacker's irreverent take on Longfellow's melancholy Indian story, is said to have originated at the University of Glasgow in the early 1980s. However, the lines, which closely imitate Longfellow's numbing rhythms, still speak to every computer user's experience today:

> First, he sat and faced the console
> Faced the glowing, humming console
> Typed his login at the keyboard

Typed his password (fourteen letters)
Waited till the system answered
Waited long and cursed its slowness
(Oh that irritating slowness—
Like a mollusc with lumbago) . . . [96]

Parodies like the one above attest to how much Longfellow still is part of popular culture. In 1989, the avant-garde singer and composer Laurie Anderson, in a song titled "Hiawatha" on her album *Strange Angels,* acknowledged that the difference between America's first pop poet and the King of Graceland, between Longfellow's lines about the "shores of Gitche Gumee" and "Love Me Tender," might be one of degree but not of kind: "And I said: Hello Operator / Get me Memphis Tennessee."

Art and Artifice

Philander Doestick's critique of American materialism struck close to home. American Victorians were obsessed with things, defining themselves and others through what they owned or didn't (yet) own. We have seen how some of this fascination with things also surfaces, a bit unexpectedly, in *Hiawatha.* From the toys he gave his children to the antique bookshelves he acquired for his library to the multicolored wine bottles on his dinner table, Longfellow took an unabashed pleasure in well-made objects. What delighted him was not how much they cost but the effort, workmanship, and control of the material they represented. The final section of this chapter will present readings of two late Longfellow works specifically concerned with the making of things, "Kéramos" (1877), a celebration of the global history of human craftsmanship (in which the beautiful artifact has always been more important than the artificer), and the verse play *Michael Angelo,* unfinished at the time of Longfellow's death, which evokes the plight of the "subjective" artist, driven by the ambition to surpass his predecessors rather than by an intrinsic interest in his material.

Victorian American parlors, in the modern imagination at least, were artificial, convention-laden, overstuffed, and uncomfortable.[97] But precisely because this culture was so profoundly shaped by the desire to imitate and impress, the things that appeared there served complex purposes.[98] Far from being mere parlor props, they played central roles in everyday life, indicating not just the owner's status, wealth, and sophistication but also telling tales about his or her past and future aspirations. A revealing scene from *The Barclays of Boston* (1854), the bestselling novel written by "Mrs. Harrison Gray Otis" (Eliza Henderson Otis), one of Longfellow's contemporaries and social peers, shows us how the drama of self-presentation played out in these homes. During a dinner party at Mr. Egerton's residence, the host's china becomes one of the liveliest conversation topics. No wonder: Mr. Egerton's cabinet of cups and plates—first compiled by his father, the India merchant, and then supplemented by Egerton himself during his early years in China—was a sight "sufficient to drive a collector of curiosities quite mad." Stocked with "every variety of the old burnt china, so valuable even in its own land, the curiously cracked, with the rare colors, and the transparent biscuit," it inspires the narrator to some of her most enthusiastic prose. Reveling in what she assumes will be also her reader's mounting excitement, she exclaims, "There were dinner services innumerable and tea to match, and such superb desserts! In fact, there was no end of the beauty and value of these treasures."

When this precious dinnerware arrives on Egerton's table, the assembled guests hasten to profess themselves, in various ways, to be "china-fanciers." Delightedly they point out how many of these precious objects can be found in the homes of Americans, as opposed to those of Europeans ("We are all surrounded, in this country, by such quantities of the material"), and with animation they enter into a debate about "the different degrees of excellence of various countries" in the production of porcelain.[99] Mr. Egerton's valuable dinner set, apart from serving as a convenient conversation piece, also identifies his guests as belonging to the same social circle, just as it confirms others in their role as outsiders. Mr. Egerton's black servant Dinah, for example, though she diligently cleans her "Massa's" crockery, has neither the intellectual capacity nor the cultural competence to understand its "intrinsic worth." Or so the narrator would have us believe.

Otis's china enthusiasts get their wares from abroad. The paltriness of American-made porcelain at the 1876 Centennial Exposition in Philadelphia spurred American ceramicists to redouble their efforts. When Longfellow, in the summer of 1877, wrote "Kéramos," his poem on pottery, he was directly responding to this new-found interest in ceramics. The poem was so timely that *Harper's* editor Henry Mills Alden didn't have to think twice about paying Longfellow $1,000 for the right to print it.

Harper's published the poem in December 1877 in a rather lavish format, with each of its ten pages accompanied by illustrations especially commissioned from the mural painter and illustrator Edwin Austin Abbey (and a second artist, "A.F.," whom I have not been able to identify). Featuring brawny craftsmen, pretty damsels, delicate landscapes, and dainty flowers (fig. 16), these rather conventional illustrations were, with one exception, not the ones that Longfellow had wanted for his poem. His letter

FIGURE 16

Longfellow, "Kéramos," *Harper's* 56 (December 1877), 65.
By permission of Houghton Library, Harvard University.

of August 4, 1877, to Alden reveals that he felt that pictures of the artifacts themselves, rather than "artsy" representations, would provide the best commentary on his poem (*Letters* 6:289).

Longfellow's protest was appropriate: "Kéramos," his last great poetic apotheosis of the values of craftsmanship, is less the expression of a poet's facile fantasizing than the result of painstaking research about the objects represented in the poem. Drawing on books like Albert Jacquemart's *History of the Ceramic Art* and Arthur Beckwith's *Majolica and Fayence*,[100] Longfellow used ceramics as an exact correlative for his own, "objective" text-making.

"Kéramos" begins with a conceit that epitomizes the philosophy of the entire poem, namely that the maker's hand and the substance it shapes are made of the same material. Still, the potter (note Longfellow's emphasis on the creator's hand rather than his intellect) is in control of the material, determining what the finished product will look like:

> *Turn, turn, my wheel! Turn round and round*
> *Without a pause, without a sound:*
>   *So spins the flying world away!*
> *This clay, well mixed with marl and sand,*
> *Follows the motion of my hand;*
> *For some must follow, and some command,*
>   *Though all are made of clay!* (3:247)

The key image of clay is introduced as part of a lilting refrain-like interlude that recurs seven times in the course of the poem, on each occasion with a different moral or interpretive message ("*All things must change*"; "*All life is brief*"; "*A touch can make, a touch can mar*"; "'*T is nature's plan / The child should grow into a man*"; "*The human race . . . Are kindred*"; "*To-morrow will be another day*"; "*All are ground to dust at last*"). The exhortative phrase at the beginning of the poem, "*Turn, turn, my wheel!*" is repeated verbatim until the end, where it changes to, appropriately, "*Stop, stop, my wheel!*" All the "refrains" end either with the word "clay" or some other word that rhymes with it ("*away*," "*they*," "*day*"). The alternation between the refrains and the different parts of the main narrative, each of them a vignette devoted to pottery in a different part of the world, creates a recognizable, if idiosyncratic, pattern—a subtle effect of sameness-in-difference, which makes the poem "Kéramos," as a textual object, not unlike the things about which it speaks.

The first vignette paints a portrait of the potter at work. Remarkably, the poet-speaker does not immediately cast himself in the role of the potter, preferring instead to describe his activities from an external perspective ("I stood in silence and apart"). We see the potter bent over his wheel, his workshop sheltered by a hawthorn tree in bloom. The branches of the tree sway in the breeze, and the ensuing play of light and shade over the potter's face and black-aproned body anticipates the combination of dark clay and bright fire involved in the manufacture of a piece of pottery. This potter is no longer simply Mr. Dodge from Portland, Maine, whom Longfellow had identified as the immediate inspiration behind his lines.[101] Represented only by his singing voice and his moving hand, Longfellow's potter is less a person than a principle, "a conjurer without book or beard." His creativity, Longfellow suggests, is indistinguishable from the rhythms of nature itself, which in him, the artisan, has created, or "woven," her own artifact:

> Thus sang the Potter at his task
> Beneath the blossoming hawthorn-tree,
> While o'er his features, like a mask,
> The quilted sunshine and leaf-shade
> Moved, as the boughs above him swayed,
> And clothed him, till he seemed to be
> A figure woven in tapestry,
> So sumptuously was he arrayed
> In that magnificent attire
> Of sable tissue flaked with fire. (3:247)

In the section following the next interlude ("*Turn, turn, my wheel! All things must change / To something new, to something strange*"), the speaker finally, at least in his imagination, joins the potter. Continuing the textile imagery begun earlier, Longfellow describes the union of the two as the "weaving" of "foreign" matter into one of nature's works of art, a humble bird's nest:

> Thus still the Potter sang, and still,
> By some unconscious act of will,
> The melody and even the words
> Were intermingled with my thought,
> As bits of colored thread are caught
> And woven into nests of birds. (3:248)

As was the case at the beginning of *Hiawatha,* the purpose of such metaphorical stage-setting is to de-emphasize human agency and, more specifically, divert attention from the fact of Longfellow's authorship. In the anonymous potter's work, the difference between nature and art becomes irrelevant (the Greek word chosen for the title refers both to the material—clay, for example—as well as the product made from that material). Likewise, the line separating the artisan and the object he produces is erased. Although the potter exerts absolute control over the pots he makes while he is making them, ultimately both the producer and the product are merely earth transformed: formed of the same stuff to which all things will finally return.

This was perhaps not a startlingly new idea. Longfellow could have found it (as I am sure he did) in Edward FitzGerald's translation of Omar Khayyám's *Rubáiyát,* where the speaker overhears the vessels in a potter's workshop having a lively debate about their likely future. Had they been shaped from the "common earth" only to be trampled back into it again? Could their maker consider himself exempt from the fate that will befall the things he makes? Or, as a small pot in Khayyám's simulated workshop summarized these concerns, "Who is the Potter, pray, and who the Pot?"[102]

What renders "Kéramos" interesting is that Longfellow applies the small pot's question about pottery-making to the making of poems. As he saw it, even a poem is not necessarily meant for eternity, as the timeless expression of an artist's individual will and talent. We shape a piece of pottery, burn it, glaze it, use it, break it, and then discard and replace it. Similarly, few poems will outlive their usefulness: *"Behind us in our path we cast / The broken potsherds of the past, / And all are ground to dust at last"* (3:261). Put positively, however, a poem, like a pot, is never a cheap copy of some elusive "reality"; rather, it speaks, though indirectly or impersonally, of its maker, his or her desire to make a shape that might benefit or please somebody else. Similarly, "Kéramos" is both product and process. Longfellow's round poem begins when the potter begins his work and ends when his day's work is over. Performing several circles or "revolutions" itself, it not only imitates the circular motions of the potter's wheel but also gestures toward the cycles of decay and renewal that Longfellow finds at work in both human and natural history: *"The mist and cloud will turn to rain, / The rain to mist and cloud again, / To-morrow be to-day"* (2:248).

Longfellow's highly evocative introduction prepares the reader for the main part of the poem's narrative, a *voyage imaginaire* around the world in search of examples of the potter's work. The speaker of the poem travels "with restless speed," holding onto the potter's "magic cloak," an allusion to Aladdin's magic carpet. Venturing into ever more remote regions and traveling gradually back in time, he moves from more familiar countries and cultures to less familiar terrain.

The first vignette transports the reader from Portland, Maine, to Delft in the Netherlands. With a few casual strokes of the pen, Longfellow paints a picture of a sun-filled country in which water turns into land and land into water. Almost imperceptibly, the panoramic view of the country, seen from above ("land of sluices, dikes, and dunes"; "this water-net, that tessellates / The landscape"), is replaced with a view of the country from down below—a nuance that demonstrates Longfellow's skill as a poet. In the soft, hazy afternoon light, tulips can be seen straining through latticed fences, ships "float high" on dikes that seem to cut across green fields, and "over all" the sails of windmills "sink and soar" like the wings of sea gulls in the breeze.

Inside the houses of Delft, a similar light illuminates the rooms, emanating now from the world of things, the shining porcelain plates, the translucent flagons and flasks, the colorfully ornamented walls of the chimney. Though indoors, all of them share in the luminescence of the landscape itself, with the only difference that these images of nature are not subject to the changing seasons. In a manner reminiscent of "To a Child," the poem mentioned earlier in this chapter, the poet's view has narrowed down to the size of the smallest single painted tile, "beautiful with fadeless flowers" (2:249).

Soaring high over the world, going "southward," the poet now gives us a glimpse at the studio in Saintes, France, of potter Bernard Palissy, whose mad determination in the search for some new enamel he admires. Passing over the red-roofed towns of Majorca, he then takes us to Italy. We appreciate the metallic luster of Italian pottery, notably the majolica paintings of Francesco Xanto Avelli in Urbino, who attempted to transform Raphael's "translucent grace" into the "fictile fabric" of earthenware.[103] And Maestro Giorgio Andreoli of Urbino receives praise for his spectacular polychromatic plate designs, speckled with mother-of-pearl and adorned with golden arabesques, which interweave "birds and fruits and flowers and leaves / About some landscape, shaded brown, / With olive tints on rock and town" (3:253).

Longfellow evidently enjoys the descriptive precision his subject demands from him, the focus on the glittering, gleaming material world that a poem about vases and plates requires. He knows that, for all their splendor, he cannot treat these objects as the expression of a single artistic personality, that the notion of individual authorship makes little sense here. In a long passage visualizing a stunningly beautiful cup from the manufactory of Gubbio (fig. 17), Longfellow accordingly describes the artifact purely as an object, not as the expression of an artist's will and vision. He ends with a reminder of the highly specific use it once had when it was given away.

> Behold this cup within whose bowl,
> Upon a ground of deepest blue
> With yellow-lustred stars o'erlaid,
> Colors of every tint and hue
> Mingle in one harmonious whole!
> With large blue eyes and steadfast gaze,
> Her yellow hair in net and braid,
> Necklace and ear-rings all ablaze
> With golden lustre o'er the glaze,
> A woman's portrait; on the scroll,
> Cana, the Beautiful! A name
> Forgotten save for such brief fame
> As this memorial can bestow,—
> A gift some lover long ago
> Gave with his heart to this fair dame. (3:253)

Note the skill with which Longfellow represents the plate as an iridescent play of correspondences: against the background of a blue sky filled with yellow stars we see the face of a blue-eyed woman with yellow hair! And

FIGURE 17

Illustration (fig. 25) from Arthur Beckwith, *Majolica and Fayence* (New York: D. Appleton, 1877). Author's collection.

the preciousness of the cup with its golden sheen matches the brilliant golden jewelry worn by the woman depicted on it. One material object refers to, or quotes, another. "A most harmonious piece," declared Longfellow's source.[104] Longfellow had asked that a picture of this cup ("as handsome as possible") accompany his poem in *Harper's,* and this was in fact the only one of his suggestions they used. As the last two lines of the passage make clear, Longfellow's point here is not that a beautiful work of art should be considered as self-contained, as inhabiting a world apart from the observer. Art, for Longfellow, is arti*fact:* a "made" product, intended to be remade by its user.

What Longfellow's speaker admires most in Italian ceramics are actually the oldest examples of it, the ancient vases, urns, and bas-reliefs of the Romans. A reproduction of a terra cotta relief of Hercules ("Alcides") taming the Cretan bull in Jacquemart's book caught his eye, and he now describes it in lines consisting of little more than a noun accompanied by an adjective or adverbial phrase. They match the stark expressiveness of the relief, in which the bull's muscular neck, strained virtually to bursting, lets the awed viewer wonder how strong its human conqueror must have been. In "Kéramos," particles like "almost" and "still" do not describe, as they did in Keats's "Ode on a Grecian Urn," the boundary that separates us from the hermetically sealed world of art. Instead, they indicate a promise of communication and communion soon to be fulfilled—if not in reality then at least in the viewer's (and the reader's) mind:

> Figures that almost move and speak,
> And, buried amid mould and weeds,
> Still in their attitudes attest
> The presence of the graceful Greek,—
> Achilles in his armor dressed,
> Alcides with the Cretan bull,
> And Aphrodite with her boy,
> Or lovely Helena of Troy,
> Still living and still beautiful. (3:254–55)

These Roman artifacts are not like Keats's Grecian urn, tantalizing the viewer yet never letting go of its secrets. To Longfellow, they are fully readable, accessible transcripts of a time that the speaker easily relives, even as his imagined travels take him farther away, onward to Egypt and China.

It is no coincidence that, at this point in the poem, Longfellow leaves the western world behind. His editor Alden had criticized him for not including more topical references to Wedgwood, Sèvres, or Dresden porcelain in his poem, but Longfellow had other ideas.[105] For him, pottery was both the expression of cultural difference (and therefore a truly international, multicultural enterprise) and the confirmation that all works of art and craftsmanship ultimately spring from the same source. And of course he also knew that potters in China, Japan, India, Persia, and Egypt were using stoneware and porcelain long before potters covered "with their elegant decorations the coarse, porous earth" of Greece (Jacquemart 3). And so we now find his speaker gazing raptly at huge earthen jars in Cairo, which he—incorrectly—associates with the receptacles that served as the uncomfortable hiding places, and then as the graves, of the forty thieves in Ali Baba's house. Moving onward to China, he very effectively compares himself (in what the rhetoricians would call a polyptoton) to a bird in rapid flight: "Bird-like I fly, and flying sing." Longfellow even allows himself a moment of sly humor when, in a section marked by strong masculine end rhymes, he pairs "wing" with the Chinese factory town "King-te-tching" (Jingdezhen in the Jiangxi province):

> O'er desert sands, o'er gulf and bay,
> O'er Ganges and o'er Himalay,
> Bird-like I fly, and flying sing,
> To flowery kingdoms of Cathay,
> And bird-like poise on balanced wing
> Above the town of King-te-tching . . . (3:257)

The poem's last vignette is set in Japan, where Longfellow takes the reader to the workshops near the villages of Imari. As was the case in Holland, there is a direct relationship between the landscape and the artifacts. Again, the movement from original (the landscape) to copy (the decorations on the porcelain) does not mean anything is lost. "The stork, the heron, and the crane" that the speaker has seen flying "through the clear realms of azure drift" reappear painted on the jars of Imari:

> Again the skylark sings, again
> The stork, the heron, and the crane
> Float through the azure overhead,
> The counterfeit and counterpart
> Of Nature reproduced in Art. (3:259)

In fact, in this section Longfellow almost mocks the reader's conventional views of art. Stretching one sentence out over seven lines, padding it with distracting adverbial matter and relative clauses, he effectively mingles sound (leaves rustle, reeds whisper), sight (bright flowers, bright stars, saffron dawn, sunset red), and movement (waves ripple). When he finally delivers the overdue remainder of the clause, he also supplies the adverbial phrase that identifies where all these beautiful scenes are to be found—not in nature but on a painted piece of porcelain:

> All the bright flowers that fill the land,
> Ripple of waves on rock or sand,
> The snow on Fusiyama's cone,
> The midnight heaven so thickly sown
> With constellations of bright stars,
> The leaves that rustle, the reeds that make
> A whisper by each stream and lake,
> The saffron dawn, the sunset red,
> Are painted on these lovely jars . . . (2:259)

Longfellow's "Kéramos" is carried by the poet's belief in the magic of things, whose presence and power transcends the people who made them. A reviewer writing in the *Atlantic Monthly* noticed as much when he praised Longfellow's ability in this poem to endow inanimate objects with life: "its lines are rich and lustrous with the hues of Delft, and Palissy, and Majolica, and Faenza, and China, and Imari; they flow in the matchless forms of the Greek vases." Longfellow's success lay, he said, in the poem's mesmerizing effect on the reader, an imperceptible merging not only of the identities of potter and poet but of author and audience: "The poem, when you have done, seems a reverie of your own."[106]

In her meditation on acts that "make" the world, Elaine Scarry defines an object as the "lever across which the force of creation moves back onto the human site."[107] Made by humans, it is made for other humans, for "shared sentience," in Scarry's words. In "Kéramos," the artifacts from Holland, France, Italy, Egypt, China, and Japan, like Longfellow's poem itself, ultimately exist not for their own sake but to be *shared* by readers all over the world. Thus, a plate made by Avelli can teach us more about art than the painting by Raphael that might have inspired it. Made for human consumption, as vessels fit to contain food, fragrant fruit, or cut flowers, the Italian plate or Japanese jar or Dutch flask do not flaunt their *invented-*

ness. Their power to benefit the user ultimately does not depend on wheth-er or not we recognize the maker's signature. His or her identity is irrel-evant, even detrimental, to the desired effect. Art is not personal: "Never man, / as artist or as artisan, / Pursuing his own fantasies, / Can touch the human heart" (3:260).[108]

In this sense, the poem "Kéramos" is, as the *Atlantic Monthly* reviewer realized, not categorically different from a Greek vase. Unlike Keats's well-wrought urn, Longfellow's poem does not keep its secrets to itself to cele-brate the cold self-sufficiency of art. And unlike Wallace Stevens's famous jar, it does not take dominion everywhere. Significantly, in Longfellow's source, Jacquemart's *History of the Ceramic Art,* images of simple harmony between people and the objects they make and use contrast with the au-thor's indictments of western arrogance, the damage imperialist domina-tion has done to the ancient civilizations of the East (Jacquemart 22, 78).

The main function of Longfellow's "Kéramos" is to make shareable the story of what is, by its very nature, a shareable and universal craft. It will not do to reject his philosophizing here as outdated nostalgia for the intimate, quasi-personal relationship the artisan enjoyed, in preindustrial times, with the object he or she created. Though it starts and ends with a lonely potter singing at his wheel, "Kéramos" also contains quite unam-biguous images of the factory-like effort ("Three thousand furnaces that glow / Incessantly, and fill the air / With smoke uprising") that went into the production of porcelain at a place like Jingdezhen, where each finished item bore the traces of many hands: "here . . . all individuality disappears" (Jacquemart 64). Art is the child of nature, Longfellow announces toward the end of the poem, deliberately skirting the limits of cliché: "her dar-ling child, in whom we trace / The features of the mother's face" (3:260). But the real theme of "Kéramos" is not art's mimesis of nature; it is the strange kinship between people and the things they make and use. More than a master's masterpieces, the artisan's wares (and the poet's poems, too) make tangible the ties that connect, indeed *relate,* all humans, "*of every tongue, of every place, / Caucasian, Coptic, or Malay*" (3:257). Made from clay, a potter's artifacts tell us, democratically, that we too are earth temporarily transformed—an insight that, if we go back to Mrs. Harrison Otis's nov-el *The Barclays of Boston* for a moment, applies to the porcelain-collecting "Massa" Egerton as well as to his humble servant Dinah.

Longfellow's "Kéramos" had an interesting afterlife. In October 1877, a few months after the poem was published in *Harper's,* the Cincinnati ceramic artist Mary Louise McLaughlin mixed mineral paints with liquefied clay ("slip"). As a result, she was able to achieve the rich, Rembrandtesque underglaze that Americans had admired in the works of French ceramicists.[109] In 1880, she founded her own studio in Cincinnati, the Rookwood Pottery, and became a major contributor to the American Arts and Crafts movement, tirelessly extolling the benefits of her supposedly individualistic trade over the uniformity of conventionally manufactured objects. Her enormous "Ali Baba" vase, made in 1880, was intended "to excel in size any piece of ceramic work yet produced in this country." An impressive thirty-seven inches high and seventeen inches around, it marked the mythic fervor that McLaughlin brought to her work. The inspiration for the huge vase came, I suspect, from no other source than Longfellow's pottery poem. But while Longfellow's poem had celebrated pottery as evidence that art can be practiced by everyone and everywhere, the leaders of the American Arts and Crafts movement addressed themselves to a more limited, elite segment of American society. Even the invitations to McLaughlin's receptions, printed from original designs etched in copper, were considered *objets d'art*.[110]

Longfellow's poem continued to play a minor role in pottery magazines, which were occasionally adorned with excerpts from "Kéramos." An 1885 advertisement in the *Pottery and Glassware Reporter* contains, in the round insert in the lower left corner, a rather muscular version of Longfellow's potter. The first stanza of "Kéramos" appears printed underneath (fig. 18). In the lower right corner, a quotation from the *Rubáiyát* provides the caption for the main illustration, which shows a man in the dress of a medieval artisan leaning on what seems to be the edge of a workbench. The potter seems self-absorbed, contemplating himself rather than his wares. The light emanating from the lantern above the potter's head illuminates what the engravers clearly wanted to be understood as a heroic image: the master among his wares, but not defined *by* his wares. The snippets of poetry in the picture are intended to legitimize the highly individualized reading of the potter's trade that the advertisement as a whole propagates.

"Kéramos," with its emphasis on the product rather than the producer, seems perhaps a bit more at home in a less self-consciously artistic publication, the sales catalogue of the Boston crockery dealers Abram French & Company (fig. 19). Here Longfellow's verses appear alongside pictures of plates and tureens from fancy dinner sets, to be acquired, for example, at the price of $50 for a 145–piece set (roughly $970 in current money).

"The body of the goods is a fine Porcelain," croons the catalogue, "and the decoration an underglaze border design of a delicate Gray, with Gold Trimmings." In short, "a very artistic and tasteful production." Though himself a friend of refined living, Longfellow would have been amused to see his pottery poem—which told his readers that, from the pottery-lover's perspective, all humans, "Caucasian, Coptic, or Malay," were created equal—placed next to porcelain that would have been out of reach for most of his book-loving contemporaries.

When *Kéramos and Other Poems* appeared in 1878, it contained also Long-fellow's translations of several poems by Michelangelo, whose poetry had

FIGURE 18

Advertisement from the *Pottery and Glassware Reporter,*
May 18, 1885. National Museum of American History,
Smithsonian Institution, no. 89-21067.

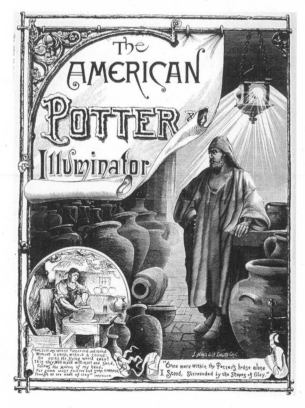

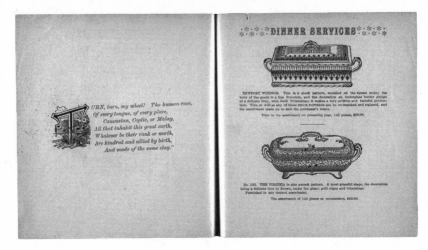

FIGURE 19

Sales pamphlet, Abram French and Company, wholesale and retail
dealers in crockery, china, glassware, silver-plated ware, and lamps,
Franklin Street, Boston. C. 1885. Harvard College Library. Courtesy
of the President and Fellows of Harvard College.

preoccupied him, in one way or another, for several years. The seven sonnets and the canzone speak of the artist's struggle with his art and his life
(two of the sonnets are devoted to old age), about his admiration for Vittoria Colonna and Dante and, finally, about the fear that, as darkness draws
near, he might have accomplished too little. All these themes appear also
in Longfellow's unfinished verse play, for which some of these translations
were originally intended, *Michael Angelo: A Fragment,* which he began in February 1872. He kept the manuscript in his drawer, adding and removing
scenes, but apparently never considered it finished enough for publication.
A reconstruction of what was supposed to be the work's last authorized
form appeared posthumously in the *Atlantic Monthly* in the spring of 1883.

Michael Angelo is a dramatic poem rather than a verse play. Longfellow is more interested in themes than in scenes, and he spends more time
on imagery than on creating dramatic tension or developing conflicts. His
portrayal of Michelangelo is usually regarded as highly autobiographical,
as an indication of a popular poet's increasing hankering after the Elysian
Fields of High Art, where he himself had never managed to walk with
ease.[111] But when we read *Michael Angelo* in the context of Longfellow's de-

flated notion of authorship as I have tried to portray it in this chapter, the text appears in a somewhat different light. Focusing on Michelangelo as an aging artist faced with the prospect of death, the poem directly reflects some of the issues that were important to Longfellow himself, notably the importance of good workmanship. But unlike the anonymous potter in "Kéramos," Longfellow's Michelangelo is never satisfied with anything he has achieved, discarding all his works as mere stepping-stones on the path to an artistic immortality he fears he will never attain.

In one of his early lectures, whose printed version Longfellow would have encountered as the lead essay of the April 1837 issue of the *North American Review,* Ralph Waldo Emerson hailed Michelangelo as "the perfect image of the artist."[112] An "eminent master in the four fine arts, Painting, Sculpture, Architecture, and Poetry," he excelled also in the practical world, namely as a military planner, engineer, and inventor of mechanical contrivances, such as the movable platform he constructed for his work on the ceiling of the Sistine Chapel. Emerson approvingly repeats what contemporaries said of Michelangelo, namely that the "marble was flexible in his hands." Throughout the essay, he emphasizes the artist's superhuman stature, declaring at one point that he was "of that class of men who are too superior to the multitude around them to command a full and perfect sympathy" (13).

Emerson's heroic portrait owes much to Giorgio Vasari's adulatory biography from 1550, which he cites frequently. The picture he paints of the dying Michelangelo, who asks that everyone feel joy at his death because he "has lived well," is appropriately glorious. The flourish that concludes Emerson's essay stresses the universality of Michelangelo's achievements, while it also strives to lessen the impression of aloofness created earlier in the essay. "He was not a citizen of any country; he belonged to the human race; he was a brother and a friend to all, who acknowledge the beauty that beams in universal nature, and who seek by labor and self-denial to approach its source in perfect goodness"(16).

Not all of Emerson's contemporaries agreed. For example, a completely different view of the artist appears in the *Fireside Travels* of James Russell Lowell, where Michelangelo is accused of having mistaken "bulk and brawn for the antithesis of feebleness." Calling him "the apostle of the exaggerated, the Victor Hugo of painting and sculpture," Lowell sees Michelangelo consumed by his competitive spirit and hampered by "the conscious intention to be original, which seldom leads to anything better than being extravagant."[113] Longfellow's view of Michelangelo is subtler than Lowell's, although he shares some of the latter's concerns. On the one hand, his Michelangelo is the prototype of the independent artist, cultivating no relationships and trusting few friends, beholden to no one but himself and his genius.[114] On the other hand, as Longfellow shows us, Michelangelo is also tortured by a very human desire to be better than others—Filippo Brunelleschi, the creator of the cupola of the Duomo in Florence, for example:

> Better than thou I cannot, Brunelleschi,
> And less than thou I will not! If the thought
> Could, like a windlass, lift the ponderous stones
> And swing them to their places; if a breath
> Could blow this rounded dome into the air,
> As if it were a bubble, and these statues
> Spring at a signal to their sacred stations,
> As sentinels mount guard upon a wall,
> Then were my task completed. (6:112)

Note the ease with which Longfellow piles image on image, skipping from the windlass hoisting stones to the giant bubble of the church's cupola to the statues of the saints popping up in their assigned places as if called for guard duty. What Michelangelo, faced with the inexorable stubbornness of his medium, cannot easily do in stone, Longfellow can do with words— create identifiable shapes out of nothing.

One of Longfellow's principal sources was Herman Grimm's biography of Michelangelo, which made a point of the special challenges posed by architecture. "No form of art," he wrote, is so "fettered" as that of the architects: "Their work depends on the soil on which it is to stand; on the materials with which it is created; on the time which the money allows; on the whim of the commissioners, who often bring forward other masters with other plans." Finally, even if all the conditions are favorable, one problem remains: "the strongest influence" exercised over the new structure by other buildings the architect has seen. No artist will find it harder not to imitate, not to copy other people's work or parts of other people's work, than the architect.[115]

And this is exactly the problem Longfellow's aging Michelangelo's faces. His work on the dome of St. Peter's marks the pinnacle of his desperate fight for originality. Haunted by the fear that "when we die, with us all art will die," he cannot accept with equanimity his fellow artist Titian's cheerful realization that all artists "must make room for others" (6:101). His friends remind him of his past achievements, but since the basis for his self-evaluation is the future, Michelangelo's sense of failure remains undiminished. His works now seem to him "as the books and slates / That school-boys leave behind them, when the door / Is opened, and they rush into the air" (6:425). He can't help wondering how posterity will look upon him, how others will "speak of me when I am gone, / When all this colorless, sad life is ended, / And I am dust" (6:97). An artist is to be measured by his results, not by his intentions or the price he paid for his accomplishments. As an unabashed aesthete, Michelangelo is interested only in the beauty of the Roman Coliseum, not in the sacrifices that were involved in its construction and the purpose for which it was intended, despite Tommaso Cavalieri's reminder that "the sand beneath our feet is saturate / With blood of martyrs; and these rifted stones / Are awful witnesses against a people / Whose pleasure was the pain of dying men" (6:130).

Death, for Michelangelo, is a warning that his art will soon be forgotten. He sees it as a devastating interruption, the unwelcome intrusion of the personal into the realm of art, and his physical limitations bother him mainly because of the innate resistance of the material with which he works both as a sculptor and an architect. If Emerson's Michelangelo found the marble "flexible," the opposite is true of Longfellow's protagonist: "The marble is too hard" (6:148). From the beginning, his life has been marked by attempts to make the reluctant stone amenable to the loftier concepts of the spirit. The first sounds he remembers hearing "were of the chisel / Chipping away the stone" (6:148). Of course, he does not want to be mistaken for a mere craftsman. Angrily Michelangelo tells the cardinals who berate him for the alleged "imperfections" of his work on St. Peter's: "I am not used to have men speak to me / As if I were a mason, hired to build / A garden wall" (6:121). He, who has spent his life "hewing stone, and painting walls of plaster" (6:426), remains adamant that handiness with marble must not be mistaken for "handicraft." Art cannot be learned, Michelangelo declares: "All men are not born artists, nor will labor / E'er make them artists" (6:149). Passionately, he draws a distinction between himself and painter Jan van Eyck: "When that barbarian Jan Van Eyck discovered / The use of oil in painting, he degraded / His art into a handicraft, and made it / Sign-painting" (6:92).

The last scene of the posthumously published fragment, dated March 12, 1872, shows the nonagenarian artist still hammering away at the stone—building, as he tells his visitor Vasari, his own tomb. In a projected final scene that Longfellow later eliminated, the dying Michelangelo cannot imagine himself *not* working, even in the afterlife: "What work can I do in the other world?" he complains. "Shall I build up aërial palaces / And churches in the air? or shape the statues / Of Saints and Martyrs in the marble clouds?" (4:426). He dies imagining the work he could not complete, his mind defeated by sluggish matter:

> The saddest thing in dying is to leave
> One's work unfinished. If now from this window
> Mine eyes could see, against the evening sky
> Saint Peter's dome, as in my mind I see it,
> Then should I die content. (6:427)

Michelangelo is, in a sense, a study of everything Longfellow was *not*—an artist consumed by, made desperate even, by his desire to have the "labor of his hand" match the grand, innovative conceptions in his head. Michelangelo is afflicted by a disease for which there is no cure: "malaria of the mind," he calls it, "the fever to accomplish some great work / That will not let us sleep" (6:76). One of the most evocative images in the dramatic poem has little to do with architecture and human ingenuity, though it suggests "new thoughts of beauty" to the architect. During his visit to the Coliseum, Michelangelo observes "a thousand wild flowers" blooming from the chinks of the stones and birds building their nests "among the ruined arches" (6:131–32). This Shakespearean image[116] resonates with a similar one in the "Dedication" Longfellow composed for *Michael Angelo,* where, fittingly, the poet compares himself to an architect, but with a difference:

> . . . from old chronicles, where sleep in dust
> Names that once filled the world with trumpet tones,
> I build this verse; and flowers of song have thrust
> Their roots among the loose disjointed stones,
> Which to this end I fashion as I must. (6:13)

Unlike Michelangelo "who creates because he has to create,"[117] Longfellow the poet in his "verse-building" is restricted ("I fashion as I must") both by past precedent ("old chronicles") and present purpose, that is, the effect he desires ("flowers of song"). There is little here of what Henry James, in one of his prefaces, called "the muffled majesty of authorship,"[118] little sense of the competitiveness, the desire for uniqueness, that were the forces driving Michelangelo to success.

Unlike the Renaissance genius who attracted and appalled him, Longfellow was reconciled to the fact that everything in this world existed at least "in duplicate" (see chapter 1). Some things might even exist in triplicate. In the 1860s, Longfellow, a poet equally interested in a child's marbles and Michelangelo's marble, drew a series of pictures for his daughters showing the trials and tribulations of a character named "Peter Quince." One of the pictures in the series shows Longfellow's alter ego Quince accompanied by two almost identical-looking friends, with whom he moves as if they were performing a strange kind of vaudeville routine (fig. 20).

All three are wearing top hats (as Longfellow did) and striped tail coats. Their postures are in almost complete synchrony: their right legs boldly stepping forward, they tiptoe on their left ones. Quince is taking his friends home with him after a fire, so frequent in the cramped streets of mid-nineteenth-century Boston, has raged through the neighborhood.

If it weren't for Peter Quince's trademark huge ears, it would be impossible to tell who is who in this picture. Imitation, said Bergson, "gives

FIGURE 20

"Mr. Peter Quince takes two friends home after the fire," from Longfellow, "Peter Quince," Longfellow Papers, Houghton Library, Harvard University, MS Am 1340 (163). By permission of the Houghton Library, Harvard University.

rise to laughter."[119] Paradoxically, to Bergson, this is not a happy response. The laughter called forth by the caricaturist's distortions masks our dismay at what we in fact see: the prospect of our own dehumanization; the dismal spectacle of movement without life; the realization that, somewhere and somehow, we too may be just like things, pathetic puppets worked by strings, acting out somebody else's designs and fantasies. But the reading of Longfellow's literary paternity that I have suggested here might tempt us to seek an alternative interpretation of this drawing: free from Michelangelo's "malaria of the mind," free from the constant pressure to make a path where no one has gone before, one may find, as Peter Quince did, that there is still good company to be had on the road most traveled.

THREE

Mad for Travel

ENRICO ABROAD

Mr. Piper's Perspective

The adventures of Peter Quince were not the only pictorial narrative Longfellow produced for the entertainment of his children. Longfellow's papers in Harvard's Houghton Library also include a small box, which, judging from the faint layer of dust that has accumulated on it, has rarely been opened. Inside is a series of quirkily captioned pencil drawings by Longfellow involving a character named "Mr. Peter Piper."[1] Not coincidentally, both "Peter Piper" and "Peter Quince" are directly concerned with one of Longfellow's favorite subjects, the experience of travel, which is, as we shall see, directly related to his egalitarian approach to authority and authorship.

One of the most memorable images in the "Peter Piper" series shows Longfellow's protagonist, of tongue-twister fame, poised on the bow of his ship as it is pulling into Le Havre de Grâce (fig. 21). Like all proper cartoon figures, Piper is an individual as well as a type, his face rendered in broad outline rather than subtle detail, suggesting enough of that puppet-like rigidity, or "inélasticité," that Henri Bergson believed was one of the sources of that which is comic.[2] With his spiky hair, pointed nose, and the hint of a broad grin on his bland face, Mr. Piper looks more like a weird snowman dressed for an evening on the town than a world traveler. His grand entry into the harbor recalls Longfellow's own joy at setting

FIGURE 21

Longfellow, "Mr. Peter Piper arrives in
Havre-de-Grace," Longfellow Papers,
Houghton Library, Harvard University,
MS Am 1340.9.1. By permission of the
Houghton Library, Harvard University.

foot, for the first time, on European soil: "I have been much pleased with
this city," he wrote to his brother Stephen upon his arrival in Le Havre de
Grâce in 1826, "because everything about it is perfectly novel to me" (*Letters* 1:160).

If Longfellow's contemporaries Emerson and Thoreau had expressed
their misgivings about any benefits of travel abroad, they were worried
especially about the challenges such peregrinations would bring to the still
fragile identity of a nation they wanted to be independent culturally as well
as politically. Travel doesn't broaden the mind, they lamented, but flattens
it; what looks like an expansion of our mental horizons in fact shrinks
the self to dimensions that prevent us from realizing our full possibilities as inhabitants of the United States of America. "Though all the fates
should prove unkind," rhymed Thoreau in *A Week on the Concord and Merrimack Rivers*, "Leave not your native land behind."[3] In the "Conclusion"
to *Walden*, he encouraged his readers to be "the Mungo Park, the Lewis
and Clarke and Frobisher, of your own streams and oceans," rather than
going round the world to "count the cats in Zanzibar" (578). For Emerson, traveling was, as he said mockingly, "a fool's paradise," the "symptom
of a deeper unsoundness" affecting our entire intellectual system.[4] Travel

stifles our desire to be ourselves. Swamped with external stimuli, sights to see and people to meet, we eschew originality for the wish to fit in, to be like everybody else, to be the same rather than provocatively different. When in Rome, do as the Romans do.[5] For Emerson, the fervent advocate of self-reliance, such an attitude spelled certain disaster, as it did for Melville's Tommo, who, shacking up with the Typee (said to be cannibals) on a remote island in the South Seas, ultimately fails to adjust to their lifestyle because he has never confronted the emptiness in his own heart.

With his moronic grin and exaggerated exuberance, Peter Piper seems as if he were intended to confirm Emerson's worst fears about the effects of traveling on American "self-culture."[6] Peter Piper's creator had traveled extensively himself. He first went abroad when he was barely nineteen years old. For three years he roamed through France, Spain, Italy, and Germany, emptying his father's coffers and perfecting, through willing immersion in native habits and habitats, his command of foreign languages. He wanted to be prepared for his new job as a professor of modern languages at his former alma mater, Bowdoin College. Such abandonment to foreign terrain was in and of itself a bold move for a traveler from the United States, a country where, in Longfellow's own uncharitable assessment, shared with Alexander Slidell in 1829, "nobody . . . pretends to speak anything but English—and some might dispute them even that prerogative" (*Letters* 1:323). But what the young man from Portland, Maine, striving after "future eminence in literature" (as he had told his father in December 1824; *Letters* 1:94), might have lost in self-assurance when abroad, he quickly regained in terms of cultural and linguistic flexibility. Within a couple of years, Longfellow had mastered French, Spanish, German, and Italian—the latter apparently with such fluency that, as he boasted in one of his letters home, he had to produce his passport to convince a Venetian hotelkeeper that he was indeed American (*Letters* 1:287). And he had acquired at least a working knowledge of, and reading competence in, Danish, Swedish, Dutch, and Portuguese.

Newton Arvin, in his book on Longfellow, mentions disdainfully the "guidebook strain" in the poet's work. He quotes, with approval, John Betjeman's unfriendly little poem "Longfellow's Visit to Venice (To Be Read in a Quiet New England Accent)," a stinging (and quite Eurocentric) parody of what Betjeman identifies as Longfellow's naïve confidence that through vigorous transatlantic sightseeing Americans could become honorary Europeans.[7] But Longfellow in fact loathed the tourist's hectic mentality: "spare me from thus travelling with the speed of thought," he writes in *Outre-Mer,* poking fun at the idea of "trotting, from daylight until dark, at the heels of a cicerone, with an umbrella in one hand, and a guide-book and plan of the city in the other" (7:277). He saw himself as head and shoulders above the stereotypical, bewildered Americans vacationing abroad as they were spoofed, for example, in George William Curtis's 1853 satire *The Potiphar Papers.* In this book, the multilingual travel companion of the Potiphars is Kurz Pacha, a diplomat from the upper African country of Sennaar (probably also an allusion to the "land of Shinar" in Genesis 11:2, on which the city of Babylon was built) and a "reputed savage" himself. But even he cannot suppress a smile after observing how a profusely sweating Mr. Potiphar on his vacation in Paris struggles with the intricacies of French pronunciation ("Kattery vang sank"). "Here you are," he comments, "speaking very little French, in a city where the language is atmosphere . . . with all French life shut out from you."[8]

What of course separated Longfellow from most of his American compatriots abroad was his capacity to perform, with ease, the verbal mimicry that stymied the likes of Paul Potiphar. An indestructible, cheerful world-traveler, Peter Piper seems as if intended to mock the rather strained attempts at pedagogical entertainment made in a popular illustrated textbook Longfellow's children would have encountered in school, *Peter Piper's Practical Principles of Plain and Perfect Pronunciation* (the first American edition, promising its readers "Puzzling Pages, Purposely to Please the Palates of Pretty Prattling Play Fellows," was published in Massachusetts in 1830.)[9]

There is, to be sure, little that is plain or perfect about Longfellow's Peter Piper. At the beginning of the story, in a kind of overture to what follows, we watch him going "a-hunting" (fig. 22). At first, all seems well, even though it is hard not to notice that Longfellow's hero, in place of a whip or the obligatory gun, carries a walking stick, an instrument of limited use when riding a horse. The inevitable comes to pass—like Humpty-Dumpty in the nursery rhyme, Longfellow's dandy-turned-hunter takes a great, and graceless, fall, walking stick, sportsman's cap, and all. Unlike his British predecessor, however, Mr. Piper has no trouble putting himself back together again. And here the ornamental cane acquires unforeseen importance, as Longfellow's hero, after wiping his brow, laboriously regains control of his battered limbs. In the last picture of the miniseries, Mr. Piper once more walks, as Longfellow notes, "with ease." As Longfellow's daughter Alice, who eagerly awaited each new installment in the series, later remembered about the wonderfully resilient Mr. Piper, "all the possibilities of life were before him."[10]

This note of cheerful optimism underlies the rest of the series, too, as we observe Mr. Piper, always both in and out of place, engaged in a variety of activities of increasing absurdity. As Longfellow himself did in 1826, Mr. Piper embarks on the Grand Tour. Unlike his creator, however, who in his letters home professed that he remembered little of the actual voyage ("a dreary blank," *Letters* 1:159), Peter Piper takes a more active part in the proceedings, foolishly leaving his ship for a solitary row on choppy waters, where he soon finds himself pursued by a surprisingly realistic-looking shark, jaws agape (figs. 23 and 24). In one of the most dramatic pictures from the sequence, Peter Piper "helps to take in sail" (fig. 25). We see Longfellow's hero, again dressed to the nines, the trademark walking stick tucked tight under his right arm, poking his carrot nose into matters of no immediate concern to him. He is precariously perched in the rigging of the ship, his high-heeled boots looking hilariously incongruous in this lofty environment. Piper's bland face, drawn in profile, is turned toward the bowlegged sailor next to him, who, unlike Longfellow's hero, is in fact at work, hauling in, as well he should, the sails of the ship. While Peter Piper's neatly shod feet point to the right, his face is directed to the left, contributing to the awkwardness of his elevated position. The downward diagonal of the mast beam in the foreground forms an effective contrast with the upward-reaching diagonals of the masts, thinner than matchsticks, of the other sailboats floating in the background. With a few casual strokes and some rough outlines, Longfellow creates an image of spatial depth; the most distant ship is indicated by a simple line. The humorous effect of the image is enhanced by the fact that the masts of the two vessels in the middle ground seem to be pointing more or less directly at the posteriors of the two men perched above.

Such clumsiness notwithstanding, when Mr. Peter Piper finally arrives in France, he without further ado and quite smoothly transmogrifies into the suave "M. Pierre Piper." Soon we meet him nearly in the nude, reposing in a spacious bathtub. Pierre takes a bath ("prend un bain chaud") in a quaint French bathroom with a beautifully tiled floor (fig. 26). Then we see him at the barbershop enjoying a French haircut, administered with panache by a dapper French hairdresser, who, himself carefully coiffed, is characterized in a wonderful French euphemism as an "artiste en cheveux" (fig. 27). The inevitable hat and walking stick are always prominently displayed, either on

FIGURE 22

Sequence of illustrations from
Longfellow's "Mr. Peter Piper,"
Longfellow Papers, Houghton
Library, Harvard University,
MS Am 1340.9.1:
"Mr. Peter Piper goes a-hunting";
"Mr. Peter Piper catches a fall";
"Mr. Peter Piper picks himself up";
"Mr. Peter Piper tries to walk";
"Mr. Peter Piper walks with ease."
By permission of the
Houghton Library,
Harvard University.

Mr Peter Piper tries
to walk.

Mr Peter Piper walks with
ease.

a chair or on the floor in the foreground. How different, though, is Mr. Piper's experience from that recorded, a bit later, in Mark Twain's travel narrative *The Innocents Abroad,* where Twain's alter ego suspects that the Parisian barber he visited, "like the genius of destruction," had his mind set not on shaving but rather "skinning" him. "Foreigner, beware!" shouts Twain, rising in his chair and angrily reversing the terms of the encounter in which traveling tourist meets native professional. Twain vows "dark and bloody revenge" the next time a French barber approaches him in this manner: "from that day forth that barber will never be heard of more."[11]

Twain's anxiety that an unauthorized Frenchman might "skin" him is, of course, highly symbolic. For Longfellow, on the other hand, shedding one's old skin, divesting oneself of one's accustomed self and exchanging it for a different identity while traveling abroad, was a highly desirable move. As far as he was concerned, the purpose of travel was the eventual affirmation of familiar prejudices (as it was for Twain, despite the thick layers of irony in which he cloaks his narrative) but in the playful exploration of alternative possibilities of being.

Longfellow's writings about travel are part of a neglected discourse in nineteenth-century American literature that runs counter to Emersonian

FIGURE 23

Longfellow, "Mr. Peter Piper goes out alone in a boat," Longfellow Papers, Houghton Library, Harvard University, MS Am 1340.9.1. By permission of the Houghton Library, Harvard University.

FIGURE 24

Longfellow, "Mr. Peter Piper is chased by the shark," Longfellow Papers, Houghton Library, Harvard University, MS Am 1340.9.1. By permission of the Houghton Library, Harvard University.

exceptionalism. Like Lydia Sigourney, whose fascinating narrative *Pleasant Memories in Pleasant Lands* (first published in 1842) he later used when compiling his *Poems of Places,* Longfellow believed that traveling was a salutary corrective to American self-esteem. "Go pitch your tent among a people of strange language," Sigourney wrote. "Walk solitary along their crowded streets, be sad, be sorrowful, be sick, where 'no man careth for your soul.' Go forth among the millions, and weigh yourself, and carry the humbling result onward with you through life." But unlike Sigourney—who, after all, preferred the "Mother-Land" England, where everybody understood the meaning of "home comfort," to all those other European places where she would find herself "mid foreign idioms"—Longfellow was genuinely attracted to the possibilities for self-invention and self-transcendence that foreign travel seemed to hold in store for him.[12]

While in Paris in 1826, Longfellow signed one of his letters home "Henri." Inwardly he was still a "Jonathan," he told his brother, but outwardly he had already assumed "a little of the Parlez-vous": "a long-waisted thin coat—claret-coloured—and a pair of linen pantaloons:—and on Sundays and other fête days—I appear in all the glory of a little hard French hat—glossy—and brushed—and rolled up at the sides" (*Letters*

FIGURE 26

Longfellow, "M. Pierre
Piper prend un bain chaud,"
Longfellow Papers, Houghton
Library, Harvard University, MS
Am 13140.9.1. By permission of
the Houghton Library, Harvard
University.

FIGURE 27

Longfellow, "M. Pierre Piper
se fait couper les cheveux,"
Longfellow Papers, Houghton
Library, Harvard University, MS
Am 1340.9.1. By permission of
the Houghton Library, Harvard
University.

1:173). Thus splendidly attired, he promenaded "amongst the crowds" in the Jardin du Luxembourg. To which description Longfellow's father replied, unmoved, that such mimicry was not only expensive but also ideologically suspect: "You should remember that you are an American, and as you are a visitor for a short time only in a place, you should retain your own National Costume" (*Letters* 1:205 n. 7).

If Longfellow's earlier self still needed such adjustments, the central point of his later narrative is that, to become Monsieur Pierre Piper, Mister Peter Piper doesn't even have to undergo a visible change—no costume necessary. Watching his antics, we might recall the characterization of the French language in Longfellow's anthology *Poets and Poetry of Europe*. There Longfellow had claimed that French, while perhaps less suitable for the expression of tragic sentiments and higher aspirations, was superior to all other languages in terms of sweetness, pliability, and "colloquial elegance."[13] Obviously, "Peter Piper," composed at a time when Longfellow's own children were studying French, also served as a kind of advertisement for the advantages of the "Parlez-vous."

But Longfellow's Peter Piper, with his swift change of identity, his rapid transformation from American innocent to French savant, is not just a funny character in a series of doodlings produced for the purposes of family entertainment. In an early journal dedicated to his impressions of Italy and Germany—written, interestingly, in French—Longfellow quoted the words Shakespeare's Rosalind hurls at Jaques Farewell: "Monsieur Traveller: Look, you lisp and wear strange suits; disable all the benefits of your own country; be out of love with your nativity . . . or I will scarce think you have swam in a gondola" (*As You Like It* 4.1.33–38). Repeated professions of love for things foreign inevitably raise questions about the extent of the love one feels for one's own country. We are wont to associate calls for a national American culture, as distinct from the tired traditions of the Old World, with nineteenth-century iconoclasts such as Melville and Whitman. But if this view of American intellectual history is correct, what was then regarded as provocative might, ironically, define the conservative consensus today. No American writer should write like a Frenchman, thundered Melville in his famous Hawthorne review of 1850, anticipating eagerly the "political supremacy among the nations, which prophetically awaits us at the close of the present century."[14] The restaurant owner in West Palm Beach who in February 2003, angered by the French refusal to rush to war against Iraq, poured all his French wine into the gutter would have applauded.[15]

In mid-nineteenth-century America, though we might find it hard to believe, Melville's endorsement of American superiority was more acceptable than Longfellow's lingering attachment to foreign *savoir vivre*. For example, in a letter to Charles Sumner dated March 27, 1852, a despondent Longfellow reports on his attempts to convince his colleagues at Harvard to sign a petition for cheap "ocean postage." But nobody there "cared a pin," he said, "as nobody else seems to have any foreign correspondence." Harvard's president, James Walker, proudly announced that "he had never had but one letter from Europe and he hoped he should never have another" (*Letters* 3:337). Longfellow's protracted struggles to improve the teaching of modern languages at Harvard demonstrate how far from the academic mainstream his interest in literary works written in languages other than English really was (and these were the languages spoken, for the most part, by the new immigrants to the United States).[16] In 1846, when Walker's predecessor, Edward Everett, called Longfellow into his office to announce plans to cut his budget and lay off the Spanish instructor, Longfellow's sarcastic response, as recorded in his journal, came in the form of a quotation from one of those dreaded modern foreign languages: "Do as you please, Gentlemen! Like a bird, as Victor Hugo says, I feel the branch bend under me, but fear not; 'j'ai des ailes!'" (November 5, 1846).[17]

Obviously, the Peter Piper drawings spoke to more serious issues on Longfellow's mind. One of the most frequent charges against him was that he seemed too much "indebted to the Old World for his mental furniture; that his culture, his taste, his habitual cast of thought, were foreign."[18] In the supremely adaptable Peter Piper, Longfellow was indeed wittingly commenting on his own alleged "unreliability" as a truly American writer, on his confusing versatility as a poet, critic, and multilingual translator and his notorious readiness to adapt and imitate, with perfection, the styles, themes, and forms of others. But what appears as a loss of self is in fact a gain in richness of perspective and breadth of insight. Stripped of the usual tributes to the "bright land" of America,[19] Longfellow's "transnational" conception of American literature and culture draws from many other traditions than the Anglophone one.[20] In many of his most successful works, notably *Evangeline* and *Hiawatha,* travel was an important plot element. But in the course of his writing career it also became one of his chief metaphors, an expression of his desire to journey vicariously or, as he put it in "Travels by the Fireside," the poem he chose to introduce his anthology of *Poems of Places,* to walk with "another's feet" and to see with eyes other than "mine own."[21]

In his thinking about travel, Longfellow was perhaps influenced by Goethe's writings and his theory of a "Weltliteratur" or "grand cosmopolitan literature," as Sarah Austin translated the term in her *Characteristics of Goethe,* which Longfellow mined extensively for his Harvard lectures.[22] A keen traveler and famous Italianophile himself, Goethe believed that personal contact between writers from different nations was essential for bringing about the kind of global literature he saw emerging.[23] Longfellow, who admired Goethe's *Italienische Reise,* would have agreed. But he would also have noticed that Goethe's lack of personal exposure to the Middle East had not kept him from writing his paean to Persian culture and the poet Hafiz, the *West-Eastern Divan.* In fact, Longfellow too was plotting ways in which it might be possible for him to hunker down in front of his fireplace at home yet imagine himself at large in the wide world outside. He wondered if one could not also be a cosmopolite while *at home,* in one's armchair, reading and relishing other "poets' rhymes." In "Travels by the Fireside," the form of Longfellow's stanzas—the "common meter" better known today from Emily Dickinson's work—beautifully illustrates this notion. Whereas the longer first and third lines of each stanza suggest expansion, a kind of reaching out, the second and fourth lines indicate contraction, a movement directed inward or, if you will, homeward. The poem thus uses a form that is "homespun" and local as well as transnationally familiar (and therefore, indeed, "common"):

> I journey on by park and spire,
>   Beneath centennial trees,
> Through fields with poppies all on fire,
>   And gleams of distant seas.
>
> I fear no more the dust and heat,
>   No more I feel fatigue,
> While journeying with another's feet
>   O'er many a lengthening league.
>
> Let others traverse sea and land,
>   And toil through various climes,
> I turn the world round with my hand
>   Reading these poets' rhymes.

From them I learn whatever lies
Beneath each changing zone,
And see, when looking with their eyes,
Better than with mine own. (3:86)

Rather than merely a biographical fact, travel in Longfellow's work became a complex metaphor for an author's refusal to let himself be limited by language or place.

As we shall see, Longfellow was far from regarding the desire to be elsewhere, either in fact or in imagination, as un-American. Thomas Gold Appleton, his peripatetic brother-in-law, who spent his life alternating between periods of travel and leisurely contemplation in the posh comfort of his souvenir-filled Boston home, saw an almost spiritual need behind it: "More and more the world needs, and learns to value, its vacation."[24] For Appleton, this was a particularly important message in the modern United States, where the "wheels of activity" were threatening to crush "every wayside lounger" beside the railroad track (176–77). Extensive travel *to* the Old World was America's chance to distinguish itself *from* the Old World, the "Europe of toil." Americans were poised to become citizens of the world, but they had to be taught how. In Longfellow's eyes, too, travel was not about leaving, arriving, taking in sights, and then going home again. Rather, it was an attitude, the relaxed cultivation of a state of mind that didn't stop at artificially imposed borders. But, as will become clear in the following section, Longfellow's cosmopolitanism crucially depended on what Tzvetan Todorov has described as "a plunge into the particular," the willingness to get to know, describe, and respect, in all their uniqueness, different *local* traditions, customs, languages, and literatures.[25] Enter Toni Toscan, gondolier in Venice.

Mediterranean Metamorphoses

Obviously, what distinguished Longfellow from other American travelers was his keen interest in acquiring proficiency in the languages of his host countries. The foreign language that attracted him the most was Italian, perhaps also because he continued to feel intimately connected with Italy as a country. "I chanced to cast my eyes this morning upon a map of Italy," he wrote wistfully on April 2, 1846, "where my old route was marked in red, the red vein of my young life-blood."

Among the earliest published documents of Longfellow's fascination with Italy is a long article, "History of the Italian Language and Dialects," published in October 1832 in the *North American Review*.[26] Acutely aware of his position as professor of modern languages at Bowdoin, Longfellow confidently began his essay by identifying the "study of languages" as "one of the most important" tasks that can "occupy the human mind." But it is not nearly enough to speak a language well, he went on. We need to know its history, too. Words are like the "armor and weapons of the Middle Ages," exhibiting "very clearly and forcibly not only the character of the times, but also the stature and physical strength of those who wore and wielded them." Like artifacts in a museum they remind us, "in a clear and vivid light," how the intellect of a nation has developed over time. And, in Longfellow's opinion, no language can make such historical research more pleasant than Italian (283).

Longfellow's encounter with the Italian language and culture contributed perhaps most significantly to his later vision, now forgotten, of a multilingual, "well-traveled," or, as he called it in a diary entry, "composite" American literature. The longest of his sojourns in any one foreign country was in Italy, from December 1827, when he arrived in Genoa, to December 1828, when he left Venice for Dresden. Evidence, in subsequent years, of Longfellow's enduring fascination with the Mediterranean can be found in his scholarship, in his travel writing, in his preoccupation with Dante, in his generous inclusion of Italian material in *Tales of a Wayside Inn,* and, last but not least, in the several volumes he devoted to Italy in his mega-anthology, the thirty-one-volume collection *Poems of Places* (which I will discuss more extensively in the last section of this chapter).

It was in Italy that the seeds were planted for Longfellow's decidedly anti-Romantic notion of the writer as a redistributor of common cultural goods. While Herman Melville was encouraging his fellow writers to condemn all imitation of foreign writers, "though it comes to us graceful and fragrant as the morning" ("Hawthorne" 546), Longfellow rejected the idea that, to paraphrase one of his characters in *Tales of a Wayside Inn,* the literary sun rises and sets in one's backyard only (4:276). In this chapter, I am especially interested in one encounter that helped the young Longfellow along in his developing notion of literature as a cosmopolitan enterprise. It took place, now more than 150 years ago, between him and a Venetian gondolier and, in a sense, Lord Byron. In order to relive this encounter, we need to allow Longfellow to guide us back to the Venice of September 1828. And there is no better way to let him do that than returning to his "History of the Italian Language."

With its references to medieval weapons and knights in shining armor, Longfellow's essay at first sight seems to display the same mixture of pedantry and ponderousness that marks and mars the other articles Longfellow wrote for the *North American Review* during the same period— "Origin and Progress of the French Language," "Spanish Language and Literature," and "Spanish Devotional and Moral Poetry." Longfellow himself admitted that some readers had been less than excited by his "Italian article," which they found "*dull and* LEARNED" (*Letters* 1:406). After all, Professor Longfellow was a language teacher as well as a poet, and the former of his identities seems to have prevailed in these pages.

During his first year at Bowdoin College, Longfellow translated a French grammar textbook, edited two Spanish adaptations of tales by Washington Irving, and compiled an anthology of dramatic sketches in French.[27] Two years later, he added to this already impressive roster of textbooks an Italian grammar (written in French!) and an anthology of Italian prose pieces, both intended to aid students in their quest for fluency in Italian.[28] These frantic editorial activities underscore the sorry state of language instruction at American colleges at the time. Privately, Longfellow doubted that the professors at Bowdoin could really speak the languages they were supposed to teach (to Stephen Longfellow, February 27, 1829; *Letters* 1:297).

The pride Longfellow takes in his own superior knowledge of foreign languages and cultures is palpable on every page of "History of the Italian Language." In the first part of the article, he reviews some theories about the origin of Italian and, playing it safe, endorses the "most generally received opinion," namely that the language was created when the illiterate and uncultured northern conquerors superimposed their dialects on the fragments of the Latin language they had picked up from the people they had subdued. But, as Longfellow admits, quoting Saverio Bettinelli, "the origin of this, like the origin of most things else, is uncertain, confused, and undetermined; for all things spring from insensible beginnings, and we · cannot say of any, *here* it commenced" (289).[29]

In the pages that follow, Longfellow does offer a kind of potted history of Italian literature that takes such skepticism seriously. Characteristically, his overview stresses influence and dependency rather than innovation and originality. Even the three *"gran maestri del bel parlar Toscano,"* Dante, Petrarca, and Boccaccio, in Longfellow's estimation were not so much bold innovators as expert sculptors giving shape to the crude material from which the Italian language had sprung: "They did not strike the first spade into the soil, but they drew the stone from the quarry, set the landmarks, polished the rough marble, and piled and cemented the misshapen blocks, till beneath their hands the noble structure rose, majestic, towering, beautiful" (295).

In the bulk of his essay, though, Longfellow leaves literary history alone and focuses on the present state of the Italian language. He provides his readers with a detailed list of dialects to be found in Italy, ranging from south to north, from the Sicilian to the Sardinian, from the Calabrian to the Corsican. In the sections devoted to individual dialects, brief comments on the most typical deviations from standard Italian are followed by examples from popular poetry, ranging from the "Soldier's Song" sung in Naples ("Who knocks,—who knocks at my door?") and the "Tarantella Trasteverina" ("Amorous youth of Rome's fair city / I have here a new-made ditty") to the more somber reflection on the sadness of love by a poet from Genoa, Gian Giacomo Cavalli ("To part from one's own life, / *Cara Bella,* oh what a death!").

Ironically, then, Longfellow's essay as a whole somewhat undermines the historical claims trumpeted at its beginning. Just as the study of literary history does not inevitably take us on a triumphant march toward greater and greater originality, learning a foreign language does not automatically provide the traveler with a master key to a nation's history. Longfellow stresses regions rather than the nation, diversity rather than unity. Like pieces of armor in a museum, to use Longfellow's own metaphor, his linguistic exhibits, battle-worn from frequent use, tell us not one but many stories. Instead of one national language we get multiple dialects, with significant differences between them. Often these dialects are themselves subdivided, as the example of the "Lingua Sarda" shows, where the dialect spoken in the city differs so considerably from that used by the peasants in the country that the two versions of the Lord's Prayer reprinted by Longfellow don't even share a word for God: "Pare" in the city, "Babbu" in the country (341).

Upon closer inspection, then, Longfellow's "History of the Italian Language" is more than just an example of a young man posing as a data-col-

lecting professor. This becomes especially clear in the section on the Venetian dialect, "the most beautiful of all the Italian dialects." It is here that
Longfellow the poet inconspicuously enters into the essay and scholarship
yields to autobiography. Longfellow begins by attributing the "soft" and
"pleasant" pronunciation of Venetian to the location of the city, nestled as
it is "in the bosom of the Adriatic" (322). Lovingly, he describes how the
dialect, fanned by the warm breezes of the Mediterranean, "grew up soft,
flexible and melodious." The anthropomorphic imagery sets the stage for
the appearance of an actual writer, the embodiment of the spirit of a city in
which, to the young American tourist, everything seems both old and new.
Longfellow's excitement is directly reflected in the poems that he goes on to
quote at length: "The two following specimens of this dialect were written
by Toni Toscan, a Venetian gondolier," he explains. And Toscan wasn't any
old gondolier. "One of the few who can still sing a stanza from Tasso," he
had once even been "in the service of Lord Byron" (323).[30]

A couple of decades later, Mark Twain would make fun of the
shrill "caterwauling" of the gondoliers, whom he called "barefooted
guttersnipe[s],"[31] but Longfellow's Toni Toscan represents the most exciting aspects of the Serenissima. This simple "barcariòl"[32] appears, from the
beginning, embedded in past and recent literary history, a devotee of the
sixteenth-century poet Torquato Tasso as well as of the recent expatriate
English poet Byron, who likewise had been a fan of Tasso. (Since Byron's
amorous exploits in Venice crucially depended on the availability of ef-
ficient, discreet transportation, we may assume that he was less interested
in Toni's literary preferences than in his services as a gondolier.) But Toni
insists that he has never been just a servant: "we made numerous inquiries
concerning the Noble Poet, all of which he answered somewhat in detail,
and concluded by informing us, that, 'like master like man,' he was himself
a little given to rhyme." And so the young traveler Longfellow finds himself studying not the literary remains of Lord Byron but the lines penned
by Toni the very-much-alive gondolier.

In true *improvvisatore* fashion, Toni's poetic tribute to the American
tourist, "Ottova Al Nobil Signor—Merican," talks mostly about the immediate reasons for its own existence. Born of the moment, it is written to
commemorate the moment. Here is Longfellow's translation as it appeared
in "History of the Italian Language":

By chance one day at Venice,
    as I stood at the Ferry
    there asked for me a person
    who was an American.
And I replied to him
    with ready service,
    I am Toni Toscan,—
    to this famous stranger,
    who is exactly the American.
Forthwith he inquired of me
    concerning the noble Byron,
    who is my good Patron
    when he is in Venice.
At our own time and leisure,
    floating along the grand canal
    he did again request me,
    and two stanzas of Tasso
    I forthwith sang to him.
Full of humility and respect
    I take off my hat
    and, from my heart, I bow my head
    to — —.

    ("History" 324)

An interesting and rather complicated nexus of relationships emerges from this little text, "une composition bien curieuse," as Longfellow aptly called it in his diary.[33] A former servant of the Tasso-admiring Byron writes a poem in which he quotes Tasso to a Byron-admiring American. Composed in Longfellow's presence, Toni's poem—called an "octave," though the poet handles the form very loosely—is also dedicated to him. Strangely, as if in sudden deference to the rules of disinterested scholarship, Longfellow omits his name from the title as well as the text of the poem. The Italian rhymes are not replicated in Longfellow's translation. But even if we didn't have the handwritten original, preserved in Longfellow's travel diary (fig. 28),[34] the name of the dedicatee, at least in its Italian pronunciation ("Longfello"), clearly resonates also in the text Longfellow published in "History of the Italian Language," as the rhyme word corresponding to "cappello."

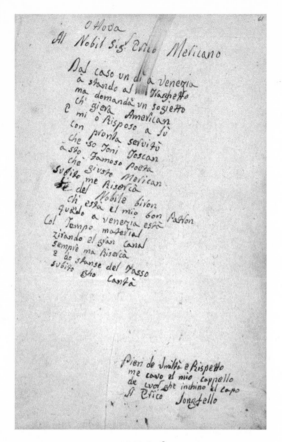

FIGURE 28

Toni Toscan, "Ottova Al Nobil Sig.ʳ Erico Mericano,"
from Longfellow's 1828–29 Journal, Longfellow Papers,
Houghton Library, Harvard University, MS Am 1340 (178).
By permission of the Houghton Library,
Harvard University.

It is not clear if the encounter between the American and the Venetian was, as Longfellow claims, an accident or if Longfellow had indeed,
as Toscan suggests, actively sought him out. In any case, Longfellow was
sufficiently intrigued by this versifying gondolier to sketch his portrait. His
drawing captures Toscan's dark looks, his chiseled features and the profusion of curls spilling out from under his cap (fig. 29). The caption was

supplied by Toni himself, who proudly identifies himself as a poet of the people of Venice ("Poeta Natural che Venizian").

A second, unpublished poem by Toscan, "All' Destinto Merito del Signor Erico Longfello," inserted into Longfellow's journal right after the page with Toni's portrait, fulsomely expresses the gondolier's gratitude for Longfellow's artistic efforts (fig. 30) and makes him an honorary Venetian: "Erico" is the local form of "Enrico" (Boerio 254). Although Toscan is

FIGURE 29

Longfellow, Portrait of Toni Toscan, from his 1828–29 Journal, Longfellow Papers, Houghton Library, Harvard University, MS Am 1340 (178). By permission of the Houghton Library, Harvard University.

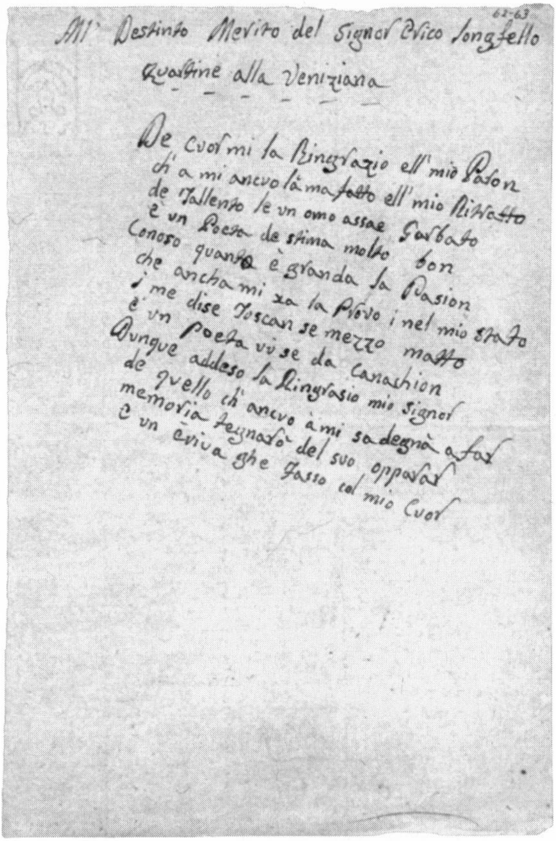

FIGURE 30

Toni Toscan, "All' Destinto Merito del Signor Erico
Longfello," from Longfellow's 1828–29 Journal,
Longfellow Papers, Houghton Library, Harvard University,
MS Am 1340 (178). By permission of the Houghton
Library, Harvard University.

conscious of the social gulf that separates him from the American tourist,
this poem, with all its irregularities of grammar and spelling, nevertheless
confidently establishes a bond between Toni the dialect-writing "poeta da
canachiòn" (the "poet of base expression")[35] and Longfellow the "poeta
de stima molto bon" (the "poet of great esteem"):

De cuor mi la Ringrazio ell' mio Paron
    ch' a mi ancuo la m' a fatto ell' mio Ritratto
    de Tallento le un omo assae Garbato
    e un Poeta de stima molto bon
Conoso quanto è granda la Pasion
    che ancha mi xa la Provo i nel mio stato
    i me dise: Toscan se mezzo matto
    e un poeta vu se da canachion
Dunque addeso la ringrazio mio Signor
    de quello ch' ancuo à mi sa degnà a far
    memoria tegnarò del suo opparar
    e un eviva ghe Fasso col mio cuor.

From the bottom of my heart I thank my patron, who has made a portrait of me. He has talent and is a well-mannered person and a poet of great esteem; I know well how great his passion is, because I, too, already feel it in my low state. They tell me: Toscan, you are half mad and you are a poet of base expression. Therefore I thank now my Signor for what you deigned to do. I will remember what you have done and I cheer you with all my heart.[36]

Entirely personal in nature, this text never made it into the pages of Longfellow's published essay. But in "History of the Italian Language," Longfellow offers his readers another sample of Toscan's art, a poem written in honor of the gondolier's former master, Byron: "All' Destinto Merito del Nobil Signor Biron, Soneto a la Veneziana." Clearly, Longfellow had his own reasons for doing so. The excerpt from Toni's Byron poem first invokes the latter's greatness and fame. It then ends with the speaker toasting Lord Byron ("I take in my hand a glass of good wine, and *viva, viva* the great *Norde biron* [Lord Byron]") and ceremoniously kissing his hand ("History" 325).

The three poems by Toscan—two written to praise Longfellow, one to praise Byron—must be read in conjunction. In the cracked mirror of Toni's poetic effusions, the identities of his new "noble" and his old "noble" master merge. Under the modest cloak of anonymity, Longfellow, the young American poet who had yet to publish a book, slips into the role of his illustrious English predecessor and literary hero Byron. With the blessing of Toni Toscan's final baptismal verses, Henry Wadsworth Longfellow, the twenty-one-year-old American tourist from Portland, Maine, could begin to think of himself as "Erico" or "Enrico," the "well-esteemed" poet. And this is how he signed his name, twice, next to a pencil sketch of himself in his "Italian Sketchbook" (fig. 31).

Longfellow's poetry-producing Toni Toscan is *not,* as a historian of Venice sensibly suggested when I approached him for advice, a "Romantic conceit." First, he has little in common with Wordsworth's speakers taken from "low and rustic life," their language "purified . . . from what appear to be its real defects."[37] Moreover, he did in fact exist, a descendant of a line of poetic gondoliers.[38] Lord Byron, his former employer, had come

FIGURE 31

Longfellow, self-portrait as "Enrico," from the Italian Sketchbook (1828), Longfellow Papers, Houghton Library, Harvard University, MS Am 1340 (177). By permission of the Houghton Library, Harvard University.

to Venice in November 1816. Instantly at home in "the greenest island of my imagination," Byron hurled himself into frenetic activity, as if to celebrate his release from the social constraints placed on him in that other, "tighter" island of his birth.[39] Relishing the wasted, worldly charms of a city that had survived Napoleon, Byron engaged in furious lovemaking, wild horseback-riding on the Lido, late-night theatergoing, and compulsive partying, all intermixed with bursts of extraordinary poetic creativity. Sex for Byron in those days seemed to have acquired an almost athletic quality, and he depended on his gondolier to keep the appointments coming and to provide, in his gondola, a place "where none can make out what you say or do" (*Beppo* 19).[40]

A review of the numerous notes to and from Byron's lovers yields a reference to Toni, in a letter sent to her dear "Giorgio" by the Venetian opera singer Arpalice Taruscelli, whom the indefatigable Byron had added to his collection of lovers in May 1819.[41] Sometime during the summer, La Taruscelli wrote to Byron that she would be coming later than planned. Like her other notes to "mio matto," as she affectionately called Byron, this one mixes logistical considerations—when, where, and how to rendezvous safely—with the promise of sexual gratification. La Taruscelli normally relied on the services of Byron's gondolier to send him her messages, but this time she apparently couldn't wait and sent her maid. "Instead of your sending me Toni, I am sending you Eleonora, to inform you that today, because of the great Heat, and the Bath I shall take in a little while, I find it impossible to come, deferring until this evening at the usual time, and thus the pleasure of seeing and kissing you will be redoubled." Even after being replaced by Eleonora on at least this occasion, Toni still remained present—in La Taruscelli's postscript: "P.S. With regard to Toni, here he is even in this note, as usual."[42]

In Longfellow's journal, the indispensable Toni speaks in his own voice and, perhaps for the first and only time in literary history, shows his face. And what a colorful journal it is: apart from the portrait and the two poems addressed to Longfellow, the manuscript also contains, in Longfellow's transcription, Toni's poem written for Byron, preceded by Longfellow's own comments on Toni written in *French* ("Il n'avait pas une belle voix,—mais pourtant il me faisait bien du plaisir"), into which we find embedded an *Italian* quotation, the lines from Tasso's poem that Toni had sung when Longfellow first met him.[43]

During his European travels, Longfellow had buried himself in Byron's poetry, so much so that the editor of his letters believes he was suffering from a "Childe Harold complex."[44] A self-portrait from Longfellow's Spanish diary, drawn with a mixture of skill and wishful thinking, shows the dashing, frock-coated poet astride his horse on the road from Malaga to Granada, over a caption taken from *Childe Harold's Pilgrimage* ("To horse—to horse—he quits, forever quits / A scene of peace though soothing to his soul"),[45] intended to emphasize the seriousness and fierce resolution of Longfellow the traveler (fig. 32). Still, with his much tamer instincts and sensibilities, the young man from Maine also knew how to distance himself from Byron. Arriving in Seville, for example, he instantly remembered lines from *Don Juan* ("a pleasant city / Famous for oranges and women") but decorously added that, really, the oranges were sweeter.[46]

Longfellow accidentally left his copy of *Childe Harold* in Rome, but wherever he subsequently went, the memory of Byron's lines was still with him. He saw Venice first on a bright, moon-soaked night, when his boat entered the Grand Canal and thousands of lights flitted across the water, a scene out of a fantasy world, recorded in French in Longfellow's diary.[47] Everything was silent then, except for the ringing of an occasional bell, the soft splashing of the oars in the still water, and the muffled voices of the gondoliers. A magician seemed to have pulled all these wonderful sights and sounds up from the bottom of the sea, said Longfellow, and he half expected it would all vanish again "dans le sein des eaux" (literally, in the bosom of the waters). Of course he was thinking here of lines from *Childe Harold:* "I saw from out the wave her structures rise / As from the stroke of the enchanter's wand" (Byron 227). Like Byron, he admired the sleek gondolas (fig. 33), praising the casual professionalism of the gondoliers as well as the comfortable leather upholstery inside, though their funereal black color repelled him. And like Byron, who said he found it especially "pleasing in the mouth of a woman" (Moore 2:53), Longfellow enjoyed the soft, sensual sounds of the Venetian dialect.

But unlike his counterpart in *Childe Harold,* Longfellow's gondolier is not "songless" (Byron 227). And Longfellow's one close encounter with a Venetian working-class woman has little to do with sexual pleasure: as he is sketching the Bridge of Sighs, a chambermaid, from a window in an adjacent palazzo, empties a pitcher of cold water over his head and he almost tumbles into the canal (*Letters* 1:289). Longfellow's Venice, in short, is not Byron's "Sea-Sodom."[48] It is not the mecca of feverish sex, a place of limitless pleasures, where sluggish waves lap at the crumbling foundations of

FIGURE 32

Longfellow, self-portrait, from his "Journal in Spain"
(1827), Longfellow Papers, Houghton Library, Harvard
University, MS Am 1340 (172). By permission of the
Houghton Library, Harvard University.

[Handwritten journal page in French, "La Gondole"]

A Venise on ne peut pas avoir un bel équipage. Tout le monde va à pied ou en gondole. La gondole Vénitienne est un petit bateau léger, tout noir; avec une petite cabane placée au milieu, couvert d'un drap noir. A premier vue, elle a une apparence bien triste: mais on s'accoutume facilement à cela. Les rameurs ou gondoliers sont extrêmement adroit; et d'ailleurs la gondole est si commode, et s'élance si doucement sur l'eau, que celui qui est dedans ne s'apperçoit presque pas du mouvement qu'elle fait. La cabane est tendue en dedans en noir, et on s'asseoit sur des coussins de maroquin: de manière qu'on est très bien dans ces drôles de petites machines.

FIGURE 33

Longfellow, "La Gondole" (p. 54) from Longfellow's 1828
Journal, Longfellow Papers, Houghton Library, Harvard
University, MS Am 1340 (178). By permission of the
Houghton Library, Harvard University.

stained palazzos and swift, phallic gondolas hurry into dark alleys, carrying their masked passengers to secret trysts, where women with burning eyes, "insatiate of love" (Moore 2:153), give themselves freely to desirous men, often with the knowledge of their husbands, who have made their own extracurricular amatory arrangements, since they belong, as Byron phrased it in a letter to Augusta Leigh, "to any body's wives—but their own."[49]

Longfellow's Venice is not inhabited by people as much as it is by texts—texts that have generated other texts, thereby mixing the languages as well as the identities of the authors. Writing about Venice, Byron, too, admitted that "Otway, Radcliffe, Schiller, Shakspeare's art / Had stamp'd her image in me" (Byron, *Complete Poetical Works,* 229). But Longfellow's notes radicalize the notion of "intertextual" Venice, as Rosella Mamoli Zorzi has called it.[50] The city speaks directly to Longfellow, and it speaks in tongues. He writes down what he sees and hears: the Latin inscription on a black curtain in the Palazzo dei Dogi meant to commemorate the fate of Marino Falieri, and the words scratched, in Italian, by a prisoner on the walls of his cell in the Prigioni—words that preach silence yet, by the very fact of being there, disregard what they say: "Confide in no one—think and be silent, if thou wishes to escape the snares and treacheries of spies. Sorrow and repentance avail not here."[51] Most important, though, there are Toni Toscan's poems, inscribed in Longfellow's diary in the gondolier's own hand, in clumsy letters, the lines slanting down the tattered page.

Ingrid Rowland has said that in Venice, variety creates its own aesthetic color.[52] Longfellow's Venetian notes seem written as if to prove this observation. It is here that we see the first stirrings of what Newton Arvin has termed Longfellow's "demotic" approach to writing. How fitting that not Byron himself but a "raven-voiced" Venetian native with literary leanings, a dialect-writing, Byron-adoring, Tasso-quoting gondolier, should have been his mentor.

For Longfellow, writing poems would come to mean not Romantic self-expression but participation in a public conversation conducted across decades, cultures, classes, and languages. Lord Byron, writing from Venice to his publisher John Murray in June 1818, had emphatically defended his view that poetry was an art, *not* a "profession" (Moore 2:177). But it was exactly as such that Longfellow, the future canny manipulator of copyrights and royalty payments, would come to see *his* writing. Remember how pleased Longfellow was when his daughter Annie, remembering the fishermen of Nahant, commended him for having chosen a trade that one can also "do in the winter."

It is interesting to compare Longfellow's response to Toni Toscan with the treatment of a Venetian gondolier in a travel book Longfellow read a few years later, George Sand's *Lettres d'un voyageur* (1834–36).[53] Sand, "that wonderful woman of genius strange and mild" (May 9, 1846), was a particular favorite of Longfellow (we know he wanted to meet her when he was in Paris in 1842).[54] When one thinks of the popular image of the cigar-smoking, crossdressing, unabashedly bisexual Sand writing her books "with one wheel over the abyss and glass in hand," she seems an unlikely candidate for the cautious Longfellow's admiration.[55] Deep down, Longfellow probably realized that he shouldn't really approve of Sand's sensuality.[56] But he couldn't help admiring her writing.

Although *Lettres d'un voyageur* is a thinly veiled account of Sand's affair with the much younger doctor Pietro Pagello, recreated in languid detail to make her lover de Musset jealous, Longfellow recognized that it was much more than a *chronique scandaleuse*. He began reading Sand's book on December 15, 1847, on a day "soft, with mists" like "Venise" itself. (Longfellow inadvertently used the French spelling here, and we can picture him under the influence of Sand's pliable prose as, late at night, he is writing in his diary.) He enjoyed Sand's descriptions of Venice in the spring, when everything appears to be covered with emerald dust and the lagoons, carpets of velvet verdure, lap lazily against palazzi whose bases are covered richly with oysters and mosses of the tenderest green (Sand 52). The book went on and on like that, noted Longfellow, "over wide wastes of glowing rhapsodies without an end." But he loved its "delicious style." The double columns of the edition he had been using seemed to him like "organ-pipes from which flow stupendous harmonies, accompanying the reader's voice and setting all her thoughts to music" (December 15, 1847).

Like Longfellow and Byron, George Sand—or, rather, her persona in the book, a young man dressed in a cotton smock and trousers—adored the "soft Venetian speech" (Sand 46). But there was one important difference: her gondoliers, masters in the art of hurling insults at each other, were definitely more rough-hewn than the poetic Toni (Sand 57). One of them, the "domestic animal" Old Catullo, suffering from a chronic infection of the trachea and therefore perpetually hoarse, was also lame in one leg (Sand 68). He, too, would reminisce about Byron, but what he had in common with him was only his limp: "Catullo . . . never fails to say, when mentioning Lord Byron: 'I saw him; he was lame!'" Comments Sand's narrator: "Alas, Alas! The divine poet Catullus was a Venetian; who knows if the crippled drunkard who steers our gondola is not his direct descendant?" (Sand 95; Catullus was, in fact, Roman).

And here Sand and her American admirer part ways. The Venice that emerged from *Lettres d'un voyageur* was the epitome of otherness, a wild, gloomy, sensual realm where gondolas skimmed over the waters like "wild ducks" and the "Moorish" buildings, when shrouded in the darkness of the night, looked more sinister than the gates of hell, "plus sombres que les portes de l'enfer" (Sand 39, 67). Longfellow, by contrast, recalled it as a place where even the gondoliers were serious about their poetry.

While Sand was working on *Lettres d'un voyageur*, Longfellow was busily compiling his own travelogue, *Outre-Mer*. In the finished book, which first appeared in 1835 (and which will be the subject of the next section of this chapter), the multilingual exuberance of the Venetian diary pages is suitably transfigured and transformed. But the somewhat predictable image of wanton, wealthy, soft and sensual Venice lying in her waters as in a "swan's nest," which Longfellow had lifted from *A Survey of the Signorie of Venice* (1651) by James Howell, is followed by a demotic Italian proverb: "Venegia, Venegia / Chi non ti vede non ti pregia; / Ma chi t' ha troppo veduto / Ti dispregia!" In Longfellow's translation: "Venice, Venice, he that doth not see thee doth not prize thee; but he that hath too much seen thee doth despise thee!" And the section ends with a familiar presence, with rough words written not by Longfellow himself but by his poet-gondolier, Toni Toscan, the very words he had written underneath his portrait in Longfellow's diary:

> Should you ever want a gondolier at Venice to sing you a passage from Tasso by moonlight, inquire for Toni Toscan. He has a voice like a raven. I sketched his portrait in my note-book; and he wrote beneath it this inscription:
>
> Poeta Natural che Venizian,
> Ch' el so nome xe un tal Toni Toscan. (7:319)

With Eyes Other Than Mine Own

Longfellow would not visit Venice again until May 1869, and then the sheer effort involved in traveling exhausted him: "I . . . long to be at home again," he wrote to his son Charles, who at the time happened to be in, well, India (*Letters* 5:284). In the decades after his youthful European sojourn, anxieties about leaving America became a constant refrain in his correspondence and journals. "Travelling has its joys," he declared in 1826, right after his return, "but happier is he whose heart rides quietly at anchor in the peaceful haven of home" (*Life* 1:178). ·

But perhaps Longfellow became a bit too firmly anchored in Portland. The next few years were, poetically speaking, the most barren of his life. Still, Americans are, as Longfellow saw it, a "book-making race,"[57] and he soon returned to a plan he had first mentioned in May 1829 in a letter to his father from Göttingen, Germany, and began work on a book of "scenes in France, Spain, and Italy" (*Letters* 1:310). The work grew in spurts, not leaps and bounds. Versions of some of the early chapters began to appear in the *New England Magazine* in 1831, though Longfellow's confidence in his own creative abilities apparently waned. "I find," he told George Washington Greene in March 1833, "that it requires but little courage to publish grammars and school-books—but in the department of *fine-writing,* or attempts at fine writing,—it requires vastly more courage" (*Letters* 1:408).

Outre-Mer: A Pilgrimage beyond the Sea, the book finally published by Harper & Brothers in 1835, was a scissors-and-paste job, fashioned out of previously written stories, diary entries, and three academic essays (but not the "History of the Italian Language") that had appeared separately in the *North American Review* in 1831 and 1832.[58] For the British edition, Longfellow added a chapter on "Old English Prose Romances" (an article first published in the *North American Review* in October 1833), which he later omitted from the second American edition, along with one of the book's original chapters, a review of Sir Philip Sidney's *Defense of Poetry.*

If Longfellow wavered as to the final shape of his book, some of the chapters in and of themselves (there are twenty-seven of them, if we don't count the "Introductory Note" and the brief epilogue) did not show much concentrated editorial effort either. One of them, a rambling meditation on life in Madrid, he titled "A Tailor's Drawer," a name "which the Spaniards give to a desultory discourse, wherein various and discordant themes are touched upon, and which is crammed full of little shreds and patches of erudition" (7:168). Another chapter, covering in the limited space of a few pages Longfellow's journey from Rome to Venice to Vienna to "the sands of Holland" (7:322), is simply headed "Note-book." Obviously, Longfellow's literary muse still required some coaxing.

On the surface at least, the book is a rather stylized account of Long-fellow's impressions of France, Spain, and Italy, the obvious model being Washington Irving's famous *Sketch-Book* (1820). Moments in which Long-fellow realized the absurdity of his situation—far away from home, play-ing at being a native in countries whose language he was just beginning to learn—are studiously suppressed. There is no mention, for example, of the Englishman at the dinner table in Tours with whom Longfellow con-versed in halting French: "—knew that he must be English by his accent—how ridiculous for us to have talked bad French together when we might have conversed in our native language." Absent, too, are the half-starved naked children of La Mancha who came running after the American trav-eler, "shouting forth and lifting up their hands most pitifully and begging a mouthful of bread for the love of God," and the Frenchwoman who on the way from Marseille to Toulon held her small child outside the carriage "to 'faire de l'eau,'" much to the surprise of the proper young man from Maine.[59]

Longfellow's prose in *Outre-Mer* almost highlights its own derivative-ness. Many times Longfellow asserts that there would be no use in describ-ing his experiences, because so many other writers before him have done so already. There is very little originality left in the experience of traveling itself, so why attempt to write an original book about it? Why discuss a Spanish bullfight when "it has been so often and so well described by other pens" (7:165)? Longfellow seems mindful of the advice to travel writers given by Laurence Sterne to leave at least some places, notably "churches and public squares," undescribed (7:155).[60] Comprehensiveness is not his goal anyway, and he is more than ready to skip those parts of his itiner-ary that are of no interest to him or, he assumes, his readers. He prefers, he says, alluding to a satire by Voltaire, "to stride across the earth like the Saturnian in Micromegas, making but one step from the Adriatic to the German Ocean" (7:322).

In many ways, *Outre-Mer* is a humorous book, too, a conscious trib-ute to the Sternian tradition of travel writing. Take the paean to sleep in-serted into Longfellow's rather disorderly collection of thoughts about life in Spain, which Longfellow admits was inspired by *Don Quixote* (what he doesn't say is that the same quotation also appears, in a similarly ironic context, in Sterne's *Tristram Shandy*): "I shall obey and indulge in the exqui-site luxury of a *siesta*. I confess that I love this after-dinner nap. If I have a gift, a vocation for anything, it is for sleeping; and from my heart I can

say with honest Sancho, 'Blessed be the man that first invented sleep!'"
(7:177).[61] Here and elsewhere in the book, Longfellow represents himself
as a not particularly alert traveler, less interested in research than in rest and
relaxation. Thus, he readily admits that he won't be able to supply a good
description of his trip from Bordeaux to Paris, because he spent much of
it lulled into sleepy forgetfulness in a snug corner of his coach, not know-
ing where fiction ends and reality sets in (7:129).

Of course, Longfellow didn't like guidebooks. *Outre-Mer* offers several stinging attacks on tourists who slavishly follow prescribed itineraries,
since their only ambition is to complete the "grand tour." And American
tourists were the worst of the lot. A man Longfellow met in Florence
"boasted how much he could accomplish in a day. He would despatch a
city in an incredibly short space of time" (7:276). The result of such boor-
ishness was that all objects assumed the same importance and memorable
sights were flattened into insignificance: "A city was like a Chinese picture
to him,—it had no perspective" (7:277).

For all its leisurely disparateness, and in spite of the vast geographi-
cal, cultural, and historical space the book traverses, some common the-
matic strands help tie *Outre-Mer* together. The most important of these
is Longfellow's role-playing. In an introductory chapter, the author casts
himself in the role of a secular pilgrim to the Land Beyond the Sea, the
"pays d'Outre-Mer."[62] He is a man with a mission. Europe was the Holy
Land of his dreams before he first laid eyes upon it, and now Longfellow
describes his arrival there as akin to seeing, for the first time, a vast cathedral: "when its shores first rose upon my sight, looming through the hazy
atmosphere of the sea, my heart swelled with the deep emotions of the
pilgrim, when he sees afar the spire which rises above the shrine of his
devotion" (7:18–19).

However, Longfellow's interest in European churches goes beyond
the merely metaphorical. In fact, the book marks the public beginning of
Longfellow's complicated love affair with Catholicism—not the practice
but the idea of it, from the first intense moment he spent inside the cathedral of Rouen ("I was transported back to the Dark Ages and felt as I
can never feel again," 7:31) to the midnight mass he attended in Genoa ("A
dazzling blaze of light from the high altar shone upon the red marble columns which support the roof, and fell with a solemn effect upon the kneeling crowd," 7:271). Throughout the book, Longfellow reveals an obsession
with the rituals of the Catholic Church, with funerals, processions, public

prayers, and last rites. One of the chapters, for example, a saccharine ac-count of the last day in the life of Jacqueline, a young girl from the vil-lage of Auteuil where Longfellow was then staying, offers a verbatim tran-script of her receiving the last rites ("Dost thou believe that by the holy sacraments of the Church thy sins are forgiven thee, and that thus thou art made worthy of eternal life?"). Before the priest's arrival, Jacqueline had listened, with rapt attention, to the sounds of the Holy Mass wafting through her open window, described in such glowing terms that it is dif-ficult to decide who is more emotionally involved here, the narrator or the girl: "The sweet tones of the organ were heard,—trembling, thrilling, and rising higher and higher, and filling the whole air with their rich, melodious music. What exquisite accords!—what noble harmonies!—what touching pathos!" (7:65).

The emphasis on Catholicism in *Outre-Mer* did help Longfellow make his Land Beyond the Sea appear more exotic, at least in the eyes of the American reader: as a dreamy region closer in spirit to the Middle Ages than anything they'd previously known, a world in which mumbled Latin prayers resound in the deep, dark interior of decaying churches. But this was not his only purpose. What fascinated Longfellow most of all was the apparent readiness of Catholics to assemble, at the tolling of the bell, in order to express their loyalty to something larger than their own individual lives. Writing about the Ave Maria prayers he heard in Galicia and Andalu-sia, Longfellow notes how life here comes to a standstill every night when "the multitude uncover their heads, and, with the sign of the cross, whis-per their evening prayer to the Virgin." There was something indescribably beautiful about this tradition, the idea that at the end of a long day, despite their separate aspirations, "the voice of a whole people, and of the whole world, should go up to heaven in praise, and supplication, and thankful-ness" (7:260). In Benedict Anderson's terms, we see Longfellow trying to balance his recognition of, and delight in, national differences with a dif-fuse but intense hankering after a sense of community that predates the emergence of nation-states: a longing for a global community with porous, indistinct boundaries that, in a way, becomes synonymous with human-kind itself.[63]

In *Outre-Mer,* the ancient traditions of the Catholic Church, change-less for centuries, are not only a cipher for the coincidence of the present and the past. They also signify the willing subordination of the individual to the dictates of a larger community. In a Catholic service, language is a mere tool, reaffirming one's adherence to a community of believers, not a vehicle for the expression of one's personal feelings. Years later, during his second European sojourn, Longfellow, deeply affected by the death of his first wife, Mary Storer Potter, wandered into a church in Düsseldorf, Germany, during the elevation of the Host. "The kneeling crowd, crossing themselves and prostrate in contrition—with the soft subduing hymn that was chanted to the sounds of an organ, both soothed and cheered me. There is much in the catholic worship, which I like" (December 2, 1835).

Longfellow's fascination with European Catholicism should not be confused with love for the Church as an institution. He has little sympathy for the fat monks who waddle through the streets of Rome, and he is withering about the sallow Carmelite friar, emaciated and exhausted from his midnight vigils, whom he encounters in Madrid: "Thou standest aloof from man,—and art thou nearer God? I know not" (7:175). In the funniest tale included in *Outre-Mer*, a lecherous red-faced friar, lusting after the fair Marguerite Franc, is accidentally killed by her husband. But the unseemly cleric refuses to be laid to rest; his bulging body keeps popping up in ever more unlikely places (Martin Franc's doorstep, the abbey's garden, a thief's sack, a butcher's shop), until, tied to a confused horse, it takes a final, graceless plunge into the river, never to be seen again ("Martin Franc and the Monk of Saint Anthony").

Longfellow's view of Catholicism has more to do with the word's etymology than with the Church's dubious representatives. Although the forms of worship differ in different European countries, Catholicism, in a way, universalizes Europe, providing an overarching framework within which to understand national differences. An interesting analogy occurs to Longfellow: like the Catholic religion, poetry, too, is a kind of *lingua franca* in Europe, cutting across class lines as well as national boundaries. The emotions are the same, regardless of the different languages in which they are expressed.[64] "How universal is the love of poetry," Longfellow exclaims at the beginning of his chapter "Ancient Spanish Ballads." Every nation boasts its share of popular songs: "The muleteer of Spain carols with the early lark, amid the stormy mountains of his native land. The vintager of Sicily has his evening hymn; the fisherman of Naples his boat-song" and, as Longfellow adds, remembering Toni Toscan, "the gondolier of Venice his midnight serenade" (7:180). Poems outlive the names of their authors, the way the centers of Catholic worship, the Gothic cathedrals of the Middle Ages, "have outlived the names of their builders"

(7:200).[65] Thus, the Catholic theme plays right into Longfellow's poetics of authorial anonymity, supporting his growing reluctance to be identified, in the traditional sense, as the sole author or originator of his work (that *Outre-Mer* came out anonymously, despite the fact that most readers knew who the author was, was just the icing on the cake).[66]

But the analogy between Catholicism and literature ends at the question of audience. In his review of Hawthorne's *Twice-told Tales,* Longfellow pointed out that while a priest may chant in whatever language he wants "so long as he understands his own Massbook," an author who wants the world to listen "will do well to choose a language that is generally understood" (7:432).[67] Longfellow's sympathy is with the faithful, not those who administer the faith. The "worthy and gentle reader" addressed in the short dedication of *Outre-Mer* is, literally, the writer's equal. *Outre-Mer* belongs to him or her, humbly offered by an author who, in a kind of preview of the religious imagery in the book, asks that all his literary sins be instantly forgiven. In the final chapter of *Outre-Mer,* "The Pilgrim's Salutation," the author, referring to Acts 5:36, insists that he is not like Theudas, recklessly "boasting myself to be somebody."[68] Longfellow wants his readers to understand that he is not the loudmouthed prophet of half-truths, a happy harbinger of American superiority abroad and fawning praiser of the European past at home, arrogantly talking down to them. He is a teller of tales that are less about himself than about what he has seen, read, and heard.

While traveling in France, Longfellow meets an old woman in the Loire Valley, dressed "like the poorest class of peasantry," who cannot understand why anyone would choose to leave his or her home. "Have you no relations in your own?" she asks him after he has explained to her that he has traveled all the way to France "to see how you live in this country" (7:93). But, as the "Pilgrim's Salutation" at the end of *Outre-Mer* demonstrates, "home" and "abroad" are not absolute terms. Every place a traveler visits is someone else's home.[69] Even more important, in order to feel really homesick, one must be away from home: "How sweet are these dreams of home in a foreign land!" (7:324). For Longfellow, traveling, then, is not merely an escapist exercise in Romantic self-oblivion, in the manner of Baudelaire's "partir pour partir," but a lesson in cultural relativism that will ultimately help the traveler better understand what is distinctive about his or her own culture.[70]

And leave home Longfellow did again, at least twice. His second extended European sojourn, from 1835 to 1836, was overshadowed by the death of his first wife in Rotterdam. Surprisingly, he mustered up enough energy to complete his studies at Heidelberg, this time in anticipation of his new position as the Smith Professor of Modern Languages at Harvard University. In 1842, he escaped once more, ostensibly to soothe his nerves, strained from the teaching of unruly undergraduates, by taking the water-cure at Marienberg on the Rhine in Germany, though he could hardly tolerate the fact that even here he now had, as he complained to Charles Sumner, the sounds of his "native language ringing in both ears all day long" (*Letters* 2:423).

Two decades passed before Longfellow, a father who took his family responsibilities very seriously, was able to travel to Europe again. Five children were, he told Henry Arthur Bright in England, "five good reasons for staying home" (March 25, 1859; *Letters* 4:127). But travel remained a constant temptation for him, a love affair of the mind, with images of distant places floating up before him, usually at particularly inconvenient moments, during dreary faculty meetings or in the classroom: "Another lovely Summer morning," he sighed, "Switzerland, the Tyrol, the North of Italy, all rise before me and seem to draw me away, away, as if bodily and in some dream, where all things are possible" (June 15, 1846). Listen to the following journal entry, in which Longfellow delays mentioning the subject of his sentence (and therefore the content of an unexpected epiphany he had) to the very end, thus both dramatizing and mocking his need to be elsewhere: "Like delicious perfume, like far-off music, like remembered pictures, came floating before me, amid college classes, as through parting clouds, bright glimpses and visions of Tyrolean lakes!" (May 28, 1848).

Such vivid sightings of Eden in "the great Prairie of a teacher's life" (June 21, 1848) remained welcome even as he became increasingly attuned to the pleasures of staying at home. ("Stay, stay at home, my heart, and rest," Longfellow would rhyme in a late poem, "Home-keeping hearts are happiest.")[71] In the summer of 1856, when he had finally mustered up his courage to book some staterooms on a steamer to Europe, he accidentally struck his knee against an iron bar on the train to Boston and quickly decided that he couldn't go. He did not seem too disappointed: "The undertaking seemed too momentous on a nearer view."[72] Dreaming about leaving America became preferable to the reality of doing it. In the back of the journal he kept during that year, he pasted a schedule of the departure dates for transatlantic steamers ("DEPARTS D'AMÉRIQUE POUR L'EUROPE des steamers Transatlantiques, du 17 Juin courant à la fin de cette année").[73] But instead of traveling abroad, Longfellow spent his summers at Nahant outside Boston, where only the sea separated him from France or England (July 3, 1856) and where he could continue his tradition of delicious after-dinner naps, periods of "unconditional repose" in the "Land of Drowsy-head," which annoyed, as he admitted, his wife Fanny "not a little" (August 1, 6, and 8, 1848). On good days at least, the weather at Nahant wasn't unlike that of Sorrento or Capri (July 12, 1851).

Longfellow's illustrated narrative about "Peter Quince" features such a devotee of dozing. Mr. Quince is much like Longfellow himself. He appreciates the rest and relaxation to be found in domesticity, at the fireside, where, sunk deep in his rocking chair, he is enjoying a quiet smoke (fig. 34). We see him in a variety of quaintly domestic scenes: having breakfast (fig. 35), his knife and fork daintily poised over his plate, or shaving in his bathroom in the morning (fig. 36), as his round, bland face is staring right back at us from the ornate mirror on the wall. But like his creator, Quince also has a marked fondness for travel, although Longfellow himself would have been appalled by his protagonist's taste for reckless adventure. (Reading John C. Frémont's *Expedition to the Rocky Mountains,* Longfellow was simultaneously enthralled and repulsed: "What a wild life! and what a fresh kind of existence. But, ah! the discomforts!" December 3, 1846.) Mounting and then riding his horse, his impressively striped back turned to the viewer, Quince is still somewhat in charge of his movements, though Longfellow achieves a subtly comical effect by giving us only the face of the horse and a rather complicated view of Quince's back (fig. 37). In the next illustration (fig. 38), the horse's rear looms large, giving it almost more character than the rider. When traveling by balloon Quince finally comes to grief, and rather spectacularly so—was he named perhaps after Shakespeare's bumbling carpenter? Longfellow illustrates the pull of gravity that brings down his hero by depicting an inverted, miniature Quince in midair: a tiny, striped, insect-like Icarus headed for the predictable plunge into the vast ocean (fig. 39). But Quince survives, unscathed. A subsequent installment in the series shows his limp, wet body after it has been retrieved from the depths of the sea (fig. 40).

But Quince doesn't give up. Again we see him running after the balloon, hoping to jump aboard, apparently not discouraged by the earlier mishap. Soon his body is hauled up into the air again. Longfellow depicts his hero's clumsy scramble for safety by drawing an ascending series of striped mini-Quinces attached to the balloon's perpendicular rope (fig. 41).

FIGURE 36

Longfellow, "Mr. Peter Quince
shaves," Longfellow Papers,
Houghton Library, Harvard
University, MS Am 1340 (163).
By permission of the Houghton
Library, Harvard University.

FIGURE 37

Longfellow, "Mr. Peter Quince
goes on his travels," Longfellow
Papers, Houghton Library,
Harvard University, MS AM
1340 (163). By permission of
the Houghton Library, Harvard
University.

FIGURE 38

Longfellow, "Mr. Peter Quince on horseback," Longfellow Papers, Houghton Library, Harvard University, MS Am 1340 (163). By permission of the Houghton Library, Harvard University.

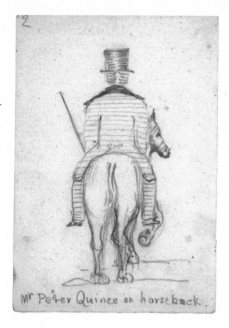

FIGURE 39

Longfellow, "Mr. Peter Quince falls out of his balloon into the sea," Longfellow Papers, Houghton Library, Harvard University, MS Am 1340 (163). By permission of the Houghton Library, Harvard University.

Mr Peter Quince comes to land

FIGURE 40

Longfellow, "Mr. Peter Quince comes to land," Longfellow Papers, Houghton Library, Harvard University, MS Am 1340 (163). By permission of the Houghton Library, Harvard University.

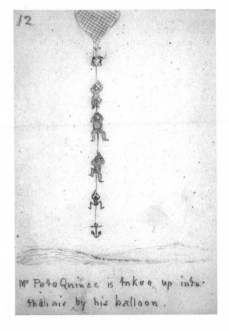

Mr Peter Quince is taken up into the air by his balloon.

FIGURE 41

Longfellow, "Mr. Peter Quince is taken up into the air by his balloon," Longfellow Papers, Houghton Library, Harvard University, MS Am 1340 (163). By permission of the Houghton Library, Harvard University.

Throughout the series, with just a few quick strokes of a pencil, Longfellow succeeds in giving Quince both a minimum of individuality and a
maximum of comic generality, a measure of his considerable talents as a
draftsman. Balloon voyages were a popular theme of children's books, and
Longfellow was perhaps also ironically alluding to the homespun moralism
and blatant nationalism of such books as *The Balloon Travels of Robert Merry
and His Young Friends, over Various Countries in Europe* (1855), allegedly edited
by Peter Parley, in reality written by Parley's creator, the tireless Samuel
Goodrich. "How little is a nation which has no other thought than to live
to-day, to eat, to drink, and to die, compared with a nation which looks beyond to-day, which considers itself God's missionary, charged with the duty
of improving, elevating, and blessing mankind," says Goodrich's balloon
traveler, Mr. Merry, comparing France, unfavorably, with his own superior
nation, the United States. While the "country and the people of France"
have a "time-worn aspect," in America "all is advancing, improving, growing." One of Merry's fellow travelers and eager pupils, Ellen, agrees: "it is
something to be an American."[74] Or is it?

Longfellow wasn't always so sure. He kept an orange tree and a lemon
tree in his study to remind himself of places other than home.[75] His songs
were, he felt, "birds of passage," always longing to go south again.[76] Not
coincidentally, he "liked the Italian beggars most," reported William Dean
Howells.[77] In 1851, Longfellow ended one of his courses on Italian literature with a passionate tribute to the country itself, a moment he proudly
recorded in his journal. He told his students that he loved not only the Italian people but also "the skies above their heads and the ground beneath
their feet!" (January 9, 1851). With every book on an Italian subject, Longfellow felt instantly transported back into the land of his dreams. One day,
having grown restless after reading Goethe's *Italienische Reise,* he embarked
on one of his long excursions into town and ended up in Boston's Hay-
market, where he found himself amid more cultural and linguistic diversity
than on all his travels in Europe. Or so it seemed to him:

> I slaked my thirst for foreign travel by driving to town on the omni-
> bus, and walking twice through the market; where the mingled and
> delicious odors of the vegetables, and the sight thereof transported
> me straightway to France. . . . On my way out stood ahwile [*sic*] on the
> bridge, looking at the waters and saying to myself, that this was a por-
> tion of the same sea that washes the shores of England and of Italy.

I then got into the omnibus and there found some some [*sic*] Spanish people, men and girls; and heard the sweet tongue again, and saw the well-known Spanish beauty of face and form, and imagined myself in Andalusia. (June 16, 1846)

Longfellow's intensely felt need for vicarious traveling found its most effective outlet in the first major work he undertook after Fanny's death, *Tales of a Wayside Inn* (1863–73). Decades earlier, in *Outre-Mer,* Longfellow had made a great effort to conjure up the time when pilgrims told tales and troubadours sang songs and delighted audiences everywhere. But he also acknowledged that "the tales which then delighted delight no longer" (7:18). *Tales of a Wayside Inn* seems written as if to challenge this assumption. The book consists of nothing but obsolete stories, told by a strange assortment of travelers staying at an old inn in Sudbury, outside of Boston, "the far-off noisy town" (though not so far off, by modern standards). From the beginning Longfellow almost willfully emphasizes the pastness of the past. Built in colonial times, when people were used to "ampler hospitality," the inn has now fallen to decay, "with weather-stains upon the wall, / And stairways worn, and crazy doors / And creaking and uneven floors" (4:13). The travelers, too, know that the stories they exchange are yesterday's news, but then they derive special satisfaction from their status as the purveyors of such antiquated lore.

The ingredients for Longfellow's plot—story-swapping followed by group discussion and literary peer review—came from Giovanni Boccaccio's *Decameron;* the setting was inspired by Geoffrey Chaucer's Tabard Inn. In an epilogue to his book, Boccaccio had cheerfully conceded that his stories—told, over a ten-day period, with the birds singing nearby and the sound of fountains in the air—were so light that they would float in water (he advised readers who expected profundity to go check out the Lamentations of Jeremiah).[78] In Longfellow's American version of the *Decameron,* there's little lightness to be had and not much fresh air either. For almost two days Longfellow's travelers (three of them from nearby Boston, three from abroad or at least of foreign descent) huddle in front of the old inn's fireplace. They come even closer together when, on the second day, a cold New England rain drenches the landscape outside. Their storytelling is serious business. One member of the party, the Theologian (based on the Harvard professor Daniel Treadwell),[79] insists that the stories they share should satisfy certain moral criteria. The "old Italian tales" simply won't do:

"They seem to me a stagnant fen,
Grown rank with rushes and with reeds,
Where a white lily, now and then,
Blooms in the midst of noxious weeds
And deadly nightshade on its banks!" (4:41)

The reference to the "white lily" among the weeds is a mealy-mouthed compliment extended to another member of the party, the Student (modeled after the Harvard student Henry Ware Wales), who has just finished telling "The Falcon of San Federico," a tale that he had taken precisely from Boccaccio's "rank" book, the *Decameron*.

While the Student's contributions tend to have a happy ending, this is not true of most of the other stories, which take the reader on a literary tour of the world, including medieval Norway and Iceland, Florence, Sicily, the Spain of the Inquisition, and the Levant, as well as colonial America. Twenty-one of the twenty-two tales have literary precedents, and the members of the party are aware of that. A tale about Charlemagne, for example, contributed by the Poet (a character inspired by the Dante translator Thomas William Parsons), is identified as having come from "an ancient tome" found "upon a convent's dusty shelves, / Chained with an iron chain, and bound / In parchment" (4:211). In the absence of female storytellers, there is not much left here of the erotically charged, radically women-centered atmosphere of the *Decameron*.

Yet I would argue that there's more to *Tales of a Wayside Inn* than meets the eye. In spite of the men's self-conscious antiquarianism, the past they evoke isn't really past yet. For starters, most of these tales aren't pretty. The air they breathe is filled with "shrieks and cries of wild despair" ("The Saga of King Olaf," 4:69). We watch "many points of iron" glisten in the sun as a large army advances, spreading "terror through the city streets" ("Charlemagne," 4:215). And after a battle fought "in fire of hell and death's frost," corpses lie "on the bloody sod / By the hoofs of horses trod," and the man who dares criticize the dead soldiers' escaping leader dies "as a stone, pushed from the brink / Of a black pool, might sink" ("Scanderbeg," 4:261–62, 264).

Several of the stories, comparable to "dark ravines / In which you grope your way" (4:148), are shrouded in the gloom of night, illuminated only by flickering torches of fanatics like the followers of the Spanish grand inquisitor Torquemada. They cast a pall over listeners like the Poet, who feels the dark and heavy atmosphere weighing on him as the sharp "arrows of the rain" shoot past the decaying inn (4:140). The Theologian, who contributed the tale about the Inquisition, afterward regrets that he ever mentioned Torquemada: his horrible ghost came to haunt him "in the dreams I dreamed, / And in the darkness glared and gleamed" (4:183).

Longfellow finished the tale of "Torquemada" in December 1862. The same month he took his sons Charley and Ernest to Boston harbor to see the ironclad battleship *Nahant,* with its glistening revolving tower. He was appalled: "How ingenious men are in ways of destruction" (December 13, 1862). Longfellow knew well "what an infernal thing war is" (September 1, 1862), and we can only imagine how horrified he was when the impulsive Charley absconded a few months later to join General Hooker's forces at the Rappahannock River in Virginia, where he would see some heavy fighting. "He is where he wants to be, in the midst of it all," wrote his despairing father (March 16, 1863), who was, at just about that time, getting the first volume of *Tales of a Wayside Inn* ready for the printer. The obsession of some of the storytellers with violence or death was not coincidental: it would have reminded the most oblivious of Longfellow's readers of the fratricidal mess outside their windows. "What are men? . . . Guests of the grave and travellers that pass" (4:225).

One of Longfellow's most accomplished tales in the first volume of *Tales* is the "Saga of King Olaf," told and, in part, performed by the Musician from Norway (Longfellow's tribute to the famous violinist Ole Bull). Drawing on the *Heimskringla,* the Musician recounts how the hard-drinking Olaf and his warriors, by sheer force and reckless slaughter, brought Christianity to Norway. Longfellow's clipped lines make the choice between Thor's hammer and Christ's cross seem a matter only of perspective. Olaf may be a "shape of the sea-mist, / A shape of the brumal / Rain, and the darkness / Fearful and formless" (4:113), but he scares the travelers enough to make them thankful, as the Theologian asserts—somewhat prematurely, as it turns out—that the "reign of violence is dead" (4:114).

Significantly, the next tale, told by the Theologian, is hardly less violent. In "Torquemada," which is set during the dark days of the Spanish Inquisition, a fanatical elderly father denounces his own daughters as heretics to the grand inquisitor and then volunteers to light the pyre on which they await their gruesome death. The Theologian feels compelled to mention that this parent from hell would "in the crowd with lighted taper stand, / When Jews were burned, or banished from the land" (4:118), a reference that strikes close to home. One of the travelers is a Sephardic Jew from Alicante (like all of Longfellow's travelers, he is based on an actual person, Israel Edrehi, a dealer in oriental goods in Boston), who always exudes a "spicy scent / Of cinnamon and sandal" (4.19). He knows such insults well, even if he hasn't experienced them personally:

> The Jew was thoughtful and distressed;
> Upon his memory thronged and pressed
> The persecution of his race,
> Their wrongs and sufferings and disgrace;
> His head was sunk upon his breast,
> And from his eyes alternate came
> Flashes of wrath and tears of shame. (4:125)

The Poet in the group attempts to lighten the mood, but his tale of the "merry birds of Killingworth," the only story in *Tales* not directly inspired by a written source, is not really all that cheerful either. It is an account of another massacre, said to have taken place "some hundred years ago" in the aptly named town of Killingworth, Connecticut. In Longfellow's poem, the "swift destruction" of "the whole race of birds" (4:128) is engineered by a violence-loving Parson ("the instinct of whose nature was to kill," 4:129), a conceited Squire, a self-righteous Deacon, and a love-struck Preceptor. The ostensible justification for their plan was that the birds wreaked havoc on the garden-beds and cornfields of the residents. But whenever Longfellow mentions "birds of passage," more is at stake. Listen to the speaker's description of the coming of spring in Killingworth:

> Across the Sound the birds of passage sailed,
>   Speaking some unknown language strange and sweet
> Of tropic isle remote, and passing hailed
>   The village with the cheers of all their fleet;
> Or quarreling together, laughed and railed
>   Like foreign sailors, landed in the street
> Of seaport town, and with outlandish noise
>   Of oath and gibberish frightening girls and boys. (4:127–28)

Readers of Hawthorne's *Scarlet Letter* will perhaps remember here the Spanish mariners arriving in Boston and the contrast between their "animal ferocity" and the gray, drab Puritan population.[80] They will realize that the birds in Longfellow's poem, "foreign" and "outlandish" as they seem and speaking an "unknown" and "strange" language, stand for everything that challenges the narrow-minded nativism of such Killingworth residents as the Squire, who is convinced that "a town that boasts inhabitants like me / Can have no lack of good society" (4:128), the Deacon, who has a "street named after him in town" (4:129), and the deer-slaying Parson, who thinks that nature is up for grabs and therefore "e'en now, while walking down the rural lane," is merrily lopping off "the wayside lilies with his cane" (4:129).[81]

Only one of the residents, the Preceptor, comes to the defense of the poor birds. Since he fancies himself a bit of a writer, too, it is left to him to make the obvious connection between them and the poets. The birds are, says the Preceptor, using a comparison particularly close to Longfellow's heart, like the wandering bards and ballad-makers of yore:

> "Plato, anticipating the Reviewers,
>   From his Republic banished without pity
> The Poets; in this little town of yours,
>   You put to death, by means of a Committee,
> The ballad-singers and the Troubadours,
>   The street-musicians of the heavenly city,
> The birds, who make sweet music for us all,
> In our dark hours, as David did for Saul." (4:130)

Longfellow adroitly rescues the Preceptor's argument from cliché by having him declare that the birds are cosmopolites, diminutive reminders that there is a world out there. They are sadly needed in a town where men "put their trust in bullocks and in beeves" (i.e., beef). Remember, says the pedagogue, "'T is always morning somewhere, and above / The awakening continents, from shore to shore, / Somewhere the birds are singing evermore" (4:131). It goes almost without saying that this interpretation had a relevance of its own at a time when Americans were busily ranking birds by their usefulness for human purposes.[82]

The Preceptor doesn't sway anyone at the town council meeting, but he wins the secret approval of another audience, the women of Killingworth. They read about his speech in the newspaper, and though they have "no voice nor vote in making laws," they assure him that he is still a "victor, vanquished in their cause." When the massacre takes place, a veritable "St. Bartholomew of Birds," it does have the dire consequences predicted by the Preceptor. The town of Killingworth (the name, though real, turns into a pun), is invaded by insects and devoured by worms, and becomes "a desert without leaf or shade" (4:134). Come fall (Longfellow's favorite season), there is none of the spectacular New England foliage to be seen here: "A few lost leaves blushed crimson with their shame, / And drowned themselves despairing in the brook" (4:134). The law is repealed, and new birds have to be imported from somewhere else, in time for the spring. When the birds do start singing again in Killingworth, it seems that their songs "were satires to the authorities addressed" (4:135).

Clearly, Longfellow's poem is itself a kind of satirical attack on those who let themselves be limited by a too-narrow sense of place. In an argument with the Theologian, the Student puts his finger on the problem. The Theologian says he prefers writers who wear homespun "singing robes," thus more or less attacking his own creator, the well-dressed and well-traveled author of *Outre-Mer*. A truly "native" poet, he thinks, should not walk around in "silk or sendal gay, / Nor decked with fanciful array / Of cockle-shells from Outre-Mer" (4:275). The Student disagrees and, in his response, contrasts Longfellow's favorite birds of passage with lowly domestic barnyard fowl:

> Poets—the best of them—are birds
> Of passage; where their instinct leads
> They range abroad for thoughts and words,
> And from all climes bring home the seeds
> That germinate in flowers or weeds.
> They are not fowls in barnyards born
> To cackle o'er a grain of corn;
> And, if you shut the horizon down
> To the small limits of their town,
> What do you do but degrade your bard
> Till he at last becomes as one
> Who thinks the all-encircling sun
> Rises and sets in his back yard? (4:275–76)

Ironically, the tale that follows, the last in the collection, is told by precisely one of those barnyard creatures, the innkeeper himself, the only one who has *not* traveled to be here. When the narrative "sword of Damocles" (4:276) finally descends upon him, the Landlord reluctantly presents the story of Sir Christopher Gardiner, which at least superficially appears to support the Theologian's challenge that "what is native still is best."

Tales of a Wayside Inn had begun with a truly American story (the irrepressible "Paul Revere's Ride"), and it seems only right that it should end with one. But what an unlikely hero the Landlord's narrative has: an exotic outsider and misfit in Puritan New England, whose habits and dress render him suspect to the upstanding citizens of Boston. Sir Christopher definitely does not don cloth "made in America":

> You should have seen him in the street
> Of the little Boston of Winthrop's time,
> His rapier dangling at his feet,
> Doublet and hose and boots complete,
> Prince Rupert hat with ostrich plume,
> Gloves that exhaled a faint perfume,
> Luxuriant curls and air sublime,
> And superior manners now obsolete! (4:277)

He hangs out with the wrong people, "roystering Morton of Merry Mount," for example, and lives in a hut outside of town, which he calls his "country seat." From the beginning, prancing through town wearing his "Prince Rupert hat" and clad in a velvet vest, Sir Christopher seems like a pathetic quotation from a feudal past:

> He had a way of saying things
> That made one think of courts and kings,
> And lords and ladies of high degree;
> So that not having been at court
> Seemed something very little short
> Of treason or lese-majesty,
> Such an accomplished knight was he. (4:277)

A sordid, male version of Hawthorne's Hester Prynne, the colorfully dressed Sir Christopher is the gaudy gadfly in the Puritan wasteland. When word gets out that this self-declared "Knight of the Holy Sepulchre" is in fact a bigamist, a warrant is issued for his arrest, and a posse of bailiffs marches out to his ramshackle home as if they were to storm a castle instead of a log cabin. They only find Sir Christopher's mistress, who, without further ado, is sent packing. Meanwhile, the Knight of the Holy Sepulchre rather ingloriously hides in the woods, until a native turns him in for a ransom.

Although Longfellow's protagonist has none of Don Quixote's aspirations to restore the splendor of a Golden Age to what has, sadly, become an "Age of Iron," Sir Christopher is reminiscent of his creator's favorite literary hero, whose head, from reading too many romances, is a sorry mess of "enchantments, quarrels, battles, challenges, wounds, complaints, amours, torments, and abundance of stuff and impossibilities."[83] For Longfellow, Don Quixote was a profoundly ambivalent character: on the one hand a foolish, deluded, irascible old man with a befuddled brain; on the other a strong, stubborn believer in the truth of the imagination, a gifted rhetorician, and a walking advertisement for the transformative power of reading.[84]

The pathetic image of the hapless Sir Christopher, truly a "knight of the woeful figure," being dragged before the magistrate, whom he then seeks to convince, with his usual eloquence, that he shouldn't be penalized, suggests that in getting rid of him the Puritans were also getting rid of much more:

> Alas! it was a rueful sight
> To see this melancholy knight
> In such a dismal and hapless case;
> His hat deformed by stain and dent,
> His plumage broken, his doublet rent,
> His beard and flowing locks forlorn,
> Matted, dishevelled, and unshorn,
> His boots with dust and mire besprent;
> But dignified in his disgrace,
> And wearing an unblushing face. (4:281)

On the unyielding Puritan governor all of Sir Christopher's sweet turns of phrase, his "speech evasive and high-flown," are wasted. Like his dubious companion Mary, he is sent home as one "unmeet to inhabit here" (4:282). The ironical point of "The Rhyme of Sir Christopher" is hard to ignore: the last "American" story in *Tales of a Wayside Inn* is about someone who doesn't belong here. Sir Christopher's bequest to the New World that rejected him is an appropriately ambiguous one:

> Thus endeth the Rhyme of Sir Christopher,
> Knight of the Holy Sepulchre,
> The first who furnished this barren land
> With apples of Sodom and ropes of sand. (4:282)

Exquisitely beautiful but dissolving into smoke and ashes when plucked, the mythical apples of Sodom, like the illusory "ropes of sand," remind us of the discrepancy between appearance and reality and its fateful consequences. Sir Christopher's duplicity, as well as his amoral posturing, were exactly the kind of disease the Puritans—resolving to be, as John Winthrop recommended, as one body—had wished would never grow on New England soil. (In his New England tragedies, *John Endicott* and *Giles Corey of Salem Farms,* Longfellow had already shown how mistaken their expectations were.) Sir Christopher might be gone, but his apples still grow and ripen in the harsh New England soil.

The Landlord's tale is the only one in the entire book that is never discussed by the others. The guests retire, leaving the empty parlor "wrapped in gloom," with only the old clock ticking, striking off "the dark, unconscious hours of night / To senseless and unlistening ears" (4:284). Early the next morning, the travelers depart, never to see each other again.

As it turns out, these tales about the past were told by people who themselves have now well-nigh disappeared into the past. Just as Longfellow's poem collapses the difference between here and elsewhere, it also reminds us that what we see as our present will, in future generations' eyes, be somebody else's past:

> Perchance the living still may look
> Into the pages of this book,
> And see the days of long ago
> Floating and fleeting to and fro,
> As in the well-remembered brook
> They saw the inverted landscape gleam,
> And their own faces like a dream
> Look up upon them from below. (4:285)

In a book in which the author has ceded much of his authority to different storytellers, the epilogue carries particular weight. *Tales of a Wayside Inn,* Longfellow seems to be telling us here, is not a simple *recherche du temps perdu,* not the expression of foolish nostalgia. Rather, it is an argument for the power of storytelling, which erases all arbitrary distinctions of time, place, and class, along with the distinction between storyteller and his audience, between author and reader. Listening to tales told about past events by travelers who are now themselves part of the past, we see ourselves reflected in those narratives—just as we once saw, somewhere else, our faces reflected in a little brook that we still remember. The past (the events that took place in other people's lives) becomes the present (our identificatory reading experience), which then becomes the past again (after we have finished the book we just read).

In 1882, the year of Longfellow's death, Ernest Renan formulated his famous concept of the nation, which for him was bound together not only by a common past (actual events, that is) but also by stories about the past that people tell each other in the present.[85] What we remember and, Renan added, what we *forget* makes us the nation we are. *Shared memories* define a nation much more than actual borders, suggesting the imagined boundaries beyond which all other nations lie.[86] Longfellow's concept of travel seems geared to explode all boundaries imposed by—and, as he would point out, therefore also *on*—the imagination. The memories his travelers in *Tales of a Wayside Inn* exchange, though they come from different parts of the world and different cultures, are easily understood by everyone, a reminder of Walter Benjamin's dictum that the goal of the storyteller is to make his own experience that of his listeners, who will then go on to tell their own stories.[87]

Obviously, Longfellow was no longer the same man who, in 1825, recommended that future American writers should derive their themes and language mostly from the "high mountains," "pleasant valleys," and "blue lake[s]" of the New World.[88] The most boisterous representative of American literary nationalism, Walt Whitman, proposed that we divide the writers of the world neatly by national affiliation: "in Egypt an Egyptian, in Greece a Greek, in Germany a German, in England an Englishman."[89] Longfellow, who had once too advocated an American poetry "as original, characteristic, and national" as possible,[90] had meanwhile reached a different conclusion. If Whitman was hoping that, with his active help, American literature would eventually become "distinct" from all others, Longfellow favored "indistinctness"—a kind of widely traveled linguistic cosmopolitanism—as one of the assets of a truly "American" tradition in literature.

"Much is said nowadays of a National Literature," Longfellow observed in 1847. "Does it mean anything? Such a literature is the expression of National character. We have or shall have, a composite one; embracing French, Spanish, Irish, English, Scotch, and German peculiarities. Whoever has within himself most of these is the truly national writer;—in other words, whoever is most universal, is also the most national" (January 6,

1847). It is a bit hard to imagine the kind of transnational-national American writer Longfellow is conjuring in this passage. He was, of course, surrounded by people who wrote in more than one language (Charles Sealsfield was one of his "favorite" writers),[91] and even his own *Hiawatha* can be seen as an experiment in literary bilingualism (see chapter 2). But a writer who is, at the same time, French as well as Spanish, Irish, English, Scotch, and German? Perhaps we shouldn't take Longfellow's thumbnail sketch too literally here. For him, American literature is, by its very nature, a mosaic of quotations, a rich, colorful, endlessly growing anthology of texts by many authors, a promise waiting to be realized.

If this vision doesn't make sense, consider the playful enactment of transnationalism Longfellow wittily proposed in a letter to his friend George Washington Greene of November 3, 1866. Sitting at home on a cold New England winter's day, Longfellow imagined himself not as the anguished producer of nation-building poems but as the cheerfully chewing consumer of foreign-sounding foods. He sketched out the first chapter of a yet-to-be-written satirical novel, a "Romance soon to be issued by Ticknor & Fields." The protagonist, the Cavaliere di San Lazzaro (Longfellow himself), upon finding himself home alone in "Castle Craigie," sits down to enjoy a multicourse repast, including fresh scallops sent from "Rhodes" (Rhode Island) accompanied by a sampling of wine from Sicily and a taste of claret from France. "O dolce frutta del Mar," exclaims Lazzaro/Longfellow. Rising from his chair "like a giant refreshed," he withdraws to his study to smoke a cigar from Brazil (*Letters* 5:92).

"A Poetic Guide-Book"

In the last decade of Longfellow's life, his vicarious traveling finally spanned the entire world. *Poems of Places,* the anthology he began publishing in 1876, is the most comprehensive evocation of the importance of place in American literature ever published, with selections ranging from England and Scotland to Africa and the Caribbean. "In Poems of Places I have travelled all the World over," Longfellow crowed on May 31, 1878, after the final volume, *Oceanica,* had gone to press (*Letters* 6:364). After decades of dreaming about going abroad, the work had tremendous personal significance for him, and he approached it with a great deal of enthusiasm. "I make it for the pleasure of making it," he announced in December 1875, in a letter to Fields, caring little that it "would take a long time to finish it"

(*Letters* 6:86). Reading and writing about other places allowed him to forget where he really was: "'Poems of Places' have shut out the dull weather," he told George Washington Greene on a cold and wet day in April 1878. "I have been in India and China and Japan, and am now in Africa, where it is hot and dry enough" (*Letters* 6:355). When the old Mr. Emerson, during a rare visit to Craigie House, found Longfellow poring over the proofs of one of his small volumes, he shook his head doubtfully: "The world is expecting better things of you than this," he said. "You are wasting time that should be bestowed upon original production."[92] But Longfellow, who thought of *Poems of Places* as one, if "many-volumed," book, was genuinely proud of his role as the "Transcriber" of poems from every corner of the world: "No politician ever sought for Places with half the zeal that I do," he wrote in a letter which he jokingly signed: "Friend and Foe alike have to give *Place* to Yours truly H.W.L." (*Letters* 6:86, 175, 91; my emphasis).

Clearly, an editor who owned not one but three editions of Virgil ("one Italian, one English, one American," *Letters* 6:248) could draw extensively on his own library. But Longfellow also depended on his many correspondents, letter-writers both here and abroad who unabashedly recommended their own works or listed poems by others that they deemed suitable. Sometimes the centrifugal quality of his projected "Poetic Guide-Book" (May 29, 1874) worried Longfellow. He was definitely surprised to find, as he told the emperor of Brazil, Pedro II, "what a vast amount of verse has been written about this world that we inhabit"—so much so that he had to give up his original notion that one volume for each country would suffice (*Letters* 6:498). And so, despite the optimism he displayed publicly, the drab detail work that was involved soon began to wear him out—the time-consuming pursuit of books and articles, the double-checking of titles, authors' names and sources, the correspondence with other writers. Though he had the help of his former publisher John Owen and of the aspiring Cambridge poet Charlotte Fiske Bates, he felt that "to get it all printed correctly" had become a task worthy of Sisyphus (*Letters* 6:89).

Then there were the copyright issues. For example, although Longfellow himself remained ever wary of his own prerogatives as a writer, he had been careless enough to reprint some poems by Tennyson without having obtained the author's permission, an oversight that sparked a brief furor in the press (*Letters* 6:181–82). In a similar incident, he had to extend his apologies to the Irish poet William Allingham for having used his work "before asking your leave" (*Letters* 6:201). Some other poems he ended up writing himself at short notice, because even with the most diligent sleuthing he couldn't fill in all the gaps. He was, he protested in a letter to a friend, an "American *professore*" not an "Italian *improvisatore*" [*sic*] like Toni Toscan (*Letters* 6:249).

Despite the fact that an American *professore* had compiled it, *Poems of Places* is far from a dry academic exercise. Even outwardly the thirty-one volumes, with their handy octavo size, resembled the famous Murray guidebooks, which Longfellow himself thought were excellent preparation for a trip to Italy.[93] In fact, using works of "belles lettres" as a kind of guide to foreign places was a well-established practice among nineteenth-century Anglo-American travelers, who, clutching their copies of Sir Walter Scott's *Lady of the Lake*, tramped out to Loch Katrine in Scotland. Longfellow's own favorite, *Childe Harold's Pilgrimage*, followed closely by Samuel Rogers's long poem *Italy*, performed a similar service for wide-eyed tourists rambling through Italy and Switzerland.[94]

Traveling became an exercise in pleasant *déjà vu*, so much so that, in some cases at least, the "ecstasy of recognition" gave way to disappointment.[95] The reproductions had been nicer than the original, Mark Twain quipped when he saw Leonardo's *Last Supper* in Milan.[96] Not surprisingly, the traditional Grand Tour began to change considerably, as travelers, no longer excited by the prospect of strolling through the picture galleries of Europe or scaling the walls of moldering castles along the Rhine, began to spread out to more remote locations. As a young man, Tom Appleton once had to pass "a dismal night on the frontier" waiting for permission to cross from Belgium into Holland.[97] Now he was delighted to see that the "tide of travel" was spilling over every border: "the grand tour has now become the globe," he exclaimed in his essay "Sight-seeing" (374).

This was great news, because it meant that people like him now got to go to Egypt and Syria. On the other hand, it wasn't such great news, because it also meant that people *unlike* Tom Appleton would now get to go there as well: "All the world travels," sighed Appleton. Again, Mark Twain's party of "pilgrims" comes to mind, strolling through the ruins of Ephesus, pocketing pretty ornamental pieces to take home with them.[98] Historians have pointed out that class differences were becoming increasingly important as nineteenth-century travel turned into tourism and affluent and educated travelers cast a cold eye on the riffraff purchasing train tickets to places where formerly they would not have been able to go: "Who knows how soon railroads may not be sending a flock of cockneys through their deserts!" cried Appleton. Travel was an art, not a pastime. Paradoxically, the globalization of travel Appleton had been observing, far from refining people's taste for the arts and sharpening their appreciation for cultural differences, was also helping, he feared, to provincialize the world, thus hastening a process that began long ago when Rome appropriated and trivialized the "hoar sublimity" of Egypt and the "sunny sweetness" of Greece.[99]

Longfellow was less concerned about upholding rigid standards. Did he remember that he himself had once behaved like the tourists Appleton despised? As a young man, Henry commemorated his visit to the old Gothic château of Chambord on the Loire by breaking off "the head of a little stone dragon which I found amongst other ornaments upon the principal staircase" and which he was hoping to bring home "as a trophy of my journey." As a rather lame excuse, he told his brother Stephen that "thousands and thousands" of other travelers before him had defaced "the walls and battlements of the old edifice entirely over with their names."[100]

Longfellow did not succeed in convincing his publisher to put out a cheap, paper-covered edition of *Poems of Places,* though the individual volumes, at $1 each, were not overpriced.[101] But the rather motley crew of poets Longfellow assembled in this anthology—where we find works aimed at travelers with the refined taste of Tom Appleton (Pindar's "Etna," for example, or Tennyson's "Ulysses") next to Spanish ballads and anonymous Russian boat songs—showed that his notion of travel had remained a rather egalitarian one. The lack of illustrations or maps left his audience with nothing but the written word: in Longfellow's collection, places are *texts* and can be accessed by anyone who is capable of turning the page. In each volume or sequence of volumes, place names were arranged alphabetically, from the Alban Hills to Villa Franca, from Aachen to Wetzlar, and from Athens to Zante. Obviously, authorship—or, for that matter, the chronology of literary history—had *not* been the guiding principle here. In several of the volumes, some last-minute additions had even been stuffed into appendices, as if to emphasize further that this anthology was far from "definitive."

But what, then, *was* Longfellow's editorial agenda? At the very least, *Poems of Places* would have served the needs of the reader looking for quick information. "Would you like to find out what the poets have had to say about Smyrna?"—"Well, check Longfellow, *Poems of Places, Asia,* vol. 2, pages 78–80." And so, seconds later, the curious reader can settle down in her easy chair with S. G. W. Benjamin's ode to the city where, as legend has it,

Homer was born ("The torches on each tapering minaret / Flash in the rippling waters of the bay," *Places* 22:78) or with Bayard Taylor's somewhat risqué tribute to a long-lashed Persian boy ("And felt the wonder of thy beauty grow / Within my brain, as some fair planet's glow," *Places* 22:80).[102] Longfellow's volumes thus acquire a weirdly democratic appeal, refusing to give "pride of place," if the pun is permitted, to any of the places selected. At first blush at least, Pisa seems no more important than Pozzuoli, and Orléans no more worthy of consideration than Oloron-Sainte-Marie. There is the occasional headnote: an extract from Murray's *Handbook of Spain,* a passage from the publications of the Irish Archeological Society, or a paragraph explaining the source of an Italian poem. But such interventions are few and far between, especially if we compare them with Longfellow's earlier venture into multicultural publishing, *Poets and Poetry of Europe* (where long introductions prefaced each of the sections) or, for that matter, his profusely annotated translation of the *Divine Comedy.* In *Poems of Places,* an anthology committed to the insight that the whole world is up for poetic grabs, the "Voice of Institutional Authority" is virtually absent.[103]

By confronting them with texts about places both familiar and unfamiliar, written by authors both unfamiliar and familiar, Longfellow encourages his readers to reflect on the many ways in which space turns into place. The programmatic motto of *Poems of Places,* neatly printed on the title page of each volume, came from one of George Crabbe's *Tales in Verse:* "It is the Soul that sees; the outward eyes / Present the object but the mind decries."[104] The world is, Longfellow tells us, a product of our own, individual imaginations. It is no coincidence that what he has collected are poems of *places* (plural) rather than of *place* (singular). Proliferation is his principle. Each reader of a volume in Longfellow's series, encountering other people's ideas about a place or a series of places, will create or re-create her own mental map of the world. It is not necessary for the reader to have personally experienced a particular place, said William Dean Howells, who liked the "gracious companionship" he had found in Longfellow's own poems of places: "'You remember Cadenabbia,' he seems to say; 'you slept at Monte Cassino; you noticed that old monk at Amalfi?' and he makes us believe him. 'Yes, yes,' we are well ready to answer, 'it was I, I was there; I am there now, for all I never was in Italy save in this verse of yours.'"[105] In Longfellow's *voyages imaginaires,* everyone is invited to come along.

Longfellow's selections range from the old to the new, from the familiar to the strange, from the political to the private, from the impressions of travelers to poems by native writers. Certainly, the editor's own preferences are evident from the extensive coverage given to some areas and the neglect with which he has treated others. Japan is dealt with in a skimpy fifteen pages and Russia and Africa get only one volume each, while Longfellow's home turf, New England, occupies two volumes, and Italy, in his own estimation "the finest portion of the work" (*Letters* 6:210), is allowed a densely packed three. But perhaps the fact that Longfellow did at all include areas like Polynesia, Mesopotamia, and Afghanistan as well as the Arctic Circle attests to his desire to go beyond the coordinates of the world he knew personally.

Within the same volume and even within the sections devoted to one place, we regularly find views that contradict each other. *America: Western States,* for example, serves up all the familiar rhetoric of settlement. "Away! far away!" shouts Charles Mackay, "let us hope for the best, / And build up new homes in the Land of the West" (*Places* 29:4). Joaquin Miller chimes in "Room! Room to turn round in, to breathe and be free, / And to grow to be giant, to sail as at sea" (*Places* 29:159). Margaret Stewart Sibley adds a personal touch, recording her rapturous experience of horseback-riding across the prairie one evening, "sweet stars above, sweet flowers beneath," when she felt compelled to ask herself, "Will life or earth e'er yield again / A joy as pure as this is?" (*Places* 29:177). The poems on San Francisco celebrate the Golden Gate as a symbol of a time to come when "all the New has leavened all the Old" and "forms familiar shall give place / To stranger speech and newer face" (Henry Morford, "At the Golden Gate," *Places* 29:197; Bret Harte, "San Francisco," *Places* 29:192).

But *Western States* also gives voice to the other side of the debate. There is a poem about Illinois, for example, by, of all people, Margaret Fuller, Longfellow's harshest critic, who greets with relief "this fair spot" untouched by busy human hands, "on which improvement yet has made no blot" (*Places* 29:16).[106] Henry Rowe Schoolcraft supplies "Indian Lament," which recalls the human losses resulting from western settlement: "my kindred are gone to the hills of the dead; / But they died not by hunger or lingering decay; / The steel of the white man hath swept them away" (*Places* 29:23). From Longfellow's own pen comes the melancholy description of "Hiawatha's Departure" into the setting sun, while the clouds are "on fire with redness" (*Places* 29:238).

Finally, there is a startlingly effective poem by the former Lowell Mills worker Lucy Larcom, "Elsie in Illinois," in which she imagines life on the prairie from the perspective of a woman longing for her eastern home (Larcom herself had lived in Illinois from 1854 to 1862). In stark, simple language, Larcom lets us share in Elsie's fear of the immense void outside her window, her not-always-successful attempts to find satisfaction in daily chores and motherhood ("Elsie's thoughts awake must keep / While the baby lies asleep"). Even when she uses more elaborate images, they are always contained by the perspective of her speaker, as when Elsie pictures the prairie as a "Garden without path or fence" or imagines it as staring at her with a frozen smile on its vast face:

> At her household work she dreams;
> And the endless prairie seems
> Like a broad, unmeaning face
> Read through in a moment's space,
> Where the smile so fixed is grown,
> Better you would like a frown.
>
> (*Places* 29:21)

Longfellow's scrupulous avoidance of editorial intervention—or, put more positively, his willingness to let his own voice be submerged into a polyphonic chorus of other writers—is particularly evident in what could have been the most overtly political volume of the series, *Southern States*. From his correspondence with the Southern poet Paul Hamilton Hayne (1830–86) we know that, for all his contempt for slaveholders, Longfellow's personal goal was reconciliation: "I have only one desire; and that is for harmony, and a frank and honest understanding between North and South" (December 4, 1878; *Letters* 6:409). Hayne grabbed the olive branch. Since his first fawning letter to Craigie House, mailed on January 24, 1872, he had worked tirelessly to win and solidify Longfellow's affection, topping off his efforts with an ode to his hero that surely deserves a permanent place in the annals of literary brown-nosing:

> And now, thou stand'st—the wings of labor furled—,
> Like some lone eagle of the mountain rocks,—
> Thine eyes turned heavenward, thy white, reverend locks
> Worn halo-wise about thy sovereign brow:—
> Thus stand'st thou, scarcely knowing that all men bow
> Before thee!—that alike thro palace halls
> And humble cottage homes, thy music calls

True hearts to fervent prayer & tender praise;—
That evermore thy pure, beneficent lays
Shall sweetly ring, re echoed [*sic*] round the World!.[107]

The strategy worked. Longfellow, who remembered a visit from Hayne a few years earlier ("too brief," Hayne lamented),[108] wrote to him for advice on what poems to include in the projected volume about the South. Hayne responded eagerly, though not without some carping ("I almost feared you had forgotten me"), and recommended warmly several poems from his own superior production as well as a few by his southern colleagues, especially those collected in *War Poetry of the South,* edited by William Gilmore Simms and published in New York in 1866.[109]

Simms's acknowledged purpose was to redefine southern poems that had been the expression of extreme sectionalism as part of a shared American national heritage: "this collection is essentially as much the property of the whole as are the captured cannon which were employed against it during the progress of the late war." His anthology began with Henry Timrod's "Ethnogenesis," written on the occasion of the meeting of the first Southern Congress in Montgomery, Alabama, in February 1861 ("Hath not the morning dawned with added light?"), and it ended with "Ashes of Glory," by A. J. Requier, a lugubrious funeral dirge for the Confederate flag ("Fold up the gorgeous silken sun, / By bleeding martyrs blest, / And heap the laurels it has won / Above its place of rest"). Simms wanted his collection to be a testament to the "genius and culture of the Southern people" and promised that, "in the event of the popular success of the present volume," he would "cheerfully" follow it up with another one "of like style, character, and dimensions."[110] The fact that *War Poetry of the South* remained without a sequel shows that Simms had probably miscalculated the public's enthusiasm.

Longfellow didn't like Hayne's suggestion. "I am afraid I could hardly use Mr Simms' war poems," he replied curtly. "I may have to insert some few pieces of the kind, but they will be as few as possible, and not of the fiercest" (April 24, 1878; *Letters* 6:352). He had little intention of compiling a volume about the South as Southerners would most like to see it represented. For example, the poems by Hayne himself that he accepted are, with one exception, indeed not overtly political but rather evoke the South as a region, a place to live. Most of these texts—"feeble stuff," as Daniel Aaron rightly calls them—employ the same dreamy voice, mur-

muring darkly about "dew-besprinkled forest paths," fields "billowing with grain," and "blissful valleys" breathing "their grateful measures to the sun."[111] Apparently, the "Longfellow of the South," as Hayne liked to be called, thought of himself as quite the nature poet.[112] There are so many "mysterious moans," "whispering waves," and "amber mists" in these murky poems that it becomes hard to say what they really are about, apart from some vaguely defined "southern" atmosphere. Imagery is not Hayne's forte. In his weepy lines we encounter the personified Twilight, who "on her virginal throat / Wears for a gem the tremulous vesper star," and we are invited to think of a squirrel as "that quaint sylvan harlequin" and (perhaps the funkiest example) to imagine the magnolia in flower as "whorls of dazzling color" that look like "sunset rainbows arched o'er perfect skies" (*Places* 28:13, 14, 29).

Ironically, when he does write about political subjects, Hayne's poetic voice suddenly acquires the precision absent in other examples of his work. "The Bombardment of Vicksburg" (*Places* 28:222–23), the one poem by Hayne about the war that Longfellow did include, describes the "hissing" enemy fire that is raining, with "a thousand forked and vengeful tongues," on the peace-loving citizens of Vicksburg. More specifically, Hayne represents Grant's siege as an attack on innocent children at play, who nevertheless remain steadfast in their faith. Hayne leaves no doubt about where he thinks God's sympathies were in this conflict:

> And the little children gambolled,—
>   Their faces purely raised,
> Just for a wondering moment,
>   As the huge bombs whirled and blazed!
> Then turned with silvery laughter
>   To the sports which children love,
> Thrice mailed in the sweet, instinctive thought,
>   That the good God watched above.
>
> (*Places* 28:223)

Obviously, in Longfellow's House of Poetry there are many mansions. Too many perhaps? Apart from Hayne's "Bombardment of Vicksburg," there are several other emphatically pro-Confederate texts in the volume, such as "Maryland, My Maryland," "The Confederate Flag," "Stonewall Jackson's Way," Henry Timrod's "Charleston" (a poem that memorably imagines the Union forces as crouching tigers in an "Orient jungle," lusting for Confederate blood), and Alethea S. Burroughs's "Savannah," a gushy celebration of her "rebel home," whose "arm of flesh is girded strong" (*Places* 28:199–200).

From a modern perspective, Longfellow's cultural and racial myopia is quite evident in some of his editorial decisions. For example, African Americans are not much represented: Longfellow's own poem "The Slave in the Dismal Swamp" is joined by Henry Howard Brownell's "The River Fight" (in which the Union soldiers marching into New Orleans see their flag held, in welcome, by the withered hand of a slave, "all outworn on our cruel land"), John Greenleaf Whittier's "Song of the Negro Boatmen," and a fleeting vision given at the end of Bret Harte's "A Second Review of the Grand Army." The most explicit celebration of African American courage comes from Phoebe Cary, whose "Ready" describes how at Rodman's Point, North Carolina, a black sailor ("no slavish soul had he") sacrificed his life to free his stranded comrades (*Places* 28: 186–87).

But then most readers would have known already where the author of *Poems on Slavery* stood politically. Longfellow once said that he could hear, wherever he went, the low murmur of the disenfranchised slaves, like the chorus in a Greek tragedy (February 15, 1861), and many of the selections seem to correspond to his own position in the matter. Cases in point are Brownell's "The River Fight" and "The Bay Fight" (the two longest poems reprinted in the book), Thomas Buchanan Read's "Sheridan's Ride" and "The Attack," Edmund Clarence Stedman's "How Old Brown Took Harper's Ferry," Richard Henry Stoddard's "Twilight on Sumter" ("when Sumter sinks at last / From the heavens, that shrink aghast, / Hell shall rise in grim derision and make room!" *Places* 28:212), and Whittier's ballad "Barbara Frietchie."

Even Longfellow's juxtapositions are often indicative of what he personally thought about the war. Consider the only poem by William Gilmore Simms that made the cut. "The Edge of the Swamp" (*Places* 28:68–69), reveling in descriptions of an oozy, fetid, rank environment, features an alligator, a "steel-jawed monster," on whose brow—a predictable, too-precious poetic conceit!—a butterfly alights after "travelling all day." But only for a moment. Upon discovering where it is, the butterfly quickly departs, counseling the nervous human traveler to leave the alligator's habitat, too, "for better lodgings, and a scene more sweet / Than these drear borders offer us to-night" (*Places* 28:69). Not much fun to be had in "Dismal Swamp, Va."

Simms's shuddering depiction of southern slime, which some northern readers would have especially enjoyed, is preceded by one of Longfellow's early antislavery poems, "The Slave in the Dismal Swamp." Here the inhabitant of the swamp is a mangled old slave who looks like "a wild beast," and the speaker leaves no doubt as to who is responsible for that. In the distance, he sees a campfire and hears the barking of a bloodhound ("The Slave in the Dismal Swamp," *Places* 28:67–68). The South as it is featured here does not appear as the most desirable of travel destinations.

But even though the presence and placement of such poems suggest where the editor's sympathies lie, Longfellow's anthology in its entirety offers no comfortable final assessments—not of any of the places in the South and not of the people inhabiting them. Depending on one's point of view, one can consider such an abdication of editorial responsibility the most problematic or the most daring aspect of *Poems of Places*. In his favorable review of the first volume, published in the *Atlantic Monthly* of March 1877, William Dean Howells mentioned the apparent "liberality" of Longfellow's editing, to which he imagined some critic less generous than him would take exception.[113] Later on, Newton Arvin was more openly skeptical, complaining about the "mingling, in these volumes, of good, mediocre and bad poems" (though he also conceded that the "sense of place" had "never been anthologized more thoroughly").[114]

Howells had a point. Even if we ignore Arvin's reservations and apply the standards of Longfellow's own time, *Poems of Places* seems too inclusive, too tolerant, too eager to please the reader—or, rather, *any* reader. As Emerson, who in his own poetry anthology, *Parnassus* (1874), had of course avoided that very mistake, would have diagnosed the problem: "too much mass and too little genius."[115] But isn't it conceivable that Longfellow, in his "poetic Guide-Books," never even wanted to provide us with the ultimate insight into the true nature of a place? That he never wanted to leave us with a definite itinerary through a region or a country? The many different voices represented in *Poems of Places* work together to show how preliminary all our imaginings of place are, and they democratically encourage the reader to add her own views to the mix.

Interestingly, women writers are prominently represented in *Poems of Places*. Besides authors who are well-known or at least still somewhat familiar (Elizabeth Barrett Browning, Phoebe Cary, Lydia Maria Child, George Eliot, Annie Fields, Felicia Hemans, Julia Ward Howe, Helen Hunt Jackson, Anna Jameson, Fanny Kemble, Bessie Rayner Parkes,

Elizabeth Stuart Phelps, Sarah Morgan Piatt, Lydia Sigourney, Harriet Prescott Spofford, Elizabeth Stoddard, Harriet Beecher Stowe, Sarah Helen Whitman) we meet poets who have long been consigned to oblivion: Cora Kennedy Aitken, Elizabeth Akers Allen, Lillie E. Barr, Esther Vernon Carpenter, Sarah Clarke, Eliza Cook, Catherine Ann Dubose, Annie Chambers Ketchum, Elizabeth F. Merrill, Lilian Rozell Messenger, Caroline F. Orne, Margaret Junkin Preston, Rose Sanborn, Charlotte Smith, Florence Smith, and Jane Taylor. Some of these poets hadn't even published before—Sarah Bridges Stebbins, for example, was known to Longfellow only because she had planned to include some of his poetry in a projected anthology of hers, to be titled "The Poetry of Pets," that was never completed (*Letters* 5:773).

The sheer variety of female authors in *Poems of Places*—ranging from the working-class poet Larcom to the sophisticated New York–born intellectual Julia Ward Howe—makes it almost impossible to resort to comfortable stereotypes about them. In *Poems of Places,* the voices of these women writers extend and qualify the more predictable selections by their male colleagues. For example, in one of the volumes about Italy, an excerpt from Shelley's "Adonais" is followed by Maria Lowell's "The Grave of Keats" ("O Mother Earth, what has thou brought / This tender frame that loved thee well?" *Places* 12:227), and Lord Byron's "Tomb of Cecilia Metella" has its counterpart in Elizabeth Stoddard's poem on the same subject ("I was Metella's wife: / I loved him,—and I died," *Places* 12:245). Sometimes female writers will even enter into a dialogue with each other, as when the New Hampshire poet Martha Perry Lowe (1829–1902) celebrates the liberating influence of the Spanish poet, novelist, and playwright Carolina Coronado (1832–1911) in a poem included under "Bajadoz," the province where Coronado was born: "She poured a tide of passion through / The sordid flats of Life's dull sea" (*Places* 14:45).

The abundance of female writers in Longfellow's anthology reflects not only the increasing "feminization" of travel in the nineteenth century[116] but also Longfellow's own conviction that women writers were on a level equal to men and therefore deserved to be included with them, instead of being segregated into a separate volume.[117] In Emerson's *Parnassus,* incidentally, only 12 out of 177 anthologized writers were women.

Here is a more detailed look at one of the women writers Longfellow mined for his anthology. In the volume on Russia, 20 out of the total 104 poems come from *A Russian Journey,* a book by the New Hampshire–born poet Edna Dean Proctor, published, as were Longfellow's books, by James Osgood in 1872. Proctor's "beautiful verses"[118] originally served as the epigraphs to the chapters of *Russian Journey,* a volume dedicated to the insight that the world is moving closer together in "a striking . . . union of countries and races."[119]

It is easy to see why Longfellow had liked the book. Proctor's travels had begun inauspiciously: whipped by the icy winds of the steppe, she musters up little sympathy for the elaborate symbols of orthodox faith she encounters in cities like St. Petersburg and Moscow. But Proctor admits that she would feel different had she been born there. Genuinely intrigued by the ethnic diversity in a country that extends from the "Pole rivers" to the "southern seas" and serves as a gateway between the west and the east, Proctor takes her attempt to understand cultural "otherness" one step further. She imagines not only what it would be like to be a Russian but what it would like to be a Tartar, and, after that, what it would like to be a Tartar thinking about the Russians: "as the Tartars, without shrine or picture, addressed their prayers to the one God, I saw how, from their point of view, they might call their Christian neighbors idolaters, and scorn to yield the Faith of their fathers" (121). Everything is a question of perspective: "What a fine pear or peach is to an American, that a slice of watermelon is to a Russian" (168). In Saratov, Proctor finds "well-executed" statuettes of Lincoln for sale, "the grave, kindly face having the same charm on the Volga as by the Sangamon" (173)—a sure sign, too, that the same basic values appeal to people in the east and the west (173). In fact, "humanity is one" (320). But sameness here does not mean identity. Traveling down the Volga, Proctor finds herself wishing that the Tartars not be westernized, which will be, she fears, the inevitable consequence of the projected Trans-Siberian railroad (160). The prospect of cultural homogeneity appalls her, and she envisions with dismay the day when there will be one "Russia from the White Sea to the Sea of Marmora, and from the Carpathians to the Pacific" (161). Like Longfellow, she was interested in cultural diversity, in seeing with "other eyes" whenever possible.

The most powerful effect of Longfellow's anthologizing, with its emphasis on heterogeneity and multiplicity rather than homogenizing predictability, is a leveling of the difference between the past and the present and between author and reader. Just as he conflates the near and the far, the native and the foreign, Longfellow removes all constraints of time and allows a dialogue to take place between the most unlikely of interlocutors, writers long dead and writers still alive. Longfellow's handling of literary history was not driven by naïve antiquarianism. While he wasn't exactly saying "No—in thunder," he did not waste time building the sepulchers of the fathers either, as Emerson would have charged (who, in his own anthology, did not go back farther than Chaucer and limited his choices to poems by English-speaking writers only).[120] For Longfellow, poetic travel-writing was less a *re*-presentation than a *presentation* of place, a process in which the *past* (historical, literary, and, less frequently, autobiographical) and the *present* act of writing or reading a poem about it become indistinguishable.

Take Longfellow's favorite sequence in *Poems of Places,* the three books on Italy, a country that, unlike Russia, he knew personally. Like Russia, Italy had been trying to shed its history of internal strife and political suppression when Vittorio Emanuele was crowned king of the newly united nation in 1861. The introductory section of Longfellow's first Italy volume reflects the dizzying contradictions of Italian history and identity. The American reader would have come across an excerpt from Virgil's *Aeneid* ("Land rich in fruits, and men of mighty name!") and Mignon's wistful song from Goethe's *Wilhelm Meisters Lehrjahre,* as well as Elizabeth Barrett Browning's declaration of love ("Our Italy's / The darling of the earth"). But there were also laments on Italy's fall from greatness, from Petrarch's despair about the "unnumbered" wounds that stain Italy's "beauteous bosom" to Giacomo Leopardi's dejected ode to his country, pictured as a woman "unveiled and with dishevelled hair," cowering disconsolately on the ground. Vincenzo da Filicaja, in a poem translated by Longfellow himself, wonders what would have happened to Italy had she been "stronger, less fair." But then the next entry, by an anonymous author, sets a different tone again: "O Land of Beauty, garlanded with pine / And luscious grapevines" (*Places* 11:15).

In the sections devoted to individual places, we see a similar dynamic at work. Poems that deplore the pastness of the past are found side by side with others that simply celebrate the delight of living in the present, the joys of being in a particular place at a particular time. Many poems collected under the heading "Rome" yearn for the city's glorious past and bemoan the amorality and dire poverty of the present, from Lucan's riff on the suicidal depravity of imperial Rome ("her hands on her own vitals seize, / And no destruction but her own can please," *Places* 12:89) to Vittorio Alfieri's denunciation of the city as a desolate void inhabited by the "mute spectres of a race" filled with "guilt, base fears, fierce and en-sanguined hate" (*Places* 12:98) to Thomas William Parsons's unpleasantly antisemitic poem about the "Ghetto di Roma" ("Where no saint's cha-pel, perfect in proportion, / Breaks the long ugliness with one fair front," *Places* 12:122). A lighter, more optimistic take on the eternal city comes in a graceful ballad by Longfellow's friend the "fascinating" Julia Ward Howe.[121] Here the speaker fantasizes that her "old friend" Horace is still having fun in modern-day Rome:

> . . . in the Ancient City
> And from the quaint old door
> I'm watching at my window
> His coming, evermore.
>
> For Death's eternal city
> Has yet some happy street;
> 'T is in the Via Felice
> My friend and I shall meet.
> (*Places* 12:181)

In poems like Howe's, the difference between Europe's literary past and the American reader's present becomes irrelevant. Centuries shrink to the narrow space between one page and the next, and the differences between then and now begin to fade away.

Longfellow's liberating "mix-and-match" approach to anthologizing is particularly evident in the section on Venice, one of the longest in the entire collection. Predictably, there are many passages from Byron's works, among them the famous beginning of canto 4 from *Childe Harold* ("I stood in Venice, on the Bridge of Sighs; / A palace and a prison on each hand"). Percy Bysshe Shelley pays tribute to the "sun-girt city," and Wordsworth ponders the "Extinction of the Venetian Republic": "Men are we, and must grieve when even the shade / Of that which once was great is passed away." George Sand's hapless ex-lover, Alfred de Musset, in clipped qua-trains conjures up a starry night in Venice when everything is still except the guards pacing outside the Arsenal, and Graf von Platen, the German romantic, weeps over the decline of Venice the "haughty queen in gold ar-ray," as Paolo Veronese had painted it (*Places* 13:143,157, 160, 206, 166). Longfellow's own contribution, a beautiful Petrarchan sonnet written specifically for *Poems of Places,* seems as if intended to catalogue all the images coined by his predecessors. It begins with, and then elaborates on, James Howell's conceit, first recycled in Longfellow's own *Outre-Mer,* of Venice lying in the waters of the lagoon as in a "swan's nest":

> White swan of cities, slumbering in thy nest
> So wonderfully built among the reeds
> Of the lagoon, that fences thee and feeds,
> As sayeth thy old historian and thy guest!
> White water-lily, cradled and caressed
> By ocean streams, and from the silt and weeds
> Lifting thy golden pistils with their seeds,
> Thy sun-illumined spires, thy crown and crest!
>
> (*Places* 13:207)

The well-worn swan metaphor is suggested, only to be abandoned and replaced with the new image of a water-lily, whose pistils and golden stamens represent the palazzi of Venice. The "ocean streams" remind us what a strange creation this city really is—a giant, beautiful flower that seems to be floating in still waters, though it is in fact surrounded by the vast sea with its "silt and weeds."

The beginning of the sestet brings an interesting development—and that this should happen right where tradition prescribes an argumentative turn in the sonnet shows how self-consciously Longfellow handles the form:

> White phantom city, whose untrodden streets
> Are rivers, and whose pavements are the shifting
> Shadows of palaces and strips of sky;
> I wait to see thee vanish like the fleets
> Seen in mirage, or towers of cloud uplifting
> In air their unsubstantial masonry.
>
> (*Places* 13:208)

In the case of Venice, traditional poetic images don't work: the city itself is already one oversized metaphor. In Venice, what would be a street in any other city is a glittering body of water; here, substanceless shadows become the sidewalks on which, for a few moments, our minds go walking. This is a "phantom city" indeed, a perfect example of the reality of the imagination. Born from dirt drifting on sluggish waters, the overwrought buildings of Venice seem airy like castles in the sky, as evanescent yet as real as the poem Longfellow has written about it.

The speaker waits until the final tercet to introduce himself, in what is the first complete sentence in the poem, and then does so only to announce that there will be more waiting—waiting, that is, for the city, which the reader now realizes is an emblem for poetry itself, to vanish again before our very eyes. The past has, almost imperceptibly, become the present, but a present that also will soon be past. The carefully crafted language of the sonnet shows how hard Longfellow has worked to give substance, if only temporarily, to what he himself describes as "unsubstantial masonry." The reader finds herself enmeshed in a web of sound effects ("*White swan of cities, slumbering in thy nest*"; *shifting / shadows of palaces and strips of sky*"), which make the poem a musical experience rather than a history lesson. While the perfect end rhymes emphasize the sense of repose introduced by the initial image of the slumbering swan, the enjambments keep the poem moving forward. In the sestet, the line breaks begin to happen at particularly crucial points ("streets / Are"; "shifting / Shadows"; "fleets / Seen"). The poem obviously picks up speed as it rushes toward its suspended ending, where we pause and wait, just as the city, as if forever, seems to pause and wait.

Going abroad, for Longfellow, did not mean the acquisition of pictures to hang in the halls of Memory, as Sigourney defined her goal in *Pleasant Memories of Pleasant Lands*.[122] As he saw it, travel was not a mad scramble for a specific destination but a state of mind, a feeling remembered and now again present to us as if we were there and not here. For Longfellow, travel was the joy that comes from imagining interesting places with eyes other than our own. I am sure that this is also what Elizabeth Bishop, another well-traveled poet, had in mind when, in an only superficially calm and accepting poem, she spoke of the terrifying possibility that you might forget "places where you meant to travel."[123]

Grappling with a similar fear, perhaps, Longfellow penned one poem for the Italy sequence of *Poems of Places* that revealed a hankering for more stability than his other travel poems usually permit. Longfellow wrote "The Old Bridge at Florence" (*Places* 11:149–50) in January 1875, at a time when he was reminiscing, "as I very often do," about Dante's Florence (*Letters* 6:12). The beautifully wrought Petrarchan sonnet has a surprising speaker: Florence's Ponte Vecchio, the old, covered passageway between the banks of the Arno, which, like Longfellow himself, has survived the ravages of time. "Taddeo Gaddi built me. I am old, / Five centuries old." Listen to how Longfellow conveys a sense of gravity here by simply repeating the adjective "old." Built in 1345, the Ponte Vecchio still plants its heavy "foot of stone" upon the winding Arno river, just as Saint Michael had once placed his on the body of the dragon he had conquered: "Fold by fold / Beneath me as it struggles, I behold / Its glistening scales." Like an old geezer hungry for attention, the bridge brags about its victory over the river of time and revels in memories of the past, the expulsion of the Medici, for example, and, even further back, the feud between the Ghibellines and the Guelphs that drove Dante into exile.

Longfellow sent his sonnet, along with a photograph of his "rather sad and wrinkled face," to a friend in Florence, Arabella Duffy (*Letters* 6:12). In his letter he admitted that the ancient bridge, a solid, lifeless, unmoving thing, was a metaphor for old age, specifically *his* old age: the dragon he was slaying here was that of his own mortality. Inner need had turned into external fact, private grief into public poetry. Nevertheless, this is also first and foremost a poem about a *bridge,* a fitting symbol for someone who spent his life forging connections—between the past and the present, Europe and America, the world of poetry and the man or woman on the street. (Nineteenth-century travelers noticed with amazement that the Ponte Vecchio, covered as it was with the shops of goldsmiths and jewelers, was in fact a busy market square).[124]

A few days after finishing "The Old Bridge at Florence," Longfellow rewrote the sonnet in Italian and called it "Il Ponte Vecchio di Firenze." Self-translation was, he said to Duffy, "one way of visiting Florence, and I fear the only one for me" (*Letters* 6:12). Now almost seventy, Longfellow, using (like his Peter Piper) a language not his own, had traveled back to Italy in a poem. Significantly, the bridge in Longfellow's poem is made worthy not so much by whoever created it ("Gaddi mi fece") but by those who have used it. What quickens it into a sense of its value is someone's touch. The reader, mentally traveling—like Longfellow himself—all the way to Florence, delightedly walking past the gold and the gems that glitter in the jewelers' displays, can almost imagine the cold stone feeling still warm where, moments ago, the hand of the great Michelangelo himself must have lain:

Florence adorns me with her jewelry;
    And when I think that Michael Angelo
    Hath leaned on me, I glory in myself.
      (3:226; *Places* 11:149)

Fiorenza i suoi giojelli m' ha prestati;
    Equando penso ch' Agnolo il divino
    Su me posava insuperbir mi sento. (3:227)

FOUR

"It Whirls Me Away"

LONGFELLOW AND TRANSLATION

The Art of Translation

As Longfellow's "Il Ponte Vecchio" reminds us, translations allow texts to travel from one culture and language to another. Made for the overwhelming majority of readers with little or no knowledge of a foreign language, they address themselves to constituencies beyond a narrow circle of experts.[1] And this is exactly what Longfellow liked about them—that translations were not for the sophisticates among the readers, those who spoke and read foreign languages easily and therefore didn't need any help. Nevertheless, and herein lies the crux of the matter, he did not want them to be simplifications of a foreign text either.

As we will see in this chapter, Longfellow refused to make a choice between the two options that, according to the German philosopher Friedrich Schleiermacher, existed for the translator. Not inclined to "take the author to the reader" and to assimilate a foreign text to American culture, he also eschewed the more elitist approach favored by Schleiermacher: "taking the reader to the author," which would have meant forcing her to endure the foreign text in its full, often alienating, complexity.[2] Longfellow's many translations were part and parcel of his reader-friendly poetics, as I have been describing it in this book. Longfellow also quickly became one of the most frequently translated authors of his day, and while the Italian, French, and German versions of his poetry I will discuss later in this chapter underscore his widespread popularity and international appeal, they also help us see what might be unique about his own practice as a translator.

For Longfellow, the old bridge he evoked in "Il Ponte Vecchio" was more than a casual metaphor. Remembering Michelangelo's touch on the stone, his poem/translation turned into a metaphorical handshake across the centuries. And what a strange handshake this was! They were an unlikely match, as my discussion of Longfellow's *Michael Angelo* in chapter 2 has shown: the American poet who answered fan mail with a red rose in his buttonhole, had a taste for Mouton Cadet, imported his cigars, and could not, as his friend Howells once said, "do anything other than gently,"[3] and the broken-nosed Renaissance artist who slept with his boots on, had a passion for nude bodies, and a reputation for sexual deviance. But Longfellow liked Michelangelo's rough-talking poetry, which others before him had found so hard to re-create in English. William Wordsworth, for example, went on record as having said that, since Michelangelo had "put so much meaning into so little room," he found the difficulty of translating him "almost insurmountable."[4]

That did not deter Longfellow. Among the Michelangelo translations he chose to include in *Kéramos and Other Poems* was, characteristically, a sonnet that talks about the limits placed on the artist's divine power, making him more or less, if not quite, like all of us. "Non ha l' ottimo artista" is generally believed to have been addressed to Vittoria Colonna, the only (and safely elusive) woman of any importance in Michelangelo's life. The poem is based on an extended comparison between on the one hand the work of the sculptor who is trying to hew a rough, resistant hunk of stone into the shape of a statue and on the other hand the speaker's obsession with the lady he adores:

> Non ha l' ottimo artista alcun concetto
>   Ch' un marmo solo in se non circoscriva
>   Col suo soverchio, e solo a quello arriva
>   La man che obbedisce all' intelletto.
> 5   Il mal ch' io fuggo, e 'l ben ch' io mi prometto
>   In te donna leggiadra, altera, e diva,
>   Tal si nasconde; e per ch' io più non viva
>   Contraria ho l'arte al desiato effetto.
> Amor dunque non ha, nè tua beltate,

10   O fortuna, o durezza, o gran disdegno
        Del mio mal colpa, o mio destino, o sorte,
     Se dentro del tuo cor morte, e pietate
        Porti in un tempo, e che 'l mio basso ingegno
        Non sappia ardendo trarne altro che morte.[5]

Famous even in Michelangelo's lifetime, the poem expounds his theory of potential form or "pietra viva," the Neoplatonic notion "that the rocks in the quarry wait for the sculptor to liberate their inner form."[6] The sculptor's tool reveals what is inherent in the stone as well as in his God-given mind, releasing it from the rough covering ("soverchio") that veiled it. But Michelangelo adds an interesting twist to this familiar theme. His sculptor fails miserably in his endeavor—and so does, by implication, the lover. Here is Longfellow's translation:

> Nothing the greatest artist can conceive
>   That every marble block doth not confine
>   Within itself; and only its design
>   The hand that follows intellect can achieve.
> The ill I flee, the good that I believe,
>   In thee, fair lady, lofty and divine,
>   Thus hidden lie; and so that death be mine,
>   Art, of desired success, doth me bereave.
> Love is not guilty, then, nor thy fair face,
>   Nor fortune, cruelty, nor great disdain,
>   Of my disgrace, nor chance nor destiny,
> If in thy heart both death and love find place
>   At the same time, and if my humble brain,
>   Burning, can nothing draw but death from thee. (6:348)

Longfellow begins with an inversion that ever so slightly changes the Italian original, placing emphasis not on the subject of the sentence, the artist, but on *the artist's work*. This shift forces him to turn the noun "concetto" into a verb, "conceive." The surprising, hardly perceptible effect of Longfellow's modification (obvious only to those who know Italian) is that the English line now recalls the sound patterns of the Italian original. And although they won't realize it, readers not familiar with Italian will get both—a readable English sentence and an inkling of what Michelangelo's Italian sounds like:

Nothing the greatest *a*rtist *c*an *c*on*c*eive
*N*on ha l' ottimo *a*rtista al*c*un *c*on*c*etto

Poet John Frederick Nims, who wasn't shy about pointing out the deficien-
cies of his predecessors among the Michelangelo translators, liked Longfellow's rearrangement of the first line so much that, over a hundred years
later, he repeated it almost verbatim in his own Michelangelo translation
("Nothing the best of artists can conceive . . .").[7] In Longfellow's *Divine
Comedy,* we will encounter further examples of his desire to remind the reader, in an English translation, of the actual sounds of the foreign original, an
anticipation of the "phonemic" mode of translation carried to such a glorious extreme in Louis and Celia Zukofsky's English renderings of Catullus.[8]

With the exception of the beginning, Longfellow also follows Michelangelo's syntax faithfully, reproducing even the caesura in line 3 where it
occurs in the Italian text. Sometimes his sentences seem to become even
more convoluted than Michelangelo's. Take the complicated translation
of lines 7–8: "so that death be mine, / Art, of desired success, doth me
bereave," which, though not easy to understand, gives the English reader
an idea of how tortured Michelangelo's argument is here. Longfellow expresses well the artist's agonizing realization that he lacks the skill to coax
from his block of marble (or, by analogy, from the woman he loves) the
result that he so much desires. One of Longfellow's predecessors, the Michelangelo biographer John S. Harford, simply and blandly rewrote these
two lines as a main clause: "I, death-struck, / Fail in my efforts to attain that Good," a solution preferred also by modern translators. James
M. Saslow, for example, adds a fancy prepositional phrase, but the rest of
his sentence sounds equally dispassionate, even downright clinical: "but,
to my mortal harm, / my art gives results the reverse of what I wish."[9]
Longfellow has been charged with confusing cause and effect in his translation of this passage,[10] but the subordinate clause he has chosen ("so that
death be mine"), besides gesturing at the sentence pattern of the original,
captures vividly the sense of perverse inevitability that the artist and the
lover experience in their parallel quests for perfection. In a similar vein,
Longfellow's separation of the adjective "guilty" from its object ("of my
disgrace") in the penultimate tercet of the sonnet imitates the placement
of words in Michelangelo's original, where the verb ("ha") is separated
from its object ("colpa") by a catalogue of reasons, each one immediately
rejected as insufficient, for the speaker's despair:

Amor dunque non ha, nè tua beltate,
O fortuna, o durezza, o gran disdegno
Del mio mal colpa, o mio destino, o sorte

Love is not guilty, then, nor thy fair face,
Nor fortune, cruelty, or great disdain,
Of my disgrace, nor chance nor destiny

Interestingly, Ralph Waldo Emerson once tried his hand at the same Michelangelo sonnet—a somewhat unlikely choice for someone who believed in the liberating power of poetry. Indeed, Emerson quickly proves that he can transform even a poem about the limitations of art into an affirmation of its power. More motivated to create an Emersonian poem than to produce a faithful translation of another writer's work, he also picks a rather unconventional rhyme scheme (*aabab ccdd eee ff*):

Never did sculptor's dream unfold
A form which marble doth not hold
In its white block; yet it therein shall find
Only the hand secure and bold
Which still obeys the mind.
So hide in thee, thou heavenly dame,
The ill I shun, the good I claim;
I alas! not well alive,
Miss the aim whereto I strive.
Not love, nor beauty's pride,
Nor Fortune, nor thy coldness, can I chide,
If, whilst within thy heart abide
Both death and pity, my unequal skill
Fails of the life, but draws the death and ill.[11]

In Emerson's version, the artist's failure appears almost as a personal shortcoming. If only his hand were "bold" enough and he himself sufficiently "skilled," the sculptor's mallet could turn into a tool of liberation, the instrument by which mind asserts itself over matter. This is a misreading, of course, but a deliberate one. Obviously, it was important to Emerson that the speaker's frustration not be taken as a general statement about the insufficiency of art but as a specific case of an artist "missing his aim."

Like Emerson, Longfellow was still using Michelangelo the Younger's expurgated edition, in which male pronouns had been exchanged for female ones to expunge all traces of the famous artist's homosexuality or "amor virile." In a note he added in *Kéramos,* Longfellow did offer an apology of sorts for his failure to use a reliable text,[12] but that did not spare him the opprobrium of the British poet and critic John Addington Symonds, whose ambitious Michelangelo translation was published in London later the same year. Symonds dismissed Longfellow's translations, along with the "specimens" produced by Wordsworth and Southey, as based on an antediluvian state of scholarship. Fortunately for us, the meddling hands of Michelangelo's nephew had left "Non ha l' ottimo artista" virtually intact, so that we can fairly compare Longfellow's translation with that produced by Symonds, the British aesthete and prophet of gay liberation:

THE LOVER AND THE SCULPTOR
Non ha l' ottimo artista

The best of artists hath no thought to show
    Which the rough stone in its superfluous shell
    Doth not include: to break the marble spell
    Is all the hand that serves the brain can do.
The ill I shun, the good I seek, even so
    In thee, fair lady, proud, ineffable,
    Lies hidden: but the art I wield so well
    Works adverse to my wish, and lays me low.
Therefore, not love, nor thy transcendent face,
    Nor cruelty, nor fortune, nor disdain,
    Cause my mischance, nor fate, nor destiny;
Since in thy heart thou carriest death and grace
    Enclosed together, and my worthless brain
    Can draw forth only death to feed on me.[13]

Like Longfellow, Symonds has a penchant for archaisms such as "doth" and "thee." While the verbal phrase in line 7 ("lies hidden") probably came from Longfellow's translation, line 5 ("the ill I shun") might have been lifted from Emerson's text. But the significant changes in the poem's imagery are entirely Symonds's doing, such as the characterization of the stone as "rough" in line 2, the reference to the "marble spell" to be broken by the sculptor in line 3, the evocation of the lady's "transcendent" face in line 9 and, finally, the metaphor of death slowly "feeding" on the sculptor whose art cannot help win the lady's grace. The last image, emphasizing the self-destructiveness of the speaker's love that, as it were, eats him up, illustrates well Symonds's approach: he brilliantly reinterprets rather than preserves the original's meaning. What began as a Michelangelo sonnet ends up as a poem written, under more difficult circumstances, by Symonds himself.

In fact, Symonds is really less worried about the sculptor's problems than about those of the lover, who finds himself in a situation in which all his talents are of little use to him. His choices as a translator—the emphasis on the speaker's lowness ("lays me low"; "worthless") and on the "worthless brain" that fails the lover (note that Symonds avoids the closer English word "intellect")—make this sonnet, despite its heterosexual surface appearance, sound like the story of homosexual self-discovery frequently told, if only covertly, in Symonds's own poetry.[14]

Manifestly less interested than either Emerson or Symonds in creating *his* version of Michelangelo, Longfellow the translator is as literal as he needs to be and as liberal as he can be. To him, the work of translation was more than a refuge for someone with problems in the originality department. He knew that, for some of his readers at least, translating was "like leaning on another man's shoulder."[15] But then Longfellow wouldn't have regarded that argument as criticism: he was, as my previous chapters have demonstrated, quite the opposite of a writer reveling in the power of authorial sovereignty. In fact, his translating was what helped him *create*. He told his friend and fellow translator Ferdinand Freiligrath that translation really was "like running a plough share through the soil of one's mind; a thousand germs of thought start up (excuse this agricultural figure) which otherwise might have lain and rotted in the ground" (November 24, 1843; *Letters* 2:551).

The sheer number of translations that bear Longfellow's name—from the poem by Luis de Góngora he chose for his first attempt in 1829[16] to the Dante translation of the 1860s to his last, posthumously published translations from the French—ought to be proof enough that this activity satisfied a deep-seated need. "A translated text," Lawrence Venuti has argued, "should be the site where the different culture emerges, where the reader gets a glimpse of a cultural other."[17] And this was exactly what Longfellow, dreaming as he was of a "composite" American literature, hoped he would accomplish—that, handled carefully by the translator, the "foreignness" or "otherness" of a text would begin to speak to him and, by implication, to his readers.

Naturally, Longfellow's own work didn't remain unaffected by all the translations he did. Readers noticed with amazement that volumes bearing Longfellow's name were composed of a large number of works by other writers. At least one loyal fan was under the impression that some of the original poems in Longfellow's *Voices of the Night* had also been translated from another language.[18] It's hard to blame him. *Voices of the Night* contained only a handful of recent poems by Longfellow but as many as fifteen works he had translated, from the Spanish, the French, the Italian, and the German, ranging from Lope de Vega's "The Good Shepherd" to Johann Gaudenz von Salis's "Song of the Silent Land." And his poetic farewell, *In the Harbor* (1882), included a rather diverse offering of poems translated from the French, a ballad by Charles Coran ("Little sweet wine of Jurançon, / You are dear to my memory still"), an anonymous poem praising "The Quiet Life" ("I, leaving not the home of my delight, / Far from the world and noise will meditate"), and Xavier Marmier's expression of his longing for his hometown ("All things smiled on the happy boy").

The critics fretted a bit about all this foreign stuff that seemed to have crept in. Writing in the *North American Review* in 1840, an anonymous reviewer singled out Longfellow's translation of Ludwig Uhland's ballad "The Black Knight," feeling compelled to "utter a word of protest against a form of speech ... which is threatening to invade us from Germany." What specifically bothered this critic was the "omission of the personal pronoun" in sentences like "Am a prince of mighty sway"—a mannerism that was "too foreign to the English idiom to be defensible." Quick action was needed, "as translations are notoriously the great corrupters of the purity of a language."[19]

But by this point Longfellow was already hooked. His early translation attempts were, according to Gary Scharnhorst, "instrumental to his intellectual and artistic development."[20] Later on, of course, Longfellow would pick nonnative speakers as the protagonists of several of his most widely known works—think of Evangeline and her fellow Acadians, Hiawatha as well as the Spanish Jew, Ole Bull, and the Sicilian in *Tales of a Wayside Inn*. But what is perhaps less well-known today is that the first book he ever published was, yes, a translation. *Coplas de Don Jorge Manrique* (1833) contained poems by the medieval Spanish poet Jorge Manrique as well as Longfellow's article "The Moral and Devotional Poetry of Spain," now reprinted as the introduction to the new volume.[21] Longfellow also included the Spanish text in his edition—"*le texte en regard,* as we say in France"[22]— thus making *Coplas* one of the first, if not *the* first, bilingual volume of poetry in American literature.

Translation was, as Longfellow acknowledged in the preface to *Coplas,* an impossible balancing act, the art of "rendering literally the words of a foreign author" in another language while also preserving, as faithfully as possible, the "spirit" of the text. He knew that critics had been quarreling for a long time over "how far a translator is at liberty to embellish the original before him." Cautious as always, Longfellow expressed his own views about the matter by way of an analogy, which, coincidentally or not, takes us back to the Michelangelo sonnet discussed at the beginning of this chapter:

> The sculptor, when he transfers to the inanimate marble the form and features of a living being, may be said not only to copy, but to translate. But the sculptor cannot represent in marble the beauty and expression of the human eye; and in order to remedy this defect as far as possible, he is forced to transgress the rigid truth of nature. By sinking the eye deeper, and making the brow more prominent above it, he produces a stronger light and shade, and thus gives to the statue more of the spirit and life of the original, than he could have done by an exact copy. So, too, the translator. (*Coplas* [iii]–iv)

Longfellow's comparison is a tricky one. His sculptor is not at all like the powerful artist Michelangelo as the public saw him: a lofty genius who, divinely inspired, frees the work of art from the superfluous, inert matter that imprisons it. Rather, he is a patient imitator, doggedly bent, like "l' ottimo artista" in the sonnet, on reproducing a reality that is *not* stone, his work always falling short of the living, breathing essence of the original. Incapable of representing life as it is, the sculptor is driven to exaggeration. He even changes, for better effect, some of the original's most salient features. But look what he achieves: the "life" and the "spirit" of the original return and inhabit its copy, however much the latter might differ from it in its details.

The sculpture analogy has interesting ramifications for Longfellow's understanding of the translator's task. Instead of devaluing his work as merely supplementary to the real business of artistic production, Longfellow uses a deliberately deflated definition of the artist's capacities—limited by his own skills and the requirements of his material—to suggest that translation, too, is a form of art.

English Isn't English

Despite the efforts of Longfellow and others, translated books were a somewhat endangered species in mid-nineteenth-century America. And yet American readers needed them. Aware of their debt to their different parent cultures, attached in different ways to the countries from which they or their ancestors had come, they were naturally also intent on carving out their own new zone of "native" speech, one that would help identify them as a distinct (and non-European) culture. At the same time, they were also looking for ways to preserve at least some link with their various pasts. Each translated work—a novel originally written in French, a song from Germany, an Italian sonnet—gestures at, and repeats, the precarious passage from "foreign" to "native" that has taken place in the history, distant or recent, of every non-English American family. Translation can thus be seen as a metaphor for the balancing of "descent" against "consent" that Werner Sollors has identified as the essence of American culture.[23]

Modern translation theorists like to stress the violence that is part of the act of translation. After yanking a text out of its natural habitat, the translator strives to make the "foreign" acceptable to the culture to which his or her readers belong. Translation, in this reading, equals domestication; it means rewriting cultural otherness in terms of what is instantly familiar, easily recognizable to the folks at home.[24] Or, as *Putnam's* summarized the problem, long before the controversy about translation had reached the halls of academe:

> It is not sufficient to furnish literal equivalents, word by word, for the matter of the original. Nor is it even necessary, or always allowable, to retain the structure of the sentences, or of the paragraphs. The office of the translator is to render the foreign thought into the native thought; and, to that end, the garments of the languages must be altogether and entirely exchanged. This demands acquaintance not only with the mere relative lexicography of the two tongues, but with the genius and style of thought peculiar to each, and the equivalent thoughts in each.[25]

Now the success of such an exchange, as George Steiner has pointed out more recently, is far from certain: "No language, no traditional symbolic set or cultural ensemble imports without risk of being transformed." The "bringing home" will always be fraught with risk. What may look like incarnation can turn into infection.[26]

The influx of foreign matter was a latent but potent fear in the 1850s, when a new pride in "Saxonism" began to emerge.[27] The worry that the health of America might be contaminated by an invasion of books in translation loudly flaunting their cultural otherness is a recurring theme in the periodical literature of the time. For example, a reviewer for the *Atlantic Monthly,* although he admitted he liked the "smooth consecutive English" into which Jean Paul's *Titan* had been translated, felt that the German writer's belief in "a love that one man can have for another" was downright "nauseous." Americans did not want to read about such things.[28]

In their shared paranoia regarding the baneful influence of foreign literature, the "Young Americans" were not fundamentally different from their Whiggish opponents. Not persuaded by the "wholesome English" into which a recent book by Longfellow's favorite French novelist, George Sand, had been translated, a reviewer for the *United States Democratic Review* in October 1847 declared that he was put off by the very notion of a "female reformer." Clearly, such ideas didn't need to be imported. While Americans still seemed "like men rowing in a boat with our faces turned all the time to Europe," they were in fact receding, as they should, "farther and farther from it." Happily, those who "borrow their ideas from abroad" were getting less numerous by the day.[29]

In March 1847, a long, rambling article in the *American Whig Review,* provocatively titled "Shakespeare *versus* Sand," denounced American readers of the French novelist as "sand-blind." Against those foreign books that "muddle the mind" the writer held up the established canon of books written in English by writers who had all displayed "good common sense" and had never tried to unsettle the brains "of us who find it easier to believe in . . . things as we find them." Reading Sand was like washing one's hands in mire. Not to worry, the writer exclaimed, "we have yet confidence in our Saxon blood."[30] Circumspect as he was in matters of public conduct, even Longfellow himself in his weaker moments wasn't immune to such doubts about the effects of translation, as, for example, when he expressed his reservations about the translation of Goethe's provocative novel *Elective Affinities* undertaken by his friend Bernard Rölker: "It is a strange thing altogether; and will smell very offensively in this climate, whatever it may do in Germany." This was not to say that Rölker shouldn't go ahead and finish his translation of the novel if he liked it. "But he had better act alone publishing it."[31]

As it happened, many established publishers handled translations only gingerly anyway. The early history of Longfellow's own publishing house, Ticknor, is a case in point.[32] It's a nice fact that the first genuine book they ever published was a translation, *Caspar Hauser: An Account of an Individual Kept in a Dungeon* (1832), by the German criminologist Paul Johann Anselm von Feuerbach. Over the next two decades, William Ticknor stuck to translations of textbooks or nonfiction books of interest to a general reader. If his preferences are any indication, mid-nineteenth-century Americans were more interested in seashells, female anatomy, and epidemic diseases than in foreign novels and poems. Representative Ticknor titles included Jean-Baptiste Lamarck's *Genera of Shells* (1833), translated by the conchologist Augustus Gould; Louis Charles Kiener's *General Species and Iconography of Shells* (1837), translated by the Boston ichthyologist and physician David Humphreys Storer; Jacques Lisfranc de St. Martin's *Diseases of the Uterus* (1839), translated by the Boston doctor Giles Henry Lodge, M.D.; Auguste Ambroise Tardieu's *Treatise on Epidemic Cholera* (1849), translated by Samuel Lee Bigelow, a doctor from Worcester, Massachusetts; and *The Art of Prolonging Life* (1853), by the illustrious German physician Christoph Wilhelm Hufeland, the father of macrobiotics.

It's good to remember here that the first *literary* translation released by Ticknor was Longfellow's very own *Coplas de Don Jorge Manrique*. Unfortunately, the book sold so little that the firm never recovered its expenses. Sand's novel *Consuelo*, translated by Francis G. Shaw and published in 1846, did somewhat better: the firm put out a three-volume paperback edition a year later, with a comparatively large print run of three thousand copies. Goethe was a pretty safe bet as well. Abraham Hayward's translation of *Faust*, first published in 1840 and reprinted in 1850, became a staple in the catalogue over the next few years, until it was replaced by Charles Timothy Brooks's versified rendering, for which the translator received a remarkable 20 percent per copy. Carlyle's translation of *Wilhelm Meister* followed in 1851, with a print run of four thousand copies (customers, if so inclined, could purchase both *Wilhelm Meister* and *Faust* in two volumes for $2.50). But a collection of literary fables by the Spanish eighteenth-century poet Tomas de Iriarte (*Literary Fables of Iriarte*), translated by George Devereux and published in December 1855, had such embarrassingly low sales that, out of the five hundred copies printed, a whopping 234 copies remained unsold by the end of October 1858, when Ticknor sent the translator the kind of letter dreaded by all struggling writers, announcing that the remainder would be returned to him forthwith, at cost.

All in all, these were slim pickings. Obviously, translations weren't risk-free for a profit-oriented publisher. Still, American readers were grateful for them, as the charge records of the New York Society Library show. Data collected by Ronald Zboray prove that among the books checked out more than four times by women between 1847 and 1849 and from 1854 to 1856, Goethe ranked second, while on the list of books borrowed by men, *The Count of Monte Cristo* occupied a respectable thirteenth place (out of a total of sixty-three titles).[33] A striking example of the wide-ranging, eclectic interest in foreign literature is the narrator's (hypothetical) wife in Donald Grant Mitchell's tremendously popular sentimental novel, *Reveries of a Bachelor: A Book of the Heart* (1850). Mitchell's description also points to the unconscious male fear that reading might empower women or at least distract their attention from the affairs of the home. Instead of tending to the baby, "Peggy" destroys the narrator's valuable first editions by—God forbid—*reading* them:

> Peggy loves you—at least she swears it, with her hands on the Sorrows of Werther. . . . You never fancied when you saw her buried in a three volume novel, that it was anything more than a girlish vagary; and when she quoted Latin, you thought innocently, that she had a capital memory for her samplers. But to be bored eternally about Divine Danté [*sic*] and funny Goldoni, is too bad. Your copy of Tasso, a treasure print of 1680, is all bethumbed and dogs-eared, and spotted with baby gruel. Even your Seneca—an Elzevir—is all sweaty with handling. She adores La Fontaine, reads Balzac with a kind of artist-scowl, and will not let Greek alone. . . . The nurse is getting dinner; you are holding the baby; Peggy is reading Bruyère.[34]

For Longfellow, translations were more than occasional windows unto exotic cultures, more than small escape routes out of domestic drabness. He loved to think about the similarities and differences between languages, noting with delight that the "very English expression 'As flat as a pancake'" had an exact counterpart in the Danish language ("Saa flak som en Pandekage")[35] or relishing, in a letter written two months before his death, the

Dutch word for sonnet, *klinkdicht,* which seemed equally evocative as the Latinate English word: it "certainly has a tinkling sound" (*Letters* 6:761).

He knew that translations were never exact. The evocative Italian image "ruscelletto gorgoglioso" could never be adequately captured by the English equivalent, "gurgling brooklet," and a metaphor like "garrulous birds" would fade when held against the wonderfully musical Spanish original, "pájaros vocingleros." But, Longfellow suggested, for an Italian or Spanish ear, the English words "gurgling brooklet" and "garrulous birds" would probably seem "equally beautiful."[36] Seeing through different eyes, listening to different sounds, abandoning facile distinctions between "original" and "imitation," one begins to see in a new light what supposedly makes up one's "own" culture. True, there was a certain element of elitism inherent in the business of translation; after all, the translator had to be more familiar than his readers with foreign literatures and languages. But its real purpose—to make texts accessible to everyone—was profoundly democratic.

This insight was the organizing principle behind Longfellow's eight-hundred-page compilation *The Poets and Poetry of Europe,* published in 1845 and then reissued, with additions and corrections, in 1871. As an anthology of translations, the volume was intended, Longfellow explained in the preface, "to bring together, into a compact and convenient form, as large an amount as possible of those English translations which are scattered through many volumes, and are not easily accessible to the general reader" (*Poets* [v]). With the help of his wife Fanny, who because of the bad state of Longfellow's eyes during those years did most of the actual reading and transcribing, Longfellow had collected poems from ten different languages and national literary traditions. Each of the ten sections of the anthology presented the poems in roughly chronological order, and each of them was preceded by a general introduction, written by Longfellow himself. Individual authors were introduced by short biographical headnotes, "a large portion" of which, Longfellow acknowledged in his preface, had come from the pen of his Harvard colleague, the classicist Cornelius Conway Felton. All in all a substantial volume. He did not really expect "a very rapid sale for such a work," Longfellow wrote to a New York publisher, C. S. Francis & Company, in 1856, who was interested in reprinting it, "but I think it will continue to be in demand for some time to come, as it contains much information not easily accessible elsewhere" (*Letters* 3:530).

What strikes the modern reader of *The Poets and Poetry of Europe* is the unabashed emphasis on works that would have found favor with a wide readership, rather than on those deemed important by the *cognoscenti*. This explains, perhaps, the presence of the many minor poets in the volume, technically accomplished writers (like the sixteenth-century Spanish writer and guitar-player Vicente Espinel) who were "not distinguished by originality" but wrote "pleasing and melodious" songs abounding in "beautiful images and descriptions" (*Poets* 687). Even in the case of more established writers, the appreciation accorded them by the proverbial "man on the street" becomes almost as important as their literary accomplishments. Twice we are reminded how much Lope de Vega had been a part of his country's popular culture: "Crowds gazed at him in the streets; children followed with shouts of delight; every thing that was fair assumed his name;—a bright day was called a Lope day; a rare diamond, a Lope diamond; a beautiful woman, a Lope woman" (*Poets* 630).

That said, Longfellow does not shy away from authors with a more serious, even radical agenda. Take the selections from Georg Herwegh, "recently . . . one of the celebrities of Germany," who is represented by his "Song of Hatred," in which he asks his fellow citizens to "fight tyranny, while tyranny / The trampled earth above is," and by "The Protest," in which the speaker claims that he had hardly begun to be in "breeches dressed" when he "began to shout and roar / And mightily protest" (*Poets* 369). But even in Herwegh's case, Longfellow's emphasis is on accessibility rather than on intrinsic literary merit. As he saw it, the identity of the author wasn't the main guarantee of a literary work's relevance anyway, as demonstrated by the generous space he gave to anonymous works, from *Beowulf* to Italian popular songs to the Spanish *cancioneros* and *romancieros*. This anthology hadn't been compiled for the writers but for the readers of poetry—especially those who lacked the time, as well as the knowledge of foreign languages, that would allow them to immerse themselves in the literature of a foreign country. Occasionally, Longfellow even appears to make fun of the somewhat unscholarly nature of his own project which, inevitably, reduces texts to representative snippets. At one point, he compares himself to Christina of Sweden, "who clipped two of the finest paintings by Titian, in order to fit them into the panels of her gallery" (*Poets* 516).

Longfellow's passion for European writers has been taken as evidence of his lukewarm commitment to the creation of an authentic American literature, as an expression of his uncritical adulation for everything non- and perhaps even *un*-American. But Longfellow never really forgets that in *Poets and Poetry of Europe* he is addressing an *American* audience. The editorial comments, for example, reveal remarkably little ambition to awe the reader into open-mouthed admiration of foreign literary refinement. Heinrich Heine, for example, is lambasted for his "implacable hatred of his foes": no man, we are told, "should write to another as he permits himself at times" (*Poets* 350). August von Kotzebue's plays are debunked as full of "theatrical clap-traps and false and sickly sentimentality" (*Poets* 319). And Longfellow/Felton don't mince words about Pierre Ronsard's "perverted taste" (*Poets* 411) or the dismally long "caravan of sonneteers" who traversed the literary wasteland of the Portuguese seventeenth century (*Poets* 733).

The headnotes are refreshingly unacademic too. Many of them rely on extensive quotations, taken from works by other writers, such as John Adamson's *Lusitania Illustrata* (1842), Thomas Carlyle's *Lectures on Heroes and Hero-Worship* (1840), Pierre-Luis Ginguené's *Histoire littéraire d'Italie* (1811–12), and the seventh edition of Friedrich August Pischon's *Leitfaden zur Geschichte der deutschen Literatur* (1843). Longfellow's collaborator Felton drew freely on his own translation of Wolfgang Menzel's compendium *German Literature* (1840), while Longfellow himself plundered, without acknowledgment, his earlier essays from the *North American Review*. The off-the-cuff, improvised directness of the editors' writing is especially evident in passages that show a more personal take on their subject, such as the following note about the site of the old French court in the Quartier Marais in Paris, apparently composed for the benefit of the American tourist: "there is no sign of a court now. Under the arcade are shops and fruit-stalls, and in one corner sits a cobbler, seemingly as old and deaf as the walls around him. Occasionally you get a glimpse through a grated gate into spacious gardens, and a large flight of steps leads up into what was once a royal palace and is now a tavern" (*Poets* 412–13).

Some of Longfellow's selections were also made with an American audience in mind. For example, he included one of Schiller's least familiar works, the "Nadowessische Totenklage" ("Indian Death-Song," *Poets* 313), probably because he hoped it would grab an American reader's attention. And the long introduction to Goethe's works includes a generous excerpt from an interview in which the Master himself professed to have an interest in the weather in America (*Poets* 283). On an even lighter note, a poem by Hoffmann von Fallersleben ("German National Wealth") mocks the pretensions of German immigrants in America:

> What shall we take to our new land?
> All sorts of things from every hand!
> Receipts for tax, toll, christenings, wedding, and funeral;
> Passports and wander-books great and small;
> Plenty of rules for censors' inspections,
> And just three million police-directions.
> Or when to the New World we come,
> The German will not feel at home.
>
> (*Poets* 353)

But Longfellow doesn't merely want to *please* his American readers (though the odd chuckle here or there is certainly welcome), he also wants to *change,* if ever so slightly, the way they think about other cultures and, by implication, about themselves. In the first section of *Poets and Poetry,* on "Anglo-Saxon Language and Poetry," Longfellow, in a rather bold move, tells his readers that, well, even *English isn't English:* "The Anglo-Saxon language was the language of our Saxon forefathers in England, though they never gave it that name. They called it English." It is from murky beginnings that modern English arose, from "voices, half-understood; fragments of song, ending abruptly, as if the poet had sung no farther, but died with these last words upon his lips," as Longfellow puts it beautifully (*Poets* 3). By defamiliarizing, as it were, the one linguistic tradition that English-speaking Americans, including the editor of the anthology himself, would have claimed as their own, Longfellow cleverly opens the door for the kind of cultural and linguistic diversity that his collection as a whole is intended to illustrate.

Longfellow's introductory essay, essentially a reprint of the article "Anglo-Saxon Literature," published in the *North American Review* in 1838, begins with the story of how King Alfred, when a mere "boy at his mother's knee," was so excited when he saw an ancient manuscript that he wanted to learn the letters of the Saxon alphabet. And while Longfellow's reader imagines the young Alfred looking at the manuscript, she suddenly finds the old king, crowned, bearded, careworn, looking back at her from the illuminated initial letter of the first chapter of an old book written by Alfred himself that Longfellow says he has just opened, a book "so beautifully printed, that it might tempt any one to learn not only the letters of the

Saxon language, but the language also." The power of literature bridges centuries as well as continents (*Poets* [1]).

But the real point of the anecdote comes next. That fateful first manuscript the young Alfred saw planted the seeds for his later attempts to transform the "book-Latin" of writers like Boethius into modern, plain Anglo-Saxon. Alfred had become a translator. Longfellow's innocent-seeming introduction thus sets the tone for a volume that not only tells the story of how the literatures of ten prominent European countries have developed over several centuries but also how there has always been considerable traffic between these emerging nations and their different languages. *Poets and Poetry of Europe* is not merely a collection of translations from almost a dozen different languages, it is in and of itself a plea for the necessity of translation as a means of intercultural exchange, engineered to educate the monolingual American reader.

Translations, ensuring as they do the traffic of ideas between cultures, are the most visible expression of Goethe's "Weltliteratur." By the same token, they also help nations develop a sense of their own distinctiveness. If the birth of the English language was due to several translations produced by the literature-besotted King Alfred, modern High German came into being when Martin Luther translated the Bible. Spanish literature got a major boost when Alfonso saw to it that the Bible became available in the Castilian language (*Poets* 637), and a flurry of translations—of Aesop's fables, *Reineke Fos,* and Hans Sachs's poetry—marked the beginning of modern Danish literature (*Poets* 60).

As far as individual authors are concerned, a staggering number of them took time off from their own writing projects in order to produce translations from foreign languages, a fact noted in many of the biographical introductions. True, not every one of them was as compulsive as Johann Heinrich Voss, who translated everything that he could lay his hands on: the *Iliad* and the *Odyssey* as well as the complete works of Virgil and Horace, then Hesiod, Theocritus, Tibullus and Lygdamus, Aristophanes and Aratus of Macedonia and, finally, even some Shakespeare. Voss's translations, as everyone knew, were shockingly literal. In love with all manner of stylistic and grammatical oddities, producing lines, as Anne Bradstreet would have said, that ran more "hobbling than is meet," his renderings continually reminded readers that the texts had their origins abroad. But in *Poets and Poetry of Europe,* the final assessment of Voss's translations, or at least of the theory that informs them, is quite positive, anticipating some of the comments Longfellow himself would later make about his own work as a translator: "whatever may be the defects of Voss's style as a translator, he at least led the way to a more close and faithful adherence to the original than had been common before his day. He was the first to show that the proper object of translating is, not to reproduce the work as it may be imagined the author would have written it, had he written in the language of the translator, but to reproduce it just as it is in the language in which the author actually wrote" (*Poets* 300). Translation isn't appropriation; it is an expression of, and a sign of respect for, linguistic and cultural differences.

Among the writers included in the section devoted to German poetry are Johann Jacob Bodmer, who took on Milton's *Paradise Lost,* and Christoph Martin Wieland, who translated twenty-eight of Shakespeare's plays. Carl Ludwig von Knebel, an "excellent translator," devoted himself to Propertius and Lucretius, while Friedrich Leopold Graf zu Stolberg, not to be outdone, tackled parts of the *Iliad* and four tragedies of Aeschylus and "many other miscellaneous works" (*Poets* 297). Predictably, many writers focused on the classics, because this seemed a great way of honing one's metrical skills (Schiller's poetic career began when, at the age of sixteen, he published a "translation of part of the 'Aeneid,' in hexameters," *Poets* 305). And recent authors weren't neglected either: Ludwig Theobul Kosegarten, for example, translated Richardson's *Clarissa,* and Adalbert von Chamisso, whose own "Peter Schlehmil" became famous in English translation, rendered Pierre-Jean de Béranger's poems into German. The Viennese poet Joseph Christian von Zedlitz translated *Childe Harold's Pilgrimage,* while the Swabian Gustav Pfizer, not content with translating "the greater part of Byron's poems," added "several of Bulwer's novels" to his repertoire (*Poets* 359). Longfellow's own future translator, Ferdinand Freiligrath, was no slouch either: he democratically brought his "remarkable skills" to bear on both William Shakespeare and Felicia Hemans and was currently occupied, the reader learns, "with a volume of selections from the American poets" (*Poets* 359). And, as the example of Friedrich Rückert, an "excellent translator from the Oriental languages," proves easily, these efforts were not limited to western literature (*Poets* 314). Many of these writers were comfortable enough to translate from more than one language, though few perhaps knew as many as Graf von Platen, who was fluent in "the Latin, Greek, Persian, Arabic, French, Italian, Spanish, Dutch, and Swedish languages" (*Poets* 349).

German poets were, of course, not the only ones who felt the urge to translate. Longfellow's favorite Dutch author, for example, the poet Willem Bilderdijk, knew "Hebrew, Arabic, and Persian" and translated from these three languages (*Poets* 394). In France, Clément Marot contributed to a translation of the psalms; Rémi Belleau translated the Odes of Anacreon as well as portions of the Old Testament; and Jean Antoine de Baïf produced French versions of Sophocles' *Antigone* as well as of Plautus and Terence. In Italy, Ippolito Pindemonte's first stab at literary fame was a translation of Racine's *Bérénice*. Some writers, like Adam Gottlob Oehlenschläger in Denmark or Gil Vicente in Portugal, wrote in more than one language anyway. And, at the other end of the spectrum, even lack of linguistic knowledge did not keep these poets from trying their hands at foreign texts. Longfellow's anthology records one rather serious case of translator's itch, Vincenzo Monti's rendition of the *Iliad*. "In executing the latter task, as he was ignorant of the Greek, he was obliged to avail himself of the existing literal translations, and of the able assistance which Mustoxidi, a Greek friend, disinterestedly rendered him" (*Poets* 607).

When *Poets and Poetry of Europe* was published, critics were quick to praise the "original design" of the collection and, especially, the service it provided to the linguistically challenged American reader: "Within a moderate compass, it gives him the means of gaining a connected view, and one as perfect as can be obtained without a knowledge of the original tongues, of the poetical literature which exists in ten languages."[37] Opinions about the translations Longfellow had picked were a bit more mixed. Some critics felt he had not done enough to acknowledge the role of translators. For information on who had translated a specific poem, the readers of Longfellow's anthology had to turn to a separate list of "Translators and Sources," an arrangement the *American Whig Review* found deeply unsatisfactory. It could "never be a matter of indifference to the reader by whom the version before him was executed," wrote the reviewer. And then he offered his own take on the process of translation: "Two elements enter into every translation: the author and the translator. If you would understand aright the nature of the compound, you must take into account both these elements." In fact, for better or worse, the translator was almost more important than the author. We're stuck with him (or her): "It is his influence which predominates. The compound takes its character chiefly from him." In Pope's version of Homer, for example, "the Greek is nothing—the Englishman everything."[38]

The *North American Review* presented a similar thumbnail sketch of the translator's role, but in more positive terms. The reviewer of *Poets and Poetry of Europe,* editor Francis Bowen, began by mocking those scholarly types who, brandishing the banner of word-for-word accuracy, still believed that a translator was merely a "literary slave," "a dealer in nothing but words," who had "no right to any ideas but his own," a meek merchant charged with importing goods from overseas, "allowing them to suffer as little as possible during the passage." He then developed his own theory, emphasizing the democratic potential of translations. American readers not conversant in foreign languages were entitled to English translations that could stand on their own as poems, to creative imitations rather than pale copies. Apparently, not all of Longfellow's selections in this anthology fulfilled Bowen's main criterion for a good translation—namely that the translator had to be a poet himself, whose "first purpose" was to produce "a beautiful English poem."[39]

Longfellow steered clear of such discussions. His own translations, several samples of which were included in *Poets and Poetry of Europe,* show that, above all, he wanted to produce a readable English text while also preserving as much of the "foreignness" of the original poem as possible. A successful example is his version of a little ballad by Gustav Pfizer, "Der Junggesell" ("The Two Locks of Hair"), essentially a story of how an irresponsible bachelor, besieged by a recurrent dream of family obligations in which he also begins to visualize the death of his imaginary wife and child, is inconveniently reminded of his own mortality. The first stanza gives a taste of Longfellow's approach:

> Ich bin ein leichter Junggesell
> Und wandre durch die Welt,
> Nomaden gleich, erbau' ich schnell
> Und breche ab mein Zelt.[40]

> A youth, light-hearted and content,
>   I wander through the world;
> Here, Arab-like, is pitched my tent,
>   And straight again is furled.
>   (*Poets* 359)[41]

Longfellow easily comes up with perfect equivalents for Pfizer's *abab* rhymes. The first line he translates freely (he omits any reference to the speaker being a bachelor and adds that he was "content") and the second very literally. He retains the final image of the stanza (which he then steals for a poem of his own, "The Day Is Done," discussed in chapter 1), though he also slightly modifies the syntax, changing a sentence in the active voice to the passive. Interestingly, he translates Pfizer's "Nomaden gleich" with the less accurate (and, at least for modern ears, stereotypical) "Arab-like," because he realized that the dark-sounding "nomad-like" would have interfered with the sprightly tone of the stanza. The result is both *literal* (Longfellow exactly reproduces Pfizer's alternation of eight-syllable and six-syllable lines) and *liberal*.

A somewhat more challenging text is "Wohin" ("Wither?") by the German Romantic Wilhelm Müller.[42] The poem paints an evocative scene in which a gushing brook induces a traveler to leave everything behind and follow its course, for reasons he doesn't fully understand himself:

> I heard a brooklet gushing
> From its rocky fountain near,
> Down into the valley rushing,
> So fresh and wondrous near.

In the fourth stanza, Müller puns on the double meaning of "Rausch," which signifies both the sound of the brook and a state of intoxication, an effect impossible to replicate in English: "Du hast mit Deinem Rauschen / Mir ganz berauscht den Sinn." With the fortuitously chosen verb "murmur," which brings nice alliterative resonance to his translation, Longfellow succeeds in giving readers a sense of the German poem's playfulness as well as a plausible explanation for the traveler's disorientation:

> Is this the way I was going?
> Wither, O brooklet, say!
> Thou hast, with thy soft murmur,
> Murmured my senses away.
> (*Poets* 349)

Longfellow did not subscribe to a single, coherent theory of translation. Neither as an editor of translations by other writers nor as a translator did he feel he had to sift the high from the low and the good from the bad. He approached foreign texts like Pfizer's "Junggesell" pragmatically, asking whether they were entertaining and interesting enough for his readers, but also with the firm conviction that neither complete foreignization (retention of a text's original features regardless of the problems it creates for the target language) nor relentless domestication (pretending that the text wasn't foreign at all) were the appropriate responses. He was, he said later, not "quite in favor of the Nessus-shirt style of translation, which clings so close to the original as to take all life out of it" (*Letters* 5:165).[43]

But he was also wary of translators who modified and assimilated their sources too much. Foreign texts needed to retain some of their strangeness even in English dress. "I feel sorry to lose any of the Homeric epithets, how often soever they may occur," he wrote to Sir John Frederick Herschel, son of the famous astronomer and an accomplished scientist in his own right, who had sent him a copy of his recent translation of the *Iliad* (August 2, 1867; *Letters* 5:165). Mistakes in translations, to him, were an even less pardonable sin because they unnecessarily impeded the process of cultural diffusion. He scorned translators who appeared to be not fully familiar with the language of their source texts, mocking, for example, the blunders made by Eliza Buckminster Lee in her translation of Jean Paul's *Flegeljahre,* in which an "angelic smile" ("englisches Anlächeln") had morphed into an "English smile."[44]

Longfellow's *Poets and Poetry of Europe* fared well with American readers. When the book was reprinted in 1855, the year Whitman's *Leaves of Grass* came out, a reviewer for the *United States Democratic Review* praised the editor for demonstrating that "the art of poetry . . . is confined to no race or country, to no theme or school." The flip side of the multinational coin was that Longfellow, the American editor of the anthology, had essentially vaporized himself in the process, the critic felt, "for he is as much English as American, and as much German as English." So immersed had Longfellow become in the literatures of the Old World "that it would be most miraculous if he retained any original or national characteristic."[45]

The reviewer had misunderstood Longfellow's goal. The purpose of *Poets and Poetry of Europe* was not to argue that there were no distinctions between cultures. Admire the similarities, Longfellow wanted to tell his readers, but go ahead and relish the differences too, abroad *and* at home. His sprawling collection, with its eight hundred densely packed, double-columned pages, encouraged Americans to adopt a point of view that, while respecting cultural differences, transcended all narrowly national, or national*ist,* considerations. The overarching point of view recommended by Longfellow is not the product of the work of any one translator, be she liberal or literal, but the cumulative result of all the translators' efforts taken together. And as we move beyond the limits of any one national culture, we will begin to be able to compare all of them, noting and respecting the unique features of each. Longfellow's term for such a perspective was, for lack of a better word, "American." For it would be a mistake to assume, as the *United States Democratic Review* did, that being American simply meant not being English or not being German. Be patient with America, Longfellow implored Frances Farrer of Scaleby Hall in Cumberland, England, in April 1855: "The idea, the meaning of America is very grand. She is working out one of the highest problems in the 'celestial mechanics' of man" (*Letters* 3:473).

Longfellow in Translation

A zealous editor of other people's translations, Longfellow took a hands-off approach to translations of works he had written himself. Admirers from all over the world vied for the right to import Longfellow's poems into their own languages. Translating Longfellow was not only the visible sign of their appreciation of the master's work, a labor of love that might gain them a seat at the master's table, it was also their chance to bask in the poet's glory and profit from his fame. Fanny Longfellow was told that on the day a German translation of "Excelsior" appeared in a Tyrolean newspaper, students in Innsbruck stopped the translator in the street and "embraced him and kissed him with such joy and transport that he looks upon that moment as the brightest and happiest of his life."[46]

Some hopeful translators even wrote in from abroad begging that Longfellow immediately mail them whatever new poems he had just written so that they could get to work on them. On April 10, 1878, for example, Angelo Dalmedico, the editor of *Canti del popolo veneziano* (1848) and *Proverbi veneziani* (1856), wrote to him from Venice, enclosing his "principal" translations of Longfellow's works ("I have not translated literally, because I would not estinguish [*sic*] any sparkle of my own poetical spirit"). Dalmedico owned the 1869 London edition of Longfellow and was "anxious to be informed" whether there were some more recent "beautiful things" from the master's pen that he could translate. The people of Venice were waiting. Three years later, Dalmedico wrote again, this time in Italian, imploring Longfellow to send him some as yet unpublished work, "because

I want to have as much as possible by you to translate." Would the "Maestro" please send a photograph, too?[47]

While Longfellow kept track of the translations of his work that had been completed or were still under way (they were, after all, the best confirmation he had of the broad appeal of his poetry), he refused to grant authorial endorsements. He answered freely the queries sent to him by his French translator Paul-Romain Blier, for example, but also told him that he could not, and would not, prevent any future French translations of his works: "There being no copy-right treaty between the two countries, I have no control in this matter, and some of my books have already been translated by other hands." A preface by him to Blier's work was out of the question: "if I interfered, I should be more likely to *mar* than to *make*" (February 10, 1862; *Letters* 4:265–66).

Longfellow did feel uneasy about translations of his works that sought to expunge any signs of foreignness. For example, he told Adolf Böttger that he was sorry to see he had omitted so many of the Indian names from his German translation of *Hiawatha*. Inevitably some of the "flavor of the forest" had been sacrificed (*Letters* 4:38). Longfellow knew, of course, that among contemporary translators such assimilation was indeed more or less the norm.[48] A case in point is the first Italian translation of *Evangeline*. Here, Pietro Rotondi had made every effort to "take the author to the reader," substituting Italian names not only for most American place names ("Misissipì" for "Mississippi"; "Terranuova" for Newfoundland) but for all other references that would have seemed "foreign" to the Italian reader. "Grand-Pré," for example, becomes "Granprato," the "Loup-garou" of the folk tales told by the notary is called the "lupo mannaro," and the old French songs sung by the Acadians appear now as "*I Borghesi di Chartres*" and "*Le Campane di Dunkerque.*"[49]

In his preface, Rotondi praised the "semplicità" (the simplicity) of Longfellow's tale. His translation was obviously intended to simplify the work even further. One example will suffice: when the grief-stricken Evangeline looks wistfully at the stars in the sky, Longfellow's narrator adds that most people have forgotten how to "marvel and worship" except when they see a blazing comet writing "Upharsin" on the temple's wall, a reference to Daniel 5:24–28. Rotondi, of course, would not have any of that strange Arameic in his text and refers to the writing on the wall merely as "minacciosa scritta," a "threatening inscription" (*Evangelina* 80).

One of Rotondi's successors in the flourishing field of Italian translations of Longfellow was the economist and literary dilettante Angelo Messedaglia, a member of the Italian parliament from 1866 to 1883 and the author of *Alcune poesie di Enrico W. Longfellow* (1866). In his preface to the volume, Messedaglia proudly described himself as a firm believer in the goal of fidelity ("fedeltà"). At the same time, he invoked for himself the right to all the liberties that came, he said, with a "poetic" approach to translation, as opposed to a mere "pedestrian" literalism.[50] Messedaglia's translations, indeed, give the Italian reader a rather specific version of Longfellow: a poet who is a natural ally in the cause of Italian freedom, a proponent of personal courage and collective liberty, a fighter, with the weapon of words, against slavery and political imperialism.

Fittingly, Messedaglia opens his collection with "Enceladus," a poem Longfellow wrote in February 1859 as a kind of "lament for the woes" of Italy, as he told Charles Sumner (the money the *Atlantic Monthly* paid him for publication went to the *Risorgimento* fighters).[51] Longfellow's central image here is the giant Encelados, buried under Mount Etna for his insubordination against the Olympians and now chafing, like Italy itself, at his chains.

Of the few overtly political poems Longfellow wrote, this is surely the most powerful:

> Ah me! for the land that is sown
>   With the harvest of despair!
> Where the burning cinders, blown
> From the lips of the overthrown
>   Enceladus, fill the air.
>
> Where ashes are heaped in drifts
>   Over vineyard and field and town,
> Whenever he starts and lifts
> His head through the blackened rifts
>   Of the crags that keep him down.
>
> See, see! the red light shines!
>   'T is the glare of his awful eyes!
> And the storm-wind shouts through the pines
> Of Alps and of Apennines,
>   "Enceladus, arise!" (3:66)

The fuming volcano, spreading its ashes over the land, preparing for the big fire-spewing, lava-throwing eruption that will follow, becomes a metaphor not just for the disastrous oppression of Italian independence but also for the bottled-up rage of the oppressed slaves in the United States—a connection that wasn't lost on Messedaglia, who also included Longfellow's "The Quadroon Girl" ("La Fanciulla Mesticcia") from *Poems on Slavery* in his selection.

Some of the success of Longfellow's "Enceladus" depends on his ability to represent myth in terms of the suffering of ordinary people. In Longfellow's poem, the giant with his fiery breath struggling to emerge from under the volcano is almost less interesting than the blackened fields and vineyards around the mountain, which condemn peasants to "a harvest of despair." The fact that the giant is represented only synecdochically, by references to body parts (his lips, his head, his eyes), puts the reader in the position of an eager yet terrified observer. In "Encèlado," Messedaglia deliberately emphasizes the nightmarish components of the scene. Where Longfellow's giant (a nameless "he" for most of the poem) merely breathes black dust over the landscape, Messedaglia's Titan literally vomits ("vomita") billows of hot black matter, darkening the sky ("Fa caligin dell' aere") and cluttering up the ground:*

> Ahi! per la Terra, ove un medesmo loco
>   Messi ministra e foco;
> Ove in nugoli negri il caldo cenere,
> Che dalle fauci vomita il Titano,
> Fa caligin dell' aere, e ingombra il piano . . .

Houses collapse under the weight of the lava he coughs up, and the mountain itself shakes as the giant moves his hips. When Enceladus is ready to emerge, eyes blazing, Messedaglia has Longfellow's storm-wind ("il turbine") receive some help from an earthquake, too ("la terra trema"). The concise exclamation that ends Longfellow's poem ("Enceladus, arise!") Messedaglia replaces with an unabashedly interpretive statement, in which the speaker addresses the giant directly and tells him that his hour has finally come. The two questions ("Vedi?" "Odi?"—"Do you see?" "Do you hear?"), followed by an emphatic imperative ("Sorgi!"—"Arise!"), add even more drama to a text that really isn't Longfellow's anymore:

---

* To avoid the awkwardness of retranslating into English texts that were originally written in English, my excerpts from the following translations are preceded by detailed paraphrases.

Vedi? In cielo divampa un rosso ardore:
  Dei tetri occhi è il bagliore.
Odi? Fremono l'aure, irrompe il turbine
Sull'Alpe e l'Apennin, la terra trema. . . .
—Sorgi! È giunta, o Titan, l'ora suprema.—
  (Messedaglia 2)

When Messedaglia revised his Longfellow translations for inclusion in *Alcune Poesie di E. W. Longfellow, Tommaso Moore ed altri* (1878), he offered a more literal version of the final stanza of "Enceladus," contenting himself with a mere gust of wind carrying the shout of revolution across the Alps and the Apennines instead of the meteorological catastrophe he had portrayed in the earlier version. In a note added at the bottom of the page, Messedaglia claimed that Longfellow's poem sounded as if it had been written at the time of the "spedizione dei Mille"—a reference to Garibaldi's force of one thousand freedom-fighting volunteers that landed at Marsala on May 11, 1860, and in less than three months conquered the entire island of Sicily, thus paving the way for the overthrow of the Bourbons and the union of southern Italy and Sicily with the north.

But Messedaglia went further and, with a confidence gained from historical hindsight, simply added a final celebratory line to Longfellow's last stanza noting that Enceladus had, in fact, "arisen" ("È sorto").[52] With this slight adjustment ("una leggiera infedeltà") he felt Longfellow's poem had been made even more resonant for Italians ("al caso nostro").

Upon receiving Messedaglia's book in 1866, Longfellow sent him one of his characteristically guarded letters, commending him for not "losing any essential idea or any salient point." Since Messedaglia, in the same letter, had so fulsomely praised Longfellow's Dante translation, Longfellow couldn't help pointing out that *there,* in fact, he had striven to tell, "to use the legal term . . . 'the truth, the whole truth and nothing but the truth'" (*Letters* 5:212).

Be that as it may, only one translation ever prompted Longfellow to intervene. In 1865, the French-Canadian poet Pamphile Le May (1837–1912) published his new translation of *Evangeline,* along with almost fifty of his own poems and translations of some shorter Longfellow poems, such as "The Children's Hour," "King Robert of Sicily," and "Weariness." When his *Essais poétiques* appeared, Le May was working as a translator for the Québec legislature—not such a good experience, apparently, because in his self-pitying preface he congratulated himself for pursuing his poetic dreams even in the tough environment of French Canada, where being a writer meant a life of deprivation and renunciation. How often had he envied those of his fellow countrymen, stronger and healthier than he, whose only purpose in life seemed to be the pursuit of wealth during the day and of personal happiness at night. Satisfied with the small pleasures in life, they weren't at the mercy of their vagrant imaginations, as the poet always is (Le May himself was fired from an earlier job at a store in Sherbrooke for excessive daydreaming). They'd never be caught on the bank of a brook, staring raptly at a flower, a tree, or an insect.[53]

Poets had little gain to expect for their efforts. Canadians didn't like to read and would rather borrow a book from a friend than pay money to support a man who had poured his heart's blood into writing. But then, wasn't he, as a writer, asked Le May, in an excellent position to do something good for his country? And here his translation of *Evangeline,* "une charmante poème de Longfellow," which conveniently enough was also a scathing indictment of British imperialism, became crucially important.

Motivated by a desire to see Longfellow's heroine return to her native country, Le May had undertaken a work that, if things went well, would make not only himself but also Canada and the French-Canadians look good. The glorious light emanating from his *Évangéline* would, he hoped, shine on his country, too.[54] Indeed, the political importance of Le May's translation cannot be overestimated. His *Essais poétiques* came out at a time when preparations for the union of British North America were in full sway and French-speaking Canadians were understandably concerned about the preservation of their cultural and linguistic distinctiveness in a new federal state. The struggle of the Acadians for survival in an Anglophone environment mirrored their own.[55] Five years later, Le May would publish an infamous poem glorifying the *métis* insurgent Louis Riel.

Le May's sense of ownership in Longfellow's poem was supreme. When he named his daughter, born the year he finished his translation, after Longfellow's demure heroine, he proudly announced that he now possessed "two Evangelines," his own child and the "Acadian poem" ("J'ai maintenant deux Evangelines, ma fille et le poème acadien").[56] When he finally wrote to Longfellow on September 9, 1865, Le May found it hard to contain his enthusiasm over his achievements. He claimed kinship with the author of *Evangeline,* a move that seemed to forestall even the slightest objection against his practices. While he was translating the book, he said he had felt the same sweet string vibrate in his heart that Longfellow had plucked on his lyre.[57]

Le May's confident claim to a share in the poem's authorship was not unfounded. As Longfellow discovered, Le May had indeed rewritten significant parts of his text. Perhaps the most blatant change came at the end, when Le May, sensing that his fellow citizens would prefer Evangeline the unhappy victim of British imperialism to Evangeline the pale icon of saintly endurance, made his heroine die as she was cradling Gabriel's head in her arms: "Elle avait terminé sa douloureuse vie!"[58]

Longfellow was not amused. But impressed (or perhaps intimidated) by Le May's apparent demand for co-ownership of his poem, he merely pointed out the infringement and then added, meekly, "I shall not quarrel with you about that" (October 27, 1865; *Letters* 4:514). Le May still got the message. The offending line, along with the emotional vision of Evangeline joining Gabriel in heaven "pour ne le perdre plus" ("so that she would never lose him again"), was scrapped in a new edition of the poem, which Le May published in 1870.[59] Now Longfellow was pleased: "I am glad to see that you have made the slight change" (December 24, 1870; *Letters* 5:390).

Looking at Le May's version in its entirety, one must admire Longfellow's restraint. Whether it is true or not that the English language secretly terrified Le May, as one of his friends, the poet Louis Fréchette, suggested,[60] he must have been hell-bent on transforming *Evangeline* into a French-Canadian poem. That there is a considerable difference between French-Canadian culture and the Acadian experience doesn't seem to have worried him at all (nor did it worry his fellow Québécois, who would soon pressure the few remaining Acadians to accept the fleur-de-lys flag).[61] Le May was no stickler for details. On a more formal level, his decision to convert Longfellow's mellifluous, enjambed hexameters into the meter popular with French poets since Pierre Ronsard, namely end-stopped, rhymed alexandrines, significantly affected the tone of the poem as a whole as well as its length. Longfellow's poem ends with line 1,399, whereas Le May needs thirty-two hundred lines to get the job done. Depending on one's point of view, there were some advantages to the change: Le May's end rhymes prettify the tale, giving it a concision and lilt the original arguably did not have. They also help to make individual lines more memorable. Just compare the heavy-handed ending of Longfellow's prologue with Le May's version of it: "List to the mournful tradition, still sung by the pines of the forest; / List to a Tale of Love in Acadie, home of the happy." Stripping Longfellow's exhortation of its archaisms as well as of its gloominess, Le May's rewriting provides a much more upbeat introduction to the story: "Ecoutez une histoire aussi belle qu'ancienne, / Une histoire d'amour de la terre Acadienne" ("Listen to a story as beautiful as it is old / A story of love from the land of Acadie").[62]

Perhaps buoyed by the realization that he was, in a sense, repatriating Longfellow's heroine, Le May felt authorized to make numerous changes throughout the text. He supplied tendentious epithets (while the Acadians are often referred to as "pauvres," the British soldiers, helpmates of cruel colonialism, are "féroces," "sinistres," and "sans honte") and, in some cases, added whole passages of his own invention that were meant to illustrate the predicament of the farmers of Grand-Pré. A particularly memorable example comes in the fourth section of part 1, where Longfellow likens the effect of the British commander's announcement that the Acadian men, assembled in the church of Grand-Pré, are now prisoners, to the devastating impact of a summer hailstorm on a farmer's fields. Longfellow's classically constructed epic simile begins with the comparing element, or vehicle, and supplies the tenor in the apodosis (or second part) of the period:

> As, when the air is serene in sultry solstice of summer,
> Suddenly gathers a storm, and the deadly sling of the hailstones
> Beats down the farmer's corn in the field and shatters his
>   windows,
> Hiding the sun, and strewing the ground with thatch from the
>   house-roofs,
> Bellowing fly the herds, and seek to break their enclosures;
> So on the hearts of the people descended the words of the
>   speaker. (2:47–48)

In Le May's busy hands, the storm assumes apocalyptic proportions. Rather than merely adopting Longfellow's image, he paints a picture of a parched summer landscape, littered with the withered leaves of flowers. From far away the clouds of a thunderstorm, inexorably growing in magnitude, begin to accumulate, frightening the sun away and blackening the sky. The ominous silence is interrupted only by the sound of the cicada. When the lightning and thunder come, the sky "vomits" fire (whence this obsession among Longfellow translators with metaphors of regurgitation?). "Spluttering whips" of rain and hail (Longfellow's "deadly sling") destroy everything that grows on the ground, as well as the windows in people's homes. Terrified, blaring cattle are driven out of their enclosures. After this long litany of destruction, when the original purpose of the comparison has been long forgotten, Le May allows the reader back inside the church again, where the confused villagers now appear like the fenced-in cattle themselves, reeling from the effect of the sinister words uttered by the "cruel, shameless" commander of the British invaders. Longfellow's image appears transformed into fact:

> En été quelquefois quand le soleil de juin,
> Par l'ardeur de ses feux dessèche les prairies;
> Que les fleurs des jardins, que les feuilles flétries
> Tombent, une par une, au pied de l'arbrisseau;
> Qu'on n'entend plus couler le limpide ruisseau;
> A l'horizon de flamme un point sombre, un nuage,
> Portant dans son flanc noir le tonnerre et l'orage,
> S'élève tout à coup, grandit, grandit toujours.
> Le soleil effrayé semble hâter son cours:
> Il règne dans les airs un lugubre silence:
> Le ciel est noir; l'oiseau vers ses petits s'élance;
> Et la cigale chante et l'air est étouffant;
> Le tonnerre mugit; le nuage se fend;
> Le ciel vomit la flamme; et la pluie et la grêle
> Sous leurs fouets crépitants brisent l'arbuste frêle,
> Et le carreau de vitre, et les fleurs et les blés.
> Dans un des coins du clos un moment rassemblés,
> Les bestiaux craintifs laissent là leur pâture—
> Puis bientôt en beuglant, ils longent la clôture
> Pour trouver un passage et s'enfuir promptement.
> Des pauvres villageois tel fut l'étonnement
> A cette heure fatal où le cruel ministre
> Eut sans honte élevé sa parole sinistre.
>
> (*Essais poétiques* 30–31)

Le May's embellishments of Longfellow's text mythicize rather than politicize the expulsion of the Acadians, making it appear like a force of nature. But they also enhance and dignify the reader's empathy with them. These poor farmers are not exotic relics from a remote past, reconstructed by the detached historian, but suffering fellow human beings and, more important, fellow Canadians.

Throughout his translation, Le May shows himself intent on eliminating all the details that would have stressed the text's strangeness or alienated a Canadian reader. A predictable instance occurs in the third section of the second part, where Basil the blacksmith praises his life on the prairie, welcoming the Acadian fugitives to a home "better perchance than the old one." Le May simply omits these words, framing Basil's comments on the fertile landscape he now inhabits with the assertion that the blacksmith's soul hasn't grown cold ("refroidie") toward his native country and that he still longs for the beautiful Acadia and his modest house he owned at Grand-Pré:

> "Je vous le dis encor: Soyez les bienvenus!
> "L'âme du forgeron ne s'est pas refroidie!
> "Il se souvient toujours de sa belle Acadie
> "Et de l'humble maison qu'il avait à Grand Pré!
>
> (*Essais poétiques* 76)

When Le May approached Longfellow in 1878, hoping that the famous poet could help him find an American writer interested in translating his novels, *Le Pèlerin de Sainte-Anne* (1877) and *Picounoc le maudit* (1878), he indirectly reminded him of their earlier correspondence. Self-consciously donning the part of the cultural relativist, Le May emphasized that his novels had been written entirely from the perspective of a Canadian or, even more important, a Canadian Catholic. He for one would be more than happy, he said, to implement any changes (or allow others to make them) that would render his books, "fidèles peintures des mœurs et de coutumes Canadiennes" (that is, "faithful pictures of Canadian mores and customs"), more acceptable for an American audience. As much as he wanted to hold on to *his* beliefs, he also deeply respected those of others, realizing that what pleased Canadians would perhaps raise eyebrows among Americans.[63]

Nothing came of Le May's plan. But one can imagine from Le May's comments here how justified he must have felt in making the changes he did in his translation of *Evangeline*. After all, he was not merely responding to the needs of a different audience (as he thought an American translator should in translating *his* novels). Rather, he was, literally, bringing an exiled text home to the land where he knew it really belonged.[64]

The extent of Le May's obsession with Longfellow's poem is evident from the fact that he revised his translation again decades later, essentially rewriting the entire text. In the 1912 version, the passage foreshadowing the Acadians' expulsion I discussed earlier has now been condensed from twenty-three to nineteen lines, moving the French text somewhat closer to the six lines of Longfellow's original. That said, the pale sun halting its course, the bird taking flight in the forest, the boat rushing to the safety of the shore, the leaf that has stopped turning in the still air—all details meant, of course, to prepare the reader for the coming of the storm—are fairly gratuitous additions to Longfellow's text:

> En été, quelquefois, après un jour serein,
> On voit, à l'horizon, un nuage s'étendre.
> Un grondement lointain se fait alors entendre,
> Et le soleil, pâli, semble hâter son cours.
> Tout s'agite un moment, tout cherche du secours,
> Puis tout se tait. L'oiseau sous la forêt s'envole,
> Et vers les bords ombreux s'élance la gondole.
> La feuille est immobile et l'air est étouffant.
> Mais voilà que soudain le nuage se fend,
> Le ciel vomit la flamme; et la pluie et la grêle,
> Sous leurs fouets crépitants, brisent l'arbuste frêle,
> Le chaume d'or des toits, et les fleurs et les blés.
> Alors les bestiaux se regardent troublés.
> Ils ont peur. Puis ensemble, oubliant la pâture,
> Ils s'élancent, beuglants, le long de la clôture,
> Pour s'ouvrir un passage et chercher des abris.
> Ainsi les villageois se regardent surpris,
> A cette heure fatale où le cruel ministre
> Ose leur faire part de cet arrêt sinistre.[65]

Interestingly, Le May now focuses on the Acadians' cattle, whose terror is evoked rather dramatically in the shortest sentence of the entire section (for which there is, of course, no equivalent in Longfellow): "Ils ont peur." The animals' frantic search for a way out of their pasture becomes a metaphor for the dehumanization of a people whose sufferings from the "monstrous crime" of their expulsion Edouard Richard, the author of the revisionist history *Acadia* (1895), revisited in his passionate "Préface" to Le May's new translation.

This time around, Le May admitted in a note to the reader at the beginning of the book ("A ceux qui me liront") that strict adherence to his source had never been his aim. Poetry will never let its wings get entangled in the snares of the literal, "*les terre à terre du* littéral." Besides, poems written in English tended to be more sober and less immediately appealing than works composed in French. Le May was confident he would be forgiven for all his changes. After all, all he had done was make Longfellow's lines sparkle in a form that, because more "lively," was also more congenial to the poem's subject matter. All he had done was prolong a bit his (and therefore the reader's) stay in the beautiful oasis into which Longfellow had led him. Somewhat recklessly, Le May predicted that the "immortal" Longfellow, whose dismay over Evangeline's premature death in his earlier translation he remembered well, would from his higher vantage welcome this new version of the "admirable poem" that Le May had made a permanent part of the pantheon of French-Canadian literature.[66]

Though written by an American, *Evangeline* had, in effect, become a French-Canadian poem. On November 6, 1947, the Montréal newspaper *La Presse* reported on a celebration honoring the centenary of the publication of *Evangeline,* organized by the Cambridge Historical Society at Longfellow's former residence on Brattle Street. Longfellow's grandson, Henry Wadsworth Longfellow Dana, and Le May's granddaughter, Cécile Saint-Jorre, were in attendance, along with several representatives of the Acadians from Louisiana, New England, and the Maritime Provinces. And it was clear where the focus was. When Mlle. Gaudet from Nova Scotia, costumed as Evangeline herself, sat down at Longfellow's piano and accompanied herself in some old Acadian songs, hardly an eye in the audience remained dry. "À ce moment, l'émotion était intense."[67]

Longfellow's *Evangeline* proved to be infinitely translatable. If Pamphile Le May thought that her real home was in Canada, Frank Siller, a grain merchant from Milwaukee, believed it belonged to the German Americans. In December 1877, Longfellow received a letter from Herr Siller, asking for "not exceeding an hour" of the poet's valuable time. Over the next five years, Siller kept in touch with Longfellow. He was a man on a mission: "Having as one of my aims the blending of the American with the German element of this country, I have always hailed with joy any good translation of poetry of either of these languages into the other, as a great help in that direction." Now the time had come to prove his mettle:

he was going to translate *Evangeline,* a poem that had given him much consolation on "sad days," into German.[68]

Siller, owner of the finest private library in Milwaukee, was advantageously placed for his self-elected ambassadorial task. Born in St. Petersburg to German parents, he had come to the United States in 1850, where he established himself in the shipping business in Dubuque and organized large grain deliveries "from the upper Mississippi *via* New Orleans, to Europe."[69] In 1873, Siller moved to Milwaukee, which, during those years, was widely known as "Deutsch-Athen," or the German Athens, because of the high cultural aspirations of its many inhabitants of German descent. In his memoirs, the German poet Friedrich Bodenstedt, who visited there in 1880 and was fêted as if he were royalty and the epitome of Old World cultural refinement, still remembered with envy the comfortable house, with a spectacular view of Lake Michigan, where Siller resided with his Scottish wife. In the mornings, Siller would ride into town to pursue his business deals; in the afternoons, he devoted himself to leisurely literary pursuits that included not only translations but also some original poetic works. Here is a characteristic excerpt from Siller's poem "The Song of Manitoba" (sound familiar?), which reveals that the hard-working merchant maintained a somewhat rocky relationship with the Muse: "Sound once more, thou harp of ages, the north wind tame thy strings, / To that gale which from the prairies nature's freshest fragrance brings."[70]

Siller's German translation of *Evangeline* was hardly the first to be made of Longfellow's blockbuster.[71] Either blissfully unaware of the efforts of his predecessors or determined not to be dissuaded from his lofty task, Siller, in his first letter to Longfellow, only mentioned Freiligrath, who, unaccountably, hadn't yet undertaken *Evangeline,* and Georg Herwegh, who had abandoned his plan to do so, "partly because he considered the hexameter in German much more difficult than in English, partly because he plunged too deeply into political life." Siller's casual name-dropping of course also portrayed him as a man privy even to unrealized plans and projects in the international community of German writers. Combining deference with a strong sense of entitlement, he immediately included some examples of his as-yet-unauthorized efforts:

> my love for the beautiful poem and the desire to see it translated into German, is so great, that I will attempt it, if you give me a word of encouragement. With that view I herewith send you my beginning (a

little more than the first canto). Please peruse and returning it, write me, whether I had better continue, or give up a work to which you may not consider me equal. Being *now* a merchant, I only have an occasional evening hour for the work, which thus will occupy several months, but it is a pleasant and instructive pastime to me. I also enclose a translation of the finishing lines of the poem.

Siller wasn't shy about letting Longfellow know precisely what kind of a translator he was going to be. Though he had promised to stay as close to the original text as Longfellow would require him to do, this was harder than he imagined: "Two lines in the first canto marked 'x' I was unable to translate with the same meaning they originally have and therefore substituted as well as I could." Any suggestions Longfellow might have, said Siller, "would be very gratefully received." On December 31, Siller wrote again to send return postage, which must have pleased Longfellow.

Siller's letters to Longfellow mixed serious concerns about literary translation with moments of high, if unintended, comedy. Often writing on stationery that advertised, in ornate Gothic letters, the nature of Siller's occupation, "Grain and Dressed Hogs a Specialty," Siller appeared in turn modest and self-confident, even cocky. A particularly amusing example is his attempt to denigrate the one previous translation of *Evangeline* that had been produced by a German American. The dubious Professor Karl Knortz, he claimed on January 15, 1878, had stolen the manuscript from an ex-convict known as Carl Rose, whose affidavit Siller included, along with Rose's manuscript of the entire translation (January 15, 1878). (In Rose's letter, Knortz is attacked, rather amusingly, as a "literarischer Saudieb," an invective branding the offender as, verbatim, a "thieving literary pig").

Confronted with such lurid evidence of rifts in the German American literary community, Longfellow must have resolved to do what, according to his son Ernest, he usually did best in difficult situations, namely nothing at all.[72] But he continued to take an interest in Siller's efforts. On February 12, 1879, he proposed that his enthusiastic translator reconsider two lines from the prologue and find a way of enjambing them ("Loud from its rocky caverns, the deep-voiced neighboring ocean / Speaks, and in accents disconsolate answers the wail of the forest"). His suggestion was: "Laut von den felsigen Höhlen, die dröhnende Stimme des Meeres / Spricht, und in Trauertönen des Urwalds Klage antwortet" (*Letters* 6:448). Not bad for an American. But Siller, who responded instantly (on February 16, 1879), wasn't too happy with Longfellow's use of the word "antwortet" (which translates Longfellow's "answers"). For reasons of metrical consistency, "antwortet" would have to be "wrongly" stressed on the second syllable, a practice admittedly widespread among the great old hexameter writers Klopstock, Wieland, and Goethe. But Herr Siller knew better: "with all due deference to these great masters, I cannot help saying, that, when read aloud, their verses containing such words sound somewhat forced." Siller's own version was, he was convinced, more fluent and conversational. Here the forest, instead of merely *responding* to the "deep-voiced" ocean, joins forces with it: "Während aus Felsen-Höhlen erschütternd die Stimme des Meeres / Dröhnt und dumpf sich vereint mit des Waldes düsterer Klage." (At least Siller had now enjambed the lines.) To deflect the impression that he was second-guessing the master himself, Siller explained that his ambition was to be like the meek copyist-painter Hilda in Hawthorne's novel *The Marble Faun,* that is, "to try to study and wed myself to the ideas of the author and then—to reproduce in that spirit *if possible.*"

On May 6, 1879, Siller sent Longfellow his completed *Evangeline,* hot off the presses (all proceeds were intended for "Mrs. M. F. Anneke's German school for young girls").[73] Unencumbered by the work of previous translators (whose books he asked Longfellow to send him only after he was done),[74] Siller felt he had taken a fresh approach to Longfellow's poem. In his preface, he outlined his own impressive qualifications for the job. He had, he said, traveled on the Mississippi and the Missouri in (take your pick!) a mackinaw, a birch-bark canoe, the hollowed-out trunk of a tree, and a Canadian *bateau.* He had camped on the steppes of Nebraska and roughed it in the "jungles" of the north, had smoked the peace pipe with Indian chiefs and had listened to the songs of their wives and daughters. What Longfellow had merely written about, Siller had soaked up with his own keen eyes and touched with his own eager hands—who in the world would be more qualified to translate *Evangeline,* "das wunderschöne amerikanische Gedicht?"[75]

Most of Siller's changes are tiny. Yet they are far from insignificant. A good case is his re-creation of the Acadian travelers' encounter with the intoxicating landscape of the Atchafalaya, where Siller himself had once, as he boasted in his preface, harkened to "the mysterious sounds" of the American wilderness. This is perhaps the closest Longfellow's heroine comes to a sense of fulfillment in the poem, as, inspired by the scents and sounds around her, she dreams about being reunited with Gabriel:

Faint was the air with the odorous breath of magnolia blossoms,
And with the heat of noon; and numberless sylvan islands,
Fragrant and thickly embowered with blossoming hedges of
   roses,
Near to whose shores they glided along, invited to slumber.
   (2:72)

Here is Herr Siller:

Schwül war die Mittagsluft, und der Duft der Magnoliablüthen
Wirkte betäubend fast. Unzählige, waldige Inseln,
Duftend und dicht überschattet von Dickichten blühender
   Rosen,
Welche das gleitende Boot fast berührte, lockten zum
   Schlummern.
   (Siller 56)

Each of Siller's lines ends with the exact German equivalent of the English
word found at the end of each of Longfellow's lines. Naturally, such correspondences can only be achieved by slight adjustments in vocabulary and
syntax elsewhere. Siller must have thought that Longfellow's imagery was
a bit opaque here: while it is easy to imagine the pervasive fragrance of the
magnolias filling the air, it is more difficult to see how the same air could be
made "faint" by the heat of noon. Siller's clever solution is to read Longfellow's sentence as a description of a psychological state rather than of a
natural fact. To this end, he transforms the first sentence of the passage
(before the semicolon) into two clauses. He breaks up the phrase "heat
of noon" and rewrites it as a sentence in its own right, combining the adjective "schwül" (stifling) and the compound noun "Mittagsluft" (midday
air), which fuses "noon" with the original subject of Longfellow's sentence
("air"). The reference to "faintness" comes in Siller's second clause. Only
then does he mention the near-intoxication induced in the travelers by the
odoriferous trees on the shore. Retranslated, Siller's lines would sound like
this: "Stifling was the midday air, and the scent of the magnolia blossoms
/ Seemed almost intoxicating."

Siller's declared goal was "to have the German reader touched by the
translation as the American reader is by the original" (January 3, 1877) and
so he diligently comes up with German equivalents for some of Longfel-

low's sound effects, such as alliteration ("*M*ittagsluft . . . *M*agnoliablüthen"; "*W*irkte . . . *w*aldige"; "*D*uftend . . . *d*icht . . . *D*ickichten"; "*B*oot . . . *be*-rührte"), internal rhyme ("Mittagsluft . . . Duft"), and consonance ("g*l*ei-*t*ende . . . *l*ock*t*en"). But the cleaned-up syntax of the passage also takes away some of the sensuousness that, arguably, rescues Longfellow's poem from a too-saccharine emphasis on male fortitude and female saintliness. In Siller's translation, some of the strangeness of Longfellow's *Evange-line*—a poem in Goethean hexameters about the confusing reality of the New World, with its displaced peoples, multiple cultures, and rich land-scapes, in which, yes, the stifling heat of noon may seem as palpable as the scent of flowers—is lost.

Instead of working to blend, as Siller's preface had promised he would and his own life suggested he could, elements from both the New World and the Old World, he reinvents *Evangeline* as a text that perhaps ought to have been written in German. Regionally specific terms are regularly purged from the text. "Coureurs-de-Bois" is translated as "Bewohner des Walds" (forest-dwellers), "Voyageur" as "wandernder Jäger" (nomadic hunter), and the "sweet Natchitoches tobacco" with which the blacksmith Basil, enjoying his new life in Opelousas, Louisiana, has learned to fill his pipe has turned into undefined "südlicher Taback" (southern tobacco).

Of course, Siller was perfectly entitled to his reading of *Evangeline,* as were Messedaglia and Le May. Like Miss Crannell, Mr. Hossein, and Mrs. Livingstone (the Longfellow readers discussed in chapter 1), they took from, and added to, Longfellow's poems what they thought was needed. The political activism of Messedaglia, the poetic patriotism of Le May, and the teutonic pedantry of Siller not only defined the overall purpose of their translations but also influenced the decisions they made about the smallest textual details.[76] Longfellow's approach to the translator's task was less emphatic: as a poet as well as a translator, Longfellow was more of a facilitator and less of an implementer, someone who made the Messeda-glias, Le Mays, and Sillers of this world possible. He felt that a translator, if need be, should also reproduce the original's mistakes,[77] a position that Herr Siller, for one, would have found unacceptable. What Longfellow and the grain-dealing merchant from Milwaukee would have shared, though, is an absolute commitment to customer satisfaction. Write to us, Siller's stationery announced in fancy typeface, "for an explanation of everything appearing to be unsatisfactory."

Diverse Lingue

"Too often," writes George Steiner, as if he'd known some Longfellow translators personally, "the translator feeds on the original for his own increase,"[78] heightening, overcrowding, or excessively dramatizing a text that, almost inevitably, then becomes his trophy. Longfellow's translation of Dante's *Divine Comedy* hardly seems made for that purpose. Accompanied by copious notes and supported by numerous additional readings (called "Illustrations") in the appendix, the volumes were the product of many years of detail-work and sacrifice: "How weary am I," wrote Longfellow, "of correcting, weighing, and criticizing my translation" (April 8, 1865).

He had begun perusing "the gloomy pages" of Dante's *Inferno* in Rome in midsummer 1828 (*Outre-Mer* 7:282). One of Longfellow's travel journals shows how directly his reading affected him. On December 11, 1828, he visited Rimini and filled his diary with melancholy musings about the sad fate of Dante's Francesca (fig. 42). Quoting Francesca's plaintive words from canto 5 of the *Inferno*, Longfellow pointed out the close relationship between the poet and his character ("C'est Francesca qui parle, et puis elle continue le récit, dans les paroles du poete [*sic*] 'come colui che piange e dice'")[79] and then added his own dramatic drawing of the fatal encounter between Paolo and Francesca's enraged, dagger-wielding husband Gianciotto.

Longfellow returned to the *Divine Comedy*, in earnest, for a series of lectures he gave at Harvard in the summer of 1838, when he said he could be found passing the hot days "upon a sofa, reading Dante's 'Inferno'" (May 17, 1838). In 1843, he began his translation of the *Purgatorio* (cantos 1 to 17), which he resumed again in February 1853, when he finished cantos 17 to 33. But it was only after Fanny's death in 1861 that he finally resolved to translate the entire work, as if Dante's quest for his beloved Beatrice now paralleled Longfellow's own longing for Fanny. Significantly, he began with the *Paradiso*, translating canto 20 to 33, as if he had become addicted, in little more than a month (cantos 1 to 19 were completed the next year, from February 1 to March 11, 1863).[80]

There were, of course, other reasons for Longfellow's interest in Dante. He went back to the *Divine Comedy* at a time when the country seemed to be falling apart. While he was hard at work on the *Inferno*, the first Con-

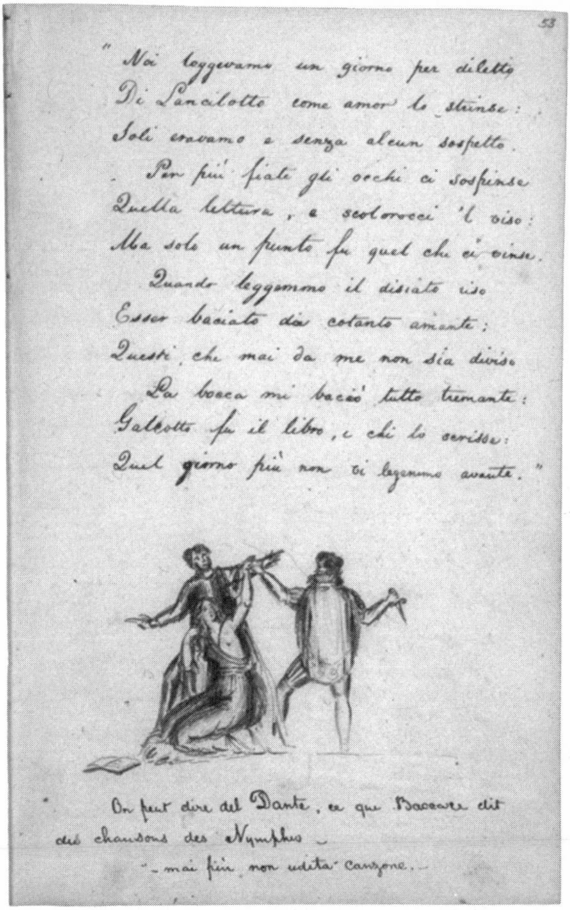

53

"Noi leggevamo un giorno per diletto
Di Lancilotto come amor lo strinse:
Soli eravamo e senza alcun sospetto.
Per più fiate gli occhi ci sospinse
Quella lettura, e scolorocci 'l viso:
Ma solo un punto fu quel che ci vinse.
Quando leggemmo il disiato riso
Esser baciato da cotanto amante;
Questi, che mai da me non sia diviso
La bocca mi baciò tutto tremante:
Galeotto fu il libro, e chi lo scrisse:
Quel giorno più non vi leggemmo avante."

On peut dire del Dante, ce que Boccace dit des chansons des Nymphes —
"— mai più non udita canzone.—

FIGURE 42

Longfellow, drawing of Paolo and Francesca, from Longfellow's 1828–29 Journal, Longfellow Papers, Houghton Library, Harvard University, MS Am 1340 (178). By permission of the Houghton Library, Harvard University.

scription Act was passed, sparking riots in working-class sections of New York, and the naval bombardment of Charleston Harbor began. Longfellow worked rapidly, translating a canto a day, for thirty-four days without a break. On the flyleaf of the volume into which he later bound the manuscript sheets of his translation, he noted, proudly: "Begun March 14. 1863. Finished April 16. 1863."[81] On May 4, Lee defeated the Union forces at Chancellorsville. Longfellow's *Purgatorio* was finished a little less than year later, on March 17, 1864, when Longfellow wrote in his journal: "Now I have the whole before me, of uniform style and workmanship." By then, Ulysses S. Grant had assumed command of the United States army.

For nineteenth-century Italians, the *Divine Comedy* was, of course, a highly political text. They saw it as a model of the unity that they desired for their own country. "Italy seeks here," claimed the patriot Mazzini about Dante's poem, "for the secret of her nationality."[82] Longfellow, too, was in awe of the Herculean proportions of Dante's self-imposed task to establish, amid the linguistic profusion of his country, a unifying *volgare illustre:* "The varieties of language common in this little corner of the world," he quoted Dante in *The Poets and Poetry of Europe,* "will amount to a thousand and even more." At the same time, Longfellow also knew that Dante's desire for a new common ground depended precisely on his recognition of the awesome diversity of his world. Dante's Italian, if firmly founded upon his native Tuscan, was "adorned and enriched by words and idioms from all the provinces of Italy" (*Poets* 502).

Even if the *Commedia* is technically not a multilingual work, it is certainly a book where people are identified by their different ways of speaking, their "diverse lingue" (*Inferno* 3), which include not only Arnaut Daniel's Provençal but also the Tuscan, Dante's own idiom. "I know not who thou art, nor by what mode / Thou hast come down here," says Count Ugolino of Pisa, now in the ninth circle of hell, to Dante, "but a Florentine / Thou seemest to me truly, when I hear thee" (*Inferno* 33; 9:183). Remember here, too, the mixture of garbled Greek and Hebrew spoken, in Hell's fourth circle, by Pluto ("Pape Satan, Pape Satan aleppe"; *Inferno* 7). When Virgil, in his first appearance, describes himself as being born "Sub Julio" or when, at the beginning of the last canto of *Inferno,* he warns Dante in Latin that the "banners of the King of Hell come forth" ("Vexilla Regis prodeunt inferni," 10:189, 366), the reader is reminded that the *Commedia* as a whole is itself an act of translation: literally, in that a classical poet is made to speak like a thirteenth-century Italian, as well as metaphorically, in that the speaker, for most of his journey, delivers himself into the hands of another writer, Virgil, whom he acknowledges as "lo mio maestro et 'l mio autore."[83]

A sketch of Virgil in the manuscript of Longfellow's *Voices of the Night,* directly inspired by one of John Flaxman's illustrations, shows the Roman poet in splendid isolation, his back turned to the viewer (fig. 43).[84] Dante was eager to please his master, Longfellow emphasized in a note he left in his working edition of the *Commedia,* next to a remark Dante makes to Virgil in *Purgatorio* 6—namely that they should hurry up since "e'en now the hill a shadow casts" (10:31). Longfellow had recognized immediately that this line was inspired by the ending of Virgil's first Eclogue ("And from the lofty mountains are falling larger shadows").[85] Mockingly, he compares the Virgil-imitating Dante to a modern poet besotted with the funereal gloom of Thomas Gray's poetry: "Dante never loses an opportunity of complimenting Virgil, by showing his acquaintance with his works, and quoting them. . . . As if we, walking with the shade of Gray, instead of saying 'It is growing late,' should say, 'The curfew tolls the knell of parting day.'"[86]

Not only as a character but as an author, too, Dante was both eclectic *and* original; his poem was both an individual creation *and* an imitation of older sources. This was the gist of an essay by Charles Labitte that Longfellow thought important enough to append, in French, to his translation of the *Paradiso.*[87] Dante's wanderings in search of Beatrice through the nine circles of Hell, the seven terraces of Purgatory, and ten heavens of Paradise are indeed also a voyage across a sea of preexisting ideas, concepts, and stories. The richly detailed notes Longfellow penned for his translation assiduously catalogue Dante's allusions to, and borrowings from, literary tradition, from Lucan, Ovid, Statius, Aquinas, and, of course, Virgil himself. But they also chart the afterlife of Dante's words, borrowings and "imitations" made, either consciously or unconsciously, by subsequent writers: the image of the sun "whitening" the night-chilled flowers with its beams, "imitated by Chaucer, Spenser, and many more" (*Inferno* 2); the description of the sunrise changing from vermilion to orange at the beginning of *Purgatorio* 2, "imitated" in Boccaccio's *Decameron;* the comparison of ghosts to "dead leaves" (*Inferno* 3), which reappears at the beginning of Shelley's "Ode to the West Wind"; Beatrice's reflections on the passing glory of childhood in *Paradiso* 28, resonating in Wordsworth's "Ode: Intimations of Immortality." The "illustrations" that follow Longfellow's notes offer generous excerpts ranging from Homer's *Odyssey* and an "Icelandic

FIGURE 43

Longfellow, drawing of Virgil (after John Flaxman),
from the manuscript of *Voices of the Night,* 1838–44,
Longfellow Papers, Houghton Library, Harvard University,
MS Am 1340 (73). By permission of the Houghton
Library, Harvard University.

Vision" of Paradise (from the *Edda*) to Ruskin's *Modern Painters* and James
Russell Lowell's article on Dante for the *American Cyclopaedia*. Dante's vast
poem thus appears embedded in a web of textual references, reaching
both back into antiquity and forward into the translator's own time.

If Longfellow's notes shift between the old and the new, his translation, neither too literal nor too liberal, likewise inhabits an intermediate space. Translating, which for him had a "great and strange fascination," was a deliberate exercise in self-abandonment: "It seizes people," wrote Longfellow to George Washington Greene, "with irresistible power, and whirls them away, till they are beside themselves" (March 7, 1879; *Letters* 6:455). In a way, Longfellow's *Divine Comedy* was never completely finished, was a process rather than a product. In February 1865, ten advance copies of the first volume of Longfellow's translation were privately issued in honor of the six-hundredth anniversary of Dante's birth. The three-volume quarto edition was finally published in the spring of 1867, but Longfellow never really stopped revising the text, making changes for subsequent printings, such as the smaller, more affordable octavo edition that appeared in 1870.

Characteristically, Longfellow's Dante translation was the result of vigorous collaboration. He welcomed the suggestions of the members of the "Dante Club" he had formed, a loose group of Italianophiles, including, at various points in time, James T. Fields, George Washington Greene, Oliver Wendell Holmes, William Dean Howells, James Russell Lowell, and Charles Eliot Norton. (This remarkable circle recently became the subject of Matthew Pearl's superb mystery novel *The Dante Club,* published in 2003). Longfellow and his collaborators met at Craigie House on Wednesday nights to review the proof sheets of the developing translation and to consume what Longfellow called "a little supper" (although the fact that his dog Trap was able to steal an entire partridge from the table—"that was his view of the *Divine Comedy*"—casts some doubt on that description).[88]

Howells has given us a memorable account of these meetings, which left him and perhaps also the frail Greene ("of lighter metal" than the rest) a bit intimidated.[89] But in spite of the combined expertise of the club members, Longfellow did not always accept their recommendations. And his manuscript drafts at Houghton Library show traces of the lively debate he had carried on with himself even before submitting it for the judgment of his peers.[90]

Poised between the past and the present, between different languages and cultures, Longellow's *Divine Comedy* is not simply an approximation, in another language, of a forever-elusive original. But neither does it stray far enough away from Dante's text to establish itself as independent from it, as a recreation in a seemingly new form. Certainly, Longfellow took some liberties with Dante's text. Perhaps most obviously, he sacrificed the terza rima. But this came less from the desire not to have his rendition, in Nabokov's unkind phrase, "begrimed and beslimed by rhyme," than from sheer expediency.[91] "In translating Dante," Longfellow wrote in his journal, "something must be relinquished." The question wasn't *if* but *what*. "Shall it be the beautiful rhyme, that blossoms all along the lines, like honeysuckle in a hedge? I fear it must, in order to retain something more precious than rhyme, namely, fidelity—truth—the life of the hedge itself" (May 7, 1864). Like William Michael Rossetti, whose translation of the *Inferno* had appeared in 1865, he reproduced Dante's meter as rhymeless English blank verse, hoping that this would allow him to follow the Italian text, as Rossetti said, "sentence for sentence, line for line, word for word."[92] At least he wasn't substituting a new, different form for the one he couldn't reproduce, as the Boston dentist Thomas William Parsons had done in his translation of the *Inferno,* in which he replaced Dante's terza rima with decasyllabic quatrains.[93]

The changes in Longfellow's manuscript show, at first sight, conflicting impulses. Sometimes fluency seems to have been the goal, and Longfellow wanted to simplify a passage without losing its beauty. "Her eyes were shining more than any star" ("Lucevan gli occhi suoi più che la stella") in *Inferno* 2 became "Her eyes were shining brighter than the stars," a line that has the same number of syllables as the previous version but sounds more idiomatic in English, though it does sacrifice one feature of Dante's text, the use of the singular ("la stella") for the plural.[94] At other times, Longfellow exchanges an obsolete or awkward word for a more common one. The "depicted people" in *Inferno* 23 (a reference to the Hypocrites in the eighth circle of hell) are now called "a painted people"; the "calid Nile" in *Paradiso* 6 becomes the "hot Nile"; and the "dulcet zephyr" in *Paradiso* 12 the "sweet west wind." Note also the substitution of the stilted "Behold, Briareus perforate by the dart" with the more readable "I saw Briareus pierced through by the dart" (*Purgatorio* 12), though the new phrase admittedly displays less of the immediacy and concision of the Italian original ("Vedeva Briareo fitto dal telo," Dante 3:90). Longfellow must have recognized the problem: "I saw Briareus *smitten* by the dart" is the version that made it into print (10:62).

On occasion, Longfellow seems to have started out with an extremely literal version, which he then gradually smoothed out. In *Purgatorio* 2, lines 67–69, for example, Dante describes the extraordinary moment when the other souls arriving in ante-Purgatory recognize that he is not one of them:

> L' anime che si fur di me accorte
> Per lo spirar, ch' io era ancora vivo,
> Maravigliando diventaro smorte
>> (Dante 3:16)

> The souls, who were aware concerning me,
>> By drawing breath, that I was still alive,
> ~~Colorless~~ Cadaverous with astonishment became.[95]

Longfellow cleans up the convoluted relative clause of his first draft and produces an English version that makes more sense than the somewhat misleading causality introduced here by other translators (according to W. S. Merwin, for example, the souls "marveled *so that* they became deathly pale").[96] Yet he also retains a sense of the importance of the occasion, and his choice of a verb ("draw breath"), which Longfellow kept for the published version, underscores the almost clinical look Dante receives here, in a world where something as ordinary as breathing becomes a mark of otherness:

> The souls, who had, from seeing me draw breath,
> Become aware that I was still alive,
> Pallid with utter wonderment became.

A passage from the *Purgatorio,* in which Dante comments on his need to use language sparingly when describing what he saw in the Earthly Paradise (29, lines 97–99), went from a rather choppy, if fairly close, translation to a version that is a marvel of linguistic economy. Longfellow had originally written:

> To trace these forms I will no farther squander
>> Reader, my rhymes for other spendings press me,
> So much, in this I cannot liberal be.[97]

> A descriver lor forme più non spargo
> Rime, lettor; ch' altra spesa mi strigne
> Tanto che 'n questa non posso esser largo;
>> (Dante 3:224)

In the new version, Dante's dramatic line break, which draws attention to the economic metaphor ("spargo / rime"), has found a suitable equivalent in English. At the same time, the cleaned-up syntax also helps tighten Longfellow's blank verse:

> Reader! To trace these forms no more I waste
> My rhymes; for other spendings press me so,
> That I in this cannot be prodigal.

A particularly elegant change takes place in *Paradiso* 8, lines 55–57, where Charles Martel of Anjou reflects on what would have become of his friendship with Dante had he but lived:

> Much didst thou love me, hadst good wherefore;
> For if below I had been, I had shown thee
> Of my affection farther than the leaves.[98]

> Assai m' amasti, e avesti bene onde;
> Che s' io fossi giù stato, io ti mostrava
> Di mio amor più oltre che le fronde.
> (Dante 4:316)

In his revision, Longfellow sheds needless verbiage in vocabulary and syntax ("good wherefore"; "if below I had been") and adds a beautiful metaphor, "the foliage of my love," which arguably strays from the original—more so, for example, than the subtle phrase "the green leaves of my love" chosen by modern translator John Ciardi.[99] But then Longfellow also recognizes that this is an emotionally tense moment for Dante, fraught with memories of what might have been yet never came to pass:

> Much didst thou love me, and thou hadst good reason;
> For had I been below, I should have shown thee
> Something beyond the foliage of my love.

Not all of these "fluency edits" survived Longfellow's own vetting or the input of the Dante Club. A case in point is Jacopo del Cassero's "Quindi fu' io" in *Purgatorio* 5, originally rendered as "From thence was I." Longfellow changed the sentence to "I was from there" in the manuscript before he went back again to the earlier, clumsy version, apparently because it more closely resembles the syntax of his source text (where the pronoun comes last). The truth is that not all of Longfellow's alterations in the manuscript make the text easier to read. Perversely, many of them create more difficult readings, by twisting the structure of a sentence or complicating the vocabulary. At times, Longfellow even sounds like Emil Jannings's poor Professor Immanuel Rath from the movie *The Blue Angel*. For example, the "fear that from her sight proceeded" ("la paura ch' uscia di sua vista"), a description of Dante's shocked reaction to the she-wolf impeding his ascent in *Inferno* 1, turns into "the affright that from her aspect came"; the lamb that "leaves the milk / of its own mother" in *Paradiso* 5 changes to the lamb "that of its mother / Leaveth the milk" ("that doth abandon / Its mother's milk" in the published version).

Longfellow's predecessor at Harvard, George Ticknor, in a perceptive letter to Longfellow written on June 1, 1867, focused on the strange combination of "extraordinary strictness" with "grace and fluency" that he had noticed in Longfellow's translation. What had especially intrigued Ticknor was Longfellow's attempt to follow Dante's original line for line and, almost, word for word: "Whether you have not encumbered yourself with heavier and more embarrassing conditions than permit the free poetical movement which an absolutely English reader covets, is a question that must be settled by the popular voice, as separate from that of scholastic lovers of Dante. On that bench of judges I can never be competent to sit; I shall always read your translation with the original ringing in my ears" (*Life* 3:90–91). But this is perhaps what Longfellow really wanted— to expose the monolingual American reader (Ticknor's "absolutely English reader") to a text that was "English plus" rather than "English only."[100] Put differently, he had no interest in offering his readers what a contemporary British reviewer of Dante translations once demanded: "a great English poem for the great Italian."[101]

One might object that with his Dante translation Longfellow had finally decided to leave the average reader behind, renouncing poetry as a public idiom (the "field of large-scale production," as Bourdieu would have called it) and catering only to the interests of his peers, such as the distinguished members of the Dante Club.[102] But such a reading would miss the point of Longfellow's project. The festivities surrounding Dante's birthday had reminded Longfellow that in Italy the *Divine Comedy* was not a "high culture" artifact. There, as Giuseppe Mazzini put it, "even the common people who cannot read know and revere his name."[103] In the country whose blossoming sense of a national identity his work had helped to shape, Dante, the prophet of the *Risorgimento,* commanded the kind of broad cultural appeal that no American writer had yet enjoyed.[104] In giving his readers an American version of the *Divine Comedy,* Longfellow also gave them a possible model of a future, truly public American poet. The success of his translation proved him right. The publication, in 1867, of the three-volume quarto edition, expertly marketed by James Fields, became one of the literary events of the season. Longfellow's *Divine Comedy* went through four printings in its first year of publication. In 1871, a one-volume edition came out, priced at $3.

Longfellow believed, as he wrote in an unpublished note, that one of the "greatest fallacies in translation is to give, not what the author really said, but what you suppose he would have said, if he had been writing in your language."[105] Long ago, in his Harvard lectures, he had claimed that all poets should be read in their native language ("It is almost mockery . . . to translate them").[106] Now, in his new Dante translation, the Italian language remained always present, at least as a point of reference. Some words Longfellow obviously chose because they directly echo words used in the Italian text, for example "dolent" for "dolente" in *Inferno* 3, "volition" for "voler" in *Inferno* 5, "champaign" for "campagna" in *Inferno* 24, "lucent" for "lucenti" in *Purgatorio* 15. In view of the many words of Romanic origin in the text, one of Longfellow's reviewers, John Fiske, claimed that an ordinary reader not familiar with the original Italian would in fact not know what to do with Longfellow's translation.[107] Such misgivings seem even more relevant when we discover that, on a few occasions, Longfellow retained Italian words even in his English text. For example, when Dante mentions the difficulty of expressing in the same language used by Italian children what he has seen in the lowest circle of Hell, Longfellow reminds the reader of just what language this is: "For 't is no enterprise to take in jest, / To sketch the bottom of all the universe, / Nor for a tongue that cries Mamma and Babbo" (*Inferno* 32; 9:178).

The Houghton manuscript reveals that Longfellow's choice of the original Italian words ("mamma e babbo") was intentional; the line at first read: "Nor for a tongue that says 'Mama, Papa.'" Other translators are remarkably less finicky here. William Michael Rossetti, in his "unconditionally" literal blank verse translation, opts for the colloquial English terms, which do indeed offer a nice contrast with the elevated and complicated beginning of the sentence but also substitute an obtrusively English frame of reference for the foreign one that he had vowed to preserve in the preface to his translation: "'tis no jesting matter to set down/ The fathomings of all the universe, / Nor for a tongue which Mammy calls and Dad."[108] John Ciardi's free translation, "tongues that only babble child's play," seems little better here than the solution offered by Longfellow's popular British predecessor, Henry Francis Cary, which probably inspired Ciardi's lines ("to describe the depth / Of all the universe . . . demands a tongue not used / To infant babbling").[109]

Robert Pinsky's recent attempt to translate this passage, on the other hand, comes remarkably close to Longfellow's proposal: "It is not jokingly that one begins / To describe the bottom of the universe—/ Not a task suited for a tongue that whines // *Mamma* and *Dadda*."[110] "Bottom" (the word Longfellow had chosen!) works much better as a translation of the Italian "fondo" than Rossetti's "fathomings," and the baby talk Pinsky uses captures at least some sense of the irony behind Dante's reminder that Hell isn't a place for wimps. A translator's worst mistake, said Walter Benjamin, is refusing to let his or her work be affected by the foreign language.[111] The reader of Longfellow's *Divine Comedy*—especially Fiske's reader "ignorant of the original Italian"—is rarely allowed to forget that she is reading a poem that came to her from abroad. Longfellow's *Divine Comedy* is a product both of America and of Italy, "the fair land . . . where the *Sì* doth sound," as Longfellow translated, in an appropriately bilingual phrase, Dante's reference to Italy in *Inferno* 33 (9:185).

As his early lecture on Dante reveals, Longfellow was generally more interested in Dante's poetry than in his theological allegory. For him, the *Commedia* was first and foremost a travelogue: "the beautiful description of the landscape," he once said, "bears the freshness of that impression, which is made on the mind of a foot-traveller, who sits under the trees at noon, and, leaves or enters towns when the morning or evening bells are ringing" (Dante Lecture 52–53). Such freshness of sight and insight he found especially in Dante's luminescent *Paradiso*. The spirits in Paradise are "clothed in light," Longfellow marveled. "Pulsations of sound and brightness," they appear as "the flashing of the sun upon the sea" and upon "precious stones" (Dante Lecture 83).

This admiration for the "steel-like polish" of Dante's language remains palpable in Longfellow's translation of these cantos. Take, for example, the beginning of canto 30, the description of Dante's ascent to the Empyrean (11:153). The poet begins with an extended metaphor for the morning breaking over Italy while it is already noon—the "sixth hour"—in India. Proving George Ticknor right, Longfellow closely follows Dante's syntax. Where he is forced to change the sequence of the words (as happens in line 4), he tries to make sure that at least some of his enjambments occur where Dante wanted them to be; see lines 5–6, where the line break "star / Ceases" exactly mirrors the Italian "stella / perde." Many of Longfellow's corrections in the Houghton manuscript (fig. 44) seem intended to make the correspondence even closer. Note, for example, line 3, where Longfellow replaces his original version, "Almost a horizontal shadow casts," with a line that matches the placement of the words in the Italian original, "Inclines its shadow almost to a level," choosing a verb, "inclines," which resembles the Italian "china" (*Paradiso* manuscript, 297–98). John Ciardi,

FIGURE 44

Manuscript page (p. 297) from Longfellow's translation of Dante's *Paradiso,* Longfellow Papers, Houghton Library, Harvard University, MS Am 1340 (113). By permission of the Houghton Library, Harvard University.

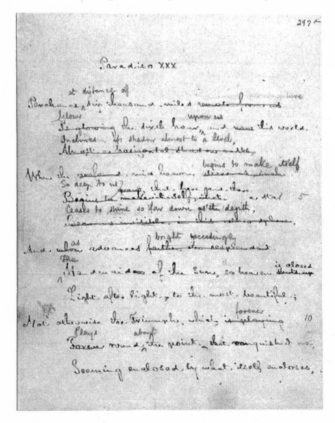

intent on rescuing at least some of Dante's rhymes for his translation, introduces a new and confusing metaphor ("the bed") here, which interferes with what Dante's passage is all about, namely the imminence of change, as Dante progresses toward the light that is God: "When, as may be, the sun's noon heat is shed / six thousand miles away, while, where we are / earth's shadow makes an almost level bed."[112]

Even Longfellow's archaisms serve a specific, strategic purpose. He made a point of defending them in his debates with the members of the Dante Club, as the Ohio journalist J. H. A. Bone confirmed, who was invited to sit in on one of the meetings.[113] Arguably, one of the most powerful moments in the *Inferno* comes at the end, when Dante and Virgil, climbing over the devil's hairy flank, emerge from Hell. "E quindi uscimmo," remembers Dante, "a riveder le stelle." Allen Mandelbaum translates this passage soberly, splitting Dante's beautiful line in two: "It was from there / that we emerged, to see—once more—the stars."[114] The "once more" seems pale, mundane, as if Dante had just come back from a trip to the store. In Longfellow's version, "Thence we came forth to rebehold the stars" (9:193), the verb "rebehold" might sound stilted, but it conveys well the excitement as well as the gravity of the experience, while it also—since it has the same number of syllables and the same initial consonant—retains a noticeable trace of the Italian original, "riveder." (When Longfellow finished his translation of *Inferno* 34, on April 16, 1863, at one o'clock in the afternoon, as he noted on the manuscript, his own exhilaration is mirrored in his double underlining of the final word, "*Stars.*")

Seen in this light, the linguistic infelicities Newton Arvin has noticed in Longfellow's translation can also be read as an intentional attempt to defamiliarize the text, to remind the reader that she is, in fact, reading not a Longfellow poem but a translation from another language, a work that is neither Italian nor English yet both. "Siede la terra dove nata fui," begins Francesca da Rimini's tearful account in *Inferno* 5, "Su la marina dove 'l Po discende / Per aver pace co' seguaci sui" (Longfellow underlined the passage in his edition; Dante 2:280). In Longfellow's reworking, the striking rhythm of the passage, descending down the lines as the river Po flows into the ocean, is subtly preserved: "Sitteth the city, wherein I was born, / Upon the sea-shore where the Po descends / To rest in peace with all his retinue" (9:46). That said, his "Sitteth" will strike some readers as needlessly ponderous. Even William Michael Rossetti, master of the deliberately odd phrase, opted for a simpler translation here: "The territory I was born in sits . . ."[115] But it seems likely that Longfellow *wanted* to sound archaic here; the manuscript (fig. 45) shows that he at first wrote "descendeth," too, though he subsequently changed his mind, perhaps to preserve a regular iambic meter. Why, then, did he keep "sitteth"? If we read the line aloud, first in the original and then in English, we'll discover that the two syllables of Longfellow's verb make it a much more effective reminder of the Italian "siede" than the comparatively lackluster "sits." One could object, too, that the rendering of the "terra" Ravenna as "city" in the same line is arbitrary and even historically incorrect—Rossetti was right, Francesca's birthplace, Ravenna, was in fact a "territory." But the crisp noun "city" is a better match for the Italian "terra" (and doesn't it also help Longfellow create a rather effective echo with "sitteth"?). Finally, the alliteration of "rest" and "retinue" in line 99 (the latter word is more suitable here than Longfellow's original choice, "followers," because of its connotations of nobility and dignity) captures some of the cohesiveness created in the original Italian by the internal rhyme of "pace" and "seguaci."

In this passage, Francesca, who is entranced with the language of courtly love, describes herself as a devotee of exactly the kind of absorptive, escapist reading that, according to his less sympathetic critics, Longfellow's poetry encouraged, too ("One day we were reading for our delight"). The book that she and Paolo read, the Old French romance *Lancelot of the Lake,* is eye-opening: they now understand they are in love with each other. In a very literal sense, poetry here *does* make something happen. Yet her account of her reading experience shows that Francesca herself is an author, not just a passive consumer of literary goods. She is a sentimental *poet* too, skilled at manipulating her audience: her words have the effect of making Dante swoon. It seems only fitting, then, that Longfellow should have given her such richly resonant lines.

From his early journal entry in Rimini on, Longfellow felt strangely drawn to this thirteenth-century lover. On occasion he even identified with her. Arguably, Francesca's identificatory reading experience is what landed her in Hell, but her ability to vocalize her suffering transcends all limitations of time and place. In the years after his wife's death, Longfellow would commemorate May 10, the anniversary of the day in 1843 on which Fanny sent him a note accepting his love, by copying into his journal Francesca's famous reply to Dante: "nessun maggior dolore / Che ricordarsi del tempo felice / Nella miseria." Or, as he translated the passage in 1863, "There is no greater sorrow / Than to be mindful of the happy time / In

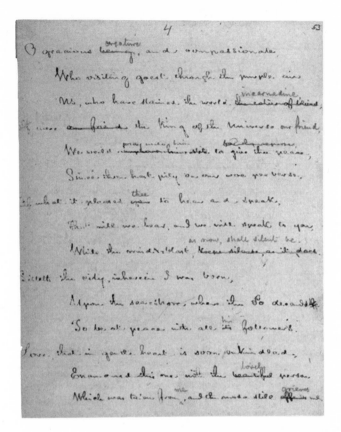

Manuscript page (p. 53) from Longfellow's translation of
Dante's *Inferno*, Longfellow Papers, Houghton Library,
Harvard University, MS Am 1340 (111). By permission of
the Houghton Library, Harvard University.

misery" (9:47). The phrase "the happy time" is heartbreaking in its simplicity. Longfellow liked Francesca's speech so much that he echoed it at the
beginning of one his most personal poems, "My Lost Youth" (discussed
in chapter 2), in which he nostalgically evoked his own birthplace: "Often I
think of the beautiful town / That is seated by the sea." As translation becomes creation, the boundaries between the "original" and its "imitation"
in another language begin to blur, and we are whirled away.

EPILOGUE

In a sequence of sonnets titled "Divina Commedia," written while he was working on his Dante translation, Longfellow compared himself to the laborer who enters a dark cathedral and, "far off the noises of the world" and "the loud vociferations of the street," kneels down to pray. Dante's vast poem, "this medieval miracle of song," is likened to the old cathedral itself, where birds build their nests in strange sculptures and "fiends and dragons" watch over the dead Christ. The past is the past.

Or is it? In the course of Longfellow's sequence, an imperceptible change takes place and the dark interior brightens. Dante, the author of the *Divine Comedy,* appears "in the gloom of the long aisles." He is no longer Virgil's docile disciple. A mentor in his own right, he guides the reader toward an apotheosis that ultimately becomes the apotheosis of literature itself, as the lines of the *Divine Comedy* cross national boundaries and are heard and repeated everywhere, by everyone in his or her own language:

> The voices of the city and the sea,
> > The voices of the mountains and the pines,
> > Repeat thy song, till the familiar lines
> > Are footpaths for the thought of Italy!
> Thy fame is blown abroad from all the heights,
> > Through all the nations, and a sound is heard,
> > As of a mighty wind, and men devout,
> Strangers of Rome, and the new proselytes,
> > In their own language hear thy wondrous word,
> > And many are amazed and many doubt. (3:150–51)

All of Longfellow's themes as I have discussed them in this book are present here: the notion that literature has the power to comfort and console, turning strangers into friends; the fascination with literary tradition, which supersedes any individual attempt at authorial self-assertion; the conviction that literature and travel are connected and that words from abroad can give us a better sense of the true meaning of home.

Longfellow returns to an image he used in his first book, the travel narrative *Outre-Mer:* the cathedral built by architects whose names, if anyone remembers them at all, are less important than the structures they have left us. And again he can't resist a quotation. The allusions to the Pentecostal wonder described by Luke in Acts 2 are obvious: the "men devout" ("from every nation under heaven," as the Bible says), the visitors from Rome, and the "new proselytes" hear Dante's words, each "in their own language." Longfellow had his reasons for choosing this particular source—the one passage in the New Testament that reimagines, and then turns upside down, the disaster of Babel, where the human tower-builders had wanted to "assure themselves, by themselves" of their uniqueness and instead found themselves scattered over the face of the earth, unable to understand the words used by their neighbors.[1]

As Longfellow must have realized, Luke could have imagined the event very differently. For example, he could have simply enabled each and everyone present to suddenly understand Aramaic. Instead, he made the spirit's message instantly accessible in the different languages of all the assembled people, thus effectively endorsing the confusion of tongues that Genesis suggests was such a tragedy.

Babel broke, in the stern words of Harvard professor Barrett Wendell, "every common bond of kinship." Everywhere except in America, wrote Wendell in his *Literary History of America,* published at the turn of the last century. America wasn't Babel. Here, "the races which should hold together through the centuries sprang afresh from men who newly spoke and newly thought and newly felt in terms of a common language," which Wendell triumphantly identified as "this English of ours."[2] Out of many languages, one. But, as his last Dante sonnet tells us, Longfellow's interpretation of what he saw as the American experiment in the "celestial mechanics of man" was different. He knew that a nation, to avoid insularity or xenophobia, must always remain capable of "imagining itself otherwise." Out of the many, many.[3] In Longfellow's hands, the Pentecostal pouring out of the spirit that enabled the apostles to speak in tongues turns into a joyous scene of instant translation, an acknowledgment of the never-ending, exciting, exhilarating diversity of the world, democratically shared by authors and readers alike.

NOTES

Introduction

1. Bruce Wexler, "Poetry Is Dead. Does Anyone Really Care?" *Newsweek,* May 5, 2003, 18.

2. See, for example, Edmund Wilson, "Is Verse a Dying Technique?" in Wilson, *The Triple Thinkers: Ten Essays on Literature,* rev. ed. (1938; New York: Harcourt Brace, 1948), 15–30; Joseph Epstein, "Who Killed Poetry?" *Commentary* 86, 2 (1988): 13–20; Dana Gioia, *Can Poetry Matter?* (New York: Graywolf, 1992).

3. A sentence from A. E. Housman, "The Name and Nature of Poetry" (1922), mocked in Cleanth Brooks, "The Formalist Critics" (1951), in *The Norton Anthology of Theory and Criticism,* gen. ed. Vincent B. Leitch (New York: Norton, 2001), 1368.

4. Karen Matthews, "A Once Unthinkable Collaboration," Associated Press News, February 4, 2002.

5. Dana Gioia, "Disappearing Ink: Poetry at the End of Print Culture," *Hudson Review* 56, 1 (Spring 2003): 21–50.

6. November 12, 1835, in *The Diary of George Templeton Strong: Young Man in New York, 1835–1849,* ed. Allan Nevins and Milton Halsey Thomas (New York: Macmillan, 1952), 113–14.

7. Charles Dickens to James Fields, July 7, 1868; James T. Fields, *Yesterdays with Authors* (Boston: Osgood, 1872), 191.

8. Virginia Jackson, "Longfellow's Tradition; or, Picture-Writing a Nation," *Modern Language Quarterly* 59, 4 (December 1998): 471–96, and Dana Gioia, "Longfellow in the Aftermath of Modernism," in *The Columbia History of American Poetry,* ed. Jay Parini (New York: Columbia University Press, 1993), 64–96.

9. From Wallace Stevens's "Adagia," in Stevens, *Collected Poetry and Prose,* ed. Frank Kermode and Joan Richardson (New York: Library of America, 1997), 906.

10. Albert J. von Frank, "Henry Wadsworth Longfellow," in *The Reader's Companion to American History,* ed. Eric Foner and John A. Garraty (Boston: Houghton Mifflin, 1991), 679–80.

11. Steven Shapin, "Personal Development and Intellectual Biography: The Case of Robert Boyle," *British Journal for the History of Science* 26 (1993): 345.

12. Mary Chapin Carpenter, "This Is Love," from her album *Stones in the Road* (Sony Records, 1994).

13. Longfellow, "Gaspar Becerra" (1849; 1:312).

Chapter 1: Strangers as Friends

1. See the letter from Eva L. Delano, Cambridge, to Longfellow, November 23, 1881, in which she invites herself and some friends to Longfellow's house, despite rumors she has heard that he might be ill: "I sincerely hope it may be untrue . . . and I also hope that we may have the pleasure of beholding the 'Poet of the Heart' face to face" (Houghton bMS Am 1340.2 [1523]).

2. Henry James, *The Aspern Papers,* in *Complete Stories 1884–1891,* ed. Edward Said (New York: Library of America, 1999), 259.

3. *Life* 1:56–57. Stephen Longfellow is right. The offending line, in which "motionless" introduces an anapestic foot into an otherwise iambic meter, appears in the sixth stanza of "Autumnal Nightfall," published in *The United States Literary Gazette,* December 1, 1824: "I stand deep musing here, / Beneath the dark and motionless beech, / Whilst wandering winds of nightfall reach / My melancholy ear" (1:332).

4. *The Cost Books of Ticknor and Fields and Their Predecessors, 1832–1858,* ed. Warren S. Tryon and William Charvat (New York: Bibliographical Society of America, 1949), A91a (p. 92).

5. Maria Susanna Cummins's novel *The Lamplighter,* for example, sold forty-thousand copies within a month of coming out, a success not matched by Longfellow's *Song of Hiawatha* (five thousand copies in the first five weeks). See Nina Baym's introduction to Cummins, *The Lamplighter* (New Brunswick, N.J.: Rutgers University Press, 1988), ix.

6. See Longfellow to Charles Sumner, December 13, 1851: "A fine state of things this, when a man cannot clap his hands without having it put into the papers" (*Letters* 3:322).

7. On April 26, 1860, Sumner had asked Longfellow for three suitable native names for "the region now known as Pike's Peak, west of Kansas, which it may bear first as Territory and then as a State." Longfellow suggested the Dakotah word "*Mazáska*" ("which means, in English, money"), as the nearest equivalent of "Eldorado," but his proposal came too late. The territory had already been named "Idaho" (*Letters* 4:174–75).

8. W. D. Howells, *Literary Friends and Acquaintance: A Personal Retrospect of American Authorship,* ed. David F. Hiatt and Edwin H. Cady (1900; Bloomington: Indiana University Press, 1968), 167.

9. Lawrence Buell, introduction to Longfellow, *Selected Poems* (New York: Penguin, 1988), xiii.

10. Ernest Longfellow reports that Colonel Harper, the owner of "Longfellow," when asked why he had given his horse the name of a poet, publicly denied there was any connection: "Poet nothing; I called him 'Longfellow' because he had such a long body." Adds Ernest: "This much amused my father." The colonel's caustic reply suit-

ed Longfellow's democratic sensibilities just fine. See Ernest Wadsworth Longfellow, *Random Memories* (Boston: Houghton Mifflin, 1922), 85. For examples of Longfellow's impact on popular culture, see Ernest J. Moyne, "Parodies of Longfellow's Song of Hiawatha," *Delaware Notes* 30 (1957): 94, and Daniel Aaron, introduction to Longfellow, *The Song of Hiawatha* (London: Everyman, 1993), xiv. In 1856, Longfellow and his sons attended the launch of the *Minnehaha* in "Donald McKay's Shipyard" in Boston, which was followed by a recitation from *Hiawatha* by Mrs. Barrow (March 22, 1856).

11. Transcribed from Fanny Brice's November 1921 recording on Victor 45203. For a fascinating analysis of Brice's song and its cultural contexts, see Alan Trachtenberg, *Shades of Hiawatha: Staging Indians, Making Americans, 1880–1930* (New York: Hill and Wang, 2004), esp. 161–62. Trachtenberg's book appeared after I completed my manuscript.

12. Annie Fields, *Authors and Friends*, 6th ed. (1896; Boston: Houghton Mifflin, 1897), 17–18.

13. *Der Sang von Hiawatha von Henry Wadsworth Longfellow*, trans. Ferdinand Freiligrath (Stuttgart: J. G. Cotta, 1857), x.

14. Quoted in George Lowell Austin, *Henry Wadsworth Longfellow: His Life, His Works, His Friendships* (Boston: Lee and Shepard, 1883), 348.

15. See Journal, December 5, 1863; Longfellow to George Washington Greene, April 3, 1881 (*Letters* 6:704); Thomas Wentworth Higginson, *Henry Wadsworth Longfellow* (Boston: Houghton Mifflin, 1902), 278.

16. See Robert Bernard Martin, *Tennyson: The Unquiet Heart. A Biography* (Oxford: Clarendon, 1980), 471.

17. See Helmut Gernsheim, *Julia Margaret Cameron: Her Life and Photographic Work* (Millerton, N.Y.: Aperture, 1975), 191.

18. Julia Margaret Cameron to Longfellow, July 26, 1868 (Houghton bMS Am 1340.2 [937]).

19. Howells, *Literary Friends*, 167.

20. Reprinted in W. Sloane Kennedy, *Henry Wadsworth Longfellow: Anecdote, Letters, Criticism* (Cambridge, Mass.: Moses King, 1882), 280–82.

21. *The Longfellow Birthday-Book*, arranged by Charlotte Fiske Bates (Boston: Houghton Mifflin, 1881); Kennedy, *Longfellow*, 126.

22. "The Universal Poet: From *The Independent*," *Youth's Companion*, May 13, 1897, 228.

23. Austin, *Longfellow*, 402.

24. Edgar Allan Poe, *Essays and Criticism*, ed. G. R. Thompson (New York: Library of America, 1984), 759–77. None of this hindered Poe from reciting Longfellow's introductory poem to *The Waif*, "The Day Is Done," in his 1848 lecture "The Poetic Principle," praising its "delicacy of expression" (*Essays and Criticism*, 80).

25. Poe, *Essays and Criticism*, 777.

26. Margaret Fuller, "Review of Henry Wadsworth Longfellow, *Poems*," *New-York Daily Tribune*, December 10, 1845, reprinted in *Margaret Fuller, Critic: Writings from the New-York Tribune, 1844–1846*, ed. Judith Mattson Bean and Joel Myerson (New York: Columbia University Press, 2000), 285–92. The quotations appear on pp. 285, 291, and

286. Fuller renewed her attack on Longfellow in "American Literature: Its Position in the Present Time, and Prospects for the Future," in her *Papers on Literature and Art* (1846), where she also described what she had in mind instead: a literature shaped by "a genius wide and full as our rivers, flowery, luxuriant, and impassioned as our vast prairies, rooted in strength as the rocks on which the Puritan fathers landed"; *Margaret Fuller, American Romantic: A Selection from Her Writings and Correspondence,* ed. Perry Miller (New York: Anchor, 1963), 231.

27. "I'm Nobody! Who are you?" (260), in *The Poems of Emily Dickinson,* ed. R. W. Franklin (Cambridge, Mass.: Belknap, 1999), 116–17.

28. By rejecting the European formal garden along with the mediocre productions of the second-rate poet, Emerson also stipulates a link between the rough American landscape and the American poet's imagination, a claim Longfellow indirectly refutes when, in his second and last novel, *Kavanagh,* his schoolmaster Churchill observes that "a man will not necessarily be a great poet because he lives near a great mountain" (8:426).

29. *The Essays of Ralph Waldo Emerson,* with an introduction by Alfred Kazin (Cambridge, Mass.: Belknap, 1987), 224.

30. See an entry written sometime during August 1853: "Longfellow, we cannot go & talk with; there is a palace, & servants, & a row of bottles of different coloured wines, & wine glasses, & fine coats"; *Emerson in His Journals,* ed. Joel Porte (Cambridge, Mass.: Belknap, 1982), 447.

31. Horace Traubel, *With Walt Whitman in Camden,* vol. 3 (1912; New York: Rowman and Littlefield, 1961), 549, 24. In "Death of Longfellow," a note included in *Specimen Days,* however, Whitman admitted that Longfellow was "the sort of bard . . . most needed for our materialistic, self-assertive, money-worshipping, Anglo-Saxon races, and especially for the present age in America"; Whitman, *Specimen Days and Collect* (Philadelphia: McKay, 1882–83), 193.

32. *The Diary of Alice James,* ed. Leon Edel (New York: Penguin, 1982), 76, 85–86.

33. Barbara Herrnstein Smith, *Contingencies of Value: Alternative Perspectives for Critical Theory* (Cambridge, Mass.: Harvard University Press, 1988), 49.

34. Anthony DePalma, "Historical Amnesia: Happy Fourth of July, Canada!" *New York Times,* July 5, 1998, sec. 4 (Week in Review), p. 4.

35. I. A. Richards, *Practical Criticism: A Study of Literary Judgment* (1929; New York: Harvest, 1969), 156–70.

36. Ludwig Lewisohn, *The Story of American Literature* (1932; New York: Modern Library, 1939), 65.

37. Herbert S. Gorman, *A Victorian American: Henry Wadsworth Longfellow* (1926; Port Washington, New York: Kennikat, 1967), 252.

38. See F. O. Mathiessen, introduction to *The Oxford Book of American Verse,* 2nd ed. (New York: Oxford University Press, 1950), xviii, and Lewisohn, *Story of American Literature,* 65. Matthiessen conceded that Longfellow's gift for storytelling "still enchants far more children than subsequently admit it" (xviii).

39. Richard Ruland and Malcolm Bradbury, *From Puritanism to Postmodernism: A History of American Literature* (New York: Penguin, 1992), 110.

40. Rochelle Gurstein, "The Importance of Being Earnest," *New Republic*, March 12, 2001, 42.

41. *The New Anthology of American Poetry*, vol. 1, *Traditions and Revolutions, Beginnings to 1900*, ed. Steven Gould Axelrod, Camille Roman, and Thomas Travisano (New Brunswick, N.J.: Rutgers University Press, 2003).

42. Barbara Everett, "Distraction v. Attraction," *London Review of Books*, June 27, 2002, 7.

43. Julia Ward Howe, *Margaret Fuller (Marchesa Ossoli)* (Boston: Roberts, 1883), 167.

44. John Crowe Ransom, "Criticism, Inc." (1938), in *The Norton Anthology of Theory and Criticism*, gen. ed. Vincent B. Leitch (New York: Norton, 2001), 115.

45. Newton Arvin, *Longfellow: His Life and Work* (Boston: Little, Brown, 1963), 3.

46. Emerson, Journal, October 13, 1838, *Emerson in His Journals*, 201.

47. See the web site of the Longfellow Institute at www.fas.harvard.edu/lowinus, and Charles Calhoun, *Longfellow: A Rediscovered Life* (Boston: Beacon, 2004).

48. Mary Louise Kete, *Sentimental Collaborations: Mourning and Middle-Class Identity in Nineteenth-Century America* (Durham, N.C.: Duke University Press, 1999), xvi, 140, 8, 113. In a similar vein, Kirsten Silva Gruesz sees Longfellow challenging "women's dominance of the domestic order"; "Feeling for the Fireside: Longfellow, Lynch, and the Topography of Poetic Power," in *Sentimental Men, Masculinity, and the Politics of Affect in American Culture*, ed. Mary Chapman and Glenn Hendler (Berkeley: University of California Press, 1999), 43–63. Like other modern Longfellow critics, Gruesz plausibly describes his work mostly in terms of what it *fails* to do, when she notes that Longfellow never directly addresses his wife's death in his later writings, where he suppresses private sentiment in favor of controlled public feeling. Gruesz's essay builds on the pioneering work of Eric L. Haralson ("Mars in Petticoats: Longfellow and Sentimental Masculinity," *Nineteenth-Century Literature* 56 [1996]: 327–55), who sees the reason for the decline of Longfellow's reputation in the new and less "feminine" models of masculinity that emerged in the latter half of the nineteenth century—not, as I do, in the impact of increasingly more restrictive definitions of the purpose of, and appropriate audiences for, literature.

49. In "Contradictions," a poem included in *The Muse among the Motors* (1904), a series of verse parodies shaped by his enthusiasm for the automobile, Kipling spoofed Longfellow's penchant for harmonious and moralizing conclusions as well his predilection for exotic name-dropping. To the poet, the roaring automobile and the "drowsy" horse-drawn carriage "Properly understood, / Are neither evil nor good— / Ormuzd nor Ahriman!" In *The Collected Works of Rudyard Kipling*, 28 vols. (Garden City, N.Y.: Doubleday, Doran, 1941), 28:134.

50. T. S. Eliot, "Rudyard Kipling," in *A Choice of Kipling's Verse Made by T. S. Eliot* (1941; New York: Anchor, 1962), 20.

51. William Charvat, *The Profession of Authorship in America, 1800–1870*, ed. Matthew J. Bruccoli (Columbus: Ohio State University Press, 1968), 109; Matthew Gartner, "Longfellow's Place: The Poet and Poetry of Craigie House," *New England Quarterly* 73, 1 (2000): 32–57.

52. Austin, *Longfellow*, 340.

53. Hans Christian Andersen to Longfellow, July 1871, Houghton bMS Am 1340.2 (140); see also *Life* 3:180.

54. See Longfellow, Journal, September 30, 1865.

55. Syud Hossein to Longfellow, April 10, 1862, Houghton bMS Am 1340.2 (2833).

56. See Longfellow to Emma Martin, May 3, 1854: "I did not write the poem on the 'Churchyard' which you have attributed to me" (*Letters* 3:430). The poem in question, "Hymn of the Churchyard," reprinted in Longfellow's anthology *The Waif,* was written by the minister George Washington Bethune (1805–62).

57. See the entry in Longfellow, Journal, July 21, 1854.

58. Daniel Aaron, "The Legacy of Henry Wadsworth Longfellow," *Maine Historical Society Quarterly* 27, 4 (1987): 49.

59. "Sometimes I make a spasmodic effort and clear the decks," he told George Washington Greene on December 8, 1851, "and in so doing I am sorry to say many letters never get answered at all, but are thrown overboard and lost forever" (*Letters* 3:319).

60. Lillian Kirk McDowell to Longfellow, December 18, 1877, Houghton bMS Am 1340.2 (3640).

61. Noah Brooks, "Lincoln's Imagination," *Scribner's* 18 (August 1879): 585.

62. See Longfellow, Journal, October 15, 1845.

63. Frances Anne Kemble to Longfellow, June 16, 1851, Houghton bMS Am 1340.2 (3140); see *Letters* 3:298–99 n. 1.

64. Caroline P. Holden to Longfellow, June 24, 1878, Houghton bMS Am 1340.2 (2774).

65. Elizabeth S. Crannell to Longfellow, June 9, 1879, Houghton bMS Am 1340.2 (1355).

66. The quotation is from *The Golden Legend,* the second part of the trilogy (5:264).

67. Ida F. M. Livingstone to Longfellow, June 18, 1880, Houghton bMS Am 1340.2 (3472).

68. Andrew Hilen's edition misidentifies Livingstone as "Livingston" (*Letters* 6:615 n. 1).

69. Ida M. F. Livingstone to Longfellow, December 29, 1880, Houghton bMS Am 1340.2 (3472).

70. Randall Jarrell, "The Obscurity of the Poet," in Jarrell, *Poetry and the Age* (New York: Knopf, 1953), 12.

71. Oliver Wendell Holmes, in a funny poem titled "Cacoethes Scribendi," imagines a world in which, though all the "pens and paper were used up," the "scribblers" would still "write, and write, and write"; *The Complete Poetical Works* (Boston: Houghton Mifflin, 1895), 300–301.

72. "The Editor's Easy Chair," *Harper's* 35, 206 (July 1867): 260.

73. Richard Henry Stoddard, "Henry Wadsworth Longfellow," *Scribner's* 17, 1 (November 1878): 14–15.

74. James Whitcomb Riley to Longfellow, November 27, 1876, Houghton bMS Am 1340.2 (4711).

75. See W. F. Cunningham to Longfellow, January 1882, Houghton bMS Am 1340.2 (1385).

76. Words spoken by Hamlet when his father's ghost asks him to have his friends Horatio and Marcellus swear on their promise not to reveal what they have seen or heard (*Hamlet* 1.5.150).

77. See, for example, Journal, February 15, 1854 ("wrote and despatched twenty letters and notes"); Lewisohn, *Story of American Literature*, 66.

78. Longfellow to George Washington Greene, October 28, 1881 (*Letters* 6:742).

79. Horace Traubel, *With Walt Whitman in Camden* (1905; New York: Rowman and Littlefield, 1961), 1:366.

80. Longfellow to Richard Boyd Davy, February 5, 1872, *Letters* 5:502.

81. "If you would kindly let us know you would receive hearty thanks from the members of 'Our Club' and especially oblige Yours Truly Ella M. Holden," Holden to Longfellow, January 18, 1879, Houghton bMS Am 1340.2 (2775).

82. George A. Sawyer to Longfellow, February 12, 1879, Houghton bMS Am1340.2 (4917).

83. Mrs. Redman Abbott to Longfellow, September 2, 1878, Houghton bMS Am 1340.2 (15).

84. Longfellow, "Book of Suggestions," 1846–82, Houghton MS Am 1340 (51). The motto inscribed on the flyleaf of the "Book of Suggestions" was from one of the dramatic fragments of Sophocles: "To have begun well what we do intend / Gives hope and prospect of as good an end." In 1864, for example, when a reader sent him a newspaper clipping about a memorable epitaph for a soldier in a Newport cemetery ("A Union Soldier Mustered Out"), Longfellow thanked her and saved the idea for a sonnet written ten years later, "A Nameless Grave" (3:224–25). See "Book of Suggestions," p. 50.

85. See J. H. Fenstermacher to Longfellow, March 20, 1877, Houghton bMS Am 1340.2 (1949).

86. See Lewis Cruger to Longfellow, n.d., Houghton bMS Am 1340.2 (1374).

87. See Albert H. Tracy to Longfellow, November 28, 1845, Houghton bMS Am 1340.2 (5599). In his reply to Tracy (a lawyer and former congressman and state senator), Longfellow diplomatically praised the poem ("a very clever one in its kind") but also said it needed a little "finish" (December 3, 1845; *Letters* 3:92).

88. On December 27, 1854, for example, he told the New York wholesale grocer and book dealer Thomas Henry Morrell, who had sent him some "ms. poems," that "the bad state of my eyes, and the delicacy of the task have forced me, for a long time, to decline all such applications" for review (*Letters* 3:458).

89. See Longfellow to William S. Martin, July 23, 1875 (*Letters* 6:52); Longfellow to Charlotte Fiske Bates, September 26, 1866 (*Letters* 5:82); Longfellow to Moody Currier, June 25, 1880 (*Letters* 6:617).

90. Longfellow to Julia Caroline Ripley Dorr, March 30, 1879 (*Letters* 6:466–67); Longfellow to James Whitcomb Riley, November 30, 1876 (*Letters* 6:204).

91. Whittier to Edward L. Pierce, April 12, 1882; Whittier to Rebecca Allinson, February 12, 1873; Whittier to Celia Thaxter, July 14, 1873, all in *The Letters of John Greenleaf Whittier*, ed. John B. Pickard, 3 vols. (Cambridge, Mass.: Belknap, 1975), 3:447–48, 289, 303.

92. Whittier to Lucy Larcom, April 16, 1867, *Letters of Whittier*, 3:152.

93. Whittier to an unidentified correspondent, November 6, 1867; Whittier to Julian Stearns Cutler, June 28, 1878; Whittier to Celia Thaxter, *Letters of Whittier,* 3:162, 394–95, 171.

94. Lydia H. Sigourney, *Letters of Life* (New York: Appleton, 1867), 368–77; 377.

95. Sigourney, *Letters of Life,* 377, 378.

96. See Joyce W. Warren, *Fanny Fern: An Independent Woman* (New Brunswick, N.J.: Rutgers University Press, 1992), 160.

97. From a column published on October 28, 1871, quoted in Warren, *Fanny Fern,* 259.

98. Fanny Fern, *Ruth Hall: A Domestic Tale of the Present Time,* ed. Susan Belasco Smith (New York: Penguin, 1997), 212, 213.

99. Warren, *Fanny Fern,* 180–81.

100. Ironically, Sigourney mailed several fan letters of her own to Longfellow, sounding not much different from the correspondents who were pestering *her* (see Houghton bMS Am 1340.2 [5085]). On April 14, 1848, she expressed her admiration for *Evangeline:* "I have just perused it anew, with two fair, young ladies, & the mingling of their enthusiasm with my awe seemed to heighten the perception of the exquisite beauty of its comparisons, and the skill of its structure." But then, chiding herself for simply assuming that her thoughts would be "very interesting" to him, she announced—quoting Longfellow, of course—that she would fold her tent "and silently steal away." On February 27, 1852, she sent Longfellow a birthday poem, in which she fulsomely praised the "Bard of Evangeline," whose "varied strains / Shall, like the honied lip of Sophocles—, / Entrance in deep delight, an unborn age." Like an "elder sister, or at least a Great Aunt," Sigourney took vicarious pride in the "frequent tributes from various lands" that Longfellow was receiving (Houghton bMS Am 1340.2 [5085]).

101. George P. Lathrop, "Literary and Social Boston," *Harper's* 17 (December 1880–May 1881): 390.

102. Robert Ferguson, *America during and after the War* (London: Longmans, Green, Reader and Dyer, 1866), 30.

103. Ferguson, *America during and after the War,* 31.

104. Ernest Wadsworth Longfellow, *Random Memories* (Boston: Houghton Mifflin, 1922), 84.

105. Howells remembers that "no one who asked decently was denied access to him," even German (least liked) and Italian beggars (his favorites); Howells, *Literary Friends,* 166–67.

106. Mrs. L. G. Abell, *Woman in Her Various Relations, Containing Practical Rules for American Females* (New York: William Holdredge, 1851), 146.

107. W. M. Fullerton in the *Boston Sunday Record* (see *Life* 3:402).

108. Gartner, "Longfellow's Place," 50.

109. Ferguson, *America during and after the War,* 28; Howells, *Literary Friends,* 161.

110. *Homes of American Authors; Comprising Anecdotical, Personal, and Descriptive Sketches, by Various Writers* (New York: Putnam, 1853), iv, 273.

111. Traubel, *Whitman in Camden,* 3:549.

112. Charvat, *Authorship,* 119, 137.

113. Fields, *Authors and Friends,* 58–59; Kennedy, *Longfellow,* 167. Fields's journal identifies the dinner guest as "the little Professor," Oliver Wendell Holmes; see M. A. De Wolfe Howe, *Memories of a Hostess: A Chronicle of Eminent Friendships Drawn Chiefly from the Diaries of Mrs. James T. Fields* (Boston: Atlantic Monthly, 1922), 47.

114. Longfellow to Mary Neal Sherwood, September 14, 1877: "This letter is as full of I's as a peacock's tail. What a pity one cannot write without so often using that objectionable pronoun!" (*Letters* 6:300).

115. Peter Gay, *The Naked Heart* (New York: Norton, 1995), 330. On "Victorianism" in the United States, see Daniel Walker Howe, "American Victorianism as a Culture," *American Quarterly* 27 (December 1975): 507–32.

116. See, for example, his account of night falling over the beach at Nahant on July 18, 1856: "I never saw a more beautiful rising of the moon. It came up round and large through smoke-colored sea-mist, through which fell on the sea beneath it a great circle of light. We watched it till late at Night; Rölker singing German songs. Far away to the north, the lightning was playing in the clouds. On the afternoon drive I had seen it on the sun-illumined white crests, like flashes of anger, heightening the color of a face."

117. See the entry for October 9, 1846: Longfellow had just begun a poem dripping with Keatsian autumnal languor ("the evening air is damp and cold / liquid, lambent, soft and wild"), when he is "called to dinner and the poem ended." Still, he seems to have had time enough to add a self-ironical literary allusion: "As the Editor inscribed at the end of 'Thealma and Clearchus, a Pastoral History, in smooth and easie Verse, written long since by John Chalkhill Esq. an acquaintant and friend of Edmund Spencer' this odd line 'And here the author died, and I hope the reader will be sorry.'" Longfellow is referring to a poem published in 1638 with a preface by Izaak Walton, of *Compleat Angler* fame, who was long suspected to be behind "John Chalkhill."

118. A phrase from Longfellow's 1875 poem "Songo River" (3:101).

119. Longfellow repeats this passage three years later almost verbatim in *Hyperion,* when he has his protagonist Flemming reject literary fame as an "indiscreet and troublesome ambition" (see 8:69 and 78).

120. The American edition of *The Diary, Reminiscences, and Correspondence of H. Crabb Robinson,* ed. Thomas Sadler, had just been published by Ticknor and Fields (Boston, 1869).

121. Fields, *Authors and Friends,* 26: "Neither Longfellow nor his wife was a brilliant talker; indeed, there were often periods of speechlessness."

122. See Emerson, "The Poet," in *Essays of Emerson,* 236.

123. Karen Halttunen, *Confidence Men and Painted Women: A Study of Middle-Class Culture in America, 1830–1870* (New Haven: Yale University Press, 1982), 50. The following discussion is also indebted to the critique of the public/private dichotomy in Karen V. Hansen, *A Very Social Time: Crafting Community in Antebellum New England* (Berkeley: University of California Press, 1994). The pun in this section's title appears in Maureen Corregan's review of *A Feeling for Books,* by Janice Radway: "Middlebrowsing," *The Nation,* November 3, 1997, 58–62.

124. See Witold Rybcynski, *Home: A Short History of an Idea* (New York: Viking, 1986), 158–61.

125. Emerson, "Self-Reliance" (1841), in *Essays of Emerson*, 47.

126. Poe, *Essays and Criticism*, 756, 764.

127. Aaron, "Legacy," 45.

128. Mark Twain, *The Innocents Abroad or The New Pilgrims' Progress* (1869; New York: Bantam, 1966), 418.

129. "Dante's Divina Commedia: From the German of Schelling," *Graham's Magazine* 36 (June 1850): 351–54.

130. Louis de Maynard de Queilhe, *Outremer*, 2 vols. (Paris, 1835); see Longfellow to Stephen Longfellow, October 25, 1835 (*Letters* 1:522).

131. Melville, "Hawthorne and His Mosses" (1850), in Melville, *Moby-Dick: A Critical Edition*, ed. Harrison Hayford and Hershel Parker (New York: Norton, 1967), 546.

132. Longfellow, "Travels by the Fireside" (3:86).

133. Longfellow, October 9(?), 1832; April 12, 1834; *Emerson in His Journals*, 86, 123.

134. Wallace Stevens, *Sur Plusieurs Beaux Sujects: Wallace Stevens' Commonplace Book*, ed. Milton J. Bates (Stanford: University of California Press, 1989), 55.

135. See James Trilling, review of *Ruskin's Venice: The Stones Revisited*, by Sarah Quill, *American Scholar* 69, 4 (autumn 2000): 146–48.

136. See Janice Radway, *A Feeling for Books: The Book-of-the-Month Club, Literary Taste, and Middle-Class Desire* (Chapel Hill: University of North Carolina Press, 1997), 217–18.

137. Wordsworth, "Preface to *Lyrical Ballads, with Pastoral and Other Poems*" (1802), in Wordsworth, *Selected Poems*, ed. John O. Hayden (Harmondsworth, England: Penguin, 1994), 441.

138. Robert Graves, *The Crowning Privilege: The Clark Lectures, 1954–1955, Also Various Essays on Poetry and Sixteen New Poems* (London: Cassell, 1955), 122.

139. See Lawrence Levine, *Highbrow/Lowbrow: The Emergence of Cultural Hierarchy in America* (Cambridge, Mass.: Harvard University Press, 1988); Richard Brodhead, *Cultures of Letters: Scenes of Reading and Writing in Nineteenth-Century America* (Chicago: University of Chicago Press, 1994); Joan Shelley Rubin, *The Making of Middlebrow Culture* (Chapel Hill: University of North Carolina Press, 1992).

140. Charvat, *Authorship*, 159.

141. For *Evangeline*, Ticknor paid Longfellow an unprecendented 25.6 percent of the retail price. Charvat, *Authorship*, 163.

142. Charvat, *Authorship*, 162.

143. See Oscar Handlin, *Boston's Immigrants*, rev. ed. (1941: New York: Atheneum, 1972), 77.

144. Abdiel Moore Caverly, M.D., *History of the Town of Pittsford, Vt., with Biographical Sketches and Family Records* (Rutland, VT: Tuttle, 1872), 534–35.

145. Poe, *The Literati of New York City*, in *Essays and Criticism*, 1172.

146. See Longfellow to Carey & Hart, April 14, 1845 (*Letters* 3:65), and Charles Sumner to Longfellow, n.d. [1845], Houghton bMS Am 1340.2 (5394). In a letter to Abraham Hart of January 19, 1846, Longfellow also mentions that "a stranger" from Reading, Pennsylvania, had urged him to go ahead with "a cheaper edition of my poems" (*Letters* 3:95).

147. [Poe], "Our Book-Shelves (3)," *Aristidean* 1 (September 1845): 240. For the attribution of this anonymous piece to Poe, see Charles F. Heartman, *A Bibliography of First Printings of the Writings of Edgar Allan Poe*, rev. ed. (1940; Hattiesburg, Miss.: Book Farm, 1943), 149.

148. See *Cost Books of Ticknor and Fields*, B 189a (pp. 381–82) and B 205.

149. According to the advertisement included in Longfellow, *Kéramos and Other Poems* (Boston: Houghton, Osgood, 1878).

150. Whitman, "Song of Myself," in Whitman, *Leaves of Grass and Other Writings*, ed. Michael Moon (New York: Norton, 2002), 31; Leo Marx, *The Pilot and the Passenger: Essays on Literature, Technology, and Culture in the United States* (New York: Oxford University Press, 1988), 274.

151. Dwight Macdonald used the term "midcult" instead of "middlebrow" to indicate an attitude toward culture that is "like taking apart Westminster Abbey to make Disneyland out of the fragments." "Masscult and Midcult" [1960], in Macdonald, *Against the American Grain* (New York: Da Capo, 1983), 38. The modern examples he cites include Hemingway's novel *The Old Man and the Sea* and Thornton Wilder's play *Our Town*.

152. Virginia Woolf, "Middlebrow" (1912), in Woolf, *The Death of the Moth and Other Essays* (1942; Harmondsworth, England: Penguin, 1961), 160, 155.

153. David Reynolds, *Walt Whitman's America: A Cultural Biography* (New York: Knopf, 1995), 311–13.

154. Traubel, *Whitman in Camden*, 3:24. Longfellow and the Philadelphia publisher George W. Childs visited Whitman in Camden on June 2, 1876. As often on such occasions, Longfellow must have kept mostly silent during the half-hour meeting. Whitman is supposed to have remarked afterward that Longfellow was "dapper and dainty and effeminate . . . like the lord whose wife was advised to keep him dressed well but never let him open his mouth." Joann P. Krieg, *A Whitman Chronology* (Iowa City: University of Iowa Press, 1998), 112.

155. Whitman, "Preface, 1872, to 'As a Strong Bird on Pinions Free,'" in Whitman, *Specimen Days and Collect*, 276.

156. Justin Kaplan, *Whitman: A Life* (1980; New York: Bantam, 1982), 22.

157. Kennedy, *Longfellow*, 222.

158. Whitman, "Sounds of the Winter" (1891), in *Leaves of Grass*, 460.

159. George Hutchinson, *The Ecstatic Whitman: Literary Shamanism and the Crisis of the Union* (Columbus: Ohio State University Press, 1986), 73. For an insightful comparison of the two poetic antipodes, see Angus Fletcher, "Whitman and Longfellow: Two Types of the American Poet," *Raritan* 10, 4 (1991): 131–45.

160. Longfellow, "My Lost Youth" (3:41).

161. Longfellow to Isaac Appleton Jewett, May 23, 1843 (*Letters* 2:538).

162. Charvat, *Authorship*, 133.

163. See Longfellow to Samuel Ward, September 30, 1841 (*Letters* 2:334).

164. According to Lennard J. Davis, the adjective "normal" as "constituting, conforming to, not deviating or differing from, the common type of standard" is first documented in English around 1840. *Enforcing Normalcy: Disability, Deafness and the Body* (London: Verso, 1995), 24.

165. A question asked by Vincenzo Cesati, professor of botany at the University of Naples and, in his own words, "Praeses to the Italian Alpine Club's Neapolitan Section," who wrote to "the renowned author of 'Excelsior'" on August 24, 1873, presenting his "best good-byes" and asking for permission to retitle the poem "adverbialiter 'Excelsius'" (bMS Am 1340.2 [1029]; *Letters* 5:712).

166. *Victorian Parlor Poetry: An Annotated Anthology,* ed. Michael R. Turner (1969; New York: Dover, 1992), 38.

167. The composition was by Jesse Hutchinson, the oldest of the Hutchinson brothers. See *Excelsior: Journals of the Hutchinson Family Singers, 1842–1846,* ed. Dale Cockrell (New York: Pendragon, 1989), 373–78, as well as John Wallace Hutchinson, *Story of the Hutchinson Singers,* ed. Charles E. Mann, 2 vols. (Boston: Lee and Shepard, 1896), 1:91–92.

168. *Excelsior, by Henry W. Longfellow,* with twelve illustrations by Fred. T. Vance (New York: Excelsior Life Insurance Company, 1872). Thanks to Elizabeth Garver of the Harry Ransom Center for the Humanities, University of Texas at Austin, for providing me with a copy of this booklet.

169. *Excelsior, Illustrated,* advertising leaflet (Springfield: D. H. Brigham, 1873), author's collection.

170. See Longfellow's letter to James Ripley Osgood, March 9, 1872, in which he refers to Charles N. Morgan, president of the Excelsior Life Insurance Company, and says that he "had no objection to his using the poem as an advertisement" (*Letters* 5:522–23).

171. Thomas Carlyle to Ralph Waldo Emerson, November 3, 1844, in *The Correspondence of Emerson and Carlyle,* ed. Joseph Slater (New York: Columbia University Press, 1964), 369. "Muddled humanity" is Van Wyck Brooks's phrase; see his "'Highbrow' and 'Lowbrow'" (1915), in Brooks, *America's Coming-of-Age* (New York: Doubleday, 1958), 1–19.

172. The essayist Edwin Percy Whipple (1819–86) was the superintendent of the newsroom at the Merchants' Exchange in Boston.

173. "Sonnet on Mrs. Kemble's Readings from Shakespeare" (1:320). See also Longfellow, Journal, January 6, 1850: "What is the use of writing *books about books?*"

174. Françoise Meltzer, *Hot Property: The Stakes and Claims of Literary Originality* (Chicago: University of Chicago Press, 1994).

175. Alexis de Tocqueville, *Democracy in America,* trans. Arthur Goldhammer (New York: Library of America, 2004), 544.

176. John Guillory, *Cultural Capital: The Problem of Literary Canon Formation* (Chicago: University of Chicago Press, 1993), 336. See also Pierre Bourdieu, "The Market of Symbolic Goods," trans. Rupert Swyer, *Poetics* 14 (1985): 13–44.

177. Austin had smuggled the book into the house. Edward Dickinson eventually discovered it and, as Emily told Thomas Wentworth Higginson, was "displeased." See Richard Sewall, *The Life of Emily Dickinson* (1974; Cambridge, Mass.: Harvard University Press, 1980), 163, 683–88.

178. Brodhead, *Cultures of Letters,* 63.

179. Israel Zangwill, "The Fate of Palestine," *Menorah Journal* 3, 4 (October 1917): 201.

180. Fanny Appleton Longfellow to Mary Appleton MacIntosh, January 2, 1855, in *Mrs. Longfellow: Selected Letters and Journals of Fanny Appleton Longfellow (1817–1861)*, ed. Edward Wagenknecht (New York: Longmans, 1956), 201.

181. *The Thousand Best Poems in the World*, ed. E. W. Cole (London: Hutchinson, n.d.). Cole, who likes the superlative mode (and calls Longfellow "one of the best poets of humanity"), interestingly reduces the claim made by his sweeping title right at the beginning of the volume: "The pieces in this collection may not at all be what a severe critic would call good poetry." Obviously, where the "heart of humanity" is concerned, criteria other than those established by academics apply.

182. H. C. Maine, "Works of Art among College Boys," *Hamilton Literary Monthly* 4 (September 1869): 60. The locket, to which I was alerted by Longfellow's biographer, Charles Calhoun, was part of the exhibition "Longfellow: The Man Who Invented America," Maine Historical Society, Portland, Maine, April 12–December 31, 2002.

183. Haralson, "Mars in Petticoats," 345.

184. Ezra Pound, *Selected Poems* (London: Faber and Faber, 1928), 25.

185. See Cowley's preface to his *Poems* (1656), in Cowley, *Poems*, ed. A. R. Waller (Cambridge: Cambridge University Press, 1905), 7.

186. Radway, *Feeling for Books*, 37.

187. James F. English, "Radway's 'Feelings' and the Reflexive Sociology of American Literature," *Modernism/Modernity* 6, 3 (1999): 145.

188. See Susan Manning, "Whatever Happened to Pleasure?" *Cambridge Quarterly* 30, 3 (2001): 227.

189. John Derbyshire, "Longfellow and the Fate of Modern Poetry," *New Criterion* 19, 4 (December 2000): 12–21.

Chapter 2: How Marbles Are Made

1. James T. Fields to Longfellow, August 1, 1860, Houghton bMS AM 1340.2 (1972).

2. Newton Arvin, *Longfellow: His Life and Work* (Boston: Little, Brown, 1963), 328.

3. He included the Mouse Tower in a little sketch of "the beautiful village of Bingen" he sent to his mother, Zilpah, on May 15, 1829 (*Letters* 1:311 and pl. 5).

4. *Poems of Robert Southey*, ed. Maurice H. Fitzgerald (London: Oxford University Press, 1909), 372. Longfellow later reprinted Southey's poem under "Bingen" in the first of his two Germany volumes for *Poems of Places* (*Places* 17:50–53).

5. Norman Holmes Pearson, "Both Longfellows" (1950), in Longfellow, *Evangeline and Selected Tales and Poems*, ed. Horace Gregory (New York: New American Library, 1964), 274.

6. The manuscript of "The Children's Hour" is contained in the box labeled "Poems from Birds of passage, flights second, third, fourth, and fifth," 1845–1870, Longfellow Papers, Houghton MS Am 1340 (128).

7. A phrase used by the New Hampshire humorist B. P. (Benjamin Penhallow) Shillaber in 1879, quoted in Gillian Brown, "Child's Play," *differences* 11, 3 (Fall 1999): 89.

8. Marina Warner, *No Go the Bogeyman: Scaring, Lulling, and Making Mock* (London: Chatto and Windus, 1998), 59.

9. When little, Emerson's children were suffered to stay in their father's study as long as they conducted themselves quietly and looked at pictures or drew them. Otherwise, Emerson was "hard at work until his walking time" (around 4 p.m.). See Edith Emerson Webster Gregg, "Emerson and His Children: Their Childhood Memories," *Harvard Library Bulletin* 38, 4 (October 1980): 429.

10. Journal, February 1, 1849.

11. Sigmund Freud, *Leonardo da Vinci: A Case Study in Psychosexuality,* trans. A. A. Brill (New York: Modern Library, 1947), 94.

12. Harold Bloom identifies the subject of his seminal study *The Anxiety of Influence: A Theory of Poetry* (1973) as a "battle between strong equals, father and son as mighty opposites, Laius and Oedipus at the crossroads," 2nd ed. (New York: Oxford University Press, 1997), 11.

13. T. S. Eliot, "What Is a Classic?" (1944), in *Selected Prose of T. S. Eliot,* ed. Frank Kermode (New York: Harcourt Brace Jovanovich, 1975), 125.

14. See Walter Jackson Bate, *The Burden of the Past and the English Poet* (1970; Cambridge, Mass.: Harvard University Press, 1991), 100.

15. Emerson, "Domestic Life," in Emerson, *Society and Solitude: Twelve Chapters* (1870; Boston: Houghton Mifflin, 1904), 107. Emerson's lecture was first delivered in the Boston Music Hall on November 13, 1859.

16. Richard H. Brodhead, *Cultures of Letters: Scenes of Reading and Writing in Nineteenth-Century America* (Chicago: University of Chicago Press, 1993), 22.

17. See Carl N. Degler, *At Odds: Women and the Family in America from the Revolution to the Present* (New York: Oxford University Press, 1980), 77–78.

18. Paula S. Fass and Mary Ann Mason, "Introduction: Childhood in America, Past and Present," in *Childhood in America,* ed. Fass and Mason (New York: New York University Press, 2000), 2.

19. Susan Warner, *The Wide Wide World* (New York: Lippincott, 1892). Warner first published her novel in 1850 under the pen name "Elizabeth Wetherell." The epigraphs range from Longfellow's version of the carpe diem motif, "It Is Not Always May," which provides the motto for the novel's very first chapter ("Enjoy the spring of love and youth / To some good angel leave the rest") to the compliantly resigned lines spoken by Evangeline when she finds her dead lover Gabriel ("All was ended now"), which preface the chapter in which Ellen learns of her mother's death, to the lines from Longfellow's evocation of the charms of youth, "Maidenhood," which introduce the chapter in which Ellen learns to obey her uncle: "Bear a lily in thy hand; / Gates of brass cannot withstand / One touch of that magic wand" (1:87).

20. Warner, *Wide Wide World,* 11.

21. Maria Edgeworth, "Toys" (1825), in Fass and Mason, *Childhood in America,* 49–51; see 49.

22. Horace Bushnell, *Christian Nurture,* ed. Luther A. Weigle (1847; New Haven: Yale University Press, 1966), 278–79; Mrs. L. G. Abell, *Woman in Her Various Relations: Containing Practical Rules for American Females* (New York: Holdredge, 1851), 228–29.

23. Degler, *At Odds,* 91.

24. *Emerson in His Journals,* ed. Joel Porte (Cambridge, Mass.: Belknap, 1982), 215.

25. Henry James, "The Point of View," in James, *Complete Stories, 1874–1884,* ed. William L. Vance (New York: Library of America, 1999), 537.

26. Shawn Johansen, *Family Men: Middle-Class Fatherhood in Early Industrializing America* (New York: Routledge, 2001), 86.

27. Johansen, *Family Men,* 136–37.

28. See Martin Duberman, *James Russell Lowell* (Boston: Beacon, 1966), 89.

29. Fanny Appleton Longfellow to Emmeline Austin Wadsworth, June 16(?), 1846, in *Mrs. Longfellow: Selected Letters and Journals of Fanny Appleton Longfellow (1817–1861),* ed. Edward Wagenknecht (New York: Longmans, Green, 1956), 122.

30. See Fanny Longfellow, entry for Friday, November 17, 1848, in "Chronicle of the Children of Craigie Castle. 1848," Archives, Longfellow National Historic Site, Cambridge, Massachusetts, LONG 21576, p. 108, and Longfellow to Frances Farrer, May 8, 1862 (*Letters* 4:284).

31. Charles Appleton Longfellow, February 22, 1854, entry in "Charley's Journal" (1854), Houghton MS Am 1340 (162).

32. Ernest Wadsworth Longfellow, *Random Memories* (Boston: Houghton Mifflin, 1922), 14.

33. Fanny Longfellow to Thomas G. Appleton, July 29, 1865, in *Mrs. Longfellow,* 204.

34. Emerson, "Domestic Life," 121.

35. Gregg, "Emerson and His Children," 429.

36. Henry Wadsworth Longfellow, "Charley's Journal," 1850, and Charles Appleton Longfellow, "Charley's Journal," 1854, Houghton MS Am 1340 (161), and (162). Charley's journals are the subject of an excellent senior thesis by my former student Elizabeth Greenwood, "Declarations of Independence: American Children's Diaries, 1820–1860" (A.B. thesis, Harvard University, 2001).

37. John Banvard (1815–91), was famous for his huge, moving panorama of the eastern shore of the Mississippi River, the largest painting in the world, which was exhibited in Boston in December 1846, when Longfellow went to check it out: "Three miles of canvas, and a great deal of merit" (December 19, 1846).

38. That is, if we ignore such occasional contributions to children's magazines as "Christmas Bells" (3:139–40), which was first published in February 1865, in the second number of Ticknor and Field's new juvenile magazine *Our Young Folks.* See James C. Austin, *James Fields of "The Atlantic Monthly": Letters to an Editor, 1861–1870* (San Marino, Calif.: Huntington Library, 1953), 94.

39. Longfellow, "Book of Suggestions," Houghton MS Am 1340 (51), p. 27.

40. Longfellow, "Little Merrythought: An Autobiography with a Portrait," Houghton MS Am 1340 (165). The Houghton Guide to the Longfellow Papers erroneously lists Charley Longfellow as the author.

41. See Longfellow, Journal, April 7, 1847.

42. Brodhead, *Cultures of Letters,* 21.

43. Miguel de Cervantes Saavedra, *The History of The Ingenious Gentleman, Don Quixote of La Mancha,* trans. Peter Motteux and ed. John G. Lockhart, 4 vols. (Boston: Little, Brown, 1856), 1:75–77.

44. Gareth B. Matthews, *The Philosophy of Childhood* (1994; Cambridge, Mass.: Harvard University Press, 1996), 122.

45. Van Wyck Brooks, *The Flowering of New England* (1932; New York: Dutton, 1952), 455.

46. Berta E. Shaffer to Longfellow, June 21, 1880 (Houghton bMS Am 1340.2 [5010]); Longfellow to Berta E. Shaffer, June 24, 1880 (*Letters* 6:617; my emphasis).

47. Johann Gottfried Herder, *Stimmen der Völker in Liedern,* 1778/79, ed. Heinz Rölleke (Stuttgart: Reclam, 1975), 248–49.

48. Herder, "Auszug aus einem Briefwechsel über Oßian und die Lieder alter Völker," in *Von deutscher Art und Kunst: Einige fliegende Blätter,* ed. Hans Dietrich Irmscher (Stuttgart: Reclam, 1968), 21.

49. Unpublished and undated prose fragment, Houghton MS Am 1340 (145).

50. Goethe apparently intimidated Longfellow. In 1846, as he was reading the *Italienische Reise,* Longfellow dreamed that Goethe had risen from the dead and had come to Cambridge to look for him: "I gave him a supper at Willard's tavern. He had a beautiful face; but his body was like the Belgian giant's; with an immeasurable black coat. I told him I thought Clärchen's song in Egmont was one of his best lyrics. The God smiled" (June 21, 1846).

51. Longfellow, "Goethe as a Man," 9th lecture, Harvard College, June 15, 1837, 1837, Houghton MS Am 1340 (49), 55. Longfellow is quoting Shakespeare, *Midsummer Night's Dream* 6.1.223, 257–59, in *The Riverside Shakespeare,* ed. G. Blakemore Evans and J. J. M. Tobin (Boston: Houghton Mifflin, 1997), 278–79.

52. Longfellow, "Goethe as a Man," 53.

53. Longfellow, "Goethe as an Author," 10th lecture, June 22, 1837, Houghton MS Am 1340 (45). See Sarah Austin, *Characteristics of Goethe; from the German of Falk, von Müller, & c., with Notes, Original and Translated, Illustrative of German Literature,* 3 vols. (London: E. Wilson, 1833), 3:76–77. Longfellow's quotation contains a revealing error: instead of "what would remain to me" in Austin's translation, his excerpt reads: "what would remain *of* me."

54. Edgar Allan Poe, *Poetry and Tales,* ed. Patrick F. Quinn (New York: Library of America, 1984), 102.

55. Whitman, *Notes and Fragments,* ed. Richard Maurice Bucke (London, Ontario: n.p., 1899), 56.

56. Emerson, "The Poet," in *The Essays of Ralph Waldo Emerson,* ed. Alfred Kazin (Cambridge, Mass.: Belknap, 1987), 224.

57. *The Poets and Poetry of Europe, with Introductions and Biographical Notices,* ed. Henry Wadsworth Longfellow (1845; New York: C. S. Francis, 1877), [v].

58. Poe, *Essays and Reviews,* ed. G. R. Thompson (New York: Library of America, 1984), 696, 702. After the publication of *The Waif,* more and more authors of the supposedly anonymous poems in the volume stepped forward to "claim their property," as Longfellow noticed with some amusement: "before long every part and parcel will find its owner, and 'The Waif' will cease to be a waif, save in name" (*Letters* 3:52).

59. See Schiller's "Das Distichon": "Im Hexameter steigt des Springquells flüssige Säule, / Im Pentameter drauf fällt sie melodisch herab"; from *Gedichte 1789–1805,* in

Schiller, *Sämtliche Werke,* ed. Gerhard Fricke and Herbert G. Göpfert, 3 vols., 3rd ed. (Munich: Carl Hanser, 1962), 1:252.

60. Margaret Fuller, "Review of Henry Wadsworth Longfellow, *Poems,*" *New-York Daily Tribune,* December 10, 1845, reprinted in *Margaret Fuller, Critic: Writings from the New-York Tribune, 1844–1846,* ed. Judith Mattson Bean and Joel Myerson (New York: Columbia University Press, 2000), 287–88.

61. Emerson, "The Poet," 224.

62. Whitman, "Song of Myself," in Whitman, *Leaves of Grass and Other Writings,* ed. Michael Moon (New York: Norton, 2002), 663.

63. Fanny Appleton (later Mrs. Longfellow), who appears in the novel, thinly veiled, as Mary Ashburton, the object of the narrator's desires, unkindly called it "a thing of shreds and patches like the author's mind"; to Emmeline Austin, August 9, 1839 (*Mrs. Longfellow,* 58).

64. *Hyperion,* bk. 4, chap. 4: "Musical Sufferings of John Kreisler" (8:271–81).

65. As in Brainard, the mockingbird's song first soars and then falls, only this time it is compared to a "crystal shower" of rain descending on the branches of a tree. See 2:75–76.

66. See Richard Crashaw's "Sospetto d'Herode" 44, in Crashaw, *The Steps of the Temple* (1646): "The house is hers'd about with a black wood, / Which nods with many a heavy headed tree"; *The Verse in English of Richard Crashaw* (New York: Grove, 1949), 71.

67. Oliver Wendell Holmes, *The Autocrat of the Breakfast-Table* (1858; Boston: Houghton Mifflin, 1881), 34.

68. Ralph Waldo Emerson, "Quotation and Originality," *North American Review* 106 (1868): 543–57.

69. Françoise Meltzer, *Hot Property: The Stakes and Claims of Literary Originality* (Chicago: Chicago University Press, 1994), 71.

70. Milton's "When I Consider How My Light Is Spent" (after 1652) ends with the reassuring line, spoken by "patience": "They also serve who only stand and wait"; in *The Complete Poems,* ed. John Leonard (London: Penguin, 1998), 84.

71. *Pluri-bus-tah: A Song That's By-No-Author, Perpetrated by Q. K. Philander Doesticks, P.B.* (New York: Livermore and Rudd, 1865).

72. Lydia Huntley Sigourney, *Pocahontas and Other Poems* (New York: Harper, 1841), 33, 37.

73. From a journal entry written before he had begun the new poem (June 22, 1854).

74. The vowels in *Hiawatha* were, Longfellow said, "nearly the same sound as in Niagara, but with different accent; the *i* like *ee,* and the *a* broad as in *father*" (to an unidentified correspondent, June 14, 1856; *Letters* 3:541).

75. See Lönnrot's preface to the first edition of the *Kalevala* (1835), in *The Kalevala, or Poems of the Kaleva District, Compiled by Elias Lönnrot,* ed. and trans. Francis Peabody Magoun, Jr. (Cambridge, Mass.: Harvard University Press, 1963), 366.

76. For Porter's charges as well as a more balanced view of the relationship between the two texts, see Ernest J. Moyne, *Hiawatha and Kalevala: A Study of the Relationship be-*

tween Longfellow's "Indian Edda" and the Finnish Epic (Helsinki: Suomalainen Tiedeakatemia, 1963).

77. Henry Rowe Schoolcraft, *Oneóta, or the Red Race of America from Original Notes and Manuscripts* (New York: Putnam, 1845). In a letter to Longfellow dated June 16, 1856, Schoolcraft reiterated his belief that Native American legends appeared to him "to furnish a new element for our literature" (Houghton bMS Am1340.2 [4950]).

78. Although she found Schoolcraft's *Algic Researches* "valuable" and conceded that the "incidents" represented there had "an air of originality," Fuller resented the "flimsy graces" and "bad taste" of Schoolcraft's style, which had so little of the "Spartan brevity and sinewy grasp of Indian speech"; Fuller, *Summer on the Lakes, in 1843,* in *The Essential Margaret Fuller,* ed. Jeffrey Steele (New Brunswick, N.J.: Rutgers University Press, 1995), 88.

79. Henry Rowe Schoolcraft, *Algic Researches, Comprising Inquiries Respecting the Mental Characteristics of the North American Indians. First Series: Indian Tales and Legends,* 2 vols. (New York: Harper, 1839).

80. Schoolcraft, *Algic Researches,* 1:150–51.

81. Thomas Jefferson, *Writings,* ed. Merrill D. Peterson (New York: Library of America, 1984), 266.

82. Robert F. Berkhofer, *The White Man's Indian: Images of the American Indian from Columbus to the Present* (1978; New York: Vintage, 1979), 88.

83. Arvin, *Longfellow,* 166, 173.

84. Berkhofer, *White Man's Indian,* 90.

85. Longfellow, "Notes for *Hiawatha:* Indian Words and Names," Houghton MS Am 1340 (92).

86. Angus Fletcher, "Whitman and Longfellow: Two Types of the American Poet," *Raritan* 10, 4 (1991): 141.

87. Claude Lévi-Strauss, *Tristes Tropiques,* trans. John and Doreen Weightman (1974; New York: Penguin, 1992), 298.

88. Longfellow to William Stuart Appleton, February 11, 1877 (*Letters* 6:244).

89. See Virginia Jackson, "Longfellow's Tradition; or, Picture-Writing a Nation," *Modern Language Quarterly* 59, 4 (December 1998): 471–96.

90. Sigourney, *Pocahontas,* 31, 21.

91. Ernest J. Moyne, "Parodies of Longfellow's *Song of Hiawatha,*" *Delaware Notes* 30 (1957): 95.

92. Lewis Carroll, "Hiawatha's Photographing," in Carroll, *Rhyme? and Reason?* (New York: Macmillan, 1883), 66.

93. W. Sloane Kennedy, *Henry W. Longfellow: Biography, Anecdote, Letters, Criticism* (Cambridge, Mass.: Moses King, 1882), 215.

94. George Augustus Strong, *The Song of Milkanwatha: Translated from the Original Feejee. By Marc Antony Henderson, D.C.L.* (Cincinnati: Tickell and Grinne, 1856), [v]–vi. Well-known parodies of *Hiawatha* not mentioned in this chapter include *The Song of Drop o' Wather, By Harry Wandsworth Shortfellow,* a pseudonym for Mary Cowden Clarke (London: Routledge, 1856); Charles M. Walcot, *Hiawatha: or, Ardent Spirits and Laughing Water. A Musical Extravaganza* (New York: Samuel French, [1856]); James W. Ward, *The*

Song of Higher-Water (New York: Johnston, 1868), as well as the Shirley Brooks parody in *Punch* (January 12, 1856, 17), which Longfellow professed to like. A list of parodies up to 1904 is included in Henry E. Legler, "Longfellow's *Hiawatha:* Bibliographical Notes Concerning Its Origins, Its Translations, and Its Contemporary Parodies," *Literary Collector* 9 (November–December 1904): 1–19.

95. Mortimer Neal Thomson wrote letters from Niagara Falls ("Doesticks on a Bender"), supplied rhymed police court reports, and produced a series of sketches of New York fortune-tellers for the *Tribune* (published as *The Witches of New York* in 1859). He married Fanny Fern's daughter and became nationally famous for his report on the Pierce Butler sale of slaves in 1859, first printed in the *Tribune* and then circulated as an abolitionist tract. His pseudonym "Q. K. Philander Doesticks, P.B.," stood for, he claimed, "Queer Kritter, Philander Doesticks, Perfect Brick." See *Dictionary of National Biography,* 9:487–88.

96. F. X. Reid, *The Song of Hakawatha,* available at www.cis.strath.ac.uk/~sinclair/hakawatha.html.

97. Katherine C. Grier, *Culture and Comfort: Parlor Making and Middle-Class Identity, 1850–1930* (Washington, D.C.: Smithsonian Institution Press, 1988), 65.

98. Kenneth L. Ames, *Death in the Dining-Room and Other Tales of Victorian Culture* (Philadelphia: Temple University, 1992), 236, 240.

99. Mrs. Harrison Gray Otis [Eliza Henderson Otis], *The Barclays of Boston* (Boston: Ticknor, Reed, and Fields, 1854), 234, 238.

100. Albert Jacquemart, *History of the Ceramic Art: Descriptive and Philosophical Study of the Pottery of All Ages and All Nations,* trans. Mrs. Bury Palliser, 2nd ed. (1873; London: Sampson Low, Marston, Searle and Rivington, 1877); Arthur Beckwith, *Majolica and Fayence: Italian, Sicilian, Majorcan, Hispano-Moresque and Persian* (New York: D. Appleton, 1877). Longfellow refers to both works in his letter to Henry Mills Alden of August 4, 1877 (*Letters* 6:289).

101. "As a boy, I often saw this potter at work under a great thorn-bush," he told Carille Winthrop Atwood, a high-school student in San Francisco, who had written to him for clarification (February 13, 1881; *Letters* 6:687).

102. Edward FitzGerald, *The Rubáiyát of Omar Khayyám: The Five Authorized Versions,* ed. Gordon S. Haight (Roslyn, N.Y.: Walter J. Black, 1942), 40. The first (limited) American edition of FitzGerald's translation was published in 1870, but the *Rubáiyát* became more widely available in the United States in 1878, when Longfellow's publisher, James R. Osgood, released a reprint of the third English version. The first extensive review, by Longfellow's friend Charles Eliot Norton, appeared in the *North American Review* in October 1869. Thomas Sergeant Perry published a longer article, "Mr. Edward Fitzgerald's Translations," in the June 1877 issue of the *Atlantic Monthly,* just around the time when Longfellow was working on "Kéramos." The similarity between Longfellow's poem and the *Rubáiyát* was first noticed by a reviewer in *Scribner's;* "Culture and Progress: Recent American Poetry," *Scribner's* 16, 3 (July 1878): 441–42.

103. Longfellow clearly takes delight in the rare adjective "fictile" (defined by the *Oxford English Dictionary* as "of or pertaining to pottery"), which also gives him an opportunity for alliteration.

104. Beckwith, *Majolica and Fayence,* 83.

105. Longfellow to Henry Mills Alden, September 13, 1877 (*Letters* 6:298).

106. "Recent Literature," *Atlantic Monthly* 42 (July 1878): 120–21.

107. Elaine Scarry, *The Body in Pain: The Making and Unmaking of the World* (New York: Oxford University Press, 1985), 307.

108. Some of the potters Longfellow mentions seem to have known and accepted their own insignificance: Bernard Palissy, for example, the sixteeenth-century French master potter who spent fifteen years struggling to make the enamels needed for his "rustic" pieces, appears never to have signed his works.

109. Garth Clark, *American Ceramics: 1876 to the Present* (New York: Abbeville, 1987), 13.

110. See Mary Warner Blanchard, *Oscar Wilde's America: Counterculture in the Gilded Age* (New Haven: Yale University Press, 1998), 103. I owe to Blanchard the reference to the advertisement from the *Pottery and Glassware Reporter,* discussed in the next paragraph of my chapter (see Blanchard, *Oscar Wilde's America,* 36).

111. See, for example, William Charvat, *The Profession of Authorship in America, 1800–1870,* ed. Matthew J. Bruccoli (Columbus: Ohio State University Press, 1968), 153.

112. Ralph Waldo Emerson, "Michael Angelo," *North American Review* 94 (January 1837): 2.

113. James Russell Lowell, *Fireside Travels* (1864; Boston: Houghton and Mifflin, 1894), 307.

114. This is how Michelangelo was portrayed in Herman Grimm's biography, *Life of Michelangelo,* trans. Fanny Elizabeth Bunnétt, 2 vols. (Boston: Little, Brown, 1865).

115. Grimm, *Michelangelo,* 2:362–63.

116. Note the allusion to Shakespeare's description of aging ("bare ruin'd choirs, where late the sweet birds sang"), in sonnet 73, in *The Riverside Shakespeare,* 2nd ed., ed. G. Blakemore Evans and J. J. M. Tobin (Boston: Houghton Mifflin, 1997, 1856).

117. Charvat, *Authorship,* 153.

118. Henry James, "Preface to *The Golden Bowl,*" in James, *The Art of the Novel* (New York: Scribners, 1934), 328.

119. Bergson, *Laughter,* in *Comedy,* ed. Wylie Sypher (New York: Doubleday Anchor, 1956), 81.

Chapter 3: Mad for Travel

1. Longfellow, "Peter Quince," Houghton MS Am 1340 (163); Longfellow, "Peter Piper," Houghton MS Am 1340 (9.1).

2. Henri Bergson, *Laughter* (1900), in *Comedy,* ed. Wylie Sypher (New York: Doubleday Anchor, 1956), 67.

3. H. D. Thoreau, *A Week on the Concord and Merrimack Rivers, Walden, The Maine Woods, Cape Cod,* ed. Robert F. Sayre (New York: Library of America, 1985), 117.

4. Ralph Waldo Emerson, "Self-Reliance" (1841), in *The Essays of Ralph Waldo Emerson,* with an introduction by Alfred Kazin (Cambridge, Mass.: Belknap, 1987), 46.

5. See Herman Melville, *Typee: A Peep at Polynesian Life,* ed. John Bryant (1846; New

York: Penguin, 1996), 209: "When at Rome, do as the Romans do, I held to be so good a proverb, that being in Typee I made a point of doing as the Typees did." Longfellow and his wife read Melville's *Typee* in 1846; from Longfellow's recorded response, it seems unlikely that they noticed the irony in Melville's portrayal of his self-obsessed protagonist: "a curious and interesting book, with such glowing descriptions of Life in the Marquesas, as to inspire a fancy for trying it" (Journal, July 29, 1846).

6. One of Mr. Peter Piper's distant ancestors is "Wiggins" from the whimsical drawings included in Thackeray's *Book of Snobs* (1848). "Rigid proud self-confident inflexible" Wiggins, a "bully of an Englishman," when vacationing goes "trampling Europe under foot, shouldering his way into galleries and cathedrals." He is not impressed by anything he sees: "Art, Nature pass, and there is not a dot of admiration in his stupid eyes." A humble shopkeeper at home, Wiggins strikes heroic poses when abroad. One of the drawings shows him being sick at sea. Longfellow, who had met Thackeray in 1852, admired him for his honesty (*Life* 3:388). Presumably, the supremely adaptable American, Mr. Peter Piper, who knows his way around a ship, was at least in part designed as a response to Thackeray's caricature of the British traveler. William Makepeace Thackeray, *The Book of Snobs,* ed. John Sutherland (St. Lucia, Australia: University of Queensland Press, 1978), 112–13.

7. John Betjeman, "Longfellow's Visit to Venice (To be Read in a Quiet New England Accent)," in *John Betjeman's Collected Poems,* ed. Lord Birkenhead (Boston: Houghton Mifflin, 1958), 261–62; see Newton Arvin, *Longfellow: His Life and Work* (Boston: Little, Brown, 1963), 118 n.

8. George William Curtis, *The Potiphar Papers* (New York: Putnam, 1853), 203, 207.

9. *Peter Piper's Practical Principles of Plain and Perfect Pronunciation* (Philadelphia: Willard Johnson, 1836). The preface states that Peter Piper "Prays Parents to Purchase this Playful Performance, Partly to Pay Him for his Patience and Pains; Partly to Provide for the Profit of the Printers and Publishers; but Principally to Prevent the Pernicious Prevalence of Perverse Pronunciation." The book, which offers a colorful woodcut illustration to go with each letter of the alphabet, ends with a hymn. The original edition was published by J. Harris (London, 1913).

10. See Alice Longfellow, "Longfellow with His Children," *Youth's Companion,* September 2, 1897, 405.

11. Mark Twain, *The Innocents Abroad or The New Pilgrims' Progress* (1869; New York: Bantam, 1966), 89.

12. Lydia H. Sigourney, *Pleasant Memories of Pleasant Lands,* 3rd ed. (1842; Boston: James Munroe, 1856), 386, 256, 390. In an emblematic episode, Sigourney asserts the close ties she has with England, which in fact make her less of a foreigner there than elsewhere in Europe. Walking through an exhibition of George Catlin's paintings of Native Americans ("our own red Indians"), in London's Egyptian Hall, she witnesses one of Catlin's staged buffalo dances, "with the most horrible tramping, and contortions of the agile personages enveloped in the skin of that ungainly animal." A little girl watching the antics of these "dark-browed actors," when she hears that Sigourney is from America, turns to her mother and exclaims: "Why, mamma, look! Mrs. Sigourney is white" (351)—and thus, we may add, more like "us" than "them."

13. Longfellow, *The Poets and Poetry of Europe, with Introductions and Biographical Notices* (1845; New York: C. S. Francis, 1877), 404.

14. "Hawthorne and His Mosses," in Melville, *Moby-Dick: A Critical Edition,* ed. Hershel Parker and Harrison Hayford (New York: Norton, 1966), 546.

15. David B. Caruso, "French Resistance to Iraq War Effort Leads to U.S. Boycotts, Bashing," *Orlando Sentinel,* February 21, 2003, A11.

16. A point emphasized in Matthew Pearl's preface to his new edition of Longfellow's translation of the *Inferno* (New York: Modern Library, 2003), xii.

17. Literally, "I have wings." The sentence does not occur in Hugo's work until much later, but Longfellow might be alluding to a section of "Soleils couchants," from Hugo's collection *Les Feuilles d'automne* (1832), which he was reading in 1844 (see *Letters* 3:24–25). The poem begins: "Oh! sur des ailes dans les nues / Laissez-moi fuir! Laissez-moi fuir" (Oh! On wings into the skies / Let me escape! Let me escape!); in Hugo, *Œuvres poétiques,* ed. Pierre Albouy, 2 vols. (Paris: Pléiade, 1964), 1:788.

18. O. B. Frothingham, "Henry Wadsworth Longfellow," *Atlantic Monthly* 49 (1882): 821.

19. A reference to William Cullen Bryant's advice to the Hudson River School painter Thomas Cole to "bear to Europe's strand / A living image of our own bright land"; "To Cole, the Painter, Departing for Europe," 1829, in *Poems by William Cullen Bryant* (New York: D. Appleton, 1854), 174.

20. See Randolph Bourne, "Trans-National America," *Atlantic Monthly* 118 (July 1916): 86–97. In an aside that would have amused the multilingual Longfellow, Bourne suggests that while recent immigrants might not have come on the *Mayflower,* they did come "upon a 'Maiblume,' a 'Fleur de Mai,' a 'Fior di Maggio,' and a 'Maiblomst.'" Bourne's concept of "transnationalism" has been given new substance by Werner Sollors and his collaborators; see especially *Multilingual America: Transnationalism, Ethnicity, and the Languages of American Literature,* ed. Werner Sollors (New York: New York University Press, 1998). Longfellow's engagement with *hispanidad,* specifically his "transnational" influence on Latino-American writers and translators, is the subject of Kirsten Silva Gruesz's fine essay "El Gran Poeta Longfellow and a Psalm of Exile," *American Literary History* 10, 3 (Winter 1998): 395–427, as well as of chap. 3, "Tastes of the Translator," in Gruesz, *Ambassadors of Culture: The Transamerican Origins of Latino Writing* (Princeton: Princeton University Press, 1999).

21. The anthropological ramifications of this position are explored by Helmuth Plessner, *Mit anderen Augen: Aspekte einer philosophischen Anthropologie* (Stuttgart: Reclam, 1982), 164–82.

22. Sarah Austin, *Characteristics of Goethe, from the German of Falk, von Müller, & c., with Notes Original and Translated, Illustrative of German Literature,* 3 vols. (London: E. Wilson, 1833), 3:307. From Austin's miscellany, Longfellow would have also learned that Goethe, "equally a master of Italian, French, and English," kept himself "*au courant* of all the important works that appeared in the three languages" (Austin 3:70), that he "took the liveliest and most generous interest in the literature and art of other countries" and "enriched his pages with songs from the modern Greek, the Scotch, Irish, old Bohemian and Serbian, and with poems from the Persian and Indian" (Austin

3:309–10), and, finally, that he was firmly convinced that poetry, regardless of national origin, belonged to "*the whole race of man*" (Austin 2:246). For Longfellow's lecture notes, see "Life of Goethe," "Illustrations of the Faust," "Goethe as an Author," "Goethe as a Man," and "Faust," Houghton MS Am 1340 (49).

23. Goethe's notion of "Weltliteratur" was based on the hope "that the living and dying authors meet one another and resolve, on the basis of their own inclinations as well as of sound communal sense, to become politically active. This project is more effectively accomplished by travelers than by correspondence, since truthful relationships between human beings can only be established and confirmed in actual face-to-face encounters" (my translation). See Goethe, "Die Zusammenkunft der Naturforscher in Berlin" (1828), in *Sämtliche Werke (Gedenkausgabe),* 17 vols. (Zürich: Artemis, 1948–71), 14:909–10.

24. Thomas Gold Appleton, "The Philistine," in Appleton, *Chequer-Work* (Boston: Roberts, 1879), 172.

25. Tzvetan Todorov, *On Human Diversity: Nationalism, Racism, and Exoticism in French Thought,* trans. Catherine Porter (Cambridge, Mass.: Harvard University Press, 1993), 251.

26. Longfellow, "History of the Italian Language and Dialects," *North American Review* 35 (October 1832): 283–342.

27. Longfellow, *Elements of French Grammar, by M. Lhomond, Translated from the French with Additional Notes for Schools* (Boston: Gray and Bowen, 1830); Longfellow, ed., George Washington Montgomery, *Novelas españolas: El serano de las alpujarras y El cuadro misterioso* (Brunswick, Me.: Griffin, 1830); Longfellow, ed., *Manuel de proverbes dramatiques* (Portland, Me.: Samuel Coleman, 1830).

28. Longfellow, *Syllabus de la grammaire italienne* (Boston: Gray and Bowen, 1832); *Saggi de' novellieri italiani d'ogni secolo; tratti da' piu celebri scrittori, con brevi notizie intorno alla vita di ciascheduno* (Boston: Gray and Bowen, 1832).

29. From chapter 4 of *Risorgimento d'Italia* (1775), where Bettinelli declares that it cannot be determined in what work, and by whom, the Tuscan dialect was first used. Was it an account book, a bill, a doctor's note for someone who didn't understand Latin? "Anche questo principio è, come gli altri, incerto, confuso, indeterminato, perché insensibilmente tutto è prodotto, né si può dir qui comincia"; Bettinelli, *Risorgimento d'Italia negli studi, nelle arti e ne' costumi dopo il Mille,* ed. Salvatore Rossi (Ravenna: Longo, 1976), 193–94.

30. Toscan has so far attracted no one's attention; in *Young Longfellow, 1807–1843,* Lawrance Thompson altogether ignores Longfellow's Venetian experiences (1938; New York: Octagon, 1969).

31. Twain, *Innocents Abroad,* 161.

32. "Barcariòl" is the Venetian word for "barcaruolo" or "gondolier." See Giuseppe Boerio, *Dizionario del Dialetto Veneziano,* 2nd ed. (1829; Venice: Giovanni Cecchini, 1856), 64. When Longfellow wrote to classical scholar Charles Folsom to ask for definitions of words in the Roman and Neapolitan dialect that he needed for his *North American Review* article, Folsom consulted Boerio's dictionary (see *Letters* 1:372 n. 4).

33. Longfellow, Journal, April 10, 1828–April 7, 1829, Houghton MS Am 1340 (178), p. 64.

34. Longfellow, Journal 1828–1829 [p. 61].

35. "Canachiòn" is a vulgar term for "culo" (bottom, ass); see Boerio, *Dizionario del Dialetto Veneziano,* 126.

36. Longfellow, Journal, 1828–1829, pp. 62–63. Translated by the author, with the help of Rosella Mamoli Zorzi and Marino Zorzi, Venice.

37. William Wordsworth, "Preface to Lyrical Ballads, with Pastoral and Other Poems" (1802), in Wordsworth, *Selected Poems,* ed. John O. Hayden (Harmondsworth, England: Penguin 1994), 433–34.

38. Rosella Mamoli Zorzi, Venice, letter to the author, November 19, 2001. Toni Toscan was still producing poems as late as 1843; see his canzone celebrating the regatta of "gondolini," *In Ocasion Dela Corsa e Gara de Gondolini a Do Remi, Fata nel Canal Grando dela Regia Città di Venezia el zorno 5 Zugno 1843. Canzon ala Veneziana Composta da Toni Toscan Sarvitor da Barca* (Venice, 1843), Biblioteca Nazionale Marciana, Venice.

39. Thomas Moore, *Letters and Journals of Lord Byron: With Notices of His Life,* 2 vols. (London: John Murray, 1830), 2:52.

40. George Gordon, Lord Byron, *Complete Poetical Works,* ed. Frederick Page, rev. ed., ed. John Jump (Oxford: Oxford University Press, 1970), 626.

41. Donald H. Reiman and Doucet Devin Fischer, eds., *Shelley and His Circle, 1773–1822,* vol. 7 (Cambridge, Mass.: Harvard University Press, 1986), 322.

42. "Mio Matto. Bondì[.] Invece che tu mi mandi Toni, io ti mando Eleonora, per avvertirti che oggi, per il gran Caldo, e per il Bagno che farò frappoco, trovo impossibile che possi venire, riserbandomi a stassera all' ora solita, e sarà così raddoppiato il piacere di vederti, e di baciarti. . . . P. S. A proposito di Toni, eccolo anche in questo biglietto, secondo il solito"; Reiman and Fischer, *Shelley and His Circle,* 7:320.

43. Longfellow, Journal, 1828–1829, p. 63.

44. See Andrew Hilen's comment in *Letters* 1:151. Longfellow later tried to exorcise his own ghosts when, in his 1832 essay on Sidney's *Defense of Poetry,* he piously attacked the "aping of Lord Byron" in current American literature: "no writer has done half so much to corrupt the literary taste as well as the moral principle of our country, as the author of Childe Harold"; "The Defence of Poetry," *North American Review* 34 (1832): 76.

45. Byron, *Childe Harold's Pilgrimage* 1.28, in Byron, *Complete Poetical Works,* 185.

46. Byron, *Don Juan* 1.8, in *Complete Poetical Works,* 638.

47. Longfellow, "Venise," Journal 1828–1829, p. 55.

48. Byron, *Marino Faliero, Doge of Venice* 5.3, in *Complete Poetical Works,* 452.

49. Byron, *Selected Letters and Journals,* ed. Leslie A. Marchand (Cambridge, Mass.: Belknap, 1982), 146.

50. Rosella Mamoli Zorzi, "The Text Is the City: The Representation of Venice in Two Tales by Irving and Poe and a Novel by Cooper," *Rivista di Studi Anglo-Americani* 6 (1990): 285–300.

51. Longfellow's own translation; see *Letters* 1:289.

52. Ingrid Rowland, "The Nervous Republic," *New York Review of Books,* November 1, 2001, 12–15.

53. Letter 2 of *Lettres d'un voyageur,* from which I have taken most of the following

quotations, was first published on July 15, 1834, in the *Revue des deux Mondes,* a periodical Longfellow read avidly.

54. See Annie Fields, *Authors and Friends,* 6th ed. (1896; Boston: Houghton Mifflin, 1897), 43.

55. George Sand, *Lettres d'un voyageur,* new ed. (1837; Paris: Lévy, 1869), 286: "une roue dans l'abîme, et le verre à la main." These and the following quotations are my translations.

56. When he read *Elle et Lui,* Sand's tell-all novel about her relationship with Alfred de Musset, Longfellow found it "sufficiently disagreeable" (May 19, 1859).

57. Longfellow to Alexander Slidell Mackenzie, January 7, 1830 (*Letters* 1:334).

58. These chapters were "The Trouvères" (based on "Origin and Progress of the French Language," *North American Review,* April 1831); "The Devotional Poetry of Spain" (which first appeared in the *North American Review* of April 1832 and was later also included in Longfellow's translation of *Coplas de Don Jorge Manrique* [Boston: Ticknor, 1833]), and "The Defence of Poetry."

59. Longfellow, Journal in France, October 11, 1826, Houghton MS Am 1340 (171); Journal in Spain, entry made in September 1827, Houghton MS Am 1340 (172); entry made in December 1827, Journal December 16, 1827–April 24, 1829, Houghton MS Am 1340 (173).

60. Laurence Sterne, *The Life and Opinions of Tristram Shandy, Gentleman* (1760–67; New York: New American Library, 1980): "Now I think it very much amiss—that a man cannot go quietly through a town, and let it alone, when it does not meddle with him" (390).

61. "I wish I could write a chapter on sleep. . . . God's blessing, said Sancho Pansa, be upon the man who first invented this selfsame thing called sleep" (Sterne, *Tristram Shandy,* 233–34). See also Cervantes, *The History of the Ingenious Gentleman, Don Quixote de la Mancha,* trans. Peter Motteux and ed. John G. Lockhart, 4 vols. (Boston: Little, Brown, 1856), 4:321 (pt. 2, chap. 68).

62. In *Lettres d'un voyageur,* Sand's (male) persona identifies himself as a wanderer who is, like Dante, "midway between heaven and earth" (14). Bayard Taylor, in his popular *Views A-Foot, or Europe Seen with a Knapsack and Staff* (1846; Boston: Joseph Knight, 1848), picked up the age-old metaphor, emptying it of all its spiritual connotations and offering tips on how to survive a pedestrian tour of Europe (a "truly pilgrimlike journeying") on a shoestring budget.

63. These terms come from Benedict Anderson, "Cultural Roots," chap. 2 of Anderson, *Imagined Communities: Reflections on the Origin and Spread of Nationalism* (London: Verso, 1983). Jenny Franchot, in *Roads to Rome: The Antebellum Protestant Encounter with Catholicism* (Berkeley: University of California Press, 1994), accounts for the love affair of New England Protestants with European Catholicism, marked both by "a fear of corruption and a hunger for communion" (xxiii). For Franchot, *Evangeline* expresses the Unitarian Longfellow's sad longing for "an unrecoverable Catholic community" (205). She does not discuss *Outre-Mer* or the links that I see between Catholicism and Longfellow's understanding of authorship.

64. In his novel *Kavanagh,* completed in 1849, Longfellow imagines Arthur Kava-

nagh's conversion from Catholicism to Protestantism as passing "from one chapel to another in the same vast cathedral." Though officially an apostate, Kavanagh was "still beneath the same ample roof, still heard the same divine service chanted in a different dialect of the same universal language" (8:412).

65. Years later, Fanny Longfellow read to her husband an "interesting article from the Quarterly Review on the Cathedral of Cologne." Longfellow was impressed: "Strange enough, that the name of the architect of this greatest work of Gothic Architecture should be irretrievably lost!" (December 10, 1846). See also my discussion of Longfellow's interest in authorial anonymity in chapter 2.

66. See the notice of the first number of *Outre-Mer* in *New-England Magazine* 5 (1833): "It seems hardly worth to keep in the public journals, a secret which is known by all the world; so we may as well say, that this little work is the production of Professor Longfellow, of Bowdoin College" (248).

67. The Hawthorne review was to be included in *Driftwood,* a collection of essays Longfellow never managed to publish as a separate book. The essays selected for *Driftwood* appeared right after *Outre-Mer* in the first volume of the Blue and Gold edition of Longfellow's *Prose Works,* 2 vols. (Boston: Ticknor and Fields, 1857).

68. For the full passage, see Acts 5:36 (King James Version): "For before these days rose up Theudas, boasting himself to be somebody, to whom a number of men, about four hundred, joined themselves. He was slain; and all, as many as obeyed him, were scattered, and brought to nought."

69. See 7:204: "I never hear the sweet warble of a bird from its native wood, without a silent wish that such a cheerful voice and peaceful shade were mine."

70. See Baudelaire's "Le Voyage": "les vrais voyageurs sont ceux-là seuls qui partent / Pour partir"; in Baudelaire, *Les Fleurs du mal,* ed. Antoine Adam (Paris: Garnier, 1961), 155.

71. Longfellow, "Song," written in 1875 (3:125).

72. From the summary entry for June 1856, where Longfellow explains why the month had remained "unrecorded."

73. See endpaper of Longfellow's journal, January 1, 1856–December 31, 1857, Houghton MS Am 1340 (207).

74. *The Balloon Travels, of Robert Merry and His Young Friends, over Various Countries in Europe, Edited by Peter Parley* (New York: J. C. Derby, 1855), 74.

75. Longfellow to Frances Farrer, May 8, 1862 (*Letters* 4:283).

76. See Longfellow, "Birds of Passage," written on November 1, 1845 (3:9–10).

77. William Dean Howells, *Literary Friends and Acquaintance,* ed. David F. Hiatt and Edwin H. Cady (1900; Bloomington: Indiana University Press, 1968), 167.

78. Giovanni Boccaccio, "Conclusione dell' autore," in *Decameron,* ed. Antonio Enzo Quaglio, 2 vols. (Milan: Garzanti, 1974), 2:943–48; see 947.

79. For more on the real-life models of Longfellow's storytellers, see John Van Schaick, *Characters in Tales of a Wayside Inn* (Boston: Universalist, 1939).

80. Nathaniel Hawthorne, *The Scarlet Letter,* ed. Seymour Gross, Sculley Bradley, Richmond Croom Beatty, and E. Hudson Long (New York: Norton, 1988), 157.

81. In the conclusion to *The Wayside Inn,* Longfellow compares his tales to the biblical "lilies that neither toil nor spin" (4:283).

82. See John James Audubon's vigorous defense of the American crow in his *Ornithological Biography* (1831–39): "The Crow devours myriads of grubs every day of the year, that might lay waste the farmer's fields; it destroys quadrupeds innumerable, every one of which is an enemy to his poultry and his flocks. Why then should the farmer be so ungrateful . . . as to persecute that friend even to the death?" In Audubon, *Writings and Drawings,* ed. Christoph Irmscher (New York: Library of America, 1999), 343.

83. *Don Quixote,* trans. Motteux, 1:105, 16.

84. On Longfellow and Cervantes, see Iris Lilian Whitman, *Longfellow and Spain* (New York: Instituto de las Españas en les Estadas Unidos, 1927), 124–32. As Longfellow saw it, there was indeed something quixotic about a writer's life. Once, when someone showed him a picture of Antonio Stradivari in his workshop, he quipped that he should have liked to make good musical instruments too. But, alas, like the Knight of La Mancha, he was spending most of his time on useless things. "Don Quixote thought he could have made good toothpicks and bird-cages, if his head had not been full of adventures" (Journal, March 10, 1862). In pt. 2, chap. 6 of *Don Quixote,* Don Quixote's niece suggests that her megalomaniacal uncle, "who knows everything," could probably build "a house as easy as a bird-cage." Answers the Knight: "Were not my understanding wholly involved in thoughts relating to the exercise of knight-errantry . . . no curiosity should escape my hands, especially bird-cages and tooth-pickers" (*Don Quixote,* trans. Motteux, 3:62).

85. Ernest Renan, "Qu'est-ce qu'une nation?" (1882), in *Oeuvres complètes,* ed. Henriette Psichari, 10 vols. (Paris: Calmann-Lévy, 1947–61), 1:887–906.

86. See Kwame Anthony Appiah, "You Must Remember This," *New York Review of Books,* March 13, 2003, 35–37.

87. Walter Benjamin, "The Storyteller: Reflections on the Works of Nicolai Leskov," in *Illuminations,* ed. Hannah Arendt and trans. Harry Zohn (New York: Schocken, 1969), 87.

88. Longfellow, "Our Native Writers" (1825), in *The American Literary Revolution, 1783–1837,* ed. Robert E. Spiller (Garden City, N.Y.: Anchor, 1967), 387–90.

89. Walt Whitman, *Notes and Fragments,* ed. Richard Maurice Bucke (London, Ontario: n.p., 1899), 56.

90. Longfellow, "The Defence of Poetry," 69.

91. A good example is Longfellow's friend Francis Lieber (1798–1872), a native of Berlin and a graduate of the university of Jena, who arrived in Boston in 1827. After editing the first edition of the *Encyclopedia Americana,* an American rehash of the German *Brockhus-Konversationslexikon,* Lieber accepted a teaching position at South Carolina College, where he stayed from 1835 until 1857, when he moved back north to teach at Columbia University. Though mainly remembered as a political scientist, Lieber frequently felt moved to express himself poetically, too, sending Longfellow "great quantities" of poems written in English and "demanding" a "candid opinion." Longfellow came to dread Lieber's "paper avalanche[s]" (Longfellow to George Stillman Hillard, April 4, 1848, *Letters* 3:168, and journal, February 10, 1848).

92. W. Sloane Kennedy, *Henry W. Longfellow: Biography, Anecdote, Letters, Criticism* (Cambridge, Mass.: Moses King, 1882), 116.

93. In 1851, writing to George Francis Richardson, a recent Harvard graduate who was about to depart for Europe, Longfellow recommended "Murray Guide Books or 'Hand-Books of Italy,' which I hear spoken of in very high terms, as being written by thorough scholars" (September 29, 1851; *Letters* 3:309).

94. See Lynne Withey, *Grand Tours and Cook's Tours: A History of Leisure Travel, 1750–1915* (New York: Morrow, 1997), 55–57.

95. See John Pemble, *The Mediterranean Passion: Victorians and Edwardians in the South* (Oxford: Oxford University Press, 1987), 115. "Ecstasies of recognition" is Robert Louis Stevenson's phrase; see Pemble, *Mediterranean Passion,* 115.

96. Twain, *Innocents Abroad:* "Maybe the originals were handsome when they were new, but they are not now" (142).

97. Susan Hale, *Life and Letters of Thomas Gold Appleton* (New York: Appleton, 1885), 229.

98. Twain, *Innocents Abroad,* 318.

99. Thomas Gold Appleton, "Sight-Seeing," in Appleton, *Chequer-Work,* 368.

100. Longfellow to Stephen Longfellow, Jr., October 26, 1826 (*Letters* 1:199).

101. "How would it do to publish a part in paper covers and consequently lower in price?" (Longfellow to James Ripley Osgood, May 3, 1876; *Letters* 6:133).

102. Longfellow erroneously lists Benjamin's full name as *Seymour* (instead of *Samuel*) Greene Wheeler Benjamin. The poem appears in Benjamin's *Constantinople, the Isle of Pearls, and Other Poems* (Boston: N. J. Bartlett, 1860), [89].

103. I have taken this phrase from Lawrence Weschler, *Mr. Wilson's Cabinet of Wonder* (New York: Pantheon, 1995), 101–3.

104. The beginning of Crabbe's "The Lover's Journey," in Crabbe, *Tales, 1812 and Other Selected Poems,* ed. Howard Mills (Cambridge: Cambridge University Press, 1967), 230.

105. William Dean Howells, "Four New Books of Poetry," *Atlantic Monthly* 37 (1876): 111.

106. From chap. 3 of Fuller, *Summer on the Lakes, in 1843,* in *The Essential Margaret Fuller,* ed. Jeffrey Steele (New Brunswick, N.J.: Rutgers University Press, 1992), 97.

107. Hayne to Longfellow, January 6, 1874, in *A Collection of Hayne Letters,* ed. Daniel Morley McKeithan (1944; Westport, Conn.: Greenwood, 1970), 147. Hayne continued to grease his way into the pantheon of American poetry with three more tributes to Longfellow, which like the present attempt show a strange obsession with Longfellow's hair: "To Henry W. Longfellow" ("The long gray locks are streaming softly down"); "To Longfellow, On Hearing He Was Ill" ("about whose locks of gray / Like golden bees, some glints of summer stray"); and "The Snow-Messengers" ("the green heart o'ertops the head of gray"). His final Longfellow poem, "Longfellow Dead," imagines the deceased poet in heaven bending over "the verge of heaven" to catch the sweet notes of some "human-hearted nightingale" (no doubt Hayne himself), singing his requiem. See *Poems of Paul Hamilton Hayne* (Boston: Lothrop, 1882), 268, 308, 292, 312.

108. Hayne to Longfellow, April 1, 1877, in *Hayne Letters,* 149.

109. Hayne to Longfellow, n.d., in *Hayne Letters,* 150–52.

110. William Gilmore Simms, ed., *War Poetry of the South* (New York: Richardson, 1866), v, vi, [7], 480.

111. Daniel Aaron, *The Unwritten War: American Writers and the Civil War* (London: Oxford University Press, 1973), 236.

112. See *A Man of Letters in the Nineteenth-Century South: Selected Letters of Paul Hamilton Hayne,* ed. Rayburn S. Moore (Baton Rouge: Louisiana State University Press, 1982), 35; Hayne to Longfellow, May 6, 1878, in *Hayne Letters,* 157.

113. [William Dean Howells], "Longfellow's Poems of Places," *Atlantic Monthly* 39 (March 1877): 375.

114. Arvin, *Longfellow,* 294.

115. Ralph Waldo Emerson, ed., *Parnassus,* 2nd ed. (1874; Boston: Houghton, Osgood, 1880), iii.

116. See Nina Baym, "Tourists in Time," chap. 7 of Baym, *American Women Writers and the Work of History, 1790–1860* (New Brunswick, N.J.: Rutgers University Press, 1995), 130–51, and Harvey Levenstein, "The Feminization of American Tourism," chap. 9 of Levenstein, *Seductive Journey: American Tourists in France from Jefferson to the Jazz Age* (Chicago: University of Chicago Press, 1998), 107–21.

117. American women poets were identified as separate and unequal in Rufus Griswold's *The Female Poets of America,* published in 1848 and, in a revised edition by Richard Henry Stoddard, in 1873 (New York: James Miller). "It is less easy to be assured of the genuineness of literary ability in women than in men," Griswold stated at the beginning of his preface. He went on to assure his readers that "the conditions of aesthetic ability in the two sexes are probably distinct, or even opposite" (3).

118. Longfellow to Edna Dean Proctor, June 14, 1877 (*Letters* 6:278). Proctor (1829–1923), a regular correspondent for the New York *Independent,* was an inveterate traveler—besides Russia, she had also traveled to Europe, Palestine, Egypt, the Pacific Coast, the Grand Canyon, Canada, and Mexico—and a prolific writer of remarkable versatility. Widely known for her Civil War poems (such as "The Virginia Scaffold" and "By the Shenandoah," which are included in Longfellow's *Southern States*), and for "The President's Proclamation" (her version of "John Brown's Body"), she also wrote sympathetically about Native Americans, the Inca, and Middle Eastern Muslims (see "The Prayer in the Desert," in *Places* 22:217–19). In 1893, Houghton Mifflin published her *Song of the Ancient People,* a narrative poem about Moqui and Zuni Indian thought, in a beautiful edition with eleven aquatints by Julian Scott and a commentary by anthropologist Frank Hamilton Cushing. One of the last poems she completed, in her ninety-first year, was about the Black Stone of the Ka'ba in Mecca. See the foreword to *The Complete Poetical Works of Edna Dean Proctor* (Boston: Houghton Mifflin, 1925), v–xviii.

119. Proctor, *A Russian Journey* (Boston: Osgood, 1872).

120. Ralph Waldo Emerson, *Nature,* ed. Warner Berthoff (1836; San Francisco: Chandler, 1968), 5.

121. See Longfellow, Journal, June 11, 1848.

122. Sigourney, *Pleasant Memories,* 390.

123. Elizabeth Bishop, "One Art," in Bishop, *The Complete Poems, 1927–1979* (New York: Farrar, Straus, and Giroux, 1983), 178.

124. See, for example, Charles Dickens, *Pictures from Italy* (1846), in Dickens, *American Notes and Pictures from Italy,* ed. F. S. Schwarzbach and Leonée Ormond (London: Everyman, 1997), 458–59.

Chapter 4: "It Whirls Me Away"

1. Lawrence Venuti, *The Scandal of Translation: Towards an Ethics of Difference* (London: Routledge, 1998), 46.

2. Friedrich Schleiermacher, "Über die verschiedenen Methoden des Übersetzens" (1813), reprinted in *Das Problem des Übersetzens,* ed. Hans-Joachim Störig (Darmstadt: Wissenschaftliche Buchgesellschaft, 1963), 38–70. See also Douglas Robinson, "The Limits of Translation," in *The Oxford Guide to Literature in English Translation,* ed. Peter France (Oxford: Oxford University Press, 2000), 18.

3. W. D. Howells, *Literary Friends and Acquaintance,* ed. David F. Hiatt and Edwin H. Cady (1900; Bloomington: Indiana University Press, 1968), 155.

4. William Wordsworth to George Beaumont, October 17, 1805, in *The Letters of William and Dorothy Wordsworth,* ed. E. de Selincourt, Alan G. Hill, Mary Moorman, and Chester L. Shaver, 7 vols., 2nd ed.(Oxford: Oxford University Press, 1967–88), 1:628–29.

5. This is the text of the sonnet as it was printed in the 1623 expurgated edition (the *rifacimento*) of Michelangelo's poetry, edited by Michelangelo il Giovane, which Longfellow used. Cesare Guasti, in the first critical edition of Michelangelo's poetry, reprinted the older version underneath his newly established "lezione originale," and it is cited here from his *Le Rime di Michelangelo Buonarroti, Pittore, Scultore e Architetto* (Florence: Le Monnier, 1863), 173. The main difference between the 1623 edition and Guasti's version, apart from slight variations in punctuation, occurs in line 10, where Michelangelo il Giovane changed the sequence of the words. Instead of "O fortuna, o durezza, o gran disdegno," the original reads: "O durezza, o fortuna, o gran disdegno."

6. Robert J. Clements, *The Poetry of Michelangelo* (New York: New York University Press, 1965), 66.

7. *The Complete Poems of Michelangelo,* trans. John Frederick Nims (Chicago: University of Chicago Press, 1998), 96.

8. See Theo Hermans, "Norms of Translation," in France, *Oxford Guide,* 11–12.

9. Originally published in John S. Harford, *The Life of M. A. Buonarroti, with Translations of Many of His Poems and Letters* (London, 1857), here cited from Ednah D. Cheney, *Selected Poems from Michelangelo Buonarroti, with Translations from Various Sources* (Boston: Lee and Shepard, 1885), 68–69; James M. Saslow, *The Poetry of Michelangelo: An Annotated Translation* (New Haven: Yale University Press, 1991), 302.

10. Lene Østermark-Johansen, *Sweetness and Strength: The Reception of Michelangelo in Late Victorian England* (Aldershot, England: Ashgate, 1998), 58.

11. Ralph Waldo Emerson, "Sonnet of Michel Angelo Buonarotti [*sic*]," in Emerson, *Poems* (Boston: Houghton, Mifflin, 1904), 298.

12. Longfellow claims that his translations were "made before the publication of the original text by Guasti" in 1863, but his diary proves him wrong; Longfellow, *Kéra-*

mos and Other Poems (Boston: Houghton, Osgood, 1878), 141. See Creighton Gilbert, "On Longfellow's Translation of a Michael Angelo Sonnet," *Philological Quarterly* 27 (1948): 389 n. 2.

13. John Addington Symonds, *The Sonnets of Michael Angelo Buonarroti and Tommaso Campanella, Now for the First Time Translated into Rhymed English* (London: Smith, Elder, 1878), 46.

14. Symonds was the first scholar to insist on the true nature of Michelangelo's sexual orientation, pointing out the ways editors and art historians had conspired to clean up the master's poetry. For him, it was exhilarating that, in Guasti's edition, the "heterosexual" sonnet 151 is followed by sonnet 84, written in 1534 and addressed to the object of Michelangelo's abiding affection, Tommaso Cavalieri. Here the marble containing the form to be executed by the sculptor is compared to the ink of the writer's pen from which will flow the poem that contains the poet's ideas. And one of those ideas is the love he elicits in the heart of another man, a love whose nature ("rich" or "vile") will be determined by the writer's own imaginings: "As pen and ink alike serve him who sings / In high or low or intermediate style; / As the same stone hath shapes both rich and vile / To match the fancies that each master brings; / So, my loved lord, within thy bosom springs / Pride mixed with meekness and kind thoughts that smile." Symonds, *Sonnets of Michael Angelo Buonarroti and Tommaso Campanella*, 47.

15. Longfellow to Ferdinand Freiligrath, November 24, 1843 (*Letters* 2:551).

16. See Longfellow to George Washington Greene, June 22, 1881 (*Letters* 6:722). The poem, signed "L.," first appeared in *New England Magazine,* July 1, 1831, and then in Longfellow, ed., *Poets and Poetry of Europe, with Introductions and Biographical Notices* (1845; New York: C. S. Francis, 1877), 695.

17. Lawrence Venuti, *The Translator's Invisibility: A History of Translation* (London: Routledge, 1995), 100.

18. On August 10, 1854, Longfellow told Robert Bigsby in England that neither "The Reaper and the Flowers" nor "The Psalm of Life" were translations (August 10, 1854; *Letters* 3:443).

19. "Voices of the Night. By H. W. Longfellow," *North American Review* 50 (January 1840): 269.

20. Gary Scharnhorst, "Longfellow as Translator," *Translation Review* 12 (1983): 24.

21. Longfellow, *Coplas de Don Jorge Manrique, Translated from the Spanish, with an Introductory Essay on the Moral and Devotional Poetry of Spain* (Boston: Allen and Ticknor, 1833).

22. Longfellow to George Washington Greene, July 16, 1833, *Letters* 1:421.

23. Werner Sollors, *Beyond Ethnicity: Consent and Descent in American Culture* (New York: Oxford University Press, 1986).

24. Venuti, *Invisibility*, 19.

25. "Editorial Notes: Literature," *Putnam's* 5 (January 1855): 110.

26. George Steiner, *After Babel: Aspects of Language and Translation,* new ed. (1975; Oxford: Oxford University Press, 1992), 315.

27. John Higham, *Strangers in the Land: Patterns of American Nativism 1860–1925,* 2nd ed. (1955; New York: Atheneum, 1974), 9–11.

28. "Titan: A Romance. From the German of Jean Paul Friedrich Richter. Translated by Charles T. Brooks," *Atlantic Monthly* 11 (January 1863): 138.

29. "Gossip of the Month," *United States Democratic Review* 21 (October 1847): 347.

30. "Shakespeare *versus* Sand," *American Review* 5 (1847): 481.

31. Longfellow added, in German, as if to emphasize that Goethe's scandalous novel should remain confined to its original language, "Schöne Natur! du bist gar zu natürlich!" ("Beautiful nature! You are far too natural!" July 27, 1851). Rölker, an immigrant born in Osnabrück, Germany, who had been a tutor in German at Harvard since 1837, later joined the firm of Laur and Rölker in New York City. He became an expert on contracts and wills and seems to have forgotten about Goethe's novel. Rölker's translation, if completed, was never published.

32. The following data are derived from *The Cost Books of Ticknor and Fields and their Predecessors, 1832–1858,* ed. Warren S. Tryon and William Charvat (New York: Philosophical Society of America, 1949).

33. Ronald J. Zboray, *A Fictive People: Antebellum Economic Development and the American Reading Public* (New York: Oxford University Press, 1993), 164–67.

34. Ik Marvel [Donald Grant Mitchell], *Reveries of a Bachelor: Or A Book of the Heart,* new ed. (1850: New York: Scribner, 1869), 28–29.

35. See Longfellow's Journal, October 29, 1835.

36. Fragment, from Longfellow, Unpublished Prose Fragments, 1840–82, Houghton Am MS 1340 (145).

37. "*The Poets and Poetry of Europe, with Introductions and Biographical Notices.* By Henry W. Longfellow," *North American Review* 61 (1845): 199.

38. "Longfellow's Poets and Poetry of Europe," *American Review* 4 (November 1846): 496–507. Of course, Longfellow's decision to list the translators' names separately rather than with the poems also reflects the fact that, in many cases, he hadn't been able to ascertain the translator's identity; many had been reprinted from anonymous articles in journals.

39. See "*The Poets and Poetry of Europe,*" *North American Review,* especially 201–2.

40. *Gedichte von Gustav Pfizer: Neue Sammlung* (Stuttgart: Paul Neff, 1835), 160–61.

41. "The Two Locks of Hair" (also in 6:275–77) was included in a letter to Samuel Ward dated June 24, 1841 (*Letters* 2:309–10), and first appeared in the *Token and Atlantic Souvenir* (Boston, 1842). See Writings 6:275 n.

42. Longfellow's Müller translation was published in the second part of his novel *Hyperion* (bk. 2, chap. 7; see 8:132–33).

43. When Howells's friend Eugenio Brunetta proposed an interlinear translation of *Evangeline,* for example, the mere idea made Longfellow shudder (to Howells, July 23, 1870; *Letters* 5:366).

44. Mrs. Lee had made her blunder worse by attaching a footnote, "Jean Paul often expresses his admiration of the frank English smile" (Journal, January 9, 1846). For the passage in *Flegeljahre,* see Johann Paul Friedrich Richter [Jean Paul], *Werke,* ed. Norbert Miller and Gustav Lohmann, 6 vols. (Munich: Carl Hanser, 1959–63), 2:1040.

45. "The Poets and Poetry of Europe," *United States Democratic Review* 36 (February 1855): 68–70.

46. Fanny Longfellow to Samuel Longfellow, May 7, 1860, in *Mrs. Longfellow: Selected Letters and Journals of Fanny Appleton Longfellow (1817–1861)*, ed. Edward Wagenknecht (New York: Longmans, 1956), 222.

47. Angelo Dalmedico to Longfellow, April 10, 1878, and Dalmedico to Longfellow, December 9, 1881, Houghton bMS Am 1340.2 (1439).

48. In his preface to his 1872 translation of *Hiawatha* and in an amusingly mean-spirited report of his first visit to Longfellow, translator Karl Knortz said that Long-fellow's Chippewa, derived from Schoolcraft's faulty knowledge of the language, was so flawed that he simply had to replace all of the Indian words with new and improved versions, after consulting a few original Indians, of course; "Einleitung," *Der Sang von Hiawatha*, trans. Karl Knortz (Jena: Costenoble, 1872), 15–17; "Mein erster Besuch bei Longfellow," in Knortz, *Aus der transatlantischen Gesellschaft: Nordamerikanische Kultur-bilder von Karl Knortz* (Leipzig: Schlicke, 1882), 25–26.

49. *Evangelina, Novella di E. W. Longfellow, tradotta da Pietro Rotondi* (Florence: Le Monnier, 1857), 41.

50. See *Alcune Poesie di Enrico W. Longfellow, traduzione dall' inglese di Angelo Messedaglia* (Padoa: Prosperini, 1866), [1].

51. See Longfellow to Charles Sumner, August 4, 1859 (*Letters* 4:141), as well as Longfellow to James Fields, August 12, 1859 (*Letters* 4:144).

52. Angelo Messedaglia, *Opere scelte di Economia e altri scritti*, 2 vols. (Verona: Accademia d'agricoltora, scienze e lettere di Verona, 1921), 2:640.

53. "Plus robustes et plus forts que moi, ils n'ont d'autres soucis que de faire une bonne journée de travail, et, le soir, ils reviennent un peu fatigués, peut-être, mais l'esprit en repos, le cœur gai et satisfait. Peu de choses suffisent à leur bonheur: ils ne sont pas le jouet de leur imagination; ils ne sont pas enchaînés, comme par enchante-ment, sur le bord d'un ruisseau, devant une fleur, un arbre, un insecte!" Léon Pamphile Le May, "Au lecteur," in *Essais poétiques* (Québec: Desbarats, 1865), vii.

54. "Puissé-je avoir servi mon pays en faisant ce travail! Puisse mon livre faire rejail-lir un reflet de gloire sur mon cher Canada!" (Le May, "Au lecteur," xi).

55. On the uses and abuses of the Evangeline story in Nova Scotia, see M. Brook Taylor, "The Poetry and Prose of History: *Evangeline* and the Historians of Nova Sco-tia," *Revue d'études canadiennes / Journal of Canadian Studies* 32, 1–2 (1988): 46–67.

56. Maurice Pellerin, "Biographie de Léon-Pamphile Le May," in Maurice Pellerin and Giles Gallichan, *Pamphile Le May écrivain et bibliothécaire* (Montréal: Bibliothéque nationale du Québec, 1987), 35.

57. Léon Pamphile Le May to Longfellow, September 9, 1865, as printed in Alfred Ayotte, "Cambridge célèbre les cent ans d' 'Évangéline,'" *La Presse* (Montréal), No-vember 6, 1947, 16.

58. "She has ended her doleful life"; see Le May, *Essais poétiques*, 105.

59. See Longfellow, *Evangeline, avec une traduction en français* (Toronto: McClellan, 1962), 125.

60. Pellerin, "Le May," 34.

61. See Naomi Griffiths, "Longfellow's *Evangeline*: The Birth and Acceptance of a Legend," *Acadiensis* 9, 2 (Spring 1982): 39.

62. Le May, *Essais poétiques*, 2.

63. "Cependant je n'ai aucune objection à modifier et à changer moi-même, ou à permettre aux autres de modifier et changer les passages que l'on n'aimerait point. Bien que je tienne à me croyances, je respecte celles des autres, et je sais que telles choses peuvent plaire à notre peuple naïf et croyant, qui feront sourire d'autres peuples." Léon Pamphile Le May to Longfellow, February 3, 1878, Houghton bMS Am 1340.2 (3401).

64. In a letter dated merely "June 1879," presumably the last time he was in touch with his translator, Longfellow thanked Le May for the gift of his new volume, *Une Gerbe* ("vigorous and melodious"), Fonds Pamphile Le May, Bibliothéque Nationale Québec.

65. Longfellow, *Évangéline et autres poèmes de Longfellow. Traduction libre par Pamphile Le May*, 3rd ed. (Montréal: Guay, 1912), 59–60.

66. "*La poésie anglaise, plus sobre que la nôtre, et d'allure moins vive, il me semble, ne saurait me faire un crime de quelques élans vers de rayonnements nouveaux, non plus que d'un séjour un peu prolongé dans les oasis où elle m'a conduit. Le grand poète qui m'a reproché, un jour, d'avoir fait mourir trop tôt sa douce héroïne, et qui m'a remercié, plus tard, de l'avoir fait revivre, accueillerait avec bienveillance, je n'en doute pas, cette nouvelle édition du poème admirable que je fais entrer dans notre littérature, sous l'égide de son immortalité*"; *Évangéline et autres poèmes*, [5]–6.

67. Ayotte, "Cambridge célèbre," 16.

68. Frank Siller to Longfellow, December 18, 1877, Houghton bMS Am 1340.2 (5088).

69. Frank A. Flower, *History of Milwaukee, Wisconsin, from Pre-Historic Times to the Present Date* (Chicago: Western Historical Company, 1881), 580.

70. Friedrich Bodenstedt, *Vom Atlantischen zum Stillen Ozean* (Leipzig: F. A. Brockhaus, 1882), 289; Frank Siller, *The Song of Manitoba and Other Poems* (Milwaukee: T. S. Gray, 1888), [1]. In the dedication of his anthology, *Lieder und Sprüche für das Volk* (Munich: Finsterlin, 1887), Siller described himself as a "tired wanderer," touched in the autumn of his life by the Muse's warm sunlight.

71. For a comprehensive history of German translations of *Evangeline*, see Klaus Martens, *Die ausgewanderte 'Evangeline': Longfellows epische Idylle im übersetzerischen Transfer* (Paderborn: Schöningh, 1989).

72. Ernest Wadsworth Longfellow, *Random Memories* (Boston: Houghton Mifflin, 1922), 28–29.

73. In the following years, Siller continued to ask Longfellow for help, first with a translation he had undertaken this time from German into English, which, with Longfellow's help, he hoped to place in some "first class literary Journal." Longfellow dutifully read the poem, titled "Das Thal von Yosemite," by a poet who had visited him as well as Siller, Friedrich Bodenstedt. He must have offered some advice, because on October 11, 1880, Siller thanked him warmly for "correcting the imperfections in my translation." Just two months later, he mailed Longfellow some samples from his ongoing translation of epigrams by Omar Khayyám, after a German version prepared, again, by the indefatigable Mr. Bodenstedt (December 20, 1880). "Have the kindness to make any changes you may see fit in the language," Siller urged Longfellow in a fol-

low-up letter, "and treat the M.S. as you would that of a pupil, whose style you wish to improve and then please place it where you think the best place for it, letting me know, in which magazine or other publication I may look for it" (December 30, 1880). On August 29, 1881, he begged Longfellow again to run his "master-eye" over a translation of Gottfried August Bürger's ballad "Das Lied vom braven Mann," which Siller had produced for the composer Robert Goldbeck. At least, unlike so many other of Longfellow's correspondents, he never forgot to enclose stamped envelopes.

74. See Frank Siller to Henry Wadsworth Longfellow, Milwaukee, May 6, 1879: "If it is not asking too much, I should like you now to send me by express at my expense for perusal and return at an early date the translations of Belke, Mickles [*sic*] and the Hamburg translation, all of which you mentioned about 18 months ago in a letter to me. I should like now to read them carefully." On August 22, 1879, Siller returned the books, "with many thanks." Only "the one by Nickles" (*Evangeline: Eine Erzählung aus Arcadien,* trans. Eduard Nickles [Karlsruhe: Braunsche Hofbuchhandlung], 1872), had found favor with him: "It has but one fault; the ease and freedom of the original is lacking." And Siller added, in German script: "der feine Duft, der zarte Blüthenstaub sind fort" (the subtle fragrance, the fine dust from its flowers are gone). Still, he was glad he had not seen it "before I began my translation, it would have discouraged me."

75. *Evangeline: Ein amerikanisches Gedicht von Henry Wadsworth Longfellow, in's Deutsche übersetzt von Frank Siller* (Milwaukee: Dörflinger, 1879), III–IV.

76. Kirsten Silva Gruesz discusses the interesting case of the Chilean translator of *Evangeline,* Carlos Morla Vicuña, whose 1871 rendering "catholicizes both the text and its author"; Gruesz, "El Gran Poeta Longfellow and a Psalm of Exile," *American Literary History* 10, 3 (Winter 1998): 410.

77. Knortz, "Mein erster Besuch," 26.

78. Steiner, *After Babel,* 423.

79. "Francesca speaks here, and then continues to speak through the words of the poet 'come colui che piange' [as one who weeps]." Longfellow, Journal [Italy and Germany], April 10, 1828–April 7, 1829, Houghton MS Am 1340 (178), p. 53.

80. See the note in the bound manuscript, Houghton MS Am 1340 (113), [p. 4].

81. See Longfellow, Inferno, Houghton MS Am 1340 (111).

82. Giuseppe Mazzini, "Opere Minori di Dante" (1841), in Mazzini, *Dante* (Naples: A cura del Comitato per la pubblicazione degli scritti di Giuseppe Mazzini, 1907), 72.

83. All quotations from Dante's Italian text are from Longfellow's own working edition in Houghton Library, *Opere poetiche di Dante Alighieri, con note di diversi per diligenza e studio di Antonio Buttura* (Paris: Lefevre, 1823), hereafter cited as "Dante." Longfellow inserted sheets of ruled notepaper into Buttura's two-volume edition and had it rebound in four volumes.

84. Longfellow's admiration for the Dante illustrations of the British sculptor and draughtsman John Flaxman (1755–1826), is obvious; see his Dante lecture, May 22, 1838 (Houghton, MS Am 1340 [38]), p. 15: "Flaxman surpasses all other modern artists in reproducing the severe forms of Antique beauty, and his outlines assist the reader wonderfully in giving definite shape to the visionary shapes of the poet's imagination."

85. In Longfellow's own, later translation, included in *Kéramos and Other Poems* (see 6:369).

86. See Longfellow's marginal note in his Dante edition, 3:45.

87. Wrote Labitte: "Il faudrait en rechercher les traces partout, dans la forme, dans le fond, dans la langue même de son admirable livre" (11:436).

88. Longfellow to Ernest Wadsworth Longfellow, November 17, 1865, *Letters* 4:516.

89. Howells, *Literary Friends,* 163.

90. Far from representing himself as the aloof high priest "of American cultural life" (Gruesz, "El Gran Poeta," 402), as the only one who has access to the sacred "vessels" of the originals, Longfellow regarded translation as a never-ending process of exchange, involving, at any given point, the original text, the translator, and the reader.

91. Steiner, *After Babel,* 328.

92. *The Comedy of Dante Allighieri* [*sic*], pt. 1, *Hell,* translated into blank verse by William Michael Rossetti (London: Macmillan, 1865), iii.

93. *The First Canticle (Inferno), of the Divine Comedy of Dante Alighieri,* trans. T. W. Parsons (Boston: De Vries, Ibarra, 1867).

94. See Dante Alighieri, *The Divine Comedy: Inferno,* trans. and ed. Charles S. Singleton, 2 vols. (1970; Princeton: Princeton University Press, 1977), 2:31.

95. Longfellow, Purgatorio, Houghton MS Am 1340 (112), p. 19.

96. Dante Alighieri, *Purgatorio: A New Verse Translation by W. S. Merwin* (New York: Knopf, 2001), 17; my emphasis.

97. Longfellow, Purgatorio, Houghton MS Am 1340 (112), p. 295.

98. Longfellow, Paradiso, Houghton MS Am 1340 (113), p. 78.

99. Dante Alighieri, *The Paradiso. A Verse Rendering for the Modern Reader by John Ciardi* (New York: Modern American Library, 1970), 94.

100. See Werner Sollors, "After the Culture Wars; or, From 'English Only' to 'English Plus,'" introduction to *Multilingual America: Transnationalism, Ethnicity, and the Languages of American Literature* (New York: New York University Press, 1998), 1–13.

101. A clipping collected by Longfellow; see his "Scraps and Notes for the Illustration of the Divine Comedy," Houghton MS Am 1340 (108).

102. Pierre Bourdieu, "The Market of Symbolic Goods," trans. Rupert Swyer, *Poetics* 14 (1985): 13–44.

103. Mazzini, "Opere Minori di Dante," 73.

104. See Christian Y. Dupont, "Collecting Dante in America at the End of the Nineteenth Century: John Zahm and Notre Dame," *Papers of the Bibliographical Society of America* 95, 4 (December 2001): 443–81, and Emerson, "The Poet," in *The Essays of Ralph Waldo Emerson,* with an introduction by Alfred Kazin (Cambridge, Mass.: Belknap, 1987), 239.

105. Longfellow, "Divina Commedia Notes," Houghton MS Am 1340 (110), n.p.

106. Longfellow, "Dante Lecture," Harvard College, May 22, 1838, Houghton MS Am 1340 (38), p. 122.

107. For a highly critical assessment of Longfellow's preference for "words of

Romanic origin," see John Fiske, "Longfellow's Dante," in Fiske, *The Unseen World and Other Essays* (Boston: Osgood, 1876), 243. Fiske's review apparently did not keep Longfellow from supplying him with a letter of introduction in 1879 (see Longfellow to Horace Howard Furness, October 18, 1879; *Letters* 6:526).

108. *The Comedy of Dante Allighieri* [sic], 226.

109. Dante Alighieri, *The Inferno. A Verse Rendering for the Modern Reader by John Ciardi* (New York: New American Library, 1954), 267; *The Vision of Dante Alighieri, or Hell, Purgatory and Paradise Translated by the Reverend H. F. Cary* (1805–14; London: Dent, 1908), 135.

110. *The Inferno of Dante: A New Verse Translation by Robert Pinsky* (New York: Farrar, Straus, and Giroux, 1994), 275.

111. Walter Benjamin, "The Translator's Task," in *The Translation Studies Reader,* ed. Lawrence Venuti (New York: Routledge, 2000), 16.

112. Dante, *Paradiso,* trans. Ciardi, 327.

113. See George Lowell Austin, *Henry Wadsworth Longfellow: His Life, His Works, His Friendships* (Boston: Lee and Shepard, 1883), 356–59.

114. *The Divine Comedy of Dante Alighieri: Inferno. A Verse Translation by Allen Mandelbaum* (1980; New York: Bantam, 1982), 317.

115. *Comedy of Dante,* trans. Rossetti, 34.

Epilogue

1. On the paradoxes of the Babel story, see Jacques Derrida, "Des Tours de Babel," in *Difference in Translation,* ed. Joseph F. Graham (Ithaca, N.Y.: Cornell University Press, 1985), 209–48.

2. See Barrett Wendell, *A Literary History of America* (New York: Scribner's, 1900), 3, and Alide Cagidemetrio, "'The Rest of the Story'; or, Multilingual American Literature," in *Multilingual America: Transnationalism, Ethnicity, and the Languages of American Literature,* ed. Werner Sollors (New York: New York University Press, 1998), 17–28.

3. Richard Kearney, "Narrative and the Ethics of Remembrance," in *Questioning Ethics: Contemporary Debates in Philosophy,* ed. Richard Kearney and Mark Dooley (London: Routledge, 1999), 26.

BIBLIOGRAPHY

Only published works are listed; for the numerous unpublished sources I have used, see the references in the notes. The major repository of Longfellow manuscripts is Harvard's Houghton Library, where I have consulted especially the Longfellow Papers (MS Am 1340) and the Letters to Longfellow (bMS Am 1340. 2). I have also drawn on the Fonds Pamphile Le May at the Bibliothèque Nationale Québec.

Aaron, Daniel. *The Unwritten War: American Writers and the Civil War.* London: Oxford University Press, 1973.
———. "The Legacy of Henry Wadsworth Longfellow." *Maine Historical Society Quarterly* 27, 4 (1987): 42–66.
Abell, Mrs. L. G. *Woman in Her Various Relations: Containing Practical Rules for American Females.* New York: Holdredge, 1851.
Ames, Kenneth L. *Death in the Dining-Room and Other Tales of Victorian Culture.* Philadelphia: Temple University, 1992.
Anderson, Benedict. *Imagined Communities: Reflections on the Origin and Spread of Nationalism.* London: Verso, 1983.
Appiah, Kwame Anthony. "You Must Remember This." *New York Review of Books,* March 13, 2003, 35–37.
Appleton, Thomas Gold. *Chequer-Work.* Boston: Roberts, 1879.
Arvin, Newton. *Longfellow: His Life and Work.* Boston: Little, Brown, 1963.
Audubon, John James. *Writings and Drawings.* Ed. Christoph Irmscher. New York: Library of America, 1999.
Austin, George Lowell. *Henry Wadsworth Longfellow: His Life, His Works, His Friendships.* Boston: Lee and Shepard, 1883.
Austin, James C. *James Fields of "The Atlantic Monthly": Letters to an Editor, 1861–1870.* San Marino, Calif.: Huntington Library, 1953.
Austin, Sarah. *Characteristics of Goethe; from the German of Falk, von Müller, & c., with Notes, Original and Translated, Illustrative of German Literature.* 3 vols. London: E. Wilson, 1833.

Ayotte, Alfred. "Cambridge célèbre les cent ans d' 'Évangéline.'" *La Presse* (Montréal), November 6, 1947, 16.

Bate, Walter Jackson. *The Burden of the Past and the English Poet* (1970). Cambridge, Mass.: Harvard University Press, 1991.

Bates, Charlotte Fiske, ed. *The Longfellow Birthday-Book.* Boston: Houghton Mifflin, 1881.

Baudelaire, Charles. *Les Fleurs du mal.* Ed. Antoine Adam. Paris: Garnier, 1961.

Baym, Nina. *American Women Writers and the Work of History, 1790–1860.* New Brunswick, N.J.: Rutgers University Press, 1995.

Beckwith, Arthur. *Majolica and Fayence: Italian, Sicilian, Majorcan, Hispano-Moresque and Persian.* New York: D. Appleton, 1877.

Benjamin, S.W.G. *Constantinople: The Isle of Pearls and Other Poems.* Boston: N. J. Bartlett, 1860.

Benjamin, Walter. "The Storyteller: Reflections on the Works of Nicolai Leskov." In Benjamin, *Illuminations,* trans. Harry Zohn and ed. Hannah Arendt, 83–109. New York: Schocken, 1969.

———. "The Translator's Task." In *The Translation Studies Reader,* ed. Lawrence Venuti, 15–25. New York: Routledge, 2000.

Bergson, Henri. *Laughter.* In *Comedy,* ed. Wylie Sypher. New York: Doubleday Anchor, 1956.

Berkhofer, Robert F. *The White Man's Indian: Images of the American Indian from Columbus to the Present* (1978). New York: Vintage, 1979.

Betjeman, Sir John. *John Betjeman's Collected Poems.* Ed. Lord Birkenhead. Boston: Houghton Mifflin, 1958.

Bettinelli, Saverio. *Risorgimento d'Italia negli studi, nelle arti e ne' costumi dopo il Mille* (1775). Ed. Salvatore Rossi. Ravenna: Longo, 1976.

Bishop, Elizabeth. *The Complete Poems, 1927–1979.* New York: Farrar, Straus, and Giroux, 1983.

Blanchard, Mary Warner. *Oscar Wilde's America: Counterculture in the Gilded Age.* New Haven: Yale University Press, 1998.

Bloom, Harold. *The Anxiety of Influence: A Theory of Poetry* (1973). 2nd ed. New York: Oxford University Press, 1997.

Boccaccio, Giovanni. *Decameron.* Ed. Antonio Enzo Quaglio. 2 vols. Milan: Garzanti, 1974.

Bodenstedt, Friedrich. *Vom Atlantischen zum Stillen Ozean.* Leipzig: F. A. Brockhaus, 1882.

Boerio, Giuseppe. *Dizionario del Dialetto Veneziano.* (1829). 2nd ed. Venice: Giovanni Cecchini, 1856.

Bourdieu, Pierre. "The Market of Symbolic Goods." Trans. Rupert Swyer. *Poetics* 14 (1985): 13–44.

Bourne, Randolph. "Trans-National America." *Atlantic Monthly* 118 (July 1916): 86–97.

Brodhead, Richard. *Cultures of Letters: Scenes of Reading and Writing in Nineteenth-Century America.* Chicago: University of Chicago Press, 1993.

Brooks, Cleanth. "The Formalist Critics" (1951). In *The Norton Anthology of Theory and Criticism,* gen. ed. Vincent B. Leitch, 1366–71. New York: Norton, 2001.

Brooks, Noah. "Lincoln's Imagination." *Scribner's* 18 (August 1879): 584–87.

Brooks, Van Wyck. *The Flowering of New England.* 1932. New York: Dutton, 1952.

———. "'Highbrow' and 'Lowbrow'" (1915). In Brooks, *America's Coming-of-Age,* 1–19. New York: Doubleday, 1958.

Brown, Gillian. "Child's Play." *differences* 11, 3 (fall 1999): 76–106.

Bryant, William Cullen. *Poems by William Cullen Bryant.* New York: D. Appleton, 1854.

Bushnell, Horace. *Christian Nurture* (1847). Ed. Luther A. Weigle. New Haven: Yale University Press, 1966.

Byron, Lord George Gordon. *Complete Poetical Works.* Ed. Frederick Page. Rev. ed. Ed. John Jump. Oxford: Oxford University Press, 1970.

———. *Selected Letters and Journals.* Ed. Leslie A. Marchand. Cambridge, Mass.: Belknap, 1982.

Calhoun, Charles. *Longfellow: A Rediscovered Life.* Boston: Beacon, 2004.

Carroll, Lewis. *Rhyme? and Reason?* New York: Macmillan, 1883.

Caruso, David B. "French Resistance to Iraq War Effort Leads to U.S. Boycotts, Bashing." *Orlando Sentinel,* February 21, 2003, A11.

Caverly, Abdiel Moore. *History of the Town of Pittsford, Vt., with Biographical Sketches and Family Records.* Rutland, Vt.: Tuttle, 1872.

Cervantes Saavedra, Miguel de. *The History of the Ingenious Gentleman, Don Quixote of La Mancha.* Trans. Peter Motteux and ed. John G. Lockhart. 4 vols. Boston: Little, Brown, 1856.

Charvat, William. *The Profession of Authorship in America, 1800–1870: The Papers of William Charvat.* Ed. Matthew J. Bruccoli. Columbus: Ohio State University Press, 1968.

Cheney, Ednah D. *Selected Poems from Michelangelo Buonarroti, with Translations from Various Sources.* Boston: Lee and Shepard, 1885.

Clark, Garth. *American Ceramics: 1876 to the Present.* New York: Abbeville, 1987.

Corrigan, Maureen. "Middlebrowsing." *The Nation,* November 3, 1997, 58–62.

The Cost Books of Ticknor and Fields and Their Predecessors, 1832–1858. Ed. Warren S. Tryon and William Charvat. New York: Bibliographical Society of America, 1949.

Cowley, Abraham. *Poems.* Ed. A. R. Waller. Cambridge: Cambridge University Press, 1905.

Crabbe, George. *Tales, 1812 and Other Selected Poems.* Ed. Howard Mills. Cambridge: Cambridge University Press, 1967.

Crashaw, Richard. *The Verse in English of Richard Crashaw.* New York: Grove, 1949.

"Culture and Progress: Recent American Poetry." *Scribner's* 16, 3 (July 1878): 440–42.

Cummins, Maria Susanna. *The Lamplighter.* Ed. Nina Baym. New Brunswick, N.J.: Rutgers University Press, 1988.

Curtis, George William. *The Potiphar Papers.* New York: Putnam, 1853.

Dante Alighieri. *Opere poetiche di Dante Alighieri, con note di diversi per diligenza e studio di Antonio Buttura.* 2 vols., rebound as 4. Paris: Lefevre, 1823.

———. *The Comedy of Dante Allighieri* [*sic*]. Pt. 1, *Hell.* Trans. William Michael Rossetti. London: Macmillan, 1865.

————. *The First Canticle (Inferno) of the Divine Comedy of Dante Alighieri.* Trans. T. W. Parsons. Boston: De Vries, Ibarra, 1867.

————. *The Vision of Dante Alighieri, or Hell, Purgatory and Paradise.* Trans. H. F. Cary. 1805–1814. London: Dent, 1908.

————. *The Inferno: A Verse Rendering for the Modern Reader by John Ciardi.* New York: New American Library, 1954.

————. *The Paradiso: A Verse Rendering for the Modern Reader by John Ciardi.* New York: New American Library, 1970.

————. *The Divine Comedy: Inferno.* Trans. and ed. Charles S. Singleton (1970). 2 vols. Princeton: Princeton University Press, 1989.

————. *The Inferno of Dante: A New Verse Translation by Robert Pinsky.* New York: Farrar, Straus, and Giroux, 1994.

————. *Purgatorio: A New Verse Translation by W. S. Merwin.* New York: Knopf, 2001.

————. *Inferno.* Trans. Henry Wadsworth Longfellow and ed. Matthew Pearl. New York: Modern Library, 2003.

Davis, Lennard J. *Enforcing Normalcy: Disability, Deafness and the Body.* London: Verso, 1995.

Degler, Carl N. *At Odds: Women and the Family in America from the Revolution to the Present.* New York: Oxford University Press, 1980.

DePalma, Anthony. "Historical Amnesia: Happy Fourth of July, Canada!" *New York Times,* July 5, 1998, sec. 4, p. 4.

Derbyshire, John. "Longfellow and the Fate of Modern Poetry." *New Criterion* 19, 4 (December 2000): 12–21.

Derrida, Jacques. "Des Tours de Babel." In *Difference in Translation,* ed. Joseph F. Graham, 209–48. Ithaca, N.Y.: Cornell University Press, 1985.

Dickens, Charles. *American Notes and Pictures from Italy.* Ed. F. S. Schwarzbach and Leonée Ormond. London: Everyman, 1997.

Dickinson, Emily. *The Poems of Emily Dickinson.* Ed. R. W. Franklin. Cambridge, Mass.: Belknap, 1999.

Duberman, Martin. *James Russell Lowell.* Boston: Beacon, 1966.

Dupont, Christian Y. "Collecting Dante in America at the End of the Nineteenth Century: John Zahm and Notre Dame." *Papers of the Bibliographical Society of America* 95, 4 (December 2001): 443–81.

"Editorial Notes: Literature." *Putnam's* 5 (January 1855): 105–11.

"The Editor's Easy Chair." *Harper's* 35, 206 (July 1867): 256–60.

Eliot, Thomas Stearns. "Rudyard Kipling." In *A Choice of Kipling's Verse Made by T. S. Eliot* (1941), 7–40. New York: Anchor, 1962.

————. "What Is a Classic?" (1944). In *Selected Prose of T. S. Eliot,* ed. Frank Kermode, 115–31. New York: Harcourt Brace Jovanovich, 1975.

Emerson, Ralph Waldo. "Michael Angelo." *North American Review* 94 (January 1837): 1–16.

————. "Quotation and Originality." *North American Review* 106 (1868): 543–57.

————. "Domestic Life." In Emerson, *Society and Solitude: Twelve Chapters* (1870), 101–33. Boston: Houghton Mifflin, 1904.

————, ed. *Parnassus.* 2nd ed. 1874. Boston: Houghton, Osgood, 1880.

————. *Poems.* Boston: Houghton, Mifflin, 1904.

————. *Nature.* (1836). Ed. Warner Berthoff. San Francisco: Chandler, 1968.

————. *Emerson in His Journals.* Ed. Joel Porte. Cambridge, Mass.: Belknap, 1982.

————. *The Essays of Ralph Waldo Emerson.* With an introduction by Alfred Kazin. Cambridge, Mass.: Belknap, 1987.

Emerson, Ralph Waldo, and Thomas Carlyle. *The Correspondence of Emerson and Carlyle.* Ed. Joseph Slater. New York: Columbia University Press, 1964.

English, James F. "Radway's 'Feelings' and the Reflexive Sociology of American Literature." *Modernism/Modernity* 6, 3 (1999): 139–49.

Epstein, Joseph. "Who Killed Poetry?" *Commentary* 86, 2 (1988): 13–20.

Everett, Barbara. "Distraction v. Attraction." *London Review of Books,* June 27, 2002, 7.

Excelsior: Journals of the Hutchinson Family Singers, 1842–1846. Ed. Dale Cockrell. New York: Pendragon, 1989.

Fass, Paula S., and Mary Ann Mason, eds. *Childhood in America.* New York: New York University Press, 2000.

Ferguson, Robert. *America during and after the War.* London: Longman, Green, Reader and Dyer, 1866.

Fern, Fanny. *Ruth Hall: A Domestic Tale of the Present Time.* Ed. Susan Belasco Smith. New York: Penguin, 1997.

Fields, Annie. *Authors and Friends* (1896). 6th ed. Boston: Houghton Mifflin, 1897.

Fields, James T. *Yesterdays with Authors.* Boston: Osgood, 1872.

Fiske, John. "Longfellow's Dante." In Fiske, *The Unseen World and Other Essays,* 237–56. Boston: Osgood, 1876.

FitzGerald, Edward. *The Rubáiyát of Omar Khayyám: The Five Authorized Versions.* Ed. Gordon S. Haight. Roslyn, N.Y.: Walter J. Black, 1942.

Fletcher, Angus. "Whitman and Longfellow: Two Types of the American Poet." *Raritan* 10, 4 (1991): 131–45.

Flower, Frank A. *History of Milwaukee, Wisconsin, from Pre-Historic Times to the Present Date.* Chicago: Western Historical Company, 1881.

France, Peter, ed. *The Oxford Guide to Literature in English Translation.* Oxford: Oxford University Press, 2000.

Franchot, Jenny. *Roads to Rome: The Antebellum Protestant Encounter with Catholicism.* Berkeley: University of California Press, 1994.

Freud, Sigmund. *Leonardo da Vinci: A Case Study in Psychosexuality.* Trans. A. A. Brill. New York: Modern Library, 1947.

Frothingham, O. B. "Henry Wadsworth Longfellow." *Atlantic Monthly* 49 (1882): 819–29.

Fuller, Margaret. *Margaret Fuller, American Romantic: A Selection from Her Writings and Correspondence.* Ed. Perry Miller. New York: Anchor, 1963.

————. *The Essential Margaret Fuller.* Ed. Jeffrey Steele. New Brunswick, N.J.: Rutgers University Press, 1995.

————. *Margaret Fuller, Critic: Writings from the New-York Tribune, 1844–1846.* Ed. Judith Mattson Bean and Joel Myerson. New York: Columbia University Press, 2000.

Gartner, Matthew. "Longfellow's Place: The Poet and Poetry of Craigie House." *New England Quarterly* 73, 1 (2000): 32–57.

Gay, Peter. *The Naked Heart.* New York: Norton, 1995.

Gernsheim, Helmut. *Julia Margaret Cameron: Her Life and Photographic Work.* Millerton, N.Y.: Aperture, 1975.

Gilbert, Creighton. "On Longfellow's Translation of a Michael Angelo Sonnet." *Philological Quarterly* 27 (1948): 389–404.

Gioia, Dana. *Can Poetry Matter?* New York: Graywolf, 1992.

———. "Longfellow in the Aftermath of Modernism." In *The Columbia History of American Poetry,* ed. Jay Parini, 64–96. New York: Columbia University Press, 1993.

———. "Disappearing Ink: Poetry at the End of Print Culture." *Hudson Review* 56, 1 (Spring 2003): 21–50.

Goethe, Johann Wolfgang von. *Sämtliche Werke (Gedenkausgabe).* 17 vols. Zurich: Artemis, 1948–71.

Goodrich, Samuel. *The Balloon Travels of Robert Merry and His Young Friends, over Various Countries in Europe, Edited by Peter Parley.* New York: J. C. Derby, 1855.

Gorman, Herbert S. *A Victorian American: Henry Wadsworth Longfellow* (1926). Port Washington, N.Y.: Kennikat, 1967.

"Gossip of the Month." *United States Democratic Review* 21 (October 1847): 347.

Graves, Robert. *The Crowning Privilege: The Clark Lectures, 1954–1955, Also Various Essays on Poetry and Sixteen New Poems.* London: Cassell, 1955.

Greenwood, Elizabeth. "Declarations of Independence: American Children's Diaries, 1820–1860." A.B. thesis, Harvard University, 2001.

Gregg, Edith Emerson Webster. "Emerson and His Children: Their Childhood Memories." *Harvard Library Bulletin* 38, 4 (October 1980): 407–30.

Grier, Katherine C. *Culture and Comfort: Parlor Making and Middle-Class Identity, 1850–1930.* Washington, D.C.: Smithsonian Institution Press, 1988.

Griffiths, Naomi. "Longfellow's *Evangeline:* The Birth and Acceptance of a Legend." *Acadiensis* 9, 2 (Spring 1982): 28–41.

Grimm, Herman. *Life of Michelangelo.* Trans. Fanny Elizabeth Bunnétt. 2 vols. Boston: Little, Brown, 1865.

Griswold, Rufus Wilmot, ed. *The Female Poets of America* (1848). New edition, with additions by R. H. Stoddard, New York: James Miller, 1873.

Gruesz, Kirsten Silva. "El Gran Poeta Longfellow and a Psalm of Exile." *American Literary History* 10, 3 (Winter 1998): 395–427.

———. *Ambassadors of Culture: The Transamerican Origins of Latino Writing.* Princeton: Princeton University Press, 1999.

———. "Feeling for the Fireside: Longfellow, Lynch, and the Topography of Poetic Power." In *Sentimental Men, Masculinity, and the Politics of Affect in American Culture,* ed. Mary Chapman and Glenn Hendler, 43–63. Berkeley: University of California Press, 1999.

Guillory, John. *Cultural Capital: The Problem of Literary Canon Formation.* Chicago: University of Chicago Press, 1993.

Gurstein, Rochelle. "The Importance of Being Earnest." *New Republic,* March 12, 2001, 40–45.

Hale, Susan. *Life and Letters of Thomas Gold Appleton.* New York: Appleton, 1885.

Halttunen, Karen. *Confidence Men and Painted Women: A Study of Middle-Class Culture in America, 1830–1870.* New Haven: Yale University Press, 1982.

Handlin, Oscar. *Boston's Immigrants* (1941). Rev. ed. New York: Atheneum, 1972.

Hansen, Karen V. *A Very Social Time: Crafting Community in Antebellum New England.* Berkeley: University of California Press, 1994.

Haralson, Eric L. "Mars in Petticoats: Longfellow and Sentimental Masculinity." *Nineteenth-Century Literature* 56 (1996): 327–55.

Hawthorne, Nathaniel. *The Scarlet Letter.* Ed. Seymour Gross, Sculley Bradley, Richard Croom Beatty, and E. Hudson Long. New York: Norton, 1988.

Hayne, Paul Hamilton. *Poems of Paul Hamilton Hayne.* Boston: Lothrop, 1882.

———. *A Collection of Hayne Letters.* Ed. Daniel Morley McKeithan (1944). Westport, Conn.: Greenwood, 1970.

———. *A Man of Letters in the Nineteenth-Century South: Selected Letters of Paul Hamilton Hayne.* Ed. Rayburn S. Moore. Baton Rouge: Louisiana State University Press, 1982.

Heartman, Charles F. *A Bibliography of First Printings of the Writings of Edgar Allan Poe* (1940). Rev. ed. Hattiesburg, Miss.: Book Farm, 1943.

Herder, Johann Gottfried. "Auszug aus einem Briefwechsel über Oßian und die Lieder alter Völker," in *Von deutscher Art und Kunst: Einige fliegende Blätter,* ed. Hans Dietrich Irmscher, 5–62. Stuttgart: Reclam, 1968.

———. *Stimmen der Völker in Liedern. Volkslieder* (1778/79). Ed. Heinz Rölleke. Stuttgart: Reclam, 1975.

Higginson, Thomas Wentworth. *Henry Wadsworth Longfellow.* Boston: Houghton Mifflin, 1902.

Higham, John. *Strangers in the Land: Patterns of American Nativism 1860–1925* (1955). 2nd ed. New York: Atheneum, 1974.

Holmes, Oliver Wendell. *The Autocrat of the Breakfast-Table.* (1858). Boston: Houghton Mifflin, 1881.

———. *The Complete Poetical Works.* Boston: Houghton Mifflin, 1895.

Homes of American Authors; Comprising Anecdotical, Personal, and Descriptive Sketches, by Various Writers. New York: Putnam, 1853.

Howe, Daniel Walker. "American Victorianism as a Culture." *American Quarterly* 27 (December 1975): 507–32.

Howe, Julia Ward. *Margaret Fuller (Marchesa Ossoli).* Boston: Roberts, 1883.

Howe, M. A. De Wolfe. *Memories of a Hostess: A Chronicle of Eminent Friendships Drawn Chiefly from the Diaries of Mrs. James T. Fields.* Boston: Atlantic Monthly, 1922.

Howells, William Dean. "Four New Books of Poetry." *Atlantic Monthly* 37 (1876): 105–11.

[———]. "Longfellow's Poems of Places." *Atlantic Monthly* 39 (March 1877): 375–76.

———. *Literary Friends and Acquaintance: A Personal Retrospect of American Authorship* (1900). Ed. David F. Hiatt and Edwin H. Cady. Bloomington: Indiana University Press, 1968.

Hugo, Victor. *Œuvres poétiques.* Ed. Pierre Albouy. 2 vols. Paris: Pléiade, 1964.

Hutchinson, George. *The Ecstatic Whitman: Literary Shamanism and the Crisis of the Union.* Columbus: Ohio State University Press, 1986.

Hutchinson, John Wallace. *Story of the Hutchinson Singers.* Ed. Charles E. Mann. 2 vols. Boston: Lee and Shepard, 1896.

Irmscher, Christoph. *The Poetics of Natural History: From John Bartram to William James.* New Brunswick, N.J.: Rutgers University Press, 1999.

———. "Longfellow Redux." *Raritan* 21, 3 (Winter 2001): 100–129.

———. "Mediterranean Metamorphoses: 'Enrico Longfello's' Contribution to Multilingual American Literature." In *America and the Mediterranean,* ed. Massimo Bacigalupo and Pierangelo Castagneto, 23–42. Turin: Otto, 2003.

Jackson, Virginia. "Longfellow's Tradition; or, Picture-Writing a Nation." *Modern Language Quarterly* 59, 4 (December 1998): 471–96.

Jacquemart, Albert. *History of the Ceramic Art: Descriptive and Philosophical Study of the Pottery of All Ages and All Nations.* Trans. Mrs. Bury Palliser (1873). 2nd ed. London: Sampson Low, Marston, Searle and Rivington, 1877.

James, Alice. *The Diary of Alice James.* Ed. Leon Edel. New York: Penguin, 1982.

James, Henry. *The Art of the Novel.* New York: Scribner's, 1934.

———. *Complete Stories, 1874–1884.* Ed. William L. Vance. New York: Library of America, 1999.

———. *Complete Stories, 1884–1891.* Ed. Edward Said. New York: Library of America, 1999.

Jarrell, Randall. "The Obscurity of the Poet." In Jarrell, *Poetry and the Age,* 3–27. New York: Knopf, 1953.

Jefferson, Thomas. *Writings.* Ed. Merrill D. Peterson. New York: Library of America, 1984.

Johansen, Shawn. *Family Men: Middle-Class Fatherhood in Early Industrializing America.* New York: Routledge, 2001.

The Kalevala, or Poems of the Kaleva District, Compiled by Elias Lönnrot. Ed. and trans. Francis Peabody Magoun, Jr. Cambridge, Mass.: Harvard University Press, 1963.

Kaplan, Justin. *Whitman: A Life.* 1980. New York: Bantam, 1982.

Kearney, Richard. "Narrative and the Ethics of Remembrance." In *Questioning Ethics: Contemporary Debates in Philosophy,* ed. Richard Kearney and Mark Dooley, 18–32. London: Routledge, 1999.

Kennedy, W. Sloane. *Henry Wadsworth Longfellow: Anecdote, Letters, Criticism.* Cambridge, Mass.: Moses King, 1882.

Kete, Mary Louise. *Sentimental Collaborations: Mourning and Middle-Class Identity in Nineteenth-Century America.* Durham, N.C.: Duke University Press, 1999.

Kipling, Rudyard. *The Collected Works of Rudyard Kipling.* 28 vols. Garden City, N.Y.: Doubleday, Doran, 1941.

Knortz, Karl. "Mein erster Besuch bei Longfellow." In Knortz, *Aus der transatlantischen Gesellschaft: Nordamerikanische Kulturbilder von Karl Knortz,* 22–35. Leipzig: Schlicke, 1882.

Krieg, Joann P. *A Whitman Chronology.* Iowa City: University of Iowa Press, 1998.

Lathrop, George P. "Literary and Social Boston." *Harper's* 17 (December 1880–May 1881): 381–93.

Legler, Henry E. "Longfellow's *Hiawatha:* Bibliographical Notes Concerning Its Origins, Its Translations, and Its Contemporary Parodies." *Literary Collector* 9 (November–December 1904): 1–19.

Le May, Léon Pamphile. *Essais poétiques.* Québec: Desbarats, 1865.

Levenstein, Harvey. *Seductive Journey: American Tourists in France from Jefferson to the Jazz Age.* Chicago: University of Chicago Press, 1998.

Lévi-Strauss, Claude. *Tristes Tropiques.* Trans. John and Doreen Weightman (1974). New York: Penguin, 1992.

Levine, Lawrence. *Highbrow/Lowbrow: The Emergence of Cultural Hierarchy in America.* Cambridge, Mass.: Harvard University Press, 1988.

Lewisohn, Ludwig. *The Story of American Literature* (1932). New York: Modern Library, 1939.

Longfellow, Alice. "Longfellow with His Children." *Youth's Companion,* September 2, 1897, 405.

Longfellow, Ernest Wadsworth. *Random Memories.* Boston: Houghton Mifflin, 1922.

Longfellow, Fanny Appleton. *Mrs. Longfellow: Selected Letters and Journals of Fanny Appleton Longfellow (1817–1861).* Ed. Edward Wagenknecht. New York: Longmans, Green, 1956.

Longfellow, Henry Wadsworth. *Elements of French Grammar, by M. Lhomond, Translated from the French with Additional Notes for Schools.* Boston: Gray and Bowen, 1830.

———. *Manuel de proverbes dramatiques.* Portland, Me.: Samuel Coleman, 1830.

———, ed. *Novelas españolas: El serano de las alpujarras y El cuadro misterioso,* by George Washington Montgomery. Brunswick, Me.: Griffin, 1830.

———. "The Defence of Poetry." *North American Review* 34 (January 1832): 56–78.

———. "History of the Italian Language and Dialects." *North American Review* 35 (October 1832): 283–342.

———. *Saggi de' novellieri italiani d'ogni secolo; tratti da' piu celebri scrittori, con brevi notizie intorno alla vita di ciascheduno.* Boston: Gray and Bowen, 1832.

———. *Syllabus de la grammaire italienne.* Boston: Gray and Bowen, 1832.

———. *Coplas de Don Jorge Manrique, Translated from the Spanish, with an Introductory Essay on the Moral and Devotional Poetry of Spain.* Boston: Allen and Ticknor, 1833.

———. "Dante's Divina Commedia: From the German of Schelling," *Graham's* 36 (June 1850): 351–54.

———. *Der Sang von Hiawatha von Henry Wadsworth Longfellow.* Trans. Ferdinand Freiligrath. Stuttgart: J. G. Cotta, 1857.

———. *Evangelina, Novella di E. W. Longfellow.* Trans. Pietro Rotondi. Florence: Felice Le Monnier, 1857.

———. *Prose Works.* 2 vols. Boston: Ticknor and Fields, 1857.

———. *Alcune Poesie di Enrico W. Longfellow, traduzione dall' inglese di Angelo Messedaglia.* Padoa: P. Prosperini, 1866.

———. *Der Sang von Hiawatha.* Trans. Karl Knortz. Jena: Costenoble, 1872.

———. *Evangeline: Eine Erzählung aus Arcadien.* Trans. Eduard Nickles. Karlsruhe: Braunsche Hofbuchhandlung, 1872.

———. *Excelsior, by Henry W. Longfellow.* With twelve illustrations by Fred. T. Vance. New York: Excelsior Life Insurance Company, 1872.

———. *Excelsior, Illustrated.* Advertising leaflet. Springfield, Mass.: D. H. Brigham, 1873.

———. ed. *Poems of Places.* 31 vols. Boston: James R. Osgood; Houghton, Osgood, 1876–79.

———. ed. *The Poets and Poetry of Europe, with Introductions and Biographical Notices.* Ed. Henry Wadsworth Longfellow (1845). New York C. S. Francis, 1877.

———. *Kéramos and Other Poems.* Boston: Houghton, Osgood, 1878.

———. *Evangeline: Ein amerikanisches Gedicht von Henry Wadsworth Longfellow, in's Deutsche übersetzt von Frank Siller.* Milwaukee: Dörflinger, 1879.

———. *The Complete Writings of Henry Wadsworth Longfellow.* Craigie ed. 11 vols. Boston: Houghton Mifflin, 1904.

———. *Évangéline et autres poèmes de Longfellow. Traduction libre par Pamphile Le May.* 3rd ed. Montréal: Guay, 1912.

———. *Evangeline, avec une traduction en français.* Toronto: McClellan, 1962.

———. *The Letters of Henry Wadsworth Longfellow.* Ed. Andrew Hilen. 6 vols. Cambridge, Mass.: Belknap, 1966–82.

———. "Our Native Writers" (1825). In *The American Literary Revolution, 1783–1837,* ed. Robert E. Spiller, 387–90. Garden City, N.Y.: Anchor, 1967.

———. *Selected Poems.* Ed. Lawrence Buell. New York: Penguin, 1988.

———. *The Song of Hiawatha.* Ed. Daniel Aaron. London: Everyman, 1993.

Longfellow, Samuel. *Life of Henry Wadsworth Longfellow, with Extracts from His Journals and Correspondence.* 3 vols. Boston: Houghton Mifflin, 1891.

"Longfellow's Poets and Poetry of Europe." *American Review* 4 (November 1846): 496–507.

Lowell, James Russell. *Fireside Travels* (1864). Boston: Houghton and Mifflin, 1894.

Macdonald, Dwight. "Masscult and Midcult" (1960). In Macdonald, *Against the American Grain,* 3–75. New York: Da Capo, 1983.

Maine, H. C. "Works of Art among College Boys." *Hamilton Literary Monthly* 4 (September 1869): 58–62.

Manning, Susan. "Whatever Happened to Pleasure?" *Cambridge Quarterly* 30, 3 (2001): 215–32.

Martens, Klaus. *Die ausgewanderte "Evangeline": Longfellows epische Idylle im übersetzerischen Transfer.* Paderborn: Schöningh, 1989.

Martin, Robert Bernard. *Tennyson: The Unquiet Heart. A Biography.* Oxford: Clarendon, 1980.

Marx, Leo. *The Pilot and the Passenger: Essays on Literature, Technology, and Culture in the United States.* New York: Oxford University Press, 1988.

Matthews, Gareth B. *The Philosophy of Childhood* (1994). Cambridge, Mass.: Harvard University Press, 1996.

Mazzini, Giuseppe. "Opere Minori di Dante" (1841). In Mazzini, *Dante,* 27–73. Napoli: A cura del Comitato per la pubblicazione degli scritti di Giuseppe Mazzini, 1907.

Meltzer, Françoise. *Hot Property: The Stakes and Claims of Literary Originality.* Chicago: University of Chicago Press, 1994.

Melville, Herman. "Hawthorne and His Mosses" (1850). In Melville, *Moby-Dick: A Critical Edition,* ed. Harrison Hayford and Hershel Parker, 535–51. New York: Norton, 1967.

———. *Typee: A Peep at Polynesian Life* (1846). Ed. John Bryant. New York: Penguin, 1996.

Messedaglia, Angelo. *Opere scelte di Economia e altri scritti.* 2 vols. Verona: Accademia d'agricoltora, scienze e lettere di Verona, 1921.

Michelangelo Buonarroti. *Le Rime di Michelangelo Buonarroti, Pittore, Scultore e Architetto.* Ed. Cesare Guasti. Florence: Le Monnier, 1863.

———. *The Complete Poems of Michelangelo.* Trans. John Frederick Nims. Chicago: University of Chicago Press, 1998.

Milton, John. *The Complete Poems.* Ed. John Leonard. London: Penguin, 1998.

Mitchell, Donald Grant ("Ik Marvel"). *Reveries of a Bachelor: Or A Book of the Heart* (1850). New ed. New York: Scribner, 1869.

Moore, Thomas. *Letters and Journals of Lord Byron: With Notices of His Life.* 2 vols. London: John Murray, 1830.

Moyne, Ernest J. "Parodies of Longfellow's Song of Hiawatha." *Delaware Notes* 30 (1957): 93–108.

———. *Hiawatha and Kalevala: A Study of the Relationship between Longfellow's "Indian Edda" and the Finnish Epic.* Helsinki: Suomalainen Tiedeakatemia, 1963.

The New Anthology of American Poetry. Vol. 1, *Traditions and Revolutions, Beginnings to 1900.* Ed. Steven Gould Axelrod, Camille Roman, and Thomas Travisano. New Brunswick, N.J.: Rutgers University Press, 2003.

Østermark-Johansen, Lene. *Sweetness and Strength: The Reception of Michelangelo in Late Victorian England.* Aldershot, England: Ashgate, 1998.

Otis, Mrs. Harrison Gray [Eliza Henderson Otis]. *The Barclays of Boston.* Boston: Ticknor, Reed, and Fields, 1854.

The Oxford Book of American Verse. Ed. F. O. Matthiessen. 2nd ed. New York: Oxford University Press, 1950.

Pearson, Norman Holmes. "Both Longfellows" (1950). In Henry Wadsworth Longfellow, *Evangeline and Selected Tales and Poems,* ed. Horace Gregory, 270–83. New York: New American Library, 1964.

Pellerin, Maurice, and Giles Gallichan. *Pamphile Le May écrivain et bibliothécaire.* Montréal: Bibliothéque nationale du Québec, 1987.

Pemble, John. *The Mediterranean Passion: Victorians and Edwardians in the South.* Oxford: Oxford University Press, 1987.

Peter Piper's Practical Principles of Plain and Perfect Pronunciation. Philadelphia: Willard Johnson, 1836.

Pfizer, Gustav. *Gedichte von Gustav Pfizer: Neue Sammlung.* Stuttgart: Paul Neff, 1835.

Plessner, Helmuth. *Mit anderen Augen: Aspekte einer philosophischen Anthropologie.* Stuttgart: Reclam, 1982.

[Poe, Edgar Allan]. "Our Book-Shelves (3)." *Aristidean* 1 (September 1845): 234–42.

Poe, Edgar Allan. *Essays and Criticism.* Ed. G. R. Thompson. New York: Library of America, 1984.

———. *Poetry and Tales.* Ed. Patrick Quinn. New York: Library of America, 1984.

"*The Poets and Poetry of Europe, with Introductions and Biographical Notices.* By Henry W. Longfellow." *North American Review* 61 (1845): 199–231.

"The Poets and Poetry of Europe." *United States Democratic Review* 36 (February 1855): 68–70.

Pound, Ezra. *Selected Poems.* London: Faber and Faber, 1928.

Proctor, Edna Dean. *A Russian Journey.* Boston: Osgood, 1872.

———. *The Complete Poetical Works of Edna Dean Proctor.* Boston: Houghton Mifflin, 1925.

Radway, Janice. *A Feeling for Books: The Book-of-the-Month Club, Literary Taste, and Middle-Class Desire.* Chapel Hill: University of North Carolina Press, 1997.

Ransom, John Crowe. "Criticism, Inc." (1938). In *The Norton Anthology of Theory and Criticism,* gen. ed. Vincent B. Leitch, 1108–18. New York: Norton, 2001.

The Reader's Companion to American History. Ed. Eric Foner and John A. Garraty. Boston: Houghton Mifflin, 1991.

"Recent Literature." *Atlantic Monthly* 42 (July 1878): 120–21.

Reid, F. X. *The Song of Hakawatha.* Available at www.cis.strath.ac.uk/~sinclair/hakawatha.html.

Reiman, Donald H., and Doucet Devin Fischer, eds. *Shelley and His Circle, 1773–1822.* Vol. 7. Cambridge, Mass.: Harvard University Press, 1986.

Renan, Ernest. "Qu'est-ce qu'une nation?" (1882). In *Oeuvres complètes,* 10 vols., ed. Henriette Psichari, 1:887–906. Paris: Calmann-Lévy, 1947–61.

Reynolds, David. *Walt Whitman's America: A Cultural Biography.* New York: Knopf, 1995.

Richards, I. A. *Practical Criticism: A Study of Literary Judgment.* 1929. New York: Harvest, 1969.

Richter, Johann Paul Friedrich [Jean Paul]. *Werke.* Ed. Norbert Miller and Gustav Lohmann. 6 vols. Munich: Carl Hanser, 1959–63.

Rowland, Ingrid. "The Nervous Republic." *New York Review of Books,* November 1, 2001, 12–15.

Rubin, Joan Shelley. *The Making of Middlebrow Culture.* Chapel Hill: University of North Carolina Press, 1992.

Ruland, Richard, and Malcolm Bradbury. *From Puritanism to Postmodernism: A History of American Literature.* New York: Penguin, 1992.

Rybcynski, Witold. *Home: A Short History of an Idea.* New York: Viking, 1986.

Sand, George. *Lettres d'un voyageur* (1837). New ed. Paris: Lévy, 1869.

Saslow, James M. *The Poetry of Michelangelo: An Annotated Translation.* New Haven: Yale University Press, 1991.

Scarry, Elaine. *The Body in Pain: The Making and Unmaking of the World.* New York: Oxford University Press, 1985.

Scharnhorst, Gary. "Longfellow as Translator." *Translation Review* 12 (1983): 23–27.

Schiller, Friedrich. *Sämtliche Werke.* Ed. Gerhard Fricke and Herbert G. Göpfert. 3 vols. 3rd ed. Munich: Carl Hanser, 1962.

Schleiermacher, Friedrich. "Über die verschiedenen Methoden des Übersetzens" (1813). In *Das Problem des Übersetzens,* ed. Hans-Joachim Störig, 38–70. Darmstadt: Wissenschaftliche Buchgesellschaft, 1963.

Schoolcraft, Henry Rowe. *Algic Researches, Comprising Inquiries Respecting the Mental Characteristics of the North American Indians. First Series: Indian Tales and Legends.* 2 vols. New York: Harper, 1839.

———. *Oneóta, or the Red Race of America from Original Notes and Manuscripts.* New York: Putnam, 1845.

Sewall, Richard. *The Life of Emily Dickinson* (1974). Cambridge, Mass.: Harvard University Press, 1980.

"Shakespeare *versus* Sand." *American Review* 5 (1847): 470–81.

Shakespeare, William. *The Riverside Shakespeare.* Ed. G. Blakemore Evans and J. J. M. Tobin. 2nd ed. Boston: Houghton Mifflin, 1997.

Shapin, Steven. "Personal Development and Intellectual Biography: The Case of Robert Boyle." *British Journal for the History of Science* 26 (1993): 335–45.

Sigourney, Lydia Huntley. *Pocahontas and Other Poems.* New York: Harper, 1841.

———. *Pleasant Memories of Pleasant Lands* (1842). 3rd ed. Boston: James Munroe, 1856.

———. *Letters of Life.* New York: Appleton, 1867.

Siller, Frank. *Lieder und Sprüche für das Volk.* Munich: Finsterlin, 1887.

———. *The Song of Manitoba and Other Poems.* Milwaukee: T. S. Gray, 1888.

Simms, William Gilmore, ed. *War Poetry of the South.* New York: Richardson, 1866.

Smith, Barbara Herrnstein. *Contingencies of Value: Alternative Perspectives for Critical Theory.* Cambridge, Mass.: Harvard University Press, 1988.

Sollors, Werner. *Beyond Ethnicity: Consent and Descent in American Culture.* New York: Oxford University Press, 1986.

———, ed. *Multilingual America: Transnationalism, Ethnicity, and the Languages of American Literature.* New York: New York University Press, 1998.

Southey, Robert. *Poems of Robert Southey.* Ed. Maurice H. Fitzgerald. London: Oxford University Press, 1909.

Steiner, George. *After Babel: Aspects of Language and Translation* (1975). New ed. Oxford: Oxford University Press, 1992.

Stevens, Wallace. *Sur Plusieurs Beaux Sujects: Wallace Stevens' Commonplace Book.* Ed. Milton J. Bates. Stanford: University of California Press, 1989.

———. *Collected Poetry and Prose.* Ed. Frank Kermode and Joan Richardson. New York: Library of America, 1997.

Sterne, Laurence. *The Life and Opinions of Tristram Shandy, Gentleman* (1760–67). New York: New American Library, 1980.

Stoddard, Richard Henry. "Henry Wadsworth Longfellow." *Scribner's* 17, 1 (November 1878): 1–19.

[Strong, George Augustus]. *The Song of Milkanwatha, Translated from the Original Feejee. By Marc Antony Henderson, D.C.L.* 2nd ed. Cincinnati: Tickell and Grinne, 1856.

Symonds, John Addington. *The Sonnets of Michael Angelo Buonarroti and Tommaso Campanella, Now for the First Time Translated into Rhymed English.* London: Smith, Elder, 1878.

Taylor, Bayard. *Views A-Foot, or Europe Seen with a Knapsack and Staff* (1846). Boston: Joseph Knight, 1848.

Taylor, M. Brook. "The Poetry and Prose of History: *Evangeline* and the Historians of Nova Scotia." *Revue d'études canadienne / Journal of Canadian Studies* 32, 1–2 (1988): 46–67.

Thackeray, William Makepeace. *The Book of Snobs*. Ed. John Sutherland. St. Lucia, Australia: University of Queensland Press, 1978.

Thompson, Lawrance. *Young Longfellow, 1807–1843* (1938). New York: Octagon, 1969.

[Thomson, Mortimer Neal]. *Pluri-bus-tah: A Song That's By No-Author, Perpetrated by Q. K. Philander Doesticks, P.B.* New York: Livermore and Rudd, 1865.

Thoreau, H. D. *A Week on the Concord and Merrimack Rivers, Walden, The Maine Woods, Cape Cod*. Ed. Robert F. Sayre. New York: Library of America, 1985.

The Thousand Best Poems in the World. Ed. E. W. Cole. London: Hutchinson, n.d.

"Titan: A Romance. From the German of Jean Paul Friedrich Richter. Translated by Charles T. Brooks." *Atlantic Monthly* 11 (January 1863): 136–39.

Tocqueville, Alexis de. *Democracy in America*. Trans. Arthur Goldhammer. New York: Library of America, 2004.

Todorov, Tzvetan. *On Human Diversity: Nationalism, Racism, and Exoticism in French Thought*. Trans. Catherine Porter. Cambridge, Mass.: Harvard University Press, 1993.

Toscan, Toni. *In Ocasion Dela Corsa e Gara de Gondolini a Do Remi, Fata nel Canal Grando dela Regia Cità di Venezia el zorno 5 Zugno 1843. Canzon ala Veneziana Composta da Toni Toscan Sarvitor da Barca*. Venice, 1843.

Trachtenberg, Alan. *Shades of Hiawatha: Staging Indians, Making Americans, 1880–1930*. New York: Hill and Wang, 2004.

Traubel, Horace. *With Walt Whitman in Camden*. Vol. 1 (1905). New York: Rowman and Littlefield, 1961.

———. *With Walt Whitman in Camden*. Vol. 3 (1912). New York: Rowman and Littlefield, 1961.

Trilling, James. Review of *Ruskin's Venice: The Stones Revisited*, by Sarah Quill. *American Scholar* 69, 4 (Autumn 2000): 146–48.

Twain, Mark. *The Innocents Abroad or The New Pilgrims' Progress* (1869). New York: Bantam, 1964.

Van Schaick, John. *Characters in "Tales of a Wayside Inn."* Boston: Universalist, 1939.

Venuti, Lawrence. *The Translator's Invisibility: A History of Translation*. London: Routledge, 1995.

———. *The Scandal of Translation: Towards an Ethics of Difference*. London: Routledge, 1998.

Victorian Parlor Poetry: An Annotated Anthology. Ed. Michael R. Turner (1969). New York: Dover, 1992.

"Voices of the Night. By H. W. Longfellow," *North American Review* 50 (January 1840): 266–69.

Warner, Marina. *No Go the Bogeyman: Scaring, Lulling, and Making Mock*. London: Chatto and Windus, 1998.

Warner, Susan. *The Wide Wide World* (1850). New York: Lippincott, 1892.

Warren, Joyce W. *Fanny Fern: An Independent Woman*. New Brunswick, N.J.: Rutgers University Press, 1992.

Wendell, Barrett. *A Literary History of America*. New York: Scribner's, 1900.

Weschler, Lawrence. *Mr. Wilson's Cabinet of Wonder*. New York: Pantheon, 1995.

Wexler, Bruce. "Poetry Is Dead. Does Anyone Really Care?" *Newsweek,* May 5, 2003, 18.

Whitman, Iris Lilian. *Longfellow and Spain.* New York: Instituto de las Españas en les Estadas Unidos, 1927.

Whitman, Walt. *Specimen Days and Collect.* Philadelphia: McKay, 1882–83.

———. *Notes and Fragments.* Ed. Richard Maurice Bucke. London, Ontario: privately published, 1899.

———. *Leaves of Grass and Other Writings.* Ed. Michael Moon. New York: Norton, 2002.

Whittier, John Greenleaf. *The Letters of John Greenleaf Whittier.* Ed. John B. Pickard. 3 vols. Cambridge, Mass.: Belknap, 1975.

Wilson, Edmund Wilson. "Is Verse a Dying Technique?" In Wilson, *The Triple Thinkers: Ten Essays on Literature* (1938), rev. and enl. ed., 15–30. New York: Harcourt Brace, 1948.

Withey, Lynne. *Grand Tours and Cook's Tours: A History of Leisure Travel, 1750–1915.* New York: Morrow, 1997.

Woolf, Virginia. "Middlebrow" (1912). In Woolf, *The Death of the Moth and Other Essays* (1942), 152–60. Harmondsworth, England: Penguin, 1961.

Wordsworth, William. *The Letters of William and Dorothy Wordsworth.* Ed. Ernest De Selincourt, Alan G. Hill, Mary Moorman, and Chester L. Shaver. 7 vols. 2nd ed. Oxford: Clarendon, 1967–88.

———. Preface to *Lyrical Ballads, with Pastoral and Other Poems* (1802). In *Selected Poems,* ed. John O. Hayden, 431–59. Harmondsworth, England: Penguin, 1994.

Zangwill, Israel. "The Fate of Palestine." *Menorah Journal* 3, 4 (October 1917): 196–202.

Zboray, Ronald J. *A Fictive People: Antebellum Economic Development and the American Reading Public.* New York: Oxford University Press, 1993.

Zorzi, Rosella Mamoli. "The Text Is the City: The Representation of Venice in Two Tales by Irving and Poe and a Novel by Cooper." *Rivista di Studi Anglo-Americani* 6 (1990): 285–300.

INDEX

Christoph Irmscher is a professor of English at Indiana University. The recipient of fellowships from the National Endowment for the Humanities and the Houghton Library at Harvard, he has also won book awards from the Association of American Publishers and the American Studies Network. His books include *Masken der Moderne, The Poetics of Natural History,* and an edition of John James Audubon's *Writings and Drawings.*

The University of Illinois Press
is a founding member of the
Association of American University Presses.

———————————

Composed in 11/13 Monotype Garamond
by Jim Proefrock
at the University of Illinois Press
Designed by Copenhaver Cumpston
Manufactured by Thomson-Shore, Inc.

UNIVERSITY OF ILLINOIS PRESS
1325 South Oak Street
Champaign, IL 61820-6903
www.press.uillinois.edu